CAUGHT!

The Travels and Travails of John W. Kerr, Fisheries Overseer, 1812–1888

Joel B. Kerr

FriesenPress

Suite 300 - 990 Fort St
Victoria, BC, v8v 3K2
Canada

www.friesenpress.com

Copyright © 2021 by Joel B. Kerr
First Edition — 2021

All rights reserved.

No part of this publication may be reproduced in any form, or by any means, electronic or mechanical, including photocopying, recording, or any information browsing, storage, or retrieval system, without permission in writing from FriesenPress.

ISBN
978-1-5255-8502-9 (Hardcover)
978-1-5255-8503-6 (Paperback)
978-1-5255-8504-3 (eBook)

1. BIOGRAPHY & AUTOBIOGRAPHY, HISTORICAL

Distributed to the trade by The Ingram Book Company

Table of Contents

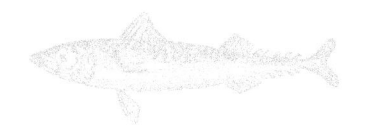

Introduction	1
Chapter 1 Early Years in Ireland	7
Chapter 2 The Royal Irish Constabulary 1832–1846	12
Chapter 3 Arrival in Canada	20
Chapter 4 The Wentworth Society for the Protection of Game and Fish	28
Chapter 5 Commercial Fishing in the Lower Great Lakes	32
Chapter 6 1864–1867 – The Battle of the Beach and the Bay	40
Chapter 7 Confederation, Peter Mitchell, and Subsequent Ministers	71
Chapter 8 1867–1873 Good Old Sir John A. – Hip, Hip Hurray!	77
Chapter 9 The Grits! (1874–1878)	98
Chapter 10 1878–1882 – The Nation Builder is Back!	126
Chapter 11 1882–1886 – England Expects Every Man to Do His Duty	167
Chapter 12 And So Mote It Be! 1887–1888	228
Chapter 13 Pollution	245
Chapter 14 Kerr and the Long Point Company	266
Chapter 15 Farming and Family	276
Chapter 16 Revenge is a Dish Best Served Cold	292
Chapter 17 Indigenous People	303

Chapter 18 Americans	307
Chapter 19 Samuel Wilmot and the Fish Hatcheries	311
Chapter 20 Ancient Order of Freemasons	337
Chapter 21 Kerr and Barton Township	343
Chapter 22 Alcohol!	358
Chapter 23 The Strange Saga of Simcoe Kerr	363
Chapter 24 A Melancholy Accident on Burlington Bay	374
Postscript	378
Conclusion	382
How I Wrote This GD Book	385
Acknowledgments	387

Introduction

At 11:00 a.m. on Tuesday May 8, 1888, John William Kerr was dead. Just six weeks shy of his seventy-sixth birthday, Kerr died of a combination of ailments in his large home on Hamilton Mountain. He was survived by his fifty-eight-year-old wife, the former Mary Elizabeth Winslow, and eight of his nine children. A front-page obituary published in the *Hamilton Spectator* on May 10 noted,

> *The genial countenance of John W. Kerr, the venerable fishery inspector, will be seen no more on the streets. He died at his residence on the mountain Tuesday at 11:00 from a complication of diseases ... In 1864 the question of better protection to the fish of the inland waters as well as the game of the country was agitated in the leading papers of this province and Mr. Kerr was appointed inspector for this district. He was then in the prime of life and he made short work of many of the poachers and trespassers ... in a few years he had all the law-breaking fishermen of this part of Canada completely under his subjection.*

The *Hamilton Evening Times* called him "a man of great intelligence, of kindly disposition and leaves hundreds who have reason to say kind things about him." The funeral was held at his house, and the burial took place at Hamilton Cemetery, across the street from Dundurn Castle. I imagine it was highly attended because Kerr knew everyone, from politicians to merchants, industrialists, and fishermen from all over.

Kerr had been appointed as fisheries overseer by the commissioner of Crown lands in 1864 and held the position continuously until his death. As such, he was tasked with the job of enforcing Canada's fishing laws, and he kept diaries and letter books of his activities for the next twenty-four years. These diaries were provided to the Royal Ontario Museum (ROM) by his son, Charles John Kerr, in 1942, and they can be easily found online if you Google "John W. Kerr fonds."

John Kerr's diaries consist of fifteen volumes of handwritten notes and copies of his many letters. The volumes run from about 500 pages to 1,000 pages, and I have read them all. John W. Kerr was my great-great-grandfather, and his third son, Charles John Kerr, was my great-grandfather. I had known about the diaries for many years and that the Hamilton Public Library had a copy on microfiche courtesy of Eleanor (Kerr) Morrow (the mother of Robert Morrow, Hamilton's longest-serving mayor).

I had determined to write this book years ago and knew I would have to read these diaries but grappled with the job of having to read them in the library on microfilm, an excruciating exercise. When I started researching seriously in early 2019, I began in the local history archives of our library and soon learned that the diaries were available on various online sites. This meant I could read them whenever and wherever I wanted, so I set up an office in an unused bedroom with my clunky former office computer and began to read. Fortunately, Kerr had excellent handwriting, and his diaries are in great condition. The last entry is for May 7, 1888, the day before his death, when Kerr wrote to the deputy minister to send him $260 in licensing fees he had received.

Kerr was born in 1812 in the town of Mullingar, County Westmeath, Ireland, and came to Canada in 1846 at age thirty-four with his twenty-year-old and probably pregnant wife. He had been an officer in the Royal Irish Constabulary (RIC) since 1832, and in leaving Ireland he was likely fleeing for his life, as we shall see.

Once in Canada he taught school for one season in Bayham Township, just north of Port Stanley on Lake Erie, and then worked for the post office in London for four years.

In 1851 Kerr moved his family to Hamilton, including his two eldest children, and worked as the chief clerk in the engineering office of the Great Western Railway (GWR), which opened in 1853. In 1858 he was fired from the GWR as a result of a political purge. This book examines some aspects of the story of the GWR, which was very important for the future growth of Hamilton. Also herein is a chapter on Kerr's attempt to derail the GWR's managing director, C. J. Brydges.

Before leaving the GWR, Kerr bought one hundred acres on Hamilton Mountain and created a farm in which he seemed to have little interest. Because the property was on the edge of the Mountain Brow, Kerr also built an access road and a large home. The house is still there and is a designated heritage property, as indicated by a plaque across the street in Mountain Park. You can also still see the remnants of the road from where Concession Street turns into Mountain Brow Boulevard. It was one hell of a steep and narrow road.

For whatever reason, Kerr's passion was fish and the sustainability of commercial fishing. He was an early fish-and-game conservationist and tried without success to get the authority to enforce the game laws that were under provincial jurisdiction, unlike the fishing laws that were under federal responsibility after Confederation.

This book is primarily an edit of his diaries about his remarkable travels throughout Southern Ontario while enforcing the fishing laws. He documented his method of travel, distance, and time on the job, and by my rough calculations, he travelled at least 200,000 miles, mostly by rail, but also on foot, by horse and buggy, horse and wagon, horse and sleigh, horseback, rowboat, sailboat, steamboat, and "bus" after the Hamilton Street Railway opened in 1874.

He worked around the clock and was frequently out on Burlington Bay all night and in all weather, looking to arrest fishermen who used lamps to attract fish to their nets, seines, or spears. His travels took him to Lake Erie, Lake St. Clair, Lake Huron, and Georgian Bay as well as numerous streams and rivers in his large district.

As the *Hamilton Spectator* noted in his obituary, he was a "man of indomitable pluck and endurance… From his residence at the turn of the Hamilton mountain he could sweep his telescope for 20 miles in all directions at early dawn, and if anything suspicious was drawn into the field of his glass he was away and would pounce on the offenders before they had properly got to work." While that may be slightly hyperbolic, there is no disputing that he was hardworking and persistent.

In addition to some discussion of the scandals of the GWR (in which he played a role), I also touch on some other topics regarding local politics in Hamilton, Wentworth County, and Barton Township (where Kerr sat on the council for many years) and the push to Confederation and how it came to be that fishing became a federal matter in the *British North America Act 1867*. For a number of years, his boss was Peter Mitchell, Canada's first Minister of Marine and Fisheries and one of the thirty-six Fathers of Confederation.

I also include some discussion of Canada's early legal system and Kerr's difficulty in enforcing the law (he rarely disguised his disdain for lawyers and certain members of the judiciary). As a retired lawyer myself, it was amusing to read his thoughts on the sometimes ridiculous submissions of lawyers and how he could never get a jury to convict a fisherman. I will also discuss his love/hate relationship with commercial fishermen, whose interest he was trying to protect by ensuring adequate fish stocks. They often hated him, and there was some crime and violence. He usually packed a handgun, and he had occasion to use it!

Kerr was an early environmentalist and frequently prosecuted mill owners and industrial concerns for polluting the water and killing fish. He often butted heads with local politicians who, not surprisingly, always seemed to be on the side of business.

I also examine his relationship with Americans, Aboriginals, the Sunday observance laws, alcohol, and fish propagation, in which he was keenly interested. He was a staunch, lifelong Conservative, and he worked actively to elect his many political friends.

Admittedly, as a direct relative, I am probably biased toward Kerr, but I think you will see that he was a supremely decent and moral man. I hope his story will resonate today in a world of climate change, environmental degradation, greed, and political extremism. If you read the 10,000 or so pages of his diaries and letter books, and you happen to disagree, feel free to write your own book!

Having read his story, mostly in his own words, I can state without any equivocation that he literally worked himself to death in service of the Federal Department of Marine and Fisheries. He was underpaid and overworked and lied to by his bosses, but his creed was "England expects every man to do his duty," a quote from Lord Nelson at the 1805 Battle of Trafalgar. There aren't any memorials to him except for the plaque across from his house, but he led an extraordinary life. He was intelligent and articulate, and I think he could have risen much higher in life if his focus had been more commercial in nature. He also had his flaws and foibles, and I have endeavoured to display these, often in a humorous manner.

Through my research I have attempted to throw a little light on the people he encountered. He knew everyone from Sir John A. MacDonald to the lowliest drunken fisherman. Most of this book comes from his own writing, so it lacks perspective, but I have tried to find alternate sources, like newspaper articles and pictures, to illustrate events. I could find no picture of Kerr himself, which irritates the hell out of me.

Finally, I should note that I am a retired lawyer, not a historian, so this book does not have the polished elegance of a professional history writer. Up to now my only published writing is a survey of Hamilton's older apartment buildings, *Carved in Stone,* which is available for free online (search "Vintage Hamilton").

I hope you will find some or all of this interesting because it is not intended as a scholarly work. If you want to read more, go to the diaries!

This book is dedicated to my first grandson, Frederick Bryant Burditt (Kerr) who is the seventh generation of Kerr to continuously occupy a portion of the Kerr farm since 1855.

OBITUARY.

Death of Mr. John W. Kerr, Fishery Overseer.

The many friends in Hamilton and Wentworth of Mr. John W. Kerr, the popular Fishery Overseer of this district, will be grieved to hear of his death, which occurred early this morning at his residence on the mountain top (Barton.) Mr. Kerr had been ailing ever since February, and his relatives and friends could see that he was failing fast, but although he had seen 76 years his indomitable pluck and spirit kept him up until the very last. His family physician says death resulted through a general breaking up of the constitution. He had serious affections of the heart and kidneys. Deceased emigrated from Ireland in the year 1848, and settled in London, Ont., where he took a situation in the post-office, remaining there for about ten years. Then he moved to Hamilton and was employed on the Great Western Railway for a long time. Subsequently he received the appointment of Fishery Overseer of this district, a position which he has held with great credit to himself and satisfaction to the Department at Ottawa for the past twenty-four years. In fact, those in authority deferred to his superior judgment on matters connected with the inland fisheries, and Mr. Kerr had many a trip to points outside his jurisdiction to put things to rights for the department. He was a man of great intelligence, of kindly disposition, and leaves hundreds who have reason to say kind things about him. Mr. Kerr was an esteemed member of the Masonic fraternity, being a life member of St. John's as well as connected with Temple Lodge. He also was a member of the Irish Protestant Benevolent Society. He leaves a widow and eight grown up sons and daughters to mourn their loss. The funeral will leave the house in Barton at 2 o'clock to-morrow for Burlington Cemetery.

Kerr's obituary from Hamilton Spectator. Hamilton Public Library

OBITUARY.

JOHN W. KERR.

The genial countenance of John W. Kerr, the venerable fishery inspector, will be seen no more on the streets. He died at his residence on the mountain Tuesday at 11 o'clock, from a complication of diseases, at the ripe age of 76 years. Mr. Kerr was a native of the county of Fermanagh, Ireland, and for some years held the position of inspector in the Irish constabulary. He removed from Ireland to Canada some 40 years ago, and first settled in London. He was employed in the postoffice of that town for ten years and then removed to Hamilton, where he was in the employ of the Great Western railway company. In 1864 the question of better protection to the fish of the inland waters, as well as the game of the country, was agitated in the leading papers of this province, and Mr. Kerr was appointed inspector for this district. He was then in the prime of life, and he made short work of many of the poachers and trespassers. He was a man of indomitable pluck and endurance, and in a few years he had all the law-breaking fishermen of this part of Canada completely under his subjection. From his residence at the turn of the Hamilton mountain he could sweep his telescope for twenty miles in all directions at early dawn, and if anything suspicious was drawn into the field of his glass he was away and would pounce on the offenders before they had properly got to work. He also traveled in different directions around the lakes, and surprised illegal fishermen from Parry sound to the Thousand islands. Mr. Kerr was a very efficient officer, but of late years he had been in failing health, and his death was not unexpected by his intimate friends. Mr. Kerr was a Conservative in politics, and in former years took an active part in county and Barton township matters. He represented the latter township for many years in its council. He leaves a widow, five daughters and three sons. He was a member of St. John's and Temple lodges, A. F. and A. M., and will be buried with Masonic rites to-day at 2 p.m.

Kerr's obituary from the Hamilton Times, Hamilton Public Library.

CHAPTER 1

Early Years in Ireland

There is no doubt that Kerr was born in Ireland, but there is some mystery about where he was born and where he grew up. The two biographical sources regarding Kerr are the *Dictionary of Hamilton Biography* and the introduction to Kerr's diaries. They are much the same in terms of details, and both are wrong about his date of birth, his place of birth, and much else.

They both indicate he was born on June 24, 1812, in County Fermanagh when, in fact, he was born June 23, 1812, at Mullingar in County Westmeath. The diaries were provided to the Royal Ontario Museum in 1940 by Kerr's son, Charles John Kerr. He had the diaries in his possession because he took over as fisheries overseer when his older brother, Frederick, died in 1902.

It is unknown if any biographical details were provided with the diaries, but when they were put on microfilm in 1981, the ROM was provided with a biography by J. W. Kerr's great-grandson, Dr. Robert Bews Kerr of Vancouver.[1]

Also in 1981, the *Dictionary of Hamilton Biography* was published under the editorship of T. Melville Bailey, a famous Hamilton historian. It contains a one-page biography of John William Kerr. I don't know whether Dr. Bailey got his information from the book or whether the

---

1   Dr. Robert Bews Kerr (Aug. 20, 1908–Dec. 19, 1997) was a distinguished medical doctor and recipient of the Order of the British Empire for his service during WWII.

book got its information from Dr. Bailey. Indeed, there could have been other sources of information of which I am not aware.

I know they are wrong because Kerr wrote in his diary that he was born in Mullingar and made several references to his date of birth (June 23) and even his hour of birth (7:00 p.m.).

Kerr made no reference to his family, other than that his mother's surname was Price and that his father and grandfather were Protestant Conservatives and Orangemen.[2] I have not done a family tree of his ancestors, but I have seen some reference to Kerr being the oldest of nine brothers. If so, he made no mention of them in his 10,000 pages of diaries and letters, and there is no apparent correspondence with anyone in Ireland after his arrival in Canada, which is unusual given his prolific letter writing.

There is also no indication that Kerr's wife had any communications with relatives in Ireland after arriving in Canada. Her family, the Winslows of County Fermanagh, were reportedly wealthy, but there is no record of any communication. Did she and Kerr leave Ireland under a cloud, or was there a fractured family situation? We will never know. Maybe there were letters, but they didn't survive. Kerr's diaries were only intended to record his business as fisheries overseer, but they also contain unrelated material, and his letters make occasional reference to extraneous events. I just find it hard to believe that over twenty-three years and thousands of pages he did not write more about his family.

Mullingar is a sleepy county town in the sleepy central-Ireland county of Westmeath. About eighty km from Dublin, it was primarily an agricultural town of maybe 3,000 people in the mid-nineteenth century. Never having been there, or indeed anywhere in Ireland, I can't say much about it except what I have read and watched on videos. It doesn't seem like much of a tourist town, and no tour buses appear to stop there. Containing a mix of Protestants and Catholics, it was noted to be primarily a nationalist (Catholic) town.

Kerr wrote nothing about what his father did for a living or about

---

2   The Loyal Orange Association was formed in 1795 as an Irish Protestant political society named after William of Orange, who defeated Catholic King James II in 1691 at the Battle of the Boyne.

any other members of his family. I have no idea where he went to school, but Kerr had a good education, as is evident from his writings, which are erudite, with generally excellent spelling and grammar. He appears to have been pretty well read, and I know from my father that he had a library in his home.[3]

In an 1882 letter to his friend, Thomas Elliot, from Niagara, Kerr made mention of his neighbourhood in Ireland and in the same sentence referred to the Dardistown River, which is an area near the airport north of Dublin. Whether he lived there or whether he was just visiting there is unclear. He gave the year as 1820, so he would have been just eight years old. He said he joined the Royal Irish Constabulary in 1832 when he was twenty years old and was sworn in at Dublin. We also know that he sailed out of Dublin for Canada in the summer of 1846.[4]

There is no mention of whether he had any farming background, but he seemed to have little difficulty farming his own one hundred acres on Hamilton Mountain. It's hard to imagine that he became an instant farmer in 1855 like some early version of Mr. Douglas from *Green Acres*, so I assume he had some farming experience in Ireland. He probably also fished and hunted as a young boy, which would be typical of the era when food was in short supply. County Westmeath is noted to this day as a popular fishing destination.

In 1884 he had an audience in Hamilton with newly installed Bishop Carberry, the third Catholic Bishop of Hamilton.[5] In a letter to his sometime Catholic friend, James "Big Jim" Cantwell, he reported, "By appointment I went to the Bishop's Palace, here on Friday last, and at 10:00 A.M. paid my respects to His Lordship, Bishop Carberry, and welcomed him to

....

3   I have a paper-bound book from the early nineteenth century that came from his library. It surveys a prospective railway line from Hamilton to Brantford.
4   The biographies claim he came to Canada in 1844, which is incorrect. He arrived on August 26, 1846.
5   James Joseph Carberry (Apr. 30, 1823–Dec. 19, 1887) was born in Mullingar, Westmeath, and was ordained as the third Catholic Bishop of Hamilton on Sept. 4, 1883. The Hamilton Diocese then consisted of Wentworth, Brant, Bruce, Grey, Halton, Wellington, and parts of Dufferin counties. Suffering from bad health, he returned to Ireland, where he died. He is buried in Limerick.

Hamilton! My own Townsman! A school boy in 1832 of about 10 years of age! I was then about 20 years old!! It is now 52 years ago! Since this happened in Mullingar. When taking my leave of His Lordship, he prayed that God might bless and keep me! He is a splendid man!"

When Kerr left Ireland in 1846, the Irish Potato Famine was just beginning, but that was not likely a factor in his leaving the country. As a Protestant and a friend of the "landlords," Kerr was not likely facing imminent starvation, as were millions of Irish Catholics who fled to North America. Kerr was no fan of Irish nationalism, but he did not engage in sectarian activities in Canada as so many other Irish did. Irish Catholics were often persecuted in Canada and were generally relegated to the lowest echelons of society. In having such a high opinion of Bishop Carberry, it is evident that Kerr did not disrespect Catholics. I imagine they talked about people and places they had known in Ireland, just as any other fellow travellers would do.

Kerr dropped occasional hints about his life in Ireland. Having a high regard for Collingwood fishermen, Kerr noted, "I have seen the Cornwall fishermen of England, from Land's End and Penzance, at Howth, County Dublin, Ireland in years gone and past, but give me Collingwood boat fishermen." Howth was a fishing village on the northern boundary of Dublin Bay. What was Kerr doing there? We will never know. He was probably a fisherman, at least recreationally, because he seemed to know a lot about fish and fishing, which was very popular in Ireland, where people were hungry.

While in the Royal Irish Constabulary, he served near the River Shannon, and we know he was put on trial and acquitted at Mullingar. He married Mary Eliza Winslow on February 19, 1846, just before leaving Ireland, and his marriage certificate indicated his status as "widower." If so, there is no mention of a first wife or any children in Ireland. The bios say that during his first winter in Canada, he stayed with an uncle, also a John Kerr, but there is only one reference to this uncle. In fact, after arriving in Port Stanley, he gave the name of the hotel he and his wife stayed in, Hutchinson House. He did teach school his first winter in Bayham County, as is correctly reported. He said he lived in the small town of Richmond, which no longer exists.

His wife was from Enniskillen, in County Fermanagh, so maybe that is where the confusion about his birthplace originates. Again, we know nothing about her from his writings. Indeed, if I didn't know her name was Mary Eliza, I would not know that from his writings, where she is only ever referred to as "Mrs. Kerr."

There is a brief reference to the Winslow's being wealthy landowners in Fermanagh, and we are told that Mary Eliza's sister married an important Irishman named William Thomas Mulvany.[6]

Kerr gave the occasional anecdote about songs he knew in Ireland and some people he was acquainted with, but other than that, crickets about his early life!

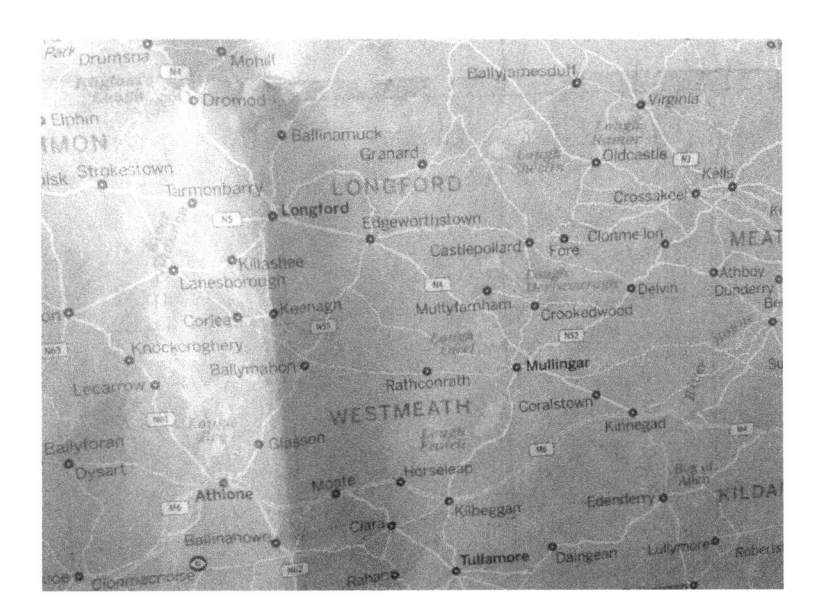

Detail of Map showing County Westmeath, Ireland. Lonely Planet, 2020.

....

6 William Thomas Mulvany (Mar. 11, 1806–Oct. 30, 1885) was born in Dublin as a Catholic, but he converted to the Church of England to enhance his educational and career prospects. He became an engineer and was responsible for planning waterways and improving commercial fishing. He married Alicia Winslow in 1832 and quit the Irish Civil Service in 1853. He moved to Germany, where he became instrumental in developing the Ruhr coal fields and was described as the "Irish King of the Ruhr."

CHAPTER 2

The Royal Irish Constabulary 1832–1846

The *Irish Constabulary Act* of 1822 marked the official beginning of what became, effectively, a national police force. By 1841 the force numbered over 8,600 men, of which Kerr was one. He was sworn in at Dublin Castle on September 1, 1832, when he was just twenty years of age. It is likely that he had been training for some time in what was like a military force with barracks and an arsenal. It was known as the Royal Irish Constabulary only after 1867 as a result of its involvement in the Fenian attacks in Ireland and elsewhere during the 1860's.

He mentioned several times that he was sworn in by Sir John Harvey (Apr. 23, 1778–Mar. 22, 1852), who was one of four inspector generals of the Royal Irish Constabulary (RIC). Harvey had an illustrious career in the British Military, and he was lieutenant general during the War of 1812 under General John Vincent. In June 1813 the British forces were camped out at Burlington Heights after being driven from Fort George at Niagara.

Harvey learned, supposedly from scout Billy Green, that the 3,500 American troops had advanced as far as Stoney Creek and were camped out near what is now known as Battlefield Park. Harvey convinced General Vincent to attempt a bold night attack and led his 700 men through what is now known as Hamilton to Stoney Creek, where the Americans were surprised and routed and their two generals captured. It was a turning point in the war. The Americans were forced to retreat to Fort George, where they were hemmed in. Had they advanced, we might all be Americans today!

Harvey returned to Canada in 1836, where he held a number of important posts, such as lieutenant governor of PEI and Nova Scotia. He died in Halifax in 1852. Kerr remarked several times that from his front door on Hamilton Mountain, he could see the battlefield of Stoney Creek, and he was intensely proud of having been sworn in by Harvey. When Kerr arrived in Canada in 1846, apparently, he had some contact with Harvey in Nova Scotia because he cryptically noted that Harvey had done him a favour. This was probably a letter of reference, for soon after he arrived in Canada, Kerr joined the Middlesex Militia as an officer.

It is likely that Kerr learned his discipline and perseverance in the RIC, where he also honed his police skills. He wrote that he was appointed as chief constable in 1838 and that he had a number of men serving under him. Apparently, he was stationed in County Westmeath, his home, which was somewhat unusual because RIC members were not usually stationed in their home county or the home county of their wives for fear that family members could be abducted.

In the 1830s and 1840s, the Catholic tenants were rebelling against the Protestant landlords, and there was a lot of sectarian violence. This probably occupied members of the RIC as much if not more than ordinary crime. As an Irish Protestant and the son and grandson of Orangemen, Kerr was clearly not on the side of the nationalists. Although not an Orangeman himself, he was clearly and fervently loyal to Britain, although he was committed to justice and "British fair play," a phrase he used frequently.

Seeking promotion in 1887, Kerr sent a letter to his boss in Ottawa in which he enclosed an article from the Mullingar newspaper of 1839, "an article in this old paper… will tell you who I was 48 years ago. Even the remembrance of these long years has its bright side up, and is pleasant sometimes to think over." The Mullingar newspapers of 1839 are not available online, but they may be available in the local library. I would love to see this article, which was probably about some law-enforcement event involving Kerr in County Westmeath. While there might have been a "bright side," there was also likely a dark side to his memories of those days.

On May 1, 1882, Kerr wrote a deeply personal letter to Samuel Wilmot at Newcastle. Wilmot had established a fish hatchery there and had at various times supplied Kerr with fry to be placed into Lake Ontario and salmon streams, such as the Credit River. Kerr was a great fan of Wilmot in his early years as fisheries overseer, revering him and frequently praising him. In later years Kerr and Wilmot had a bitter falling out. (See chapter 20.)

For sixteen years Kerr had been trying to get a fish hatchery established at Niagara-on-the-Lake in the Niagara River using a barracks attached to Fort George, which, if I am right, still exists as Navy Hall, a national historic site. He frequently tried to enlist the support of Wilmot and local politicians to get his supervisor to approve and partially fund the facility but never succeeded. By 1882 he was clearly frustrated and felt that part of the reason for the Department ignoring him might have been his Irish ancestry. To set the record straight, he sent the following letter to Wilmot, which I have reproduced here in its entirety.

Private and Confidential Hamilton 1st May 1882

My Dear Mr. Wilmot

I am in receipt of your letter and I have reported to your son about the fry for Puslinch Lake and Lake Meadad [Kerr was also frustrated that he could not secure fry for these two bodies of water that he wished to stock. Lake Puslinch fed into the Speed River and the Grand River while Lake Meadad fed into Burlington Bay through what is now Grindstone Creek.]

Except that I was born in Ireland 23rd June 1812, I have no sympathy with the Murdering class of Irish and for 65 years of my life I have known them in no other light. Of course there are a great many good men amongst them but in any case I am to be always found on the side of the Landlords [the landlords were the Protestant land owners] and nothing on Earth can separate me from them. I was very well acquainted with Mr. William Barlow Smythe (Smith) of Ballynegall,[7] Collinstown[8] Westmeath, my

---

7   Ballynagall (sometimes spelled with an "e") is a small town in County Westmeath, about four miles northeast of Mullingar.

8   Collinstown is a larger town about eleven miles northeast of Mullingar.

own native County who was recently fired at when his sister-in-law was shot and killed–what law can tolerate this! The greater part of Mr. Smythe's property was willed to him by his uncle by marriage James Gibbons Esq.[9] of Ballynegall who purchased and paid for the property. Mr. Gibbons was immensely rich his father having made a large fortune out in India.

When in 1841 I was at a place called Ballinahown[10] as Head Constable of the Royal Irish Constabulary Force I was fired at, returned the fire and wounded the man who fired at me and I took a prisoner and the gun that was fired at me. This same Mr. Gibbons was my personal friend and contributed money for counsel who assisted me. For mind you I was put in the dock as a felon at Mullingar Assizes where for 8 hours all the perjury that could be ransacked was sworn against me! I was honourably acquitted and mind you Mr. Gibbons and his nephew Mr. Smythe remained until 8:00 PM in court until the Verdict of Not Guilty was returned. And when that verdict of not guilty was handed in and cheer after cheer, the cheer that was given by Mr. Gibbons, Mr. Smythe and at least 200 other gentlemen, was astonishing and I am aware that when Mr. Gibbons and Mr. Smythe got home from Mullingar to Ballynegall, the family seat, the first expression they used was "We won. We have won!! Head Constable Kerr is Honourably acquitted." I was the Landlords friend then and I am so still.

When the late Lieutenant General Sir Duncan McGregor who was then Inspector General of the Royal Irish Constabulary sent for me he said in conversation to me that it was a deep laid conspiracy to deprive the County Westmeath of one of its most efficient officers and instead of being sent away to Cork as a preservation of my life I was retained in the County of Dublin. I had a force of 25 men

---

9   Ballynagall House was built for James Gibbons in 1808. The house is now in ruins.

10   Ballinahown is a small town in County Westmeath, about three miles east of the River Shannon.

under me at Ballinahown and I was there to protect three men, Mr. Kearan Daly, Mr. James Kennedy and a landlord agent, a Mr. Lewman and I did protect them. But while I was away from there <u>under suspension</u> and out on bail, Kennedy was fired at and wounded in the head and Kearan Daly was murdered, his throat was cut and his tongue was pulled out through the cut and was found lying on his breast when his Murdered body was found. But the murdering crew dare not touch them so long as I was protecting them while at Ballinahown.

I tell you this little incident of my life so that you will always know where to find me as regards Ireland and the Irish. Kearan Daly had been a <u>Ribbonman</u>,[11] became a land bailiff hence why he was shot and killed and his throat cut as I have described. I was wounded in my right leg by Joe Kearney who as one of an armed party of six fired at me. I returned the fire and being loaded in one barrel with 12 Swan drops[12] I shot him from head to foot. I aimed at his thighs and when I fired at him as he crossed me running for River Shannon to escape after he had first fired at me and I had called on him to stand and deliver up his gun in his hand and I could see dust fly out of his corduroy breeches and I observed him yield to the shot when I struck him at a distance of about 80 yards. It was only after I told him if he did not give up the gun I would send something heavier at him that he dropped the gun, made for the Shannon and crossed over from Westmeath to Roscommon.[13] I picked up the gun and I made and took another of the party prisoner before my own party of police except one man named Hayes got up to me. A true bill was found against Joseph Kearney for first firing at me but I was placed first on my trial and was acquitted and them I refused with the sanction of the Government to

....

11   A "ribbonman" was a member of an Irish Catholic nationalist secret society formed in 1806 to oppose the Protestant landlords.
12   Swan drops were an early type of shotgun ammunition.
13   County Roscommon lies to the west of Westmeath and is divided in places by the River Shannon.

prosecute Kearney and such a thankful man you never beheld as this man Joe Kearney proved himself to be. He promised if I came back again to Ballinahown no more outrages would be committed and that if any more shooting was in contemplation he would apprise me before hand so that I could capture the offenders.

When Kennedy was fired at and wounded Sir John Ennis[14] *who was the landlord of Ballinahown applied to the Lord Lieutenant (then) of Ireland to send me back and augment the station. MacDonnell the County Inspector to whom the application was submitted for report replied he would not recommend it for if I was sent back a person would shoot me or I would shoot somebody.*

This shooting affair happened on a Sunday when this armed party tried to steal a march and assassinate Mr. James Kennedy imagining I had permitted all the policemen under me to go to church! I was, however, equal to the attack and frustrated it.

There is no inducement on Earth could induce me to do what I have read our House of Commons done recently, pass a resolution in behalf of murderers. I can tell you a great deal more but I refuse doing so. Of course, Ireland should have a Parliament of their own but I have doubts they would enjoy it. Men who would murder or shoot an innocent lady deserve no indulgence of any kind whatever--so much for the Irish. If I happen to be Scotch instead of being unhappily born in Ireland I suppose I would have a fish hatchery at Niagara more than 16 years ago. I have had so many promises made to me and broken again about it by you, by Mr. Whitcher and Mr. Plumb [Niagara MP] that I have now come to conclusion to apply no more. If you do help me well and good, I shall never forget it to you but whether granted or not my disappointment will not be affected any.

I send you this letter as a variety from all my previous correspondence... I am loyal and true to England and our beloved Queen

---

14   Sir John Ennis (1800–Aug. 8, 1878) was an Irish Catholic politician, who sat in the English House of Commons from 1857–1865.

and I lived under 4 Crown Heads, George the 3rd, George the 4th, William the 4th and our Noble Queen Victoria and I am a sound conservative at home and abroad as my father and grandfather was before me and believe me as ever, your fraternally, J. W. Kerr

It is curious that Kerr was put on trial for this event when he did not fire first and was clearly just doing his job. I have no explanation for this and can only speculate that it may have been an attempt to mollify the Catholic majority. As Kerr stated, lies were given at trial. It is likely that the Catholics had a different version of events, probably that Kerr had fired first on unarmed tenants. Fortunately, Kerr had the backing of the Protestant landlords, who likely paid for his defence and ensured his acquittal. Had he been convicted, he would likely have been hanged or at least transported to Australia.

It seems certain that the shooting was the main reason for him leaving Ireland in 1846. It appears that he may have become unwelcome in the Irish Constabulary as a risk to himself and others. It is unclear if he quit or was fired, but in any event, he and his wife, whom he married on February 19, 1846, left the country by July, never to return. There was likely some outrage at his acquittal, and had he returned to service in Westmeath or elsewhere, there might have been a bounty on his head.

If the shooting took place in 1841, it is hard to explain why he did not leave Ireland until 1846. Trials in that era happened soon after the event, so he was likely acquitted within a few weeks or months of the shooting. So, what did he do during the five intervening years? We will likely never know, but he was possibly put on duty in Dublin where he would likely have been relatively anonymous.

There is also a bit of a mystery about Kerr's marriage status in Ireland. When he married in 1846, he listed his marital status as "widower," and yet there is no mention anywhere in his diaries about a first wife. There is a cryptic reference in a letter that he would be a third time married before an unlikely event occurred. That is it! The RIC frowned on marriage for its members, fearing that wives could be kidnapped or compromised. Marriages had to be approved by commanding officers, and permission was rarely granted, often resulting in secret marriages.

Was that what had happened to Kerr? We will likely never know.

Kerr wrote that he was in the RIC for thirteen years and eight months, which means until April 1846. It is unfortunate that we don't know more about his life in the RIC or, indeed, about his life in Ireland generally. This seems to have been a very formative period for his future in Canada, and it is mostly lost in the haze of time.[15]

One final curiosity exists about his RIC years. If you search the RIC archives (apparently, their service records are available online, although you have to join, and pay for, a membership in a genealogical outfit like Ancestry to access them), you can search by name to see if they have any information you need, but when you enter Kerr's name and service dates, you get nothing. Did he never actually belong to the RIC (which seems unlikely), or were his records expunged? I suppose another explanation might be that my frugality in not signing up has denied me even this basic information!

Emblem of Royal Irish Constabulary

....

15   Apparently, the Mullingar library has newspapers going back to the 1840s, and it is possible I could have learned more had I been able to get there and afford to spend the time to do a lot of searching. Unfortunately, Covid-19 and my own health precluded this. Maybe for a future edition!

CHAPTER 3

Arrival in Canada

When Kerr arrived at Port Stanley on August 26, 1846, he had just turned thirty-four years old, and his probably pregnant wife, Mary Elizabeth Winslow, was just twenty. It is not known why they chose to emigrate, but the situation in Ireland was not good, and the Irish Potato Famine had commenced the year before, in 1845. My suspicion, however, is that the move had more to do with his service in the RIC and the probability that he was a marked man.

Kerr and his wife left from the Port of Dublin, but they may have travelled across the Irish Sea to Liverpool, which was the English port from which most steamers departed for America. Kerr wrote that he was in Phoenix Park, Dublin,[16] on June 18, 1846, "celebrating the great victory of Wellington,[17] I was then on my way to this glorious country." The trip across the ocean to New York would have taken about twenty days, so they likely boarded sometime in mid-July. I do not know the name of the ship they travelled on, but it was probably a steam-powered paddle-wheeler assisted by sail and likely held a few hundred passengers. Most travelled in steerage, but I suspect Kerr had a cabin because he was

....

16 Phoenix Park in Dublin was a 1,750-acre enclosed park that included a British military fort. It was the scene of the shocking 1882 murder of Lord Frederick Cavendish and Thomas Burke by Irish nationalists.
17 The Battle of Waterloo was fought on June 18, 1815, between England, led by the Duke of Wellington, Arthur Wellesley (born and raised in Ireland), and Napoleon, bringing the Napoleonic wars to an end.

probably a cut or two above the poorest travellers.

After landing in New York, Kerr would have had to travel a couple hundred miles up the Hudson River to where the Erie Canal commenced near Rome, New York. He could have travelled by train, which would have taken maybe ten hours, or by boat, which could have taken a couple of days. The Erie Canal opened in 1825, and packet boats were pulled by teams of horses or mules. As long as seventy feet, they could hold forty or more passengers, and it would take another three to four days to make the 363-mile trip to Buffalo. Kerr made no mention of his voyage across the ocean or his trip to Buffalo. He did, however, mention that from Buffalo he took the steamer, *New London,* to Port Stanley, on its way to Amherstburg on the Detroit River.

Originally known as Kettle Creek, the town of Port Stanley was renamed in 1824 after a visit by Lord Stanley, who later became the prime minister of Great Britain and was the father of Frederick Stanley, the earl of Derby, who became the governor general of Canada and donated the Stanley Cup in 1893. Steamship service commenced between Buffalo and Port Stanley in 1832. Port Stanley had a large, sheltered harbour, one of the finest on Lake Erie.

Steamships had sailed on Lake Erie since 1818. In 1842 the first screw propeller was introduced on the Great Lakes, which was an advance on the older paddlewheel technology. The Buffalo-to-Detroit trip cost about eight dollars for cabin and about three dollars for steerage, and the voyage took about forty hours. Cabin got passengers a private room and meals, whereas in steerage people had to buy their own meals, and they slept on the deck or in the forward cabin, where there might have been bunks. These ships burned firewood and on a round trip would use between 100 and 200 cords of wood (a cord is 4 x 4 x 8 feet and cost about $1.75).

Kerr mentioned arriving in Port Stanley on August 26 at 6:00 a.m. to a band playing "Rule Britannia." That sounds a little strange, but I have to assume it was true. It also seems that the Kerrs were not the only British immigrants that morning and that it was an immigrant ship. I am sure the band didn't get up early just to welcome undistinguished people like Kerr and his wife. Maybe someone of distinction was on board.

Although Kerr had an uncle in the area, on his first night in Canada, he stayed at the Hutchinson House Hotel[18] in St. Thomas. Of his uncle, also John William Kerr, he made only one reference. This seems strange, but Kerr made little reference to his own family in Ireland, and I don't even know his parents' first names, although he did mention in passing that his mother's surname was "Price." Kerr noted that he taught school during the fall and winter of 1846–1847 and that he lived in the small town of Richmond in Bayham Township. Kerr moved to London, ON, in May 1847 to take a position as a clerk in the post office, but I have no idea where he lived.

There are various references to his life in London. For example, he mentioned knowing the prominent Carling family and their son, John Carling,[19] from May 1847 when Carling would have been just nineteen years old. He also referenced joining the militia in London and rising to the rank of adjutant, which is an assistant to a commanding officer.

CANADA IN THE 1840s

The British colonies of Upper Canada and Lower Canada were formed in 1791 and consisted of what are Ontario and Quebec, although both were much smaller because the Hudson Bay Company controlled all of Rupert's Land, consisting of the entire watershed of Hudson's Bay, including what is now Northern Ontario and most of Northern Quebec. Both provinces had elected legislatures and appointed executive councils. In Upper Canada the governing members were known derisively as the "Family Compact." There was much agitation for reform, and in 1837 the Mackenzie and Papineau rebellions took place. After putting down the rebels, the English government sent the Earl of Durham to

---

18   The Hutchinson House Hotel dates back to at least 1831 but appears to have originally been a modest dwelling, like a B&B of today. A more substantial structure was built in 1855, and Kerr returned to stay there again in the 1880s, with fond memories.

19   John Carling (Jan. 23, 1828–Nov. 6, 1911) moved with his family to London in 1839, and the family opened their brewery in 1843. Carling became a politician and was a Conservative MP from 1872–1891. He was postmaster general from 1882–1885, and he was later appointed to the Senate. He was also a railway man, being involved with the GWR and the London & Port Stanley Railroad.

Canada in the spring of 1838 to investigate, and he presented his *Report on the Affairs of British North America* in late winter 1839.

One of the report's recommendations was the legislative union of Upper and Lower Canada. The *Act of Union* was passed in 1840 and came into effect in 1841, creating the united Province of Canada, which consisted of Canada West (Ontario) and Canada East (Quebec). Each branch had equal representation in the legislative assembly and a governing executive council, but there continued to be a lot of pressure for truly representative government, meaning representation by population. This was eventually achieved by the passage of the *British North America Act* in 1867, of which more will be said later.

THE POST OFFICE AT LONDON

When Kerr moved to London in May 1847, he took a job as the fourth clerk in the post office. At the time London only had a population of 2,500, but the post office likely served the entire Middlesex County. In 1847 the post office was still under control of British authorities, but they were trying to divest responsibility onto the colonies. The first stamp was not used until 1851, so people probably had to go into the post office to pick up and drop off mail. Although telegraph service between Toronto and Hamilton started in 1846, in any other location, the only method of communication was by mail.

Being a clerk in a post office in 1847 was likely a pretty mundane and low-paying job. The only advantage that I can see is that one likely got to know everybody and, if one was a person of intelligence and good upbringing, one might get other opportunities. Kerr was both, so the post office may have been his springboard to better things.

During his four years there he advanced from fourth to first clerk, so someone must have recognized his potential. Needless to say, his Irish Protestant status also did not hurt.

THE GREAT WESTERN RAILWAY

In May 1851, Kerr and his family moved to Hamilton, where he was employed as the chief clerk in the engineering office of the Great

Western Railway (GWR).

The *Great Western Railway Bill* was passed by the legislative assembly of Upper Canada in 1837 to promote the construction of a line to be built from Niagara to Sandwich (now Windsor). On July 20 of that year, Sir Allan Napier MacNab of Hamilton was elected president of the company. Because of a depression from 1838 to 1843, little had been done to develop the line, which was then controlled by Hamilton backers, including MacNab and Hamilton businessmen such as George Tiffany and the brothers Peter and Isaac Buchanan.

MacNab was born in Niagara-on-the Lake in 1798. He fought in the War of 1812 as a fourteen-year-old boy. He was called to the bar in 1824 and moved to Hamilton in 1826, where he practiced law and became a land developer. In 1835 his Dundurn Castle was completed after three years of construction. In 1830 he was elected to the legislative assembly of Upper Canada, and he fought as part of the British militia against the Mackenzie Rebellion. As Hamilton's leading citizen, his two passions were the GWR and politics. He achieved his highest office as the premier of the United Province of Ontario from 1854–1856.

In August 1845 MacNab travelled to London, England, to secure investors for the GWR. About 55,000–60,000 shares were sold to the British public, who were guided by a "corresponding committee." According to Donald R. Beer's biography of Sir Allan MacNab, published in 1984, shares of the GWR "became one of the glamour stocks of the (then economic) boom."

By the fall of 1847, a full survey of the line had been completed, and on October 23, a ground-breaking ceremony was held in London, ON, attended by some 3,000 spectators and Hamilton dignitaries. On page 237 of Beer's biography, he notes that "no one deserved or received more credit than MacNab himself." Undoubtedly, Kerr was in attendance, and it was probably then that his interest in working for the railroad began.

In 1847 greater London had a population of about 5,000 and was a backwoods community inadequately served by Lord Simcoe's Dundas Road (now Highway 2) and too far from Great Lakes commerce. One of the purposes of the GWR was to provide a shortcut between Detroit and western New York State for the movement of freight and passengers, and London benefitted greatly from the line's construction. By 1855 its population had grown to 16,000 according to David R.P. Guay's 2015 book, *Great Western Railway of Canada*.

When Kerr, his wife, and their first two children moved to Hamilton in May 1851, it would have been a difficult two-day trip by horse and buggy—or by horse and wagon if they had any belongings. The first city directory for Hamilton was printed in 1853 with a dedication to Sir Allan MacNab. It notes a John Kerr living at 86 Peel Street, which is now Hunter St., and lists his occupation as "clerk," so this was undoubtedly him. On the north side of Peel Street, #86 was between Catherine Street and Walnut Street, which is now a row of old houses, but they can't possibly date back to the 1850s.

The 1853 directory contains a curious note. Under the list of municipal officers, J.W. Kerr is noted as a "firewood inspector." This was probably our Kerr and was possibly a side job from his position as clerk with the GWR. Most of the city was still heated by firewood, and the inspector's job was to ensure the wood was properly labeled and of the correct size and species. Fires were common everywhere in Ontario in the mid-nineteenth century and monitored firewood was one method of controlling the risk.

In the 1856 and 1858 city directories, John W. Kerr is listed as "City Chamberlain." A chamberlain was something like a treasurer today, responsible for collecting and distributing tax money. He also had the power to cancel licences issued to vendors who did not pay their fees. This seems like a pretty prestigious position, although in 1851 Hamilton had a population of only about 12,000. The problem is, contradictory information exists because a Robert Kerr is also listed as city chamberlain. I cannot confirm which Kerr this was, but it would have been right up Kerr's alley, with his aptitude for keeping accounts.

Railways were expensive to build and, of course, did not produce any revenue until opened for business after years of construction. This created an imperative to build them as quickly as possible, which sometimes resulted in cost cutting and shoddy safety standards. This was clearly the case with the GWR and was the cause of a curious situation that involved Kerr until 1861. (See chapter 16 on the GWR scandal in which Kerr tried to get his former boss, Managing Director C. J. Brydges, fired.)

As chief clerk in the engineering department, Kerr likely was very involved in the railway line's construction and clearly had access to all the records and accounts. Sir Allan MacNab worked tirelessly and without pay for the railway and was likely well known by Kerr. The engineering office would have been the busiest part of the enterprise, and Kerr was likely involved with acquiring equipment and material for construction, contracts, and personnel. He seemed to have a great familiarity with maps and surveys, skills he likely learned while at the GWR. He was meticulous in his account keeping and scrupulous about obtaining receipts, things that would have stood him well with his employer.

By 1852 construction was well underway, and the line was scheduled to open in August 1853. In 1852 Chief Engineer Roswell G. Benedict was dismissed because of rising costs and was replaced, at the request of the American shareholders, by John T. Clark, an American. In late 1852 Charles John Brydges, born in 1827 in London, England, was appointed managing director, and he arrived in Canada in early 1853 to assume control of the line. He was fifteen years younger than Kerr, who was then forty years old, and it is unclear what Kerr thought of this young English upstart, but clearly Kerr was in the camp of his immediate boss, John T. Clark.

Kerr wrote that he earned $1,200 a year with the GWR, which is twice what his annual salary was as a fisheries overseer.[20] At almost four dollars a day, this was about four times the average pay for a working man, so Kerr was doing very well, which probably enabled him to acquire his farm in 1854 and build his large house the following year.

Kerr reported that in May 1858 he and about forty other employees of the GWR were fired because of political infighting. As I understand the story, GWR shareholder and major businessman Isaac Buchanan backed the building of a second railroad, running between Buffalo and Windsor, to prevent the hated Grand Trunk Railroad from building that line and thereby undermining the GWR. The Grand Trunk would

---

20   He did earn quite a bit more for his "special duty" assignments, and he was paid for his expenses.

then have lines running north and south of the GWR, which would be boxed in and made superfluous for international trade.

This idea was not backed by Managing Director C. J. Brydges or the primary contractor, Samuel Zimmerman. Buchanan, who was a staunch supporter of Sir John A. MacDonald, was shoved out, and with him went all his supporters, including Kerr. Considering that the line opened in 1854, the engineering office would have probably shrunk anyway, so it was unlikely that Kerr could have had a job for life unless he was promoted. There is never a good time to get fired, but Kerr, who now had a wife and four kids to feed, probably took a financial hit as a result.

We do not know what Kerr did between 1858 and 1864 when he was appointed as fisheries overseer because he made no mention of this period in his diaries or letters except for his school board and fish-and-game society activities. He was living in Barton Township at the time, so he does not show up in the city directories. Maybe he was just building his mountain road and learning how to farm. Most mountain roads were toll roads, but I have no idea if Kerr ever made any money off his almost impossibly steep and narrow road.

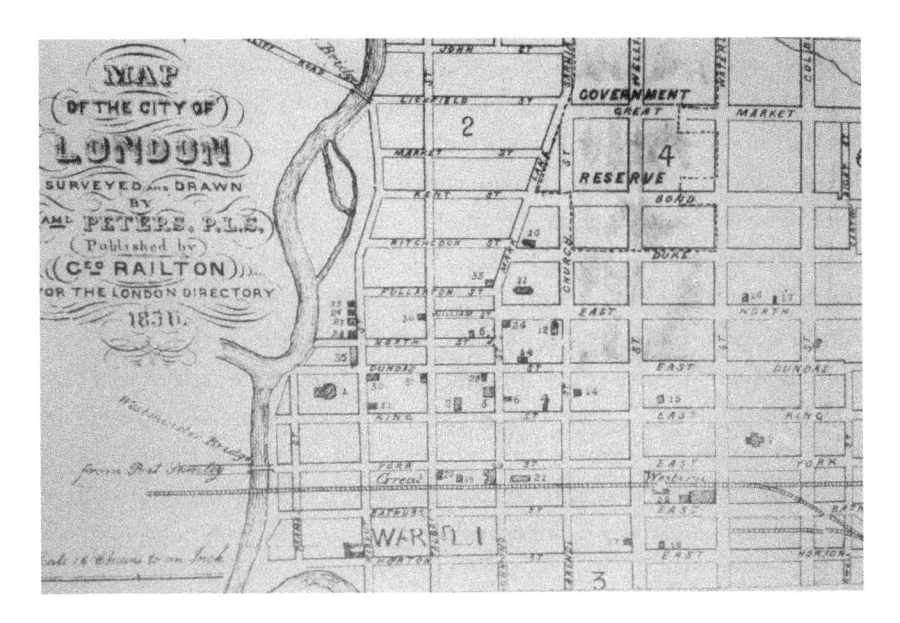

Detail from Map of London Ontario, 1856.

CHAPTER 4

The Wentworth Society for the Protection of Game and Fish

By 1860 Kerr had been on the mountain for almost five years. It is not known whether he cleared his one hundred acres or whether it was already cleared for farming, but he had a mixed farm with crops and livestock. By then he had a wife and six kids to feed, ranging in age from one to thirteen. He was probably out of work, bored with farming, or both.

It is unclear where his interest in protecting game and fish came from, but suddenly in June 1860, he initiated the Wentworth Society for the Protection of Game and Fish. The first meeting was held at Mrs. Press's saloon in downtown Hamilton at 8:00 p.m. on Tuesday June 19, 1860. The attendees included Hamilton's most famous citizen, Sir Allan MacNab,[21] whom Kerr had served under both at the Great Western Railway and as adjutant[22] to MacNab's militia regiment. Also present were nineteen other local residents, including Harcourt Bull, who later assisted Kerr in getting his appointment as fisheries overseer in 1864, and John McCuaig, who was appointed the first fisheries overseer in Upper Canada in 1850.

It's pretty clear that Kerr was the driving force behind the society because he was elected secretary of the meeting. Anybody who has ever

---

21 After MacNab's name is the word "Bart," which stands for "baronet."
22 An adjutant is a personal assistant to a military commander as an executive officer.

joined a committee knows that the secretary does about eighty percent of the work and propels the agenda.

The first item of business was to order 300 copies of the *Game Act* to be printed and posted throughout the county. The *Game Act* was passed in 1856 and prohibited hunting or possessing various species during their birthing seasons, "Indians" exempted.

The second order of business was to provide "a $5.00 dollar reward for information leading to convictions." The information was to be given to Kerr, which he would treat as confidential if so requested. Knowing how he later operated as fisheries overseer, this was probably purely Kerr's invention.

It was also adopted that fish "do form a part of the consideration of the members of the Club." A committee was struck to form a constitution, a most British formality, and then the meeting broke up at 10:30, whereupon the gentlemen likely adjourned to the saloon.

A second meeting was held on June 27 to consider the draft constitution and to set a date for a formal meeting to elect officers and pass the constitution and bylaws. A short notice of the meeting to be held on July 3 was placed in the *Hamilton Spectator*.

This meeting also took place at Mrs. Press's saloon, and the seven-article constitution was passed. Sir Allan MacNab, then sixty-two years old and in poor health, was elected president by acclamation, and Kerr was elected secretary. It was ordered that the formation of the society be noted in the *Spectator*, and Kerr wrote a lengthy piece that was published a few days later. I say Kerr wrote it because the form and content was consistent with his twenty-three years of diaries.

Typically for the time, new membership was restricted to those securing a majority vote from existing members. Membership fees were set at one dollar per year, which is about what a common workman earned in a day. The initial members seem to have been a pretty well-heeled group of Wentworth County gentry.

Curiously, article seven of the constitution set an objective of introducing prairie fowl into Upper Canada. Prairie chickens had once lived on the prairie lands of southwestern Ontario, but as land was converted to farming, they gradually lost habitat. Known as "boomers" for the mating sounds the males made, they were officially noted as having been extirpated in Ontario since 1990, although they had mostly disappeared long before then. Extirpated in bird conservation terms means not extinct but no longer occupying former habitat. Some member must have wanted these birds on the menu!

The next noted meeting took place on March 8, 1861, at which time it was agreed to write to the governor general to request the appointment of deputies to enforce the fishery laws in Burlington Bay, Dundas Marsh, and tributaries. They also increased the reward leading to convictions to ten dollars, which was a sizable amount in 1861. Kerr may have been behind these motions in his quest for employment.

Kerr also noted that Captain Glassco attended the meeting and recommended that a closed season be enacted for the protection of mink and muskrats. While Glassco is never again mentioned in Kerr's diaries, he must have been a friend or at least made some impression on Kerr. A plan of subdivision on part of Kerr's farm sets out various proposed streets, one of which was "Glassco Ave." Although it was never built, there is a Glassco Avenue in the lower city. I have no other information as to who Glassco was, but he was probably a captain in the militia unit to which Kerr belonged (the 3rd Wentworth Militia).

The day after the meeting, the committee met to draft the letter to the governor general through the commissioner of Crown lands to request that no seine or gill-net fishing be permitted on Burlington Bay or Dundas Marsh and that deputies be given the power to seize and destroy nets and other devices used to fish during the closed season. The petition, signed by Kerr and MacNab, was sent to Quebec on March 14, 1861.

The first annual meeting was held on July 2, 1861, with a considerably diminished membership. The officers were re-elected, including Kerr and MacNab, and the government response to the March 14 petition was considered, although it was not described in the minutes.

The second and apparently the last annual meeting was held on July 1, 1862, with only six members in attendance. MacNab died only five weeks later, on August 8, 1862, and was not an attendee. Oh, in case you were wondering, Mrs. Press was paid one dollar for every meeting held in her saloon. I wonder what she made on the drinks!

The Wentworth Society for the Protection of Game and Fish

Kerr's diaries make only one further mention of the society, and that is from February 1865 when Kerr mentioned Fishery Overseer McCuaig in rather negative terms.[23] Responding to a notification that he had been appointed to enforce the games laws, Kerr noted that he was instrumental in getting up the Wentworth Game Protection Society together with MacNab. Regarding his predecessor, John McCuaig, Kerr said, "his hobby was to protect and preserve the fish but he being a well-paid officer of government, I and other members had no objection provided he attended to the fish, we would attend to the game." Kerr noted that on one occasion, McCuaig deputized him to seize nets, but when Kerr discovered that McCuaig had warned the fishermen of his arrival, "I abandoned all idea of doing the duty of a well-paid government officer and so went down the Game and Fish Protection Society of Wentworth."

After he was appointed fisheries overseer, Kerr had numerous dealings with other fish-and-game clubs, some of whom claimed to be interested in protecting and preserving fish and game. Kerr found that their actual motives were usually just to shoot and kill and fish as they pleased, to the exclusion of all others. Kerr had many squabbles with such organizations over the years, and sometimes matters got quite ugly and serious.

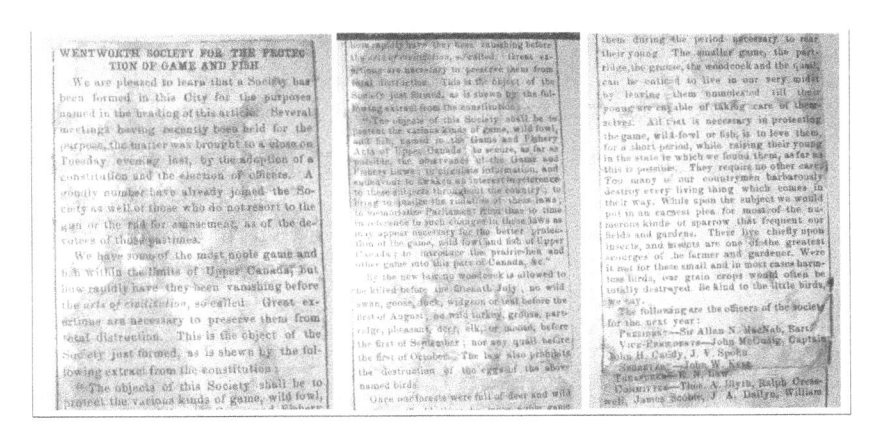

Newspaper clipping found in Kerr diary. Notice about the establishment of the Wentworth Society for the Protection of Game and Fish. ROM

....

23   Kerr's notes about the society are found at the start of volume three and are probably not a complete record.

CHAPTER 5

Commercial Fishing in the Lower Great Lakes

THE GEAR

Never having been a particularly avid fisherman (I wasn't happy unless there was something on the line every two minutes), I did not know much about fishing except that there was an awful lot of fishing tackle for sale, and somebody must have been buying it. All I knew about commercial fishing was what I saw on occasional visits to Port Dover on Lake Erie and that it involved strange-looking boats and nets. So, since John Kerr spent over twenty-three years enforcing the fishing law, I knew I would have to learn a thing or two about fishing.

Fish had managed to get up the St. Lawrence as far as Lake Ontario through the Lachine or "china" rapids, but how had they populated the upper Great Lakes through the 325-foot "impassable barrier" of Niagara Falls?. Dan Egan, in his 2017 book *The Death and Life of the Great Lakes,* describes how a 2-million-year ice age that only ended about 10,000 years ago scraped out the lakes and that the ice would ebb and flow with the climate, allowing fish to enter open water through streams and rivers.

Fish were abundant in the Great Lakes, and Indigenous people have always fished for the 15,000–20,000 years they have been here. According to a report written by A. B. McCulloch in 1987, "Indian fishermen used hooks, gill nets, weirs, spears, seines and dipnets." However, this was primarily subsistence fishing. Commercial fishing on the lower lakes didn't really begin until after the War of 1812.

> *The early fisheries were primarily inshore and river fisheries; the abundance of fish made it unnecessary to pursue fish in the deeper and more remote parts of the lakes. Commercial fisheries used seine nets, spears, dip nets, hoop nets, gill nets and hooks. The seine net was preferred because it was cheap, safe to use, required little skill and when fish were abundant, it was very efficient. However, the seine was not selective in the fish it caught and it caught all fish which it enclosed including many immature fish which were unmarketable and were wasted.*

There were many instances of wasted fish being used as fertilizer, which drove Kerr crazy, as did the act of fishermen throwing fish offal back into the water. What were these commercial fishing methods? Well, after doing a little Internet research, I am going to tell you. Most of what I learned is from the Fisheries Research Board of Canada, which published a report written many years ago by W. A. Kennedy.

Seine Nets – A seine is an oblong piece of netting with weights and floats that is set parallel to a beach and then pulled ashore, thereby enclosing fish between the netting and the beach. In the nineteenth century, seine nets were made of twine and were either bought or more often made by fishermen and their families. They were hauled in to the beach on wooden rollers, and the fish were removed. The nets were then dried and reset for the next haul. The government set the minimum size for the mesh to limit the catch of immature fish. For herring and smaller fish, the mesh was usually two inches in diameter. For larger species like whitefish and pickerel (walleye), it was four to six inches. Thus, smaller fish could swim through the mesh and avoid capture. Kerr frequently wrote to various fisheries ministers to suggest changes to the mesh size. Sometimes they listened, and sometimes they didn't.

The major problems with seine nets was that they cannot be used in rocky water and require access to a beach or shoreline.

Gill Nets – Gill nets are long lengths of netting that can be set in deep water and drawn up periodically to extract the catch. They also have different mesh sizes to catch particular types of fish. By 1890 more than a million yards of gill nets were in the lakes. Gill nets were cheap and could be used by large- or small-scale fishermen. Before the use of steam-powered tugs, nets were brought into the boat by hand, which limited their length. By the 1870s steam-powered tugs allowed boats to fish up to 60,000 yards of net. The only problem with gill nets is that the fish in them expire after a few hours, and their quality declines. They can be used anywhere, the season is longer, and they are more durable than fixed nets.

Pound Nets – These were particularly useful in the generally shallow waters of Lake Erie and involved wooden stakes that were pounded into the lake bottom and projected several feet above the water level. According to Kennedy,

> *the stakes are carefully located in a predetermined pattern. The pound net "leader" is essentially a straight fence of netting general set at right angles to the shoreline. When fish encounter it they generally head to deeper water where the "head" of the pound net is located. Fish are guided further and further into a trap from which retreat becomes difficult. Finally, they enter the "crib" or "pot" where the fish are trapped until the pot is brought to the surface where the fish are brought aboard alive with dip nets.*

Trap Nets – These were legal in American waters but not in Canada until 1950. Essentially the same as pound nets, the major difference was that stakes were not used. With weights at the bottom and floats at the top, trap nets can be set in deep water. They can be moved easily, and like pound nets, the fish are held alive until they are scooped out.

Hook Lines – In commercial fishing, a line with one hundred hooks or more was baited and dropped in the lake until they were retrieved, hopefully full of fish. The fish were dead, and the lines were inefficient because bait such as minnows had to be caught and put on the hooks. I guess they didn't have dew worms in Styrofoam containers!

Spearfishing – A spear usually had multiple prongs and was used for ice fishing and in open water. Kerr hated spearfishing because it was usually done at night using light (jack lights) to attract the fish, which gave the fisherman an unfair advantage. Spear fishing on Burlington Bay was licensed for one dollar a season. It was popular with the citizenry because it gave unemployed men something to do in the winter to provide food and perhaps make a bit of money. Every fall Kerr had to scout out the spearfishermen and try to extract their collar, which he would the dutifully send on to Ottawa.

The Fish – According to Kennedy, there were at least thirty-one species of fish in the Great Lakes. Many species went by different names. I didn't know what pickerel were because they are commonly referred to as "walleye" for some reason. In the nineteenth century, the big commercial fish were lake herring, whitefish, lake trout, and pickerel. Although salmon were in Lake Ontario, it was not a big commercial fish due to limited supply. Yellow perch was a minor commercial fish, as were sturgeon, which were caught for their roe (caviar to most) Some were reported to be as long as seven feet. Introduced or invasive species included eels, smelt, and carp.

What fishermen caught depended on where they were, how deep and cold the water was, and what kind of gear they were using. For example, Lake Erie contains three separate basins of varying depths and water temperatures, and the catch, both the quantity and the species of fish, varies in each.

In *The Death and Life of the Great Lakes,* Egan notes how the Erie and Welland canals opened the upper lakes to invasive species like lamprey eels and carp, and Kerr noted how some species were introduced by well-meaning but usually uninformed fish culturists. Egan also mentions damage done to the Great Lakes by the ballast from oceangoing vessels full of zebra and quagga mussels that arrived in the latter half of the twentieth century.

Kennedy says that lake herring, also known as ciscos, were the most important species in the fishery in the nineteenth century, followed by whitefish, pickerel, and lake trout. Sturgeon were popular for a while until they were fished out, and salmon was never really a commercial fish until they were virtually extinct in the 1890s. The largest commercial fisheries were on Lake Erie, with its shallow, warm water. Perch were a relatively minor catch in the 1800s, even though now that is practically all people get from the Great Lakes.

THE LAW

In his 1987 treatise *Commercial Fishing on the Great Lakes,* A. B. McCullough discusses Canadian fishing laws and notes,

> *Early legislation, and much of the legislation that is in force today, attempted to maintain the fishery in three ways: First, by encouraging the reproduction of existing stocks; second, by limiting the total catch; and third, by maintaining the environment. Reproduction was encouraged by protecting the spawning grounds, ensuring access by fish to them, limiting fishing during the spawning period and by artificial propagation. Until recently, no attempt was made to limit the total catch directly by means of catch limits or quotas; instead, the catch was limited indirectly by imposing conditions on the use of fishing gear. Environmental protection has largely taken the form of regulations preventing obvious pollution. Attempts to restrict more subtle forms of pollution, such a nutrient loading, have only been attempted in recent years.*

Upper Canada passed a *Salmon Protection Act* in 1807, and a major revision did not take place until 1858 when the *Fisheries Act* was passed, which regulated what and where fishing gear could be used and provided for closed seasons to protect the fish during spawning. It also provided for the licensing of fishing and perhaps most importantly, provided for the enforcement of the regulations by the province rather than municipal governments relying on informers. A fisheries superintendent was appointed in 1857, and by 1866 Kerr was one of eighteen fisheries overseers.

McCullough writes,

> *Although the staff was small, poorly paid and often poorly motivated, it made some progress towards implementing the fisheries laws. It began a systematic collection of statistics which made subsequent scientific investigations of the fishery possible. It began enforcing the law requiring fish ladders around mill dams and it had some success in limiting the dumping of sawdust. The staff were essential to the introduction of the licence system. Many fishermen assumed that they had, through long occupation, acquired a title to the fisheries which they were accustomed to exploit and resisted the imposition of licenses and leases. By the 1870s this resistance had been overcome and fishermen accepted that licenses and fishery officials were a part of the fishery.*

After Confederation, the federal government controlled the fisheries, and in 1868 the *Fisheries Act* was passed, which was largely modeled on the 1858 Act. It also provided for artificial fish propagation under the supervision of Samuel Wilmot of Newcastle. As McCullough observes, "Although there was widespread support for the hatchery system from both commercial fishermen and fishery officials, scientists were unable to prove that large numbers of the planted fish actually grew to maturity and increased the commercial catch. As early as 1883 the Commissioner of Fisheries, W. F. Whitcher, expressed doubts about the practical value of planting fish."

Whitcher was well known to Kerr as his immediate boss for many years. This position may have cost Whitcher his job because he was "superannuated" shortly after he published his article against Wilmot and the fish hatcheries. I think if Kerr were asked, his position on fish-breeding would have been that fish propagation failed because Wilmot and his son were shameless self-promoters and frauds. If Kerr had been allowed to establish his fish hatchery in the Niagara River, would things have been different? We'll never know, but ultimately, I don't think so. Hatcheries may have been useful to support sport fishing but for many reasons were unable to perpetuate commercial fishing.

Creation of closed seasons for the various fish species was useful, but as McCullough notes, "Enforcement of the Act was uneven and weak. In part, the failure to enforce the Act rigorously was the result of poorly paid officials, patronage appointments and inadequate equipment. In many cases, the major problem was a lack of political will to enforce the regulations."

Kerr was extremely keen to enforce the pollution provisions of the Act but was frequently thwarted from doing so by a lack of support from the Department and by public pressure. As McCullough points out, "Polluting industries have been economically and politically much more important than the fishery and have been able to delay attempts to reduce pollution."

Chemical pollution was committed mostly by small tanneries or oil refineries, both of which Kerr frequently took on, sometimes with success, and sometimes without success. Kerr was keenly aware of the balancing process between stopping pollution and the economic success of industry, and he often noted the number of employees and total payroll of industrial polluters. Kerr naively believed that tanneries and cotton mills used up the chemicals until they no longer had harmful qualities that would affect the fish.

The *Fisheries Act* also had a provision that prohibited fishing on Sundays, which was of questionable constitutional legality because the Sunday observance laws were a provincial jurisdiction. Kerr often used this prohibition to charge people, sometimes because he was religious, other times as a "gotcha" to punish enemies or the uncooperative. Always thinking from the perspective of the fish, Kerr often felt they deserved a holiday from overfishing at least one day a week!

As Kerr discovered, most people did not support fishing laws or take them seriously, and juries almost invariably acquitted the fishermen against whom Kerr had meticulously made a case. Judicial officials like justices of the peace, police magistrates, and judges often shared these popular views about fishing and did not take prosecutions seriously or were flat-out corrupt in favour of the fishermen.

Eventually, the federal government gave up on commercial fishing in the inland waters, and jurisdiction was shifted to the provincial governments around the turn of the century, which would have driven Kerr mad because he had witnessed provincial laxity in enforcement of the game laws and had a low regard for the generally Liberal Ontario government.

In 2018 the commercial fishing catch in Ontario was about 24 million pounds with a dockside value of $44 million and consisted mostly of walleye and perch caught in Lake Erie. It is likely to reduce further in the future with global warming and algae blooms.[24]

Could the commercial catch of other species like whitefish and herring have been protected? I doubt it because too many things were stacked against them, like population growth, pollution, and habitat loss. I think Kerr foresaw this as he frequently warned about the extinction of fish if the laws were not vigorously enforced. So, in the long run, Kerr's extraordinary efforts over twenty-three years as fisheries overseer all came to naught. However, he may have planted a kernel of concern in the popular psyche of Ontarians regarding pollution and overfishing. Today we still struggle, but we are still building on his work. We are still making progress on pollution and habitat loss, and there still is a commercial fishery in places in Ontario.

Fishermen catching a lunker at Niagara on the Lake. Photo by Joel Kerr, December 28th, 2019.

....

24   A 2020 conversation with a commercial fisherman at Port Colborne confirmed that the current catch is primarily perch and pickerel, but they occasionally bring in a whitefish or sturgeon. He maintained that due to the quota the fisheries are stable, and prices are good. He was cautiously optimistic, as am I, bordering on confident, at least in the deeper, eastern basin of Lake Erie.

Chapter 6

1864–1867 – The Battle of the Beach and the Bay

1864 – 1865

On December 16, 1864, Kerr was appointed fisheries overseer by the Department of Crown Lands, Fisheries Branch, at Quebec City. The printed notice advised "All well-disposed persons are requested to afford him whatever information and assistance they can towards carrying out the fishery laws." I am not sure what the "non-well-disposed persons" were to make of this, but there seemed to be a lot more of them than "well-disposed persons." Kerr also received a letter of instructions that has not survived. I presume this included some lessons on the law and guidelines for enforcement.

I am not sure whether Kerr officially applied for this position, but in the first volume of his diaries, he attached an undated note that he sent to the Honourable H. B. Bull, MLC:[25] [26]

---

25 MLC stands for "Member of Legislative Council," which was held in Quebec City prior to 1867.
26 Harcourt Burland Bull (June 2, 1824–Aug. 12, 1881) a fellow Irishman from Dublin, was a journalist and politician who was appointed to the Senate in 1879. He was also a coroner and examined the bodies from the 1857 Desjardins Canal accident, using photography for that purpose for the first time.

1864–1867 – The Battle of the Beach and the Bay

My Dear Sir:

Any person who will walk on the John Street Mountain in the dusk of the evening and cast his eyes in the direction of Dundurn will observe a great number of lights burning all around the head of Burlington Bay.

It appears this is done for the purpose of attracting the fish there (herring) which are taken nightly by the thousands. Will you be pleased to recommend me to the Government to be appointed local fishery guardian for the United County of Wentworth and I will soon stop the illegal destruction of the fish at this improper season.

Likely a little matter of trifling importance like this will be easily got for me on your application and recommendation.

Yours Sincerely, John W. Kerr

Kerr was clearly elated with his appointment and got right to work. He noted that on December 24 he posted notices "in order that the public may be in possession of the fact of my appointment." He morosely noted for December 25, "being another holiday I did nothing."

On December 26 he made his first official trip to Burlington Beach where most of the Hamilton fishermen resided, often in shacks on squatted land. Travelling by horse and sleigh, he likely drove down Hamilton Mountain using the access he had built from Flock Road up to his farmhouse at what is now known as 988 Concession Street.[27] He immediately found men fishing for herring without licences in Lake Ontario using gill nets ten miles north of the canal and six miles out in the lake. Leaving at 9:00 a.m., he returned home at 5:00 p.m., having travelled twenty miles.

On December 27 he was at Burlington Heights and all around the bay posting notices. The next day he was back on Burlington Beach talking to fishermen, most of whom expressed a willingness to pay an annual ten-dollar licence fee. Like a good cop, he took down all their

....

27 You can still see a part of the Kerr mountain road across Concession Street from Kerr's home, which is now 988 Concession. It was very steep and narrow.

names, many of which reappeared in his diaries over the next twenty-three years. Having been sent a copy of the *Fisheries Act,* he noted it prescribed net mesh sizes, and he found that many of the fishermen were using illegal undersized nets.

Kerr made his first mistake by deciding to prosecute the illegal fishermen. By December 29 he was at the Hamilton courthouse getting summonses signed by Police Magistrate James Cahill, another Irishman, who played a prominent role in Hamilton law enforcement until after Kerr's death in 1888.[28]

After serving the summonses, he proceeded to court on January 4, 1865, where three of the four charged were convicted and fined eight dollars each plus costs, but they were given ten days to pay, so they could write to the governor general to remit the fines. Kerr didn't mention whether they pled guilty or not guilty, and there was no mention of any lawyers being present. That would change.

Flush with an early and easy victory, Kerr decided to stop spearfishing on Burlington Bay, which was then illegal because the bay was set aside for fish propagation. Warning people at first, he quickly lost patience with their noncompliance. Enlisting the assistance of Police Constable McLogan on January 10, Kerr demolished five fishing huts and then five more on January 13. He noted, "I was obliged after repeated warnings to resort to this prompt measure and so put a final stop, if possible, to the spearing."

Kerr's entry on January 16, 1865, includes the first reference to Mr. W. F. Whitcher, Kerr's immediate boss for many years who was to play a large role in Kerr's life as fisheries overseer. Whitcher apparently wrote the book on fishing grounds and fishery licensing, and he provided Kerr with his instructions. "I would not allow any person to fish Scot free," Kerr replied. "All should in my estimation pay a little annual which amount could always be regulated by the head of the Fishery Department."

---

28   James Cahill (July 15, 1815–May 5, 1893) from Tipperary, Ireland, was a trained lawyer who was appointed police magistrate in 1850. Kerr thought so highly of Cahill that one of the streets on his plan of subdivision was "Cahill Ave." Cahill Ave. on the proposed plan was never built.

On January 17 Kerr was in court against the ten spear fishermen he had charged. To his surprise and chagrin, they had a lawyer with them, Mr. Charles A. Sadlier, who became Kerr's legal nemesis for years to come. Sadlier, another Irishman, advised the court that Kerr could not be a witness because under prevailing law he would be entitled to receive half of any fines ordered and thus was not a disinterested party or a neutral witness.

Magistrate Cahill rejected this argument but accepted Sadlier's second argument that the court had no jurisdiction to hear the case because the alleged infractions occurred in the waters off Halton County, and Cahill was only appointed for Wentworth County. Kerr later wrote the Commissioner of Crown Lands (CCL) to request that Cahill be appointed for Halton. "I will then be able to convict these 10 persons and thereof meet these flimsy objections raised solely for the express purpose of defeating the ends of justice."

To his astonishment, Kerr was then charged and convicted of unlawful destruction of the fishing huts and theft of the spears, as a result of private complaints laid by the spear fishermen. Kerr huffed, "I may perhaps have acted hasty in tearing down the spearing box, but the owner, Duncan McGilivray, had no right or authority to place it there for spearing purposes. I believe it was as much my duty to remove these spearing boxes as it would be to take away gill nets or any other nets I found in Burlington Bay for similar purposes."

Putting an improbably positive spin on this turn of events Kerr then noted, "The result of all this is most satisfactory, as well as pleasing for after a careful examination made by me today not a fishing box is to be found although at this time same period last year more than 100 spearing boxes [were on the ice]."

By January 21, 1865, Kerr had learned that most of the Burlington Beach fishermen had "combined together and subscribed money to carry on the war against the Fisheries Act." Noting that they had hired Mr. C.A. Sadlier, Kerr doubled down: "I am determined to haul them up whenever I find them acting contrary to the Act…All sorts of bad names and threats have been used against me but I am not alarmed! I will not be deterred by threats nor entreaties from doing my duty…They fish where they like, when they like and how they like and I have been informed that John Bates says no law shall prevent him from continuing to do so."

Kerr also wrote that "very few legal nets are used at this present time nor since Mr. McCuaig's discharge."

Kerr's trial was presided over by Justice of the Peace John Wesley Hopkins[29] at the "hotel" of one of the fishermen on Burlington Beach, Frederick Corey. Hopkins and Corey became frequent adversaries of Kerr over the years. After his conviction, Kerr appealed, confident of success. At the time, an appeal of a magistrate's decision was heard before a jury in the Court of General Sessions.[30]

On January 23, Kerr was approached by Fred Corey, who demanded the return of a spear that belonged to Corey's son. On Sadlier's advice, he threatened to sue Kerr if he did not do so. Kerr wrote to the CCL, saying, "my mind says let him sue away! But in such matters, I am wholly under your guidance." Kerr fired back by requesting from the Department permission to search all the nets of the Burlington Beach fishermen.

Upon his appointment, Kerr's initial jurisdiction was only for the waters of Wentworth County, which included Burlington Bay and the Lake Ontario shore from about the Burlington Canal to as far as Winona. Constantly seeking increases to his district, Kerr noted illegal fishing elsewhere and requested his jurisdiction be extended to include Halton and Lincoln Counties. It was extended, and there would be much more to come, Kerr boldly crowed. "If appointed to go and look after them there—here I am."

Kerr also stated that many of the illegal fishermen were not legitimate fishers but "intruders and trespassers—sailors in summer, poaching fishermen in winter." This state presaged never-ending disputes between licensed and unlicensed fishermen.

By late January 1865, things started to get dangerous. On January 23

....

29   John Wesley Hopkins (Dec. 14, 1825–Oct. 19, 1871) was born in Flamborough. He was a justice of the peace for Saltfleet Township.
30   Not all jurisdictions had a fixed courthouse, and trials were frequently held at local watering holes. As a young lawyer, I was involved in a small claims court trial that was held in the Grimsby Legion. During lunch break everyone had a beer together—judge, court staff, lawyers, litigants, and witnesses!

Kerr observed, "Saw a spearing house on the ice—heard it was a trap laid by one of the poaching fishermen. Did not go near it. I might get precipitated into the bay." The next day Kerr wrote to Justice of the Peace Hopkins to tell him off about the trap: "It was placed in a perilous position to entrap and drown me... it is my duty to remove fish boxes when placed on the ice to spearfish—Yours as a magistrate to remove a trap so placed for to destroy human life."

Confronting Hopkins directly on January 26, Hopkins correctly advised Kerr that it was a police matter.[31] Kerr's point was to impress upon Hopkins the consequences of his biased decisions. The incident also illustrates that Kerr sought and received information and encouraged informers, which would be a consistent theme throughout his career.

Meeting a Burlington Beach fisherman in Hamilton who claimed to be the owner of one of the broken ice huts and said that he was going to sue, Kerr retorted, "I bid him to do so and enrich the lawyers." Opining about a new *Fisheries Act,* Kerr stated, "It will be necessary in the framing of this new Fishery Act to avoid everything that may be construed to mean nothing by crafty lawyers."

On February 7, Kerr received confirmation that he had been appointed to enforce the *Game Act*. This never really became the focus of his career, and by 1867 he lost the post because under the *British North America Act,* game laws became a provincial jurisdiction, and Kerr could never get Ontario to appoint him, although he tried from time to time. On March 14, Kerr secured his first conviction of a man who

----

31 J. W. Hopkins and Peter Van Wagner (1818–1906) were JPs for Saltfleet Township. Like police magistrates they were judicial officers but had somewhat different functions. Police magistrates were usually lawyers while JPs were not. Magistrates had policing functions as well as presiding over trials and issuing summons. JPs presided over trials of less serious charges and had to sit as a pair. They operated out of their homes or other public buildings. JPs still handle numerous judicial functions, such as authorizing search warrants, conducting bail hearings for most Criminal Code charges and trials for provincial offences, such as those listed in the *Highway Traffic Act*. They were, and probably still are, patronage appointments, although these days more and more JPs are lawyers, and they make about $100,000 a year or more.

brought "a fine doe" to sell at the Hamilton market, contrary to the legal hunting season.

On February 10, Kerr got a warrant from Police Magistrate Cahill to search all fish houses and seize all spears. "By this means I will be enabled to overhaul these persons who have no fear of the law before their eyes. I find Mr. Cahill at all times ready and willing to afford me every assistance in his power to carry out your instructions and for which I feel myself so much indebted to him."

On February 13, Kerr was made aware of a petition to allow spearfishing on Burlington Bay and Dundas Marsh. Kerr was opposed, noting, "I believe angling is a sufficient fair mode of fishing for all and that the vast majority of the population support this position." Petitions were a common event during Kerr's tenure, and he usually reported that the signatories were men with ulterior motives, political opponents, people who knew nothing about the issue in question, or a combination of the three. To discredit the signatores, Kerr offered to let the Department "have the particulars about every man whose name I may find signed thereto!"

Throughout the remainder of the winter, Kerr continued his war against spearfishing, usually taking a constable with him on missions, whom he had to pay for his services. On February 18, Kerr broke up five fish houses with the help of a police constable, including some repeat offenders like John Bates, who "refused to exit his hut and threatened to put the constable in the fishing hole." Four days later Kerr was served with a summons alleging an assault on Bates. "There is not a particle of truth contained in the whole of this summons but so long as John Wesley Hopkins is endowed with magisterial authority I expect nothing but trouble from him." Sure enough, on March 6, Kerr and the officer attended trial before Hopkins, and Kerr was convicted.

Commenting on the trial Kerr noted, "such swearing made I have never witnessed." Apparently, one witness "has since cleared for the United States fearing that he might be taken up and charged with perjury." Kerr had a lawyer, Mr. R. R. Waddell, the county solicitor "who ably defended the case." Kerr recounted that "A large number of respectable persons, **friends of mine** attended the trial. They condemned the conduct of the magistrate. The Reeve of Saltfleet, Mr. Alvey Jones presided with Mr. J. W. Hopkins.[32] They were divided in their view of the case. After a scene which I hope I may never witness again in a court of justice proceedings were adjourned." Kerr was convicted and appealed.

This trial is reminiscent of his trial in Ireland regarding the shooting by the River Shannon. Kerr had a good lawyer and several friends and supporters in court to intimidate witnesses and influence the result, but alas, things were different this time, and it probably came down to the partiality of Magistrate Hopkins.

The appeal was in the Court of Quarter Sessions before a jury and was to be heard on March 14. Kerr did not expect the trial to proceed because he had been advised by Sadlier that the witnesses would not attend. Kerr noted, "It appears the appeals against J. Wesley Hopkins convictions made by my attorney have had the desired effect." But the witnesses did appear, and the case proceeded, which makes me wonder if Sadlier deliberately lied to Kerr. One lesson here is don't take advice from the opposing lawyer.

The constable and Kerr's appeals were heard on March 16 and were reported in the *Hamilton Spectator*. Curiously, one appeal trial was heard after the other by the same jury. After somewhat reluctantly convicting the constable, Kerr was also convicted. Each was fined one dollar plus thirteen dollars in costs. Kerr attached the *Spectator* article on p. 122 of volume 1. Kerr noted that, "John Bates is a very litigious character." Kerr and the constable each now had criminal convictions that could affect their future employment.

At the end of February, Kerr employed a new tactic in his "war on illegal fishing." He went to the Hamilton market and checked out the fish vendors, finding one selling 400 fish illegally speared at Long Point on Lake Erie. He could tell they were speared due to the marks left on the fish. Inspecting fish markets became a regular part of his MO. Sometimes he used the tactic to get information. Other times he

....

32   Not permitted to try cases alone, they sat with municipal officials, such as mayors or reeves.

would charge the vendors under the Act. Selling illegally caught fish was also illegal.

Undeterred by this conviction, Kerr sought the expansion of his jurisdiction to include Lake Ontario as far as the Niagara River plus the city of Welland and the counties of Haldimand and Norfolk on Lake Erie, noting, "a great quantity of fish [are caught] both in and out of season." He didn't get it all, but on March 22 he was notified that he had gotten all of Lake Ontario from Toronto Harbour to the Niagara River.

On February 27, Kerr was back on the ice near the Desjardins Canal. Walking along the GWR mainline, he saw a repeat offender lock up a fishing hut. Demanding the key, Kerr was rebuffed, so he knocked over the hut, only to find another man inside with a freshly speared bass. Curiously, no charges were laid. Kerr was probably remembering his last debacle on the bay.

Making plans for when the ice went out, Kerr wrote to CCL on March 20 to request permission to purchase "a small boat and spy glass to enable me to take up gill nets." Always concerned about money, Kerr reassured the Department that it wouldn't cost more than thirty dollars.

Aside from his swashbuckling adventures, there was also more mundane business. Whitcher wrote to him wanting to know what cisco herring were. Kerr wrote that he believed they were an introduced species entering Lake Ontario near Oswego in New York State: "They are a splendid fish, rich in flavor, fat, pleasant to eat and like the salt water herring of Dublin Bay, Ireland, always in good condition to fry and cook. Or to use a fisherman's phrase, they are good fish and need no butter."

By mid-April, Kerr had not received authorization to buy his boat. Thus, he was thwarted in his desire to seize illegal nets. He expressed his concerns to the CCL about duck hunting and net fishing in his district. Still receiving no reply by April 28, he telegrammed the CCL with the following frantic message: "Telegram me please! If you have anything to say." He also warned the Department about the cost of having to rent a boat and employ someone to row and noted that Dundas Marsh was "literally swarming with wild ducks of various kinds."

Still not hearing from the Department, he rented a boat on May 1 and began seizing illegal nets, thus opening another front on the war for Burlington Bay. He noted, "out at 11:00 a.m. in at 11:00 p.m. 18 miles. Horse and cart to take home net $1.50. Boat .50c. Charge for rower $1."

By mid-April, Kerr had heard that Hamilton fishermen intended to take their boats to Niagara and fish on the fishing stations of the licensed fishermen. Kerr wanted to get his hands on the records of the former overseer, Captain Baxter, who had died, so on May 3, he took the train to St. Catharines and then proceeded to Niagara-on-the-Lake. There he found some of the Hamilton fishermen and wanted to prosecute "these several persons as intruders and trespassers on leased property of Mr. Cantwell." Kerr also requested that his friends James Cahill and Peter Van Wagner be appointed as magistrates for the County of Lincoln. (Talk about trying to stack the deck!) Spending the night in Niagara, Kerr stayed at the Whale Inn, which was run by Thomas Elliott and his family, who would play a prominent role in his life. Kerr proceeded the next day to St. Catharines before walking to Thorald and catching "an immigrant train" back to Hamilton.

On May 5, Kerr was back on the bay, where he found 800 yards of gill nets, the property of Mrs. Baldry, a widow and perhaps the only female fisher in the Hamilton area. Kerr took the net to his home, where he dried it and rolled it up to preserve its sixty-dollar value. Kerr wrote that Baldry "pleaded very hard to get back this net but, of course, this is something that I cannot do on my own responsibility. She promised faithfully never to offend again. I really feel for the poor woman." This was the beginning of another long, tempestuous relationship and proof that Kerr could be a gullible person and a poor judge of character.

On May 6, 1865, Kerr wrote that he wanted to protect the legal fishermen from interlopers at Niagara for fear that the whole system would collapse. "Why should we pay rent when there are more than 12,000 yards of illegal nets?" they asked. Thus began his Niagara adventures.

By this time Kerr seemed to be getting things in order, and people started to pay him grudgingly for leases. He noted that on May 8 he received ninety dollars from Niagara fishermen, and even people in Hamilton began to pay. Kerr was given permission to return Mrs. Baldry's net to her, saying, "She was much pleased at getting it back again."

On May 27 he convened a meeting at the county solicitor's office with the beach fishermen to try to come to some rapprochement, but he did not state how the meeting went. On June 3, he got his spyglass (which he used for the next twenty-three years).

On June 8, Kerr made his first trip to Toronto and reported back on Toronto Harbour, the Toronto islands, and rivers like the Humber and the Credit. Toronto figured prominently in his career, and he made some friends there, such as David Ward and Patrick Gray, and some enemies, including Edward "Ned" Hanlon and pretty much every politician in town. Toronto was then a busy commercial fishery, particularly on Toronto Island, where it seemed like everybody was a fisherman. That would change, to Kerr's dismay.

By July 1865, Kerr began to hear that people were fishing on Sunday, contrary to the *Lord's Day Act,* and he wrote to the Department for instructions. The Act prohibited work on Sundays as well as certain recreational activities and provided for a $200 fine, which was a fortune at the time. Kerr was a deeply religious man and particularly in his later years frequently gave thanks to God. A good Anglican and a member of the Church of Ascension located on John Street just across from what is now St. Joseph's Hospital, Kerr was buried in the church section of the Hamilton Cemetery. Despite this apparent religious fervour, there is no mention in his diaries of him ever attending church. He also frequently worked on Sunday, which seems a bit hypocritical.

Trouble began to brew again in late July when Kerr was sent a copy of a letter from lawyer Charles Sadlier to Viscount Monck, the governor general, on behalf of Joan Baldry, complaining that as a poor widow she had been taken advantage of by Kerr in regard to a land dispute on Burlington Beach with a neighbour. Kerr fired back with his usual gusto, calling Baldry a liar who hadn't paid her lease and who owed ten dollars. He also noted that "at present Mrs. Baldry has no licence for dispensing malt liquor but I understand she does so, notwithstanding!!" Kerr concluded by saying, "I cannot help remarking that I have always found it through life that on a change of persons in authority **crafty people** always endeavour to benefit themselves at the sacrifice even of old neighbours."

On August 3, Kerr summonsed Mrs. Baldry and others for fishing on Sunday, thus opening another hornet's nest. Kerr tried to rely on the evidence of Burlington Beach fishermen who were apparently willing to testify, but they did not show up for trial, or if they did show, they changed their evidence. Most accused were acquitted, including Mrs. Baldry, who claimed it was her employees who fished and not her. Ben Foulds was convicted and fined twenty dollars. Then he appealed using Sadlier as his solicitor.

Kerr spent most of August laying charges and attending court with Sadlier and J. P. Hopkins. On August 24, Kerr wrote, "I saw Hopkins the magistrate today. He tried to frighten me—but it no go—let him commit me to goal at his peril."

On September 8, Kerr reported that he was arrested by a constable acting under a warrant issued by "John Wesley Hopkins, the magistrate whose conduct I have been so repeatedly obliged to bring under your notice." Kerr had to pay a fine and costs in the amount of $28.95, or he was off to jail.[33] He paid under protest and wrote to CCL, "In the course I shall now take I hope the Department will not interfere or control me."

On September 18, Kerr was at the Court of Quarter Sessions for the appeal of the Sunday fishermen who were convicted. Kerr was bitterly disappointed that his lawyer, Samuel Freeman, did not attend or send anyone in his place, resulting in the convictions being quashed by Judge Logie "by a mere quibble." Kerr noted, "Mr. Sam B. Freeman takes no interest in the fishing cases on behalf of the Crown. I have no confidence in him and never had!"

Asked by his boss for further particulars Kerr wrote, "I am mortified to find the case dismissed on the mere **flimsy pretext or quibble** that the conviction should have set forth that Benjamin Foulds was not an Indian." It was legal for Natives to fish on Sunday, so apparently the onus was on Kerr to prove that Foulds was not a native.

Earlier in September Kerr had his first skirmish in the "Battle of Toronto." A fisherman named Patrick Gray told Kerr that Gray and

....

33   Costs included lawyer's fees, summons, and witness fees, including police.

his men were attacked by John Hanlon, "a squatter resident on the island," and that Gray's house was seized and his men assaulted. Hanlon was acting on the permission of Alderman Vance, the chairman of the harbour and water committee of the City of Toronto, which claimed to own the island. Kerr met with the alderman and explained that in fact the Department of Crown Lands owned the island as part of the fishery reserve, "which seemed to astonish Mr. Alderman Vance."

This became another recurring theme for Kerr over the years as he fought to preserve the fisheries while Toronto wanted the lands and waters for its own purposes, primarily recreational. Kerr launched a personal attack on John Hanlon ". . . he keeps an unlicensed tavern and he was recently fined $10 for selling liquor. He was appointed constable on the island by the Corporation at a salary of $200 a year to keep the peace and order amongst the visitors there.... Mr. Hanlon, for his undue interference and misconduct should be at once served with notice to leave." So began a long-lasting grudge with the Hanlon family.

By early October Kerr began to pester the Department about the upcoming salmon-breeding season and wanted authority over Duffins Creek, near Bowmanville. He noted hearing that in one night in November 1864, two men caught 200 salmon, some weighing as much as thirty pounds and most weighing twenty pounds or more. Noting the other salmon streams on Lake Ontario, such as the Credit and Humber Rivers, Kerr stated that during spawning season, from late October to November, "I am determined to go down and spend some nights there." This became a yearly obsession with Kerr until, unfortunately, the salmon were virtually extinct despite his vigorous efforts to prevent illegal fishing.

By mid-October the "Battle for the Bay" was back on and worse than ever. Kerr reported a conversation in which the Burlington Bay fishermen threatened "they would serve John W. Kerr this winter the same way that they did Abraham Lincoln" (i.e., by assassinating him).[34] On October 14, Kerr was on Dundas Marsh at 11:00 p.m. catching men spearing fish with "jack lights" when one man threatened to shoot

....

34   Lincoln was assassinated on April 15, 1865, by John Wilkes Booth.

him. "I, of course, care very little for such foolish threats," Kerr wrote. "I never carry firearms for personal protection. A stick in my hand is quite sufficient." That would change.

On November 7, Kerr reported that "vengeance was sworn against me by the people of the Beach." On November 29, Kerr heard that a serial offender "borrowed a double barrel gun and paraded the beach vowing vengeance against me and using threats. He wound up the day by breaking the gun to smithereens—small pieces." Kerr was undeterred and spent most of October arresting men for illegal spear-fishing at night with lights.

In the fall of 1865, the government passed a new *Fisheries Act,* which Kerr believed would assist in regulating the fisheries by defining his powers and detailing his jurisdiction. He sent copies of the new Act and regulations to be posted all over his district.

On November 23, Kerr's boss, William Frederick Whitcher, visited Hamilton and spent the day with Kerr on Burlington Beach to inquire into Mrs. Baldry's grievances and to discuss "a great many other things." Kerr made no mention of his impression of Whitcher, but that changed over the next several years. Whitcher seems to have been a bit of a "good time Charlie" and wore out his welcome with more than a few people, including Kerr.

When Kerr seized fish, he would normally give them away to a local orphanage or some charitable organization. But on November 25, Kerr seized 800 herring he found in an illegal net. Being out with two constables from 6:00 p.m. to 5:00 a.m., he took the fish to the police station on James Street, presumably to be preserved as evidence. I wonder what the duty officer did with them in a time before refrigeration. It was probably cold out anyway, so maybe they were just left by the back door.

Getting paid by the Department was a continuous issue for Kerr throughout his more than twenty-three-year career. On December 7, 1865, he sent an urgent letter to the CCL.

> On the 22nd instant Mr. Whitcher when here promised to send me $100 on account of disbursements for the past and present quarter. This want of money retards my active proceedings in the discharge

> *of my duty and the want of money still due for the past quarter is keenly felt by me. Will you be pleased to let me have this $100 at once and without delay and thereof enable me to wind up the affairs of my first year as your fishery Overseer.*

This was not the last urgent letter he would write, nor would it be the last time Whitcher failed to fulfill his promises. On December 22, Kerr got a cheque from Mr. S. P. Bauset of the Department. Bauset replaced Whitcher as Kerr's boss many years later and proved to be a much more reliable man. (More about him later.)

To Kerr's annoyance, on December 14 the Department relented and agreed to allow spearfishing on the iced over bay, day and night, until March 1. Fishermen–1, Kerr–0. But this was not the end of the spearfishing saga, as we shall see…

In December Kerr got a copy of the warrant issued against him that resulted in his arrest in September. He learned from Solicitor Sadlier that the warrant had not been sought by either him or his clients but was the work of J. P. Hopkins acting on his own initiative. In a letter to the CCL, Kerr stated, "You will learn that Mr. John Wesley Hopkins has been guilty of a breach of faith by his extreme action against me." That kind of malfeasance would be sufficient to get Hopkins fired today but apparently not in the 1860s.

To this point one might think that Kerr was a total hard-ass, and while it is true that he was strict, he was always fair and could be compassionate, particularly to those in need. On December 18 Kerr wrote to the CCL about rent arrears owed by some Burlington Beach fishermen.

> *I am satisfied many of the persons are exceedingly poor and unable to pay even what you proposed and to enforce payment by law would be to inflict a great and lasting injury on the persons alluded to.*
>
> *As fishing has not been by any means so lucrative for the past three years on B. Beach as heretofore, and as material for mounting and making nets has become much dearer owing to the late trouble in the United States—I hope you will be pleased to pardon*

me if I take the liberty of recommending that the amount opposite each person's name be written off and that no further claim be made henceforth on any of the persons named but that you will be pleased to forgive them for the best and most cogent reason that they are not able to pay.

I have the Honour... John W. Kerr, F.O.

One of the topics that Kerr and Whitcher discussed was Kerr's district. On December 7, he wrote to the CCL to seek confirmation that it would expand to include the Grand River from Guelph to Port Maitland, all of Lake Erie from Long Point to the Niagara River, and Lake Ontario from Niagara to Port Union. This was something Whitcher promised that did, in fact, come about in time. On December 28, Kerr attempted to make his first trip to Port Dover but only got as far as Mount Hope due to a snowstorm. He said the trip was "deferred for another day. Went out at 9:00 a.m. came in at 3:00 p.m. miles 20."[35]

After Christmas Kerr began to prepare his annual report on the fishermen and fishing in his district. This became an annual ritual and was eventually incredibly detailed and thorough. It also provided him with an opportunity to visit every nook and cranny of his realm and spend time with his many friends and some of his enemies. Anyone wanting to know about fish catches, including quantity and value, would do well to have a look. He usually submitted his reports in January.

1866

Kerr's second full year on duty started casually enough. On January 4, he was on Burlington Bay with his seventeen-year-old son, George. This is the first mention of his family. Eventually, all four of his sons became employed in what became the family business. Even a couple of his daughters were put to work driving him to the railway station, for example.

Kerr sent in his annual report for 1865 and noted $13,249.41 in

---

35   Kerr would have travelled by horse and buggy or horse and sleigh because the railroad to Port Dover was not completed until 1879.

fish caught in his district and that he had seventeen spears stored in his house that he had seized. He also had a quantity of seized gill nets and wanted to know if he could sell them for the Department's benefit. I don't know what the answer was, but it was probably yes because the government was always hard up for money.

On Sunday, January 14, Kerr was back on the ice of Dundas Marsh, having walked there from his house when he spotted two persons in a fish house, obviously fishing illegally on the Lord's Day. Sharing a bottle of whisky, they offered Kerr a drink, but instead he inhospitably seized their spear. A struggle ensued over the spear and then "I drew a pistol from my pocket and told him if he tried to carry out his threat, I would shoot him. Finding my position although alone was not a destitute one, they took to their heels and ran away." Kerr said, "I rarely carry a pistol but was advised by my friends when I go alone to do so in future." Kerr then made a request: "Will the Department be so good as to furnish me with a good pistol. It is not likely that I shall ever have occasion to use it–but then for peace sake it is better I should have one." The pistol that he wanted to replace was likely his old Irish Constabulary service revolver.

Summarizing his first year, Kerr wrote, "I will not enter into the difficulties I have had to contend with, they are past and let them be buried in oblivion." He thanked Mr. Whitcher and Police Magistrate James Cahill who helped him "in those dark days of obstruction when I was assailed." Kerr also crowed about the $316 in fines he "inflicted" and the $331 in lease fees he collected. He also took his first opportunity to complain about his pay: "I trust that that for the present year you will be pleased to make my position such as will enable me to carry out your instructions with more satisfaction to myself in a pecuniary point of view as really and truly, I am not compensated for the duties I perform." Unfortunately, no raise was on the horizon.

On February 8, Kerr observed fifty fish houses on Burlington Bay and suggested they each pay one dollar for the privilege of spearing. That would eventually be ordered, and collecting the money from disgruntled fishermen became a rather mundane aspect of his yearly duties.

In March, Patrick Gray of Toronto Island was sent a notice of eviction

1864–1867 – The Battle of the Beach and the Bay

by the solicitors for the City of Toronto. Kerr wrote, "I am perfectly astonished that these gentlemen should be induced to act towards you as they have, for they certainly must be aware that the island opposite Toronto, on which you have built your house, is not the property of the Corporation of the City of Toronto." Kerr offered to back up Gray if any further action was taken. He also noted that "I have been very unwell for some time past… otherwise I would run down to Toronto and explain myself to Messrs Robinson and McBride."[36] [37]

Kerr had spent the winter getting licence fees for 1866 and arresting people for Sunday fishing or spearing for herring, which was not permitted. When the ice went out, he began to seize illegal gill nets belonging to Burlington Beach fishermen, who apparently had not learned their lesson. He also charged a number of men with illegal duck hunting, which no doubt further irritated them. On April 9, he was at Burlington Beach with his fourteen-year-old son, Frederick, until 3:00 a.m. It was a Monday, so I doubt if Fred made it to school!

Returning to the topic of money, on April 7, Kerr submitted his returns for the first quarter 1866 and reminded the CCL about a balance still owing from the previous year: "I want the money and I will feel greatly obliged if my small demands are settled more regularly at the expiration of each quarter." Sorry to say, that would not be.

On April 14, Kerr made his first reference to pollution. Seizing a net in Sherman's Inlet on Burlington Bay, he found it contained three pike, each about three pounds. Kerr had them cooked and noted "they tasted and smell of coal oil—the oil refinery being at the inlet… Each person

....

36   John Beverley Robinson (Feb. 21, 1820–June 19, 1896), the son of his namesake father, noted jurist and chief justice of Upper Canada, was also a lawyer and politician. He was mayor of Toronto in 1856 and served as city solicitor from 1864–1880, when he was appointed lieutenant governor of Ontario. He died at Massey Hall of a massive stroke just before he was scheduled to give a speech to a group of hostile Liberals.

37   This is the first mention of any health problems. Kerr was generally as healthy as a horse until his later years. Although I cannot find a picture of him (to my annoyance), Kerr described himself as weighing 242 pounds. Joseph Masters of Niagara-on-the-Lake described him in his diaries as "portly."

who partook of them was ill for several hours afterwards." Kerr wanted to know whether he should prosecute the refineries: "the proprietors cause the refuse and deadly stuff used for refining the oil to be thrown in to the inlet." For more info, see chapter 14, which deals with pollution.

On April 27, Kerr was back on Toronto Island, arresting two men for shooting wild ducks. They claimed they were given permission by John Hanlon, who was employed as a constable on the island. Kerr was annoyed and had them convicted anyway. They were each fined five dollars plus costs, which was about a week's pay. On May 17, Kerr reported that upon meeting with Toronto solicitor John Beverley Robinson, eviction proceedings against Patrick Gray were stayed, and Kerr was "quite satisfied he will not henceforth be subject to any annoyance." This would prove incorrect, as we shall see.

On May 18, Kerr and a constable were lying "in ambush near the fishing station of Ben Joyce about 1:00 a.m." when they saw Joyce and his son heading out on the lake to fish. Kerr "waited until they came in and then pounced on them." He seized their boat and fishing gear and proceeded to row it to Bastien's boathouse on Hamilton Bay, a distance of about four miles. After the no doubt worn-out constable left, Kerr was approached by three men, including tavern owner and fisherman John Dynes and another man professing to be a constable, seeking the return of the gear and claiming to be acting under the authority of John Wesley Hopkins. "Dynes told the constable to take me into custody and that I must go with them for stealing the net and boat and ropes." Then ensued a confrontation: "I was abused particularly by Dan McGwynn who threatened me and said if I ever attempted to take his boat I would rue it and he also called me a robber. I repeatedly forbid them from taking or touching the boat, net, oars or ropes and warned them of the consequences but they set my authority and myself at open defiance."

Somehow Kerr left the scene to find Justice of the Peace Cahill (in the middle of the night!), and Dynes and fellow fisherman McGwynn managed to get the seized objects. Finding Cahill, Kerr obtained a warrant to arrest Dynes and McGwynn "for abusive and threatening language and for acting as a constable without authority," and they were arrested and brought to court. Kerr stated, "I was employed on this duty from 8:00 p.m. on May 18th until 8:00 p.m. on May 19th, slept none and have at this present time very sore feet." After reserving his decision Cahill re-convened court on May 22 and convicted Dynes and McGwynn and ordered forfeiture of the boat and other items. Later, Hopkins claimed he had not given Dynes the authority to arrest Kerr.

Dynes and McGwynn were each fined ten dollars plus costs but appealed the decision. Shortly after this, several boats that Kerr and his assistant used were stolen and sunk or broken up, and so began a long antagonism with Dynes and McGwynn. On June 16, 1866, their appeal was heard before Judge Logie and a jury, and their convictions were quashed. Kerr complained, "it is impossible to find a jury at General Sessions who will not quash all convictions that come before them." Curiously, Kerr hired Charles Sadlier to argue the appeal (if you can't fight them, join them). Kerr wanted to have the *Fisheries Act* amended to provide for no appeals from a magistrate's decision. That did happen but not for a while.

On June 25, Kerr got Dynes to pay his arrears of rent for 1865, but Dynes refused to pay for 1866, claiming his deed gave him exclusive rights to fish, "people with bigger heads than his having stated that he held the exclusive right of the fishery." Kerr asked to see his deed, but Dynes said he did not have it, though a copy could be obtained from the registry office. So, like a good cop, Kerr trundled off to the registry office and learned that a patent had been issued to Dynes's father in 1837 for twenty-two acres but with no particulars about fishing rights. Kerr wrote to the CCL, stating, "the course I shall in future pursue towards this refractory character."

Kerr also noted that Dynes "is a squatter on about 20 acres more of the property of the government and that he illegally cuts timber off this land." Kerr suggested he be prosecuted for illegal fishing. (Dynes will crop up again in this narrative.)

On May 29, the CCL asked Kerr to examine the Grand River at Galt and report on allegations about mills polluting the waters and damming up the river to prevent fish from climbing to spawn. Kerr proceeded to Galt and met with mill and dam owner James Blaine. Together they worked out a plan to create a fishway that would allow the passage of fish but not prevent the flow of the water to disrupt the operation of the sawmill. This was an early and rare instance of cooperation between Kerr and a mill owner.

Kerr found there were nine other mills, tanneries, and factories at Galt, all of which were polluting the Grand River with sawdust, dyes, ash, lime, chemicals, and mill rubbish, killing the fish. Kerr warned the proprietors but asked the CCL, "What shall I do in those cases? The water in the river was filled with a large mixture of sawdust and mill rubbish." Kerr soon had his answer. He also sought permission to visit other mills and dams in Paris, Brantford, and Dunnville. This became an important enforcement issue for him over the next twenty-two years.

On June 16, Kerr's district was extended to Long Point on Lake Erie and to Whitby on Lake Ontario. Now fifty-four years old, he was extremely busy all summer not just on the lakes but also on rivers like the Rouge, Humber, Duffin, and Credit.

In mid-May, Kerr received a copy of a complaint made by William A. Thompson, vice president of the Erie and Niagara Railroad, that Niagara fisherman Thomas Elliot was damaging the rail line "from the operations of irresponsible persons fishing thereabouts." Kerr was asked to investigate. To prevent further damage, the railroad wanted to secure all the fishing rights to stop the fishing (or so they claimed).

Kerr found no merit in the complaint and described his new friend Elliott as a "respectable and intelligent man. The men fishing with him in his employment are orderly, industrious and well conducted and never will expose the property of the railway company to any damage." He added that "**I happen to know a little about rail roads and railway speculators!!**" Kerr observed Elliott make a few hauls and found that it would be impossible for him to cause any damage because the rail lines were on an embankment at least fourteen feet high above the water.

Quoting Thompson's complaint, "The company would prefer to pay for and hold a licence of the fishing for our own protection," Kerr snorted, "such nonsense!! I have no doubt the company would, but I strongly recommend that Mr. Thompson's proposition not be entertained nor complied with **as it looks like a little speculation.**" Noting that Elliott's father fished for a lifetime before him, this illustrates Kerr's loyalty to good fishermen and the fisheries in general. Kerr

1864–1867 – The Battle of the Beach and the Bay   61

and Elliot became good friends, and when in Niagara Kerr would stay with the Elliots at the Whale Inn they operated at the foot of King St. Unfortunately, the sad saga of Thomas Elliott began years later.

On June 18, Kerr received orders to clean up the Grand River mills. He wrote to them to warn them of prosecution under the Act for killing fish. "It will all be abated," he boasted. He was wrong.

Meanwhile in Toronto, Kerr's prediction of no more trouble for Mr. Pat Gray was about to be dispelled. Kerr met Gray in Toronto on June 28 and planned to hire a surveyor to delineate Gray's lands. The next day Kerr was confronted on the island by solicitor John Beverly Robinson, a group of Toronto officials, a police sergeant, and a reporter from the *Globe*. Kerr was told that Toronto was going to map the island and lease it to tenants. "Evidently the intention today was to overcome me but true to your orders and instructions I stand firm in my post… I would recommend that you be pleased to afford Mr. Gray every protection within your power."

In August 1866, Kerr made his first trip to Lake Erie, stopping on his way to visit the mills and dams on the Grand River below Caledonia. Having already been to Paris and Brantford, Kerr proceeded to Turkey Point and Long Point along Lake Erie. Then Kerr made his way back to Port Dover and by train to Port Colborne.[38] He reported on everything about the local fishing.

In regard to the Grand River, he complained about locks owned by the Grand River Navigation Company regulating the flow of water and preventing fish from travelling up or down stream. Unfortunately, the company was in receivership and couldn't be compelled to do anything about it. The company eventually faded into oblivion, and the locks disintegrated, thereby rectifying the problem.

Now earning $200 a year because of his expanded jurisdiction, Kerr's task was to get to know the fisheries and fishermen of his vast district

....

38 Kerr was many times at or near Port Colborne, where my wife and I have our cottage. He once foot-patrolled our beach, and I have ridden my bike on the trail that follows the path of the rail line where he used to take the train between Port Colborne and Fort Erie. When he sailed up Lake Erie to Port Stanley in August 1846, he passed right by. I wonder what he was thinking about as he first set eyes on his new home of Canada.

and to begin to rationalize the leased fishing stations. The purposes were to secure revenue, prevent squabbling and trespassing, and regulate the catch of fish. Kerr's MO was to take whatever mode of transportation was available and then spend a couple of days looking around and meeting people. Obtaining maps (tracings, as he called them) from the government, he would mark off fishing lots and then lease them to local fishermen. Writing fervently in his diaries, he noted all his observations and then sent them to Quebec in long, detailed letters. He must have known thousands of people, and he seems to have had a photographic memory for names and faces.

When establishing a "fishing station," Kerr would mark off in chains (sixty-six feet) and drive stakes into the shore on the fishery reserve. The station would then extend a prescribed distance out into the lake (typically six miles). The lessee had the exclusive right to fish the station, and it could not be sublet. Then Kerr would ensure the fishing gear (seines or gill nets) were the proper size in terms of length and mesh size (extension measure).

In September 1866, Kerr was at Long Point when he had his first encounter with the Long Point Company, which then owned about 15,000 acres on the twenty-six-mile-long spit that juts out into Lake Erie, almost to the international boundary. The Long Point Company was composed of a group of wealthy businessmen from Hamilton and St. Catharines. The Legislature granted the company its patent in August 1866, reserving the fishing rights. One of the stated purposes of the company was conservation of fish and game, so this was sympatico with Kerr. However, as sportsmen, they also liked to fish, hunt, and drink. Kerr had a generally harmonious relationship with the company over the years, but there were occasional wrinkles. After a visit in September, Kerr noted "had Long Point Hash for supper." Hash is like a stew, not the marijuana-related product! (For more info, see chapter 15.)

After a busy and relatively tranquil summer, the "Battle of the Beach" resumed in October. Joan Baldry fired the first salvo by having her neighbor, who she previously tried to screw out of his house, brought up before Justice of the Peace Hopkins on trespassing charges. Then John Dynes and an ally tried to sell land on the beach strip that they didn't own—it was part of the government lands. Kerr informed him "it was government property. He replied he was aware of it and he told me I might kiss his a__." Kerr wrote to the CCL, saying, "The fact is this man latterly is determined to create a good deal of annoyance and I would like to be furnished with authority from your department to stop such conduct at once." Kerr noted the government plan was to lease out plots on the beach strip for fishermen to grow vegetable gardens, a plan he fully supported to help the fishing families.

On October 24, Kerr was at court before Cahill as a witness in a trial against Joan Baldry and her crew for burning down her neighbour's root house. Then Kerr spent virtually every day until Christmas seizing illegal nets everywhere, arresting people for illegal fishing and fishing on Sunday, and attending before magistrates all over his district to secure convictions. Kerr appeared to be winning, but stay tuned!

On December 31, Kerr was in court in Niagara prosecuting James "Big Jim" Cantwell for throwing "a large stone into a fishery situated there with the intention of obstructing and damaging the same." We have met Cantwell before, but from this moment on he became one of Kerr's Niagara frenemies. After Kerr redistributed the Niagara fishing stations, Cantwell was obviously upset, even though Kerr made painstaking efforts to ensure all the fishermen had plenty of space.

On July 13, Cantwell hoisted a large stone from his boat into the water to hamper fishing. Seine nets are hauled in from the beach, and rocks would impede the net, possibly causing it to tear and be ruined. Cantwell's language at the time of the offence was commented on by the magistrate, who fined him eight dollars and expenses. As Kerr reported, "his expression when he heaved overboard the stone being—It will give the d n ed be gg rs something to do to get that up." In addition to the fine, Kerr suggested the Department "seriously reprimand James Cantwell for such gross misconduct." The Battle of Niagara had seen its first salvo fired.

1867 TO CONFEDERATION

It appears that by the end of 1866, the Burlington Beach fishermen had stopped fighting Kerr and started fighting one other. In a letter to the

CCL written on January 1, Kerr noted a number of recent crimes. The lighthouse keeper had been robbed of $200, Joan Baldry had 400 yards of nets stolen, and Ben Foulds had a number of geese and ducks stolen plus "a quantity of bed linen." (Off the clothesline? Who does that?) Kerr heard that Fred Corey and his sons and henchmen were behind these crimes, but he had no proof. Kerr also recorded that "a man was drowned while in a state of drunkenness. The liquor was got by him in an unlicensed house on the Beach."

In January Kerr began to notice deer being killed illegally and shipped by train. He noted carloads were shipped in bond[39] "from Detroit to New York, locked up. Eighty passed here today locked up in a box car." Meeting with Emilius Irving, the GWR solicitor, Kerr put a stop to this. Some deer were also coming from places like Ottawa, so Kerr seized one and prosecuted the intended recipient, which he discerned from the destination tag on the deer's toe. JP Cahill ruled that the deer, "a splendid buck," never reached the destination and thus was never in possession. Cahill directed Kerr to telegraph the intended recipient, so Kerr wrote, "Seized deer to your address. Do you claim it? Answer."[40] Charles Treble telegraphed back: "Yes. Send it to Fort Erie." (Oops, guilty.) The confiscated deer was instead sent to an orphans' home.[41]

By January, John Dynes was back to his old tricks. Using his brother-in-law, George Lottridge, for financial and moral support, he was trying to evict a poor fisherman who he claimed was encroaching on his land. Kerr went to great lengths to prove that it was not Dynes's land and that he had no right of eviction.

....

39   "In bond" meant travelling through Canada from one US destination to another and thus not subject to customs.

40   The telegraph came to Ontario in 1846 but was quite expensive until competition was introduced in 1868.

41   Kerr had the deer brought to court! "The deer was present in court all this time with the address fastened to a cord around his neck." Sounds like a Monty Python skit! In February Kerr discovered the confiscated deer was taken to the Industrial School and then, for some reason, to the home of Judge O'Reilly. He, in turn, gave the children "a quantity of mutton" (tough old sheep). Bad deal, kids. Kerr was upset about this. O'Reilly got a semi-fresh buck, and the poor kids got some old, rancid sheep!

In a letter written on March 8, Kerr proudly noted, "no fishermen have been fined for any infraction of the Act and I have not heard of any of them going out on Sunday." Kerr recommended that he be given discretionary power to allow limited gill-net fishing in parts of Burlington Bay. Wanting them to receive "a little indulgence," Kerr said, "until very recently I was not aware that our fishermen on Burlington Beach were so extremely poor and needy." Kerr believed they would receive this kindness with "gratitude and thankfulness." This act of kindness and compassion later got Kerr accused of favouritism and ignited a lot of hostility with competing interests. They eventually prevailed, and the minister banned net fishing in Burlington Bay.

In April, Kerr spent most of a week in Toronto seizing nets and arresting people for duck hunting. Curiously, people like David Ward and Leonard Marsh were charged, men who became Kerr's long-term friends. Even more curious is that he received assistance from Constable John Hanlon.

On April 15, Kerr took the overnight train to Ottawa, arriving there at about noon. This was his first trip to meet Mr. Whitcher at headquarters, which had evidently moved from Quebec City in anticipation of Confederation. They talked about local fishing matters and the Department's plans for the future, although Kerr gave no details.

Back in Toronto on April 19, Kerr and Constable Hanlon were arresting duck hunters, some of whom resisted arrest: "Seized three ducks in the possession of John Cubitt who struggled hard against it—the gun went off and shot a hole through the boat." He didn't say whose boat or whose gun. Presumably they were all armed.

On April 13, Kerr got his new boat, which was built in Toronto and shipped by rail to Hamilton. Thereafter he became more active in patrolling Burlington Bay and frequently employed his sons to row him.

Kerr reported a strange incident on April 22 when a Toronto cop, "Mason the whisky detective," seized the seine net of Pat Gray, who was fishing legally. Kerr proceeded to the Toronto police station to complain, and the net was immediately restored to its owner. Kerr railed on: "It is a great pity that a man like Mason should be encouraged in the manner he is. I never knew of a similar case but one that happened in Dublin in the year 1842, when the recipient, Delahunt, actually killed a man, attempted to charge an innocent person with the offence but ultimately was hanged himself for the same." It seems to me that Kerr must have been talking about Mason being a bad cop. In 1842, Kerr was still in the Irish Constabulary. Kerr finished by noting, "The majesty of our laws can be maintained without employing such rotten degrading tools! Put such people down say I." It was not his last encounter with crooked cops.

At one of the trials, a young lawyer made the argument that the magistrate had no jurisdiction because Toronto Island was not part of the city of Toronto, its limit extending only 500 yards out into the water. For once praising a lawyer, Kerr stated, "Mr. Robertson, a promising young barrister argued and I believe made a good case for his clients, sufficient at least to cause his worship to put off the decision until today." Kerr was undoubtedly chuffed because the ruling confirmed, at least for the time being, that the feds were still in control of the island.

Contrast this with his response to the ongoing case between Joan Baldry and her neighbor, James Waddell: "If lawyers were out of the way I could very shortly settle and arrange the matter." Kerr reported on the sleazy tactics of Charles Sadlier, who had the case held down in Quarter Sessions until the end of the list and then adjourned to the next sitting, three months later. The case was to be tried first, but again through Sadlier's actions, it was held down until, out of frustration, Waddell finally settled with Baldry paying him eight dollars. Because of the delays and adjournments, Waddell had to pay lawyer and witness fees totaling thirty dollars.[42]

Kerr reported how Joan Baldry tried to bribe him if he could arrange to have the lands in question conveyed to her. In this strange saga, we hear mention of a lawyer named Simcoe Kerr (no relation to J. W. Kerr) who wrote to allege that the lands in question were part of

....

42 Through my thirty-six-year career as a lawyer, I witnessed many such sleazy tricks—sometimes by lawyers, and sometimes by clients. Every adjournment or delay gives an advantage to someone, usually to the detriment of someone else. Sleazy lawyers are always known as such by other lawyers, court staff, and most importantly, by judges. Unfortunately, they are not always known as such by clients.

the "canal reserve" and thus not the government lands. Kerr noted that Whitcher told him in November 1865 that there was no such thing as a canal reserve. (Much more about Simcoe Kerr later.) Kerr refused to renew Baldry's fishing license, and eventually she sold her place and moved elsewhere.

In May, Kerr received a complaint from a Niagara fisherman, John Raynor, alleging that Kerr had been biased in favour of Jim Cantwell, of all people, in reallocating the fishing lots. Raynor provided the information used to convict Cantwell of tossing the rock into the water. Raynor seemed unhappy with the result, even though Kerr let him have half the fine. Kerr noted that Cantwell was unhappy about the subdivision of his lease. "I am aware that he has a long tongue. A barking dog never bites… I allow no fisherman to have his own way, fishing as he likes… And thus, you will see how little cause of complaint there is of undue intimacy with James Cantwell."

Back in Toronto, Kerr suggested a compromise to the ownership dispute whereby the island be granted to the City but the Department maintain a one-chain fishery reserve. "I hope Mr. Whitcher will see that our fishermen's rights are protected at the Toronto Island, not only now but for all time to come, and don't give the Corporation of Toronto any right nor control over the fisheries, nor over the Bay nor over the Marsh there as regards the fisheries—Corporations have no souls." Prescient words indeed that the Department would later ignore for political expediency.

Kerr continued to seek increases in the limits of his district. Receiving an application to fish the Holland River and Lake Simcoe, Kerr noted it was not in his district. He included in his reply, "I believe locally, it ought to be in my district." What Kerr failed to see was that the larger his turf, the less efficiently he could police it, despite his Herculean efforts. As we see repeatedly, when the cat's away, the mice will play. Kerr said, "I have been obliged to visit the Beach every night and day during the past week and endeavour by doing so to keep the fishermen up to the law."

Kerr's last pre-Confederation task was to clean up the Grand River in response to public complaints. There were five dams between Brantford and Dunnville,[43] all owned by the Grand River Navigation Company and all in need of having fishways built. Kerr also noted numerous mills of various sorts and put them all on notice not to pollute. He also planned to write to the companies to get them to construct fishways. (Good luck with that! Receivership = bankrupt.)[44]

Kerr made no mention of Confederation until much later in his diaries. Indeed, he spent July 1, 1867, in Brantford, prosecuting some men for spearfishing on our first national holiday. Humbug!

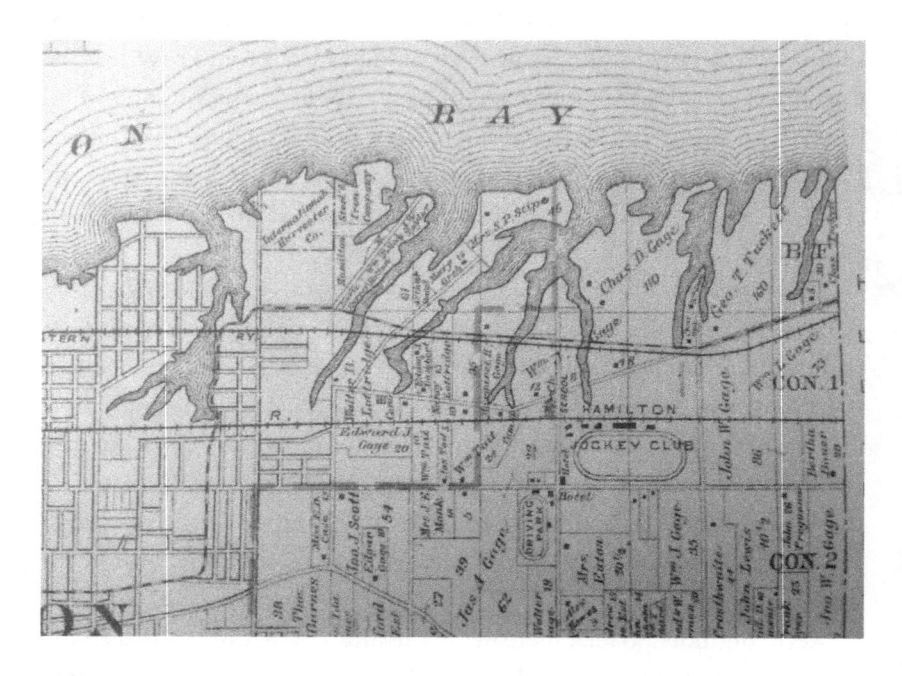

Detail of Burlington Bay map showing various inlets, c.1922. Hamilton Public Library

....

43   The dams were at Caledonia, Sims Lock, Seneca, York, and Mount Healy.
44   Five locks and dams created the navigable river system, and scows were pulled by horses or oxen from the adjacent tow path. Killed off by the railways, the system ceased to exist in 1871, and the wooden locks and dams were abandoned to rot away. The entire Grand River runs 266 km and drains 6,200 sq km as the largest watershed in Southern Ontario. If you want to know what was going on in the Grand in 1867, Kerr's description is in vol. 3 of his diaries on p. 75.

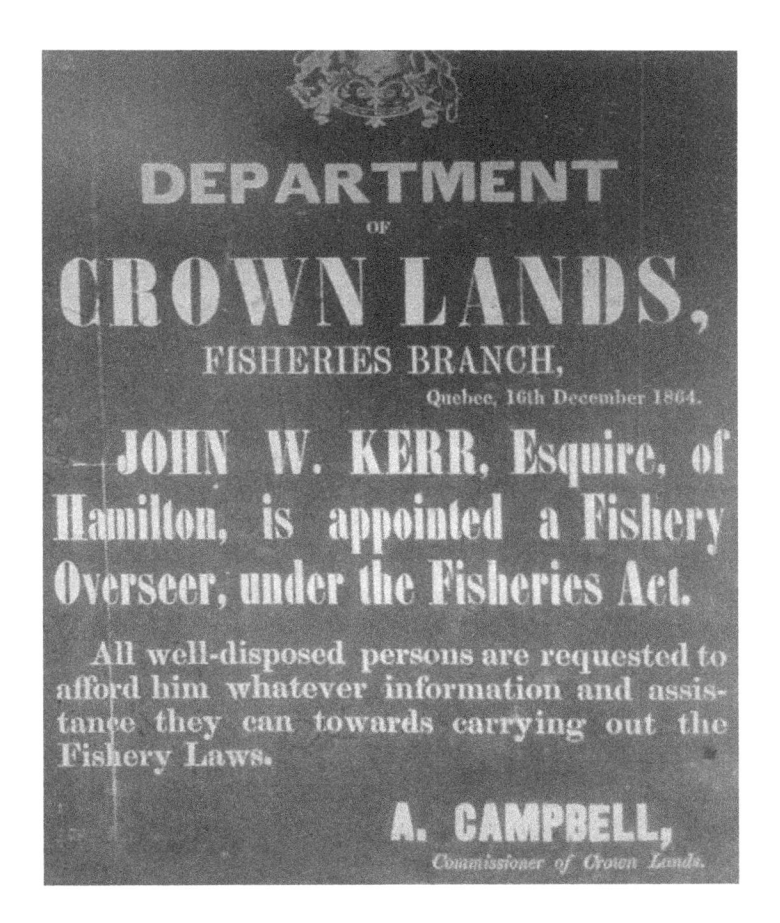

*Kerr's appointment as Fisheries Overseer, December 1864.
From introduction to Kerr diaries, ROM*

70   Caught!

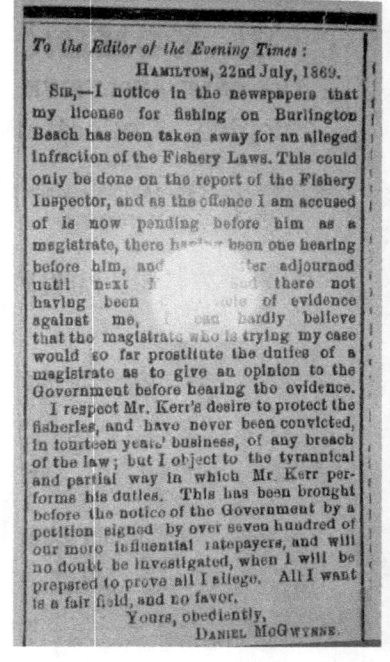

> To the Editor of the Evening Times:
>
> HAMILTON, 22nd July, 1869.
>
> SIR,—I notice in the newspapers that my license for fishing on Burlington Beach has been taken away for an alleged infraction of the Fishery Laws. This could only be done on the report of the Fishery Inspector, and as the offence I am accused of is now pending before him as a magistrate, there having been one hearing before him, and ____ ____ adjourned until next ____ ____ there not having been ____ ____ of evidence against me, I can hardly believe that the magistrate who is trying my case would so far prostitute the duties of a magistrate as to give an opinion to the Government before hearing the evidence. I respect Mr. Kerr's desire to protect the fisheries, and have never been convicted, in fourteen years' business, of any breach of the law; but I object to the tyrannical and partial way in which Mr. Kerr performs his duties. This has been brought before the notice of the Government by a petition signed by over seven hundred of our more influential ratepayers, and will no doubt be investigated, when I will be prepared to prove all I allege. All I want is a fair field, and no favor.
>
> Yours, obediently,
> DANIEL MCGWYNNE.

Newspaper clipping found in Kerr diary. Bad Boy fisherman Dan McGwynne's complaint about Kerr to the Evening Times, 1869.

Burlington Beach Lighthouse. Photo by Joel Kerr, 2019.

Burlington Beach Lighthouse keeper's house, now derelict. Photo by Joel Kerr, 2019.

CHAPTER 7

Confederation, Peter Mitchell, and Subsequent Ministers

On March 8, 1867, the *British North America Act* (*BNA*) was passed in the English Parliament and received royal assent on March 29. It was to be proclaimed on July 1, when Canada West would become the Province of Ontario and part of the Dominion of Canada.

Kerr would now be employed by the federal government in the Ministry of Marine and Fisheries. The first minister—Kerr's new boss—was Peter Mitchell of New Brunswick, a veteran politician and businessman. Kerr began to write to the honourable minister in Ottawa, although his immediate supervisor continued to be W. F. Whitcher.

Considered one of the thirty-six Fathers of Confederation, Mitchell did not attend the Charlottetown conference in September 1864 but attended the Quebec City conference in October 1864 where the seventy-two resolutions that formed the basis of the *BNA* were ratified. Mitchell left the conference a few days before it ended to attend to private business and thus is not in the official photograph.[45]

Originally intended to be a union of Canada East, Canada West, New Brunswick, Nova Scotia, PEI, and Newfoundland, for almost two years after the Quebec City conference, the colonies squabbled, and it was not until November 1866 that the delegations, minus PEI

---

45   Donald Creighton. *The Road to Confederation*. Oxford: Oxford University Press, 2012.

and Newfoundland, met in London, England, to hammer out the final details of the amalgamation. Mitchell attended this conference, although he was not a leading luminary. In fact, only the Canadians, MacDonald, Cartier, and Galt, went to Highclere Castle (the future home of the fictional *Downton Abbey*) to meet with its owner, Lord Carnarvon, the colonial secretary.[46] Mitchell did, however "clash with MacDonald over numerous points of policy beginning an acrimonious relationship between the two men that lasted for decades."[47]

In Quebec it had been agreed that the sea coast and inland fisheries would be a provincial jurisdiction, but in London an amendment to the seventy-two proclamations brought them under federal authority.[48] This was primarily due to the American cancellation of the Reciprocity Treaty between Britain and the US, which had been in effect from 1854 to 1866 and was basically a free-trade agreement. Part of the treaty provided that Americans could fish in British waters but not inland fisheries or the salmon or shad fisheries in rivers or mouths of rivers, and British subjects had reciprocal fishing rights in American seas north of the thirty-sixth latitude.[49]

Concern about America's hostility toward Britain over Britain's tacit support of the South in the Civil War and fear of the American-supported Fenians[50] were two of the main motivating factors for Confederation in 1866. Giving control of the fisheries to the feds would provide stronger enforcement of fishing rights and more vigorous negotiating powers. Had it not been for this amendment, Kerr might have

---

46   Henry Howard Molyneux Herbert (June 24, 1831–June 28, 1890) was the fourth earl of Carnarvon. He was colonial secretary from 1866–1867 and 1874–1878.

47   "Peter Mitchell," The Canadian Encyclopedia, last visited Oct. 1, 2020, https://www.thecanadianencyclopedia.ca/en/article/peter-mitchell.

48   Fisheries was one of twenty-nine defined areas of exclusive federal jurisdiction.

49   The thirty-sixth parallel runs roughly along Virginia's southern border with North Carolina.

50   The Fenian Raids took place in 1866 and from 1870–1871. In April 1866, raids took place in New Brunswick. On June 2, 1866, the Battle of Ridgeway took place near Fort Erie and resulted in the death of nine Canadian militiamen and ten Fenians. As a Protestant, Kerr was always loyal to England and vigorously opposed to Irish nationalism.

found himself unemployed.

After Confederation, Mitchell was appointed to the Senate and somehow got appointed to the MacDonald cabinet.

The Ministry of Marine and Fisheries became one of thirteen Canadian cabinet portfolios on July 1, and Mitchell was appointed minister. New Brunswick was to have two ministries, and Mitchell was a toss-up choice. One esteemed politician (Langevin) described him as a "good fellow with a badly swelled head."[51] Kerr was now writing to the boss at the newly opened Parliament Buildings in Ottawa.

Described as "innovative and aggressive" by the *Canadian Encyclopedia* and as a "colorful swashbuckler," Mitchell remained minister until McDonald's government was toppled over the Pacific Scandal in November 1873, in which bribes had been paid to conservative politicians to get the Canadian Pacific Railway built. Having run for a seat in Parliament in 1872, Mitchell was re-elected in 1874 but sat as an independent, nursing numerous grievances with MacDonald. He purchased the *Montreal Herald* in 1885 and used it to be critical of MacDonald. He was out of politics by 1896 and was found dead in his room at the Windsor Hotel in Montreal on October 25, 1899.

SIR ALBERT JAMES SMITH

Smith was Kerr's second boss during the Liberal administration of Alexander Mackenzie from 1874 to 1878. Also from New Brunswick, Smith was an able lawyer who knew the law of the sea and who had been a vigorous opponent of Confederation. Having been a "frisky bachelor," according to *The Dictionary of Canadian Biography*, "In Ottawa, Smith was at the center of affairs with Mackenzie relying on him as the maritime expert and confiding in him on many matters."[52] Following the disastrous Treaty of Washington in 1871, by which Americans were permitted to fish in Canadian waters but without a quid pro quo, the Halifax Fisheries Commission was held to determine what compensation, if any, was to be awarded to Canada. Smith represented Canada, and

....
51 Creighton 2012, 433.
52 Biography, Sir Albert James Smith, 7.

the country was ultimately awarded $5.5 million in what was described as Canada's first diplomatic victory over America. For his participation in the commission, Smith received a knighthood from Queen Victoria.

Kerr met Smith in Ottawa in December 1873 when he was called there just as the Liberals were taking office. As an ardent supporter of Sir John A. MacDonald, Kerr lost some areas of his district during Smith's ministry because patronage appointments were endemic in early Canada. Fortunately for Kerr, during the remainder of his life, Sir John A. was back in power, and Kerr's position was more or less safe. In his later years, Kerr became openly political even in his many letters to the minister and the commissioner of Fisheries.

JAMES COLLEDGE POPE

Born in PEI on June 11, 1826, this entrepreneur and politician was appointed minister of Marine and Fisheries when MacDonald returned to power in 1878. Described as "pugnacious, belligerent and vindictive," he was first elected to Parliament in 1876 and was described by his private secretary as "not an office man, nor given to the regular and methodical treatment of correspondence." According to *The Dictionary of Canadian Biography,* "many of his surviving letters concern matters of patronage."[53] (Sounds like an American president whose name rhymes with "rump.")

Following some personal and business losses, his mental and physical health deteriorated, and he took a leave of absence from cabinet in 1881. He did not contest the election of 1882, and in 1883 he was legally declared to be of unsound mind and incapable of managing his affairs. He died in 1885. During his tenure as minister, it is likely that onerous duties were placed on W. F. Whitcher and his assistant, S. P. Bauset.

ARCHIBALD WOODBURY MCLELAN

A fifty-eight-year-old Nova Scotia shipbuilder, McLelan was appointed on July 10, 1882, and served until December 9, 1885, when he was appointed minister of Finance. During his tenure with Marine and

---

53   *Dictionary of Canadian Biography,* James Colledge Pope, 7.

Fisheries, he is noted by the *Dictionary of Canadian Biography* to have been "an unusually good minister, being thoroughly familiar with the shipping business and being by nature hard working and judicious."[54] He visited all the lighthouses as far as Lake Superior "to deal more intelligently with the demands of MPs and others for lights, buoys and beacons."[55]

SIR GEORGE EULAS FOSTER

Foster, a thirty-seven-year-old from New Brunswick, became Kerr's fifth and final boss when he was appointed by MacDonald as minister on December 10, 1885. Very active in the temperance movement, Kerr probably approved of Foster for at least this reason. Foster wrote, "I became a thorough believer in the virtue of total abstinence for the individual and prohibition for the community and the State." Best known for his involvement in trying to solve various disputes between the United States and Canada, Foster was appointed minister of Finance just after Kerr died in May 1888.

There is a curious Hamilton connection with Foster in that his wife had been married to a Hamilton lawyer named Daniel Black Chisholm, who deserted her, prompting her to get a divorce in Chicago, to which he had fled.[56] As a divorced woman, even though she had been dumped, she was shunned by some in Ottawa. Peter Gwyn, in his biography of Sir John A. MacDonald, *Nation Maker,* says Foster was sent in to "social exile" by MacDonald's wife, Agnes.[57]

....

54 *Dictionary of Canadian Biography*, Archibald Woodbury McLelan, 2.
55 The Department of Marine and Fisheries was two separate divisions under one minister. Lighthouses were in the marine division. Kerr, being in the fisheries division, knew all the lighthouse keepers in his district and was periodically critical of them, particularly if they were not "good conservatives."
56 Daniel Black Chisholm (Nov. 2, 1832–Jan. 2, 1899), born in Flamboro, was a farmer who became a lawyer and was elected mayor of Hamilton in 1871. He was elected to Parliament in 1872. More about him later.
57 The *Dictionary of Hamilton Biography* notes all of Chisholm's achievements in politics and business but fails to mention the sordid end to his marriage and the fact that he also misappropriated clients' money. Kerr knew him well and one time borrowed money from him.

All five of Kerr's bosses were men from the Maritime Provinces, which suggests that inland fishing was something of an afterthought.

Chapter 8

1867–1873 Good Old Sir John A. – Hip, Hip Hurray!

After Confederation, Kerr attended to his duties, as he had done since his appointment. There were numerous prosecutions for illegal fishing all over his district and a lot of personal antipathy toward him, but Kerr smugly concluded, "The long marches I have made, the close looking after and upholding of our laws is not without its fruit and affect."

He continued to have the same problems with the same people. For example, he had another run-in with John Dynes and his crew in December 1867 when they attempted to evade Kerr's detection. He reported hearing threats that "three men on the Beach were prepared to give me a beating."

He was actively enforcing the game laws and arresting people in Hamilton and elsewhere for illegally hunting muskrats and mink as well as deer, although game protection was now a provincial jurisdiction, and I am not aware of any authority he had from the province. In fact, in April 1868 Kerr wrote to find out if he still had authority. He did not, to his chagrin.

1868

In January 1868 he was asked to investigate conditions in Sarnia, lower Lake Huron, and Lake St. Clair as well as the Thames River. He made a three-day trip and traipsed all over, making his inspection. The fishing seems to have been largely unregulated, and there were disputes between local fishermen, Aboriginals, Americans, and others. Kerr basically indicated that the whole area needed better licensing and enforcement. Encountering an Aboriginal man near Lake St. Clair selling illegal "saddles of venison,"[58] Kerr said, "I did speak to him about breaking the Game Act. His reply was that he would break my nose for me." Kerr also cautioned, "Our game are being killed off and if not nurtured and preserved will be all extinct in a few years." He proved to be correct.

In regard to the Thames, Kerr saw that mill dams were preventing the free movement of fish and that fishways should be installed: "I myself lived in London from May 1847 until April 1851 and at the time I left and during the entire period, the River Thames abounded with fish all the year round. At present, chiefly in consequence of the mill dams, there is no fish."

There were continuous money problems with the Department being constantly late in paying or questioning his disbursements. In fact, things were so bad that Kerr had to borrow five dollars from Magistrate Cahill to fund a trip to Whitby![59]

Kerr was subject to the usual complaints about nepotism and secret dealings. In regard to a March 1868 allegation, Kerr responded with his usual fervour: "I do nothing secretly! I do nothing out of my own head! I submit the Application to (the Department) and then I act in all cases according to your instructions."

During the summer of 1867, it had been agreed that the Department and James Blaine would share equally the cost of installing the fishway at Galt. By March he had submitted his account in the amount of $384.48, which seems to have been more than anticipated. The Department was quite reluctant to pay, to Kerr's consternation and embarrassment. This became the subject of many letters attempting to coax the Department to do the right thing and pay up.

By March 24, Joan Baldry was up to her old tricks. A petition was circulated to restore her fishing licence and complain about Kerr's

58   A "saddle" of venison is a loin cut of deer.
59   Imagine borrowing money from a judge! This illustrates the rather cozy nature of the relationship between Kerr and Cahill—something that would not be tolerated today.

high-handed treatment of her. It was produced by a tailor named Magnus Bruce, who Kerr alleged had a self-interest: "It appears that about 5 years ago Mrs. Baldry was taken ill and on the point of death, **as she supposed**, made a Will leaving Magnus Bruce $1,600 she had then in the bank. Mr. Bruce is no relative of Mrs. Joan Baldry, merely a visitor occasionally on Sundays."[60]

Kerr indicates that Baldry hadn't paid her lease for years and that she and her crew were repeat offenders: "The first net I seized after my appointment... was the property of Mrs. Joan Baldry. And although Mrs. Joan Baldry pledged herself never to offend again if the Department would restore to her net, I gave back the net and the evening of the same day she broke the law again and set out the net." Noting her other infractions Kerr concluded, "Evidently! The petitioners do not appear to know anything whatever about the facts of the case." Kerr howled with indignation at the assertion in the petition "that Mrs. Baldry has been in peaceable possession for the last 10 years." He noted her lawsuit against her neighbour, James Waddell, and got an affidavit signed by him setting out the details. Unfortunately for Kerr, the Department decided to grant her a lease. "I hope Mrs. Joan Baldry's tongue will now cease," Kerr wrote without apparent optimism.

By April, Kerr was in the Court of Quarter Sessions testifying in a jury trial regarding a dispute between a wealthy and prominent Hamiltonian, William Gage, and one John Bates. Gage had charged Bates with spearing on an inlet of the bay that he claimed to own.[61]

....

60   By implication, they were involved in some illicit activities. Love that Victorian language!

61   The Burlington Bay of 1868 did not look like the bay of today. It had numerous inlets that are now filled in. There were farms in Barton and Saltfleet townships at the edge of the bay. William J. Gage owned one such farm on Gage's Inlet, and he asserted ownership of the waters of the inlet and had Bates charged with trespassing. Appealing his conviction, Bates was later acquitted on the basis of Kerr's evidence that there were fish in the inlet and thus the water was owned by the government. Gage was not amused. Kerr noted, "Gage may attack me as much as he like and no doubt he will. But my instructions from the Department are to this effect. And there I shall stand firmly." Kerr and Gage reconciled their differences and became friends.

Kerr testified that the inlet was part of the fisheries and thus Crown land; therefore, Bates was not trespassing. The jury accepted this and overturned the conviction. Another day, another enemy.

Back in Toronto, Kerr reported hearing from Mrs. Len Marsh that he should be careful because "certain persons had threatened to shoot me." Kerr had no shortage of enemies in Toronto, including cops, politicians, duck hunters and the Hanlan family.

On June 13, having reflected on his lack of provincial authority to enforce the game laws, Kerr wrote, "I don't think it would be prudent for me to act in a private capacity for the protection of game. To do so without a specific authority from Ontario would only place me in a position of a public informer and bring upon me disgrace. I do not desire to make myself more notorious than I am." As previously noted, no one likes a rat.

In 1868 the *Fisheries Act* was amended to permit the minister to forgive or remit fines. This became a major tool for Kerr to effect compliance with the law. To secure good behaviour, the Department could forgive fines. It seems that the forgiveness could also be revoked for future bad behaviour if the fine was put in abeyance.

Not getting a raise prompted an outburst to the minister: "I feel disappointed. I expected promotion and was led to believe that on the completion of Confederation and the passing of the new Fishery Act my position would be bettered and my salary raised." More false promises from Mr. W. F. Whitcher.

Throughout his career, Kerr made careful observations about the habits and tendencies of the various fish species and how they could be protected. He made continuous references to net mesh sizes and when the closed season should be, plus the spawning grounds of fish, particularly the "noble salmon." His interest was always to protect the fish and preserve the successful functioning of the fisheries for the benefit of the fishermen and the general population.

One particular species that was important in the nineteenth century was whitefish. They were caught in seines and gill nets by the millions until they were virtually extinct. In 1868, Kerr noted, "Whitefish are a very tender, shy fish, **they lack pluck** and rarely, if ever, pass over the hauling lines and do not ever attempt to pass the net (seine) as long as it is in motion. Whitefish are so tender and delicate that if a portion of the scales are only slightly removed, they will die. Handling them is fatal, if only to throw them out back into the water."

Enforcement of the Sunday fishing laws was actively promoted by Kerr in his early years. It was unlawful to fish from 6:00 p.m. on Saturday until 6:00 a.m. on Monday, which seems like an excessive period of time. On Sunday, June 21, 1868, Kerr was in Toronto enforcing the Sunday laws when he found a group of soldiers fishing but declined to charge them, only warning them off: "I have since considered, as soldiers know so little about our laws but always know how to obey orders, a letter from the Department to the commanding officer at Toronto will at once make the matter all right."

However, Kerr was not so lenient with the other men and boys he found fishing "by rod, hook and line" that day, saying, "I took down the names of 59 men and boys." Some were summonsed two days later and were fined one dollar. Another fifty-two were brought before the JP a few days later. Kerr noted that there was "a much larger number" but he was only able to arrest fifty-nine of them. Kerr did recommend that some commercial fishing be permitted on Saturday evening and early Monday. To enforce the entire period "will be to virtually kill off our own fishermen."

On June 24 is the first mention of Samuel Wilmot of Newcastle, who had built a large fish-breeding operation. This was the beginning of a long, strange saga, which is the subject of chapter 20 in this book. It did not end well.

Kerr was still subject to the usual abuse. He amusingly noted an incident on Burlington Beach on July 2: "Bid George Williams, the time of day, he bid me to go to hell--I laughed at him for his bad manners."

Meanwhile, the Hamilton crowd were still at it. Kerr heard that John Dynes was fishing illegally. Kerr also noted a grisly murder on Burlington Beach in which a man was killed after being struck "on the head with a hickory broom handle." Apparently, no charges were laid "as the coroner did not investigate the case properly." The coroner was Kerr's friend, H. B. Bull, who, apparently, was not a medical doctor. Bull was also one of two coroners who examined the fifty-seven bodies from the Desjardins Canal disaster in 1857.

In May 1868, William Gage, through his solicitor, Myles O'Reilly, submitted a petition to the government to give him an exclusive licence to fish the waters adjacent to his extensive lands in the bay "in order to protect himself from the depredations of person who insist on coming on to his property… for fishing and shooting." The minister "seems disposed to grant Mr. Gage's request should no insuperable objection exist." Not surprisingly, Kerr responded, "the objections seem to me **insurmountable and cannot be overcome."**

Kerr sent in a blistering five-page letter listing thirteen objections. He pointed out that if the petition was granted, Gage would stop all boats from sailing up the inlets and prevent all fishing and spearing, "a right the public at present enjoy." He also believed Gage would close the public road and prevent all access to the inlets: "If you give Mr. Gage this exclusive lease he will at once bar everybody out, so he has informed me." The lease was not granted. Despite these negative comments, Kerr and Gage later became friends and associates.

In 1868 the government struck a Select Committee on Fisheries and Navigation. A number of the questions pertained to the inland fisheries, and Kerr wrote a detailed letter of response in which he set out full details of his district and his observations about the fisheries. Perhaps the two most interesting aspects of his six-page letter pertain to the judicial system and his dissatisfaction with his pay.

In regard to the process of appeals that resulted in a jury trial, he opined that there should be no right of appeal from a magistrate's conviction but that "persons aggrieved by such conviction may appeal by petition to the minister." He went on to say that "the convictions have invariably been quashed by the juries—Although the evidence was as clear as the noonday and the sun at meridian."

In regard to his salary, he boldly stated, "My salary at present is only two hundred dollars per year… I have unbounded confidence in Mr. W. F. Whitcher… and hope the day is not far distant when I shall be more liberally paid and so devote all my time and attention to the fisheries." His "unbounded confidence" would prove to be unfounded.

Returning to the issue of an appeal by John Dynes and others, Kerr wrote to the minister, saying, "although the evidence sustained the convictions, in all these cases the result has been and always will be the same before a jury of the County of Wentworth. It is very discouraging to me... A deep-laid conspiracy has been going on for some months past amongst Mr. John Dynes (and others) to upset the fishery laws altogether and your humble servant with them." Kerr even enlisted his own lawyer, Richard Martin, to write a scholarly letter to the minister: "Unless the legislature desire to have the Fisheries Act remain as they always have been here, the mere laughing stock of the Quarter Sessions[62] and trials for infraction of its provisions no more than a judicial farce, appeals to the Quarter Sessions must be abolished."

Martin criticized judges for their interpretation of the Act but reserved his harshest words for the jurors: "I am sure that our Quarter Session juries, who are mostly all either fishermen or relatives or friends of fishermen, will always find for the fishermen no matter how the judge charges them."[63] Today, the availability of jury trials are increasingly restricted, to the dismay of many criminal defence lawyers.

In October 1868, Kerr had his second meeting with Whitcher. After picking him up at the GWR station in Hamilton, they immediately

....

62   The Court of Quarter Sessions was so named because it only held sessions four times a year for a week or two at a time. Apparently, cases weren't scheduled for specific times, so everyone—litigants, lawyers, and witnesses—was expected to be ready whenever their case was called. Kerr reports days spent at court, waiting impatiently.

63   I did a handful of criminal jury trials in my career. I found juries inscrutable and unpredictable. Other than for murder trials where juries are generally required, most defence lawyers only elect trial by jury for lost causes in the faint hope that the jury will go off the rails and acquit. In my single civil jury trial (where there are only six jurors), they did just that. My client was suing his insurance company, who refused to pay for his stolen $10,000 truck. The jury seemed to dislike the insurance adjuster and awarded the client his money plus $250,000 punitive damages! The insurance company appealed to the Court of Appeal, who overruled the jury, taking it all away and ordering costs against my client. I was always nervous about jury trials. It was like acting in a play where I wrote the script as I performed.

left by horse and buggy for Vittoria, a town just west of Port Dover. Speaking of the forty-two-mile journey, Kerr wrote, "Done a good deal of business with Mr. W. going up to Vittoria." I would estimate the road trip to be about six hours, so that would have provided a good opportunity for a thorough discussion. I wonder what else they talked about. The next day they parted, and Whitcher boarded a steamer at Port Ryerse for an unknown destination. It may have been for Long Point because a few days later Kerr was back in the area and on return to Hamilton put four boxes of Long Point ducks on the train.

On October 29, Whitcher was back in Hamilton, and he and Kerr spent time at Burlington Bay examining the "place applied for by Mr. Gage to lease as a fishing station." The next day Kerr took Whitcher to Toronto and put his paddle, gun case, and valise on the train to Ottawa. What happened to Whitcher himself is not mentioned. My surmise is that Whitcher spent ten days hunting on Long Point.

Attending Duffens Creek, near Pickering, Kerr was elated to see salmon spawning: "Such a thing has not happened before for upwards of 20 years. Every day since my appointment my aim and object was to be able to report at some future time the pleasure I now feel of this accomplished fact." Kerr worked passionately to protect all of Toronto's streams for the next many years, but eventually, it became futile.

By late November, Kerr was frantically searching for illegal herring nets in the bay, frequently being out all night and employing two of his sons, George (age nineteen) and Fred (age sixteen), to row him around. He also appeared to be attempting to make amends with some of his adversaries. For example, he employed repeat offender Frederick Corey to assist him, and he noted he got his breakfast at William Gage's. On seizing 450 herring in an illegal net, he gave 100 to Mr. Gage. On November 27, he found men illegally fishing and wrote, "They were very daring. Had to fire my pistol to keep them from lifting their net."

On December 19, the minister sent Kerr an article about fish propagation, and Kerr for the first time expressed a wish to establish a facility of his own for such purpose. This was an unrequited dream of his for the next twenty years and the subject of much personal bitterness.

1869

Kerr had a quiet winter in 1869 and reported on April 1 that he had imposed no fines in the first quarter. However, once the ice was off the bay, he began to seize more illegal nets, including some that were the property of John Dynes. It seemed, however, that his main adversaries for the next number of years were the Turkey Point and Norfolk fishermen.

Inspecting the Grand River in April, Kerr noticed that the fishway of James Blaine at Galt had survived the "terrible freshet" (a spring flood) but that all the other dams were washed out, giving the fish an opportunity to travel from Port Maitland to Guelph "independent of the fishways."[64]

In 1869 Kerr applied to the minister to be permitted to allow limited net fishing in sections of Burlington Bay for the benefit of a few of the Burlington Beach fishermen. John Bates, a serial offender, did not get a licence and decided to stir up trouble with the assistance of his lawyer, Charles A. Sadlier.

They got an article into the Toronto *Globe* about Kerr allowing this illegal fishing and wanting to have all net fishing stopped, supposedly for the preservation of the fish. Apparently, they even persuaded Magistrate Cahill to their cause by getting him to summons one of the licensed fishermen for illegal fishing. On May 15, Kerr reported on the "strange and ridiculous proceedings" on the part of Cahill, Sadlier, and Bates stating,

> *It is the first time since my appointment the Messrs. Sadlier, Bates (and others) have taken an interest in the preservation of the fish in the B. Bay waters... The deep and lively interest taken by them to defeat me, and the Department, in almost every case of prosecution I have instituted, and in which they have always been so successful in defeating the ends of justice... will prove conclusively what the real motive and interest is of those persons.*

Kerr also noted that the citizens of the county "have been greatly benefitted by a bountiful supply of good and wholesome fish for food"

---

[64] Guelph is not on the Grand River but is on the Speed River, which is a tributary of the Grand.

as a result of the net fishing on Burlington Bay. It seems that personal grudges were big motivators for mischief in the nineteenth century.

As we have seen, fights and arguments frequently took place between the licensed fishermen, and this became particularly intense at Queenston and Niagara-on-the-Lake. One such dispute was between John Wadsworth and David Derror. Kerr wrote, "David is a coloured man with a large family to support and the fishery is his main support."[65] Kerr heard that Wadsworth had stabbed Derror twice with a pitchfork and recommended that he not be allowed to purchase a piece of ordnance land that would adversely affect Derror.[66] This had future consequences for Mr. Derror and Kerr.

On June 6, Kerr was on the Welland Canal and found thirty-seven people fishing on Sunday. Kerr had them all summonsed up to St. Catharines where their lawyer "explained that they were all perfectly ignorant of the Sunday law and if allowed to go this time would never offend again... the magistrate acquiesced, and after giving them a severe lecture, allowed them all to depart." Kerr notes that he "coincided with the favourable view taken." Ever the optimist, Kerr predicted, "I am perfectly satisfied... that the course of proceedings... will have a most salutary effect and stop Sabbath desecration for all time to come."

Tired of losing appeals and being ordered to pay costs, Kerr proposed that instead of prosecuting offenders he simply cancel their licences. How to win friends and influence people! This completely arbitrary function without the rule of law would not work unless it included a proper decision-making process and some form of appeal or review. Ultimately the department would review cancellations and sometimes ordered Kerr to re-instate licenses.

Taking his third son, Charles John Kerr (age fifteen) with him, Kerr posted notices in all the Burlington Beach bars (which I guess is where fishermen were found when not fishing) promising extreme

....

65   There was a sizable community of Black people in Niagara-on-the-Lake in the 1800s.

66   Ordnance lands were lands reserved for the military and in this case were probably near Fort George.

consequences for violations.⁶⁷

On July 7, the minister cancelled the fishing licence of Dan McGwynne, on Kerr's recommendation, for repeat offences. Already in court for an appeal of an earlier conviction, Kerr served the notice on McGwynne on July 19. At court, Kerr said, "The conduct of Charles A. Sadlier was most unbecoming, unprofessional and drunken." When the case resumed the following Monday, a "well corned" (i.e., "drunk") Mr. Sadlier assisted the "grossest display of perjury ever perpetrated or that I ever beheld since my appointment… Mr. Sadlier openly, frequently and all the time told the witnesses again and again not to answer a single word that would implicate anyone who fished upon that occasion."⁶⁸

Despite receiving the notice, McGwynne immediately resumed fishing and told Kerr that he would use a six-shooter against any person who dared to prevent him. Kerr doubled down, seized his net, and laid new charges, over McGwynne's insults and threats. Appearing in court before Cahill, "McGwynne became very penitent, cried like a child, offered his horses and wagons and money as security to Mr. Cahill for the nets and ropes." Kerr optimistically recorded that the cancelling of licenses would "forever put an end to all infractions of the fisheries act by McGwynne and all other fishermen on B. Beach." Three days later, McGwynne was seen fishing illegally again.

McGwynne hit back by sending a letter to the editor of the *Evening Times* (probably written by his sometimes-sober lawyer, Sadlier) complaining that Kerr was performing his duties in a "tyrannical and partial way." McGwynne was repeatedly fined by JP Cahill, but on September 6, Kerr wrote that McGwynne had "appealed against the Magistrate's decision, a thing he has invariably done heretofore." In his annual report in 1869, Kerr noted that, "I had 84 persons up for offenses… The Majesty of our Law has been upheld and this has been done without oppressing any person"… Oh, and Mrs. Baldry was again fishing illegal nets in the Bay… "This is the 3ʳᵈ net I have found in B. Bay belonging

....

67 Charles John Kerr (1854–1942) was my great-grandfather. His oldest son provided the diaries to the ROM just before Charles's death.

68 As I write this, the Trump impeachment trial is in the news. See any parallels here, such as shut the fuck up?

to Mrs. Baldry."

Kerr suggested to the minister that certain creeks and rivers be "set aside" for fish propagation (meaning no fishing). For example, he wanted the Credit River to be so designated.[69] Kerr noted, "There are several saw mills and mill dams: But if set apart... I will engage to get rid of the sawdust and all other obstacles during this year and I expect to report salmon back there again within three years. I don't know exactly if my district goes back as far as this, but I hope it does." It did, and he would.

By 1869 Kerr was allowed to appoint fisheries guardians under the new Act. These were low-paid locals hired for part of the year, usually during spawning season, to protect the fish (usually salmon, which spawn in late fall). Kerr's expectations of them were superhuman, and they often let him down. They generally did not share Kerr's passion for salmon and were unwilling to work long hours for low pay. Kerr attempted to secure better remuneration for them but was generally unsuccessful. He reported that by the end of 1869, five guardians were working under him. There would eventually be a lot more.

1870

In March 1870 Kerr made a second trip to the Thames River, this time inspecting from Chatham to Lighthouse Cove on Lake St. Clair. Employing his usual MO, he wrote, "met all the fishermen—expounded to them the law—laid it down everything they were to go by—received their fishing fees." Seeking to expand his already huge district, Kerr bragged, "I could, if you are pleased to appoint me to the supervision of this river... make this a valuable spring fishing and the revenue to the Department, I can perceive, can be made remunerative." He did not get the appointment, but he would be back. Mr. Farquar McCrae of Wallaceburg got the post.

On March 29, Kerr was back in Galt prosecuting mill owners "for throwing a large quantity of sawdust into the Grand River." He had prosecuted other mill owners by this time, so he knew what he was

---

69   The Credit River and its tributaries run 930 miles and drain 390 square miles before emptying into Lake Ontario at Port Credit.

doing. He vowed, "I am determined to protect and afford every protection to the fish in this river and if possible, bring it back to what it was in days gone by."

In 1870 a long-simmering dispute began between Kerr and local politicians, farmers, and anglers about Kerr allowing a small group of Burlington Beach fishermen to fish limited areas of the bay in the spring for "rough fish." This licensing rankled the local anglers who thought it was favouritism. Former Hamilton mayor, Benjamin Charleton, went to Ottawa to meet with the minister to try and put a stop to it.[70] Charleton alleged that the fishermen were obstructing the entrance and exit of fish returning to the small creeks for spawning.

Kerr was asked to comment. He fired back that Charleton's allegation was untrue and that Charleton knew it because he and Kerr had discussed the issue before he travelled to Ottawa.

> *I deny most emphatically that any truth exists in the statements he recently made to you in Ottawa ... I saw Mr. Charleton the day before he went down, and we talked over the matter, and he said if I would consent not to apply to you on behalf of the fishermen ... he would say nothing about this matter to you. Of course, I would not consent to his overtures ... I pretend I know something of the fish in B. Bay. At night during my term of office I have learned a good deal and I have often endured hunger and hardship to do so.*

Kerr launched an impassioned appeal about the fishermen.

> *How cruel it was then for Mr. Charleton to make a representation of so grave a nature against the poor fishermen of B. Beach—Men who have endured the hardship of a very severe winter, whose gardens are at present reduced one half by high water ... I often pity these men from my heart, while at the same time, it is not within my power to alleviate their sufferings except by your sanction ... I hope never to see B. Bay set apart again as a pleasure*

---

70 Benjamin Ernest Charleton (Apr. 12, 1835–Mar. 12, 1901) was a two-time mayor of Hamilton in 1867 and 1873. At the time, mayors were elected annually.

to fishing for the rich, to the exclusion of the poor fishermen and the poor.

This pretty well sums up Kerr's philosophy, which remained constant until his death.

On June 7, 1870, Kerr commenced a five-day tour of Lake Erie, starting at Port Stanley, which was now part of his district. Then he proceeded east along the lakeshore. Upon reaching Port Dover, he returned home by stagecoach. He licensed all the fishermen and noted that certain landowners were extorting the fishermen by denying them access to the beach unless they paid a fee. The beach or shore was part of the fishery reserve, thus fishermen had free access. Kerr stated, "It is a very singular way those land owners have of doing business." He put a stop to it.

At Port Rowan, near Long Point, Kerr reported on the "wanton destruction of pickerel by spearing and dip nets[71] in Big Creek."[72] Describing the pickerel as "Splendid to look at, large first-class fish. Good food," Kerr heard that as many as one hundred persons a night were fishing during the spring run, to the detriment of the licensed fishermen. Noting that Big Creek was superior to the Thames for fishing, Kerr asked that it be set aside for the natural propagation of fish and warned that if it was not protected "our pickerel fisheries at Long and Turkey Point will be completely ruined in a few years." Kerr naively concluded by predicting "we shall have only a little trouble... and then for all future time peace will reign." Wrong.

On October 1, 1870, Kerr got a $100 raise to $300 per year. It was a long time until he received another raise.

In December, a curious incident took place, the result of which saw Kerr convicted of assault: "At the railway depot and the Burlington Heights, met Joe Gates coming up from his nefarious purposes on the ice. He was insulting and jostled me. I struck him over the head with my

---

71   Like the name implies, dip nets were small hand-held nets used for fishing from boats or riverbanks.

72   Big Creek in Norfolk County runs about thirty-seven miles from above the town of Scotland into Lake Erie near Port Rowan. It drains 280 square miles.

stick and broke it in two. He pounded me on the head and took away part of the broken stick." Appearing in court before Magistrate Cahill, Kerr recorded that he was fined five dollars. There is no mention of a trial, so presumably he pled guilty. Kerr was then fifty-eight years old, and this seems uncharacteristic of him. One wonders why the minister didn't look into it further and at least admonish Kerr. In today's courts, he would have pleaded self-defence and quite possibly have been acquitted because he was jostled first, and it appears a consensual fight took place. Kerr did not specify Gates's nefarious purpose, but given the season and the location, it was likely illegal spearfishing.

1871

On May 1, 1871, the minister sent a circular to all the fisheries overseers to notify them that their disbursements would be limited to $200 per year. Kerr wrote a five-page letter in which he firmly but diplomatically indicated that "this will be the means of retarding me in my operations" and that it would be "injurious to the best interests and welfare of the fisheries."

They were also supposed to get pre-approval for any major expenses, which Kerr found ludicrous: "Frequently unforeseen and unavoidable cases of urgency may happen, where prompt action is necessary—In cases of this class, I ought certainly to be clothed by you with a discretionary power." Kerr also noted his huge district, which extended from Whitby Harbour to Port Stanley on Lake Erie, and that when he met with Whitcher in Ottawa the prior August, he was told "to do a good many things myself instead of always applying to the Department."

In requesting that the minister reconsider, Kerr was also concerned that current disbursements might not be paid: "You have left me a very small margin to work on, because altogether compelling me to fall back upon my own resources, which I can assure you, are very slim." Kerr ended by noting that the circular reminded him of an old adage: "Live, old horse, until the end of the season and then you'll get grass." The minister eventually reconsidered but not before Kerr began to pay his fishery guardians out of his own meagre salary.

In late summer 1871, Kerr returned again to the topic of enforcing the provincial game laws: "If authorized by the Provincial Government, and approved of by you, I could do much duty under the game law act, when on my tour around—For every place I go I hear of persons violating this law." Reporting on ducks being shot all over his district, he noted, "every place a wild duck is found it is Crack-Crack. The ducks are now shot indiscriminately… and why! Because the law is disregarded. There is no person to put it in force." It does not seem like the feds ever supported this request, probably because they knew Kerr already had plenty on his plate.

In October 1871, Kerr made a trip to Rondeau Bay on Lake Erie and licensed the fishermen. Kerr reported, "the fisheries seem to me to be badly neglected in this locality, for until I made my appearance there, no officer from the Department has been there during the last five years… As no officer does duty in this locality I suppose I may henceforth do so." The result was to unilaterally add about another forty miles onto his already huge district. It wouldn't last.

1872

In the news these days, we read a lot about fluctuating lake levels as if it were some new phenomenon related to climate change. Maybe it is, but Kerr's diaries make it clear that this was perhaps as much a problem in the 1870s as it is now. He frequently reported on bad storms and places like Burlington Beach contracting or expanding. For example, in February 1872, Kerr noted a "want of water in the City of Hamilton caused by the low state of the same in Lake Ontario and the filtering basin, adjacent to the same, on B. Beach." The filtering fed the 1859 pumping house which supplied Hamilton with water.

Due to this lack of water, the City was required to "put in a flume 108' long to connect the basin with the Lake." Lacking concrete, plastic or steel, the flume was built of white oak four-by-four-inch boards. Fishermen were often wiped out by high water during storms, costing them their boats, nets, and sometimes their houses. Kerr would often seek permission to reduce rentals for fishermen adversely affected by water level fluctuations or by storms. Sometimes the minister would consent, but often he would not for unknown reasons.

On February 29, 1872, Kerr received a letter of instructions to investigate the fisheries from Leamington to Windsor, Lake St. Clair, and lower Lake Huron, and he made a number of trips to do so. Traveling from Leamington to Windsor and then up Lake Huron as far as Southampton, he made detailed inquiries and reported everything to the minister in April. Probably wanting to get the area added to his district, he wanted to go to Ottawa to meet the minister and Mr. Whitcher. It didn't happen then, but he'd be back!

In May 1872, Kerr received a request from the St. Catharines Game Club to lease three small ponds off Lake Ontario near Port Dalhousie. He was told that their object was to restock the ponds and that they would keep the sandbars open, which blew in and blocked access to the ponds from the lake. Kerr thought this would promote fish spawning and restore the salmon that inhabited the ponds "in days of old," and he recommended a rare nine-year lease. He came to regret it and got a first taste of the motives of fish-and-game clubs.

Daniel Black Chisholm was a member of Parliament and former mayor of Hamilton. In September 1872, he approached Kerr about purchasing land on Burlington Beach to build a large hotel. He planned to buy the property of Joan Baldry (who seemed to have cleaned up her act) and others. He needed permission from the Department because of the fishing reserve on the bay and the beach sides. He planned to run steamships from Hamilton and spend $40,000 on the hotel and beach strip roads.

Kerr was impressed. In a letter to the minister, he observed, "The great increase of the population of the City of Hamilton demands that a place of this nature be no longer deferred. It is required absolutely for the healthy recreation of our citizens." In addition, he said, "it will be the beginning of a new and prosperous state of things to our hardy fishermen… in whose prosperity I am so deeply interested, and many of whom will hereafter get employment in various ways in connection with this establishment, besides, Mrs. Joan Baldry (and others) will get a money consideration and be allowed to move their buildings away."

(And good riddance!)

By August 1873, Chisholm had given up. Kerr wrote, "Not receiving any encouragement from the fishery department nor from the Dominion Government, he has since, to use a common phrase, backed down." However, another developer, Mr. Norris F. Birley, stepped in and bought Baldry's house and property for $2,000 with plans to build a 200-room hotel, and he apparently didn't give a fig about the Fisheries Department.[73] More to come…

Volume six of Kerr's diaries commences with some newspaper articles he cut out and glued into the journal. One is an anonymous letter from "A Reader" that is quite complimentary of Kerr and was clearly written by him or for him. Why he would feel the need to blow his own horn in this way is unknown. I guess he wanted to get some good press for a change!

Every fall Kerr was required to prepare an annual return for the year, so he would tour his entire district seeking information from the fishermen. The return was an incredibly detailed document that listed every fisherman, where they fished, how many boats they had, the length and type of their nets, and the fish they caught by barrel and value. These were then submitted to the Department and retained there, presumably with those of all other fisheries overseers. In 1872 he noted the total value of fish caught to be almost $29,000, which was a lot of money at the time.

Despite the vast expanse of his district, Kerr seemed willing to take on more territory. Sitting in his house on Christmas Day, 1872, Kerr sent a letter to the minister noting that the overseer for Lake Simcoe had died and hinted that he would like the appointment. He pointed out how easy it would be to get there as "a railway from Whitby Harbour to Port Perry is now in running order daily."[74]

Kerr also reported hearing that a man from New York City was fishing illegally all winter in Collingwood on Georgian Bay: "I believe

---

73   Norris F. Birley was a Hamilton businessman and wharf owner who built the Ocean House Hotel, which opened in 1875. It burned down in 1890.

74   The Port Whitby and Port Perry Railway fully opened in spring 1872. Never very profitable, the last service was in 1939. The rails were pulled up and used in the war effort.

there is a good deal of this kind of poaching carried on there each winter without let or hindrance." Kerr would get there eventually.

In August 1873, Kerr commented on sand and gravel being taken from Burlington Beach by wagons, intended to be used for building in Hamilton or for the glassworks. Kerr considered it to be a "wholesale plunder made upon the Government domain." He noted that "20–30 wagon loads are taken from the beach daily. Men with double teams and single wagons are making a comfortable living… They appear to have no other means of living, and they require no better, for it is a very profitable one." He concluded by predicting that "serious damage will ultimately result from this wholesale taking away from the Beach."

Somehow, the lighthouse keeper, Mr. Thompson, got his knickers in a knot about the sand being removed from the canal by Fred Corey, Kerr's occasional assistant, and warned him off. This was the start of a dispute between Thompson and Kerr, who both worked for the same ministry, though in different divisions.[75] Kerr was trying to rehabilitate Corey, a former transgressor, and felt that the sand issue was none of Thompson's business, which ultimately drew the attention of the minister, resulting in Kerr being admonished.

In the fall 1873, Kerr had a lengthy correspondence with Charles J. Atkins of Maine about salmon.[76] Like Kerr, he was particularly interested in salmon and asked Kerr a number of questions about Lake Ontario salmon. Kerr's theory was that Ontario salmon were bred in local streams and then migrated to the ocean, only to return years later to spawn. That is a long distance, but Kerr maintained "my assertion will be borne out by learned men of science and great knowledge… This is

---

75   George Thompson was the lighthouse keeper until his retirement in 1875. The old lighthouse burned down in 1857, and the current lighthouse and keeper's home were built in 1858. Kerr worked for the fisheries division of the Ministry of Marine and Fisheries, and Thompson worked for the marine division.

76   Charles J. Atkins (Jan. 19, 1841–1921) was a fish biologist and the superintendent of the Maine fish hatcheries. He is described as a visionary of early fish biology and aquatic sciences.

the true nature of salmon the world over." He may have been right.[77]

In the conclusion to his 1873 annual report, Kerr smugly reported "contentment, with very few exceptions, pervades the minds of all the fishermen of my district. I enjoy and stand on good terms with them, so far as I have the opportunity of knowing and judging, which to me is a cause of much satisfaction." It would not last.

> TRANSMITTING VENISON BY RAILWAY PROHIBITED.—Mr. J. W. Kerr, Game and Fishery Inspector, the City Police Magistrate, and Mr. Æ. Irvine, Solicitor of the Great Western Railway, had a conversation yesterday in regard to the transmitting of venison from one place to another on the Railway. They were unanimously of the opinion that if the practice was continued, the Company rendered themselves liable to be prosecuted according the law for having venison in their possession. The agents at the various stations along the line have accordingly been notified not to take any deer in charge.—This step will, we feel confident, materially assist in putting a stop to the violation of the law, which has become very general among sportsmen in almost all parts of the Province.

Newspaper clipping found in Kerr's diary.
Kerr warned the railways about transmitting illegal game (ROM).

....

77   Salmon are known as *anadromous*, meaning they hatch in fresh water, migrate to the sea, and return to fresh water to reproduce. There are numerous breeds of salmon, and they are in the same family as trout, char, and whitefish.

CAHILL, JAMES, teacher, lawyer, office-holder; b. 25 July 1815 at Clonmel, County Tipperary, Ireland; m. Louisa L. Case on 7 January 1841 and they had four sons and six daughters; d. 5 May 1893 at Hamilton, Ontario, buried in Hamilton Cemetery.

James Cahill studied at a local school in Clonmel and then at Trinity College, Dublin. He emigrated to Canada in 1833, coming to Hamilton where he took up the post of master of classics and teaching assistant at the Gore District grammar school. The following year he began a one-year term as headmaster of the school. He then left teaching and from 1835 to 1839 studied law with R.G. Beasley. He was admitted to the bar in 1840, opened his own practice, and came to be an honoured member of the Law Society of Upper Canada. In 1841 he married Louisa Case, the daughter of Dr William CASE of Hamilton.

Cahill was active in community affairs. In 1839 his signature appears on a subscription list for the laying of a footpath on James Street, from Main to Gore, and in the early 1850s he was a member of the Sons of Temperance. He represented St Patrick's ward on city council in 1852. His years of real service to the city, however, were from 1863 to 1893, when he served as police magistrate. In his thirty years of service he earned the respect and confidence of the Hamilton public

Excerpt from biography of Kerr's usually friendly police magistrate, James Cahill (Dictionary of Hamilton Biography).

CHAPTER 9

The Grits! (1874–1878)

On November 5, 1873, the government of Sir John A. MacDonald resigned as a result of the Pacific Scandal. The Liberal government of Alexander Mackenzie was sworn in on November 7, and suddenly Kerr had a new boss in Albert James Smith. Kerr's immediate supervisor, William Frederick Whitcher, was kept on, and there were few noticeable changes in Kerr's day-to-day activities. Mackenzie won the election in January 1874 and remained in power until the 1878 election when MacDonald and the Conservatives regained control, which lasted for the remainder of Kerr's career.

Kerr went to Ottawa over Christmas and met with both the new minister and Whitcher. Kerr did not reveal his impressions of Smith and made no mention of what they discussed. A lifelong Conservative, it was probably best to lie low amongst the hated Grits

The year 1874 began with Kerr sending a long letter to the minister outlining the details of his district. One topic pertained to ownership of Burlington Beach. The Ontario government had granted a ninety-nine-year lease to the City of Hamilton, so the fishermen were concerned about their ownership rights. Most of them had lived on the beach as squatters, some for as far back as the 1820s, but they had no title to their lands. At Kerr's insistence, a meeting was held, and a petition was circulated to have the minister assist in confirming their legal ownership by passage of time: "Their squatter rights, they say, should be first considered and be then respected because it has always been the custom of all Governments to do this!!"

Kerr added, "Whatever the Provincial Government in Toronto may be induced to do, if they control the Beach on your recommendation, I hope you will have our fishery rights, long since established, still maintained inviolate, so that the Corporation of the City of Hamilton may neither now, or in the hereafter be placed in a position to interfere with nor act despotic so far as the fisheries and fishermen are concerned." Kerr also commented on the proposal of Norris Birely and partners to build his hotel, Ocean House, "for accommodation of the Citizens of Hamilton during the hot and sultry days of summer." Kerr noted that he had known these gentlemen for several years and that "they are men of respectability and high social standing."

Kerr next turned his attention to the ongoing trouble in the Turkey Point and Lake Erie fisheries and pointed the finger at the Helmer brothers of Charlotteville in Norfolk County: "You will please bear in mind that these Helmers, a couple of years ago, caused excessive annoyance and trouble to the local fishery guardian. They have always been, and are now, represented to me as worthless, disagreeable men of loose fingered character who have stolen fishing lines from various fisherman and are still doing so." Kerr did not want to give them a licence. I wonder why not.

In the winter of 1874, a couple of events illustrated the struggle to preserve the fisheries and the fishermen against the burgeoning populations of Hamilton and Toronto.

On January 10, a petition was signed by Hamilton Mayor Benjamin Charleton, MP D. B. Chisholm, MP J. M. Williams, and 498 others and sent to the minister to stop the net fishing allowed on a limited area of Burlington Bay in the spring for certain "rough fish" or fish not protected under the *Fisheries Act*. Mayor Charleton had tried unsuccessfully to stop this in 1870. D. B. Chisholm was the frustrated businessman (and future scallywag) who had tried to get the Ocean House Hotel built. J. M. Williams was one of the owners of the Carbon Oil Company, which Kerr had prosecuted. All had an axe to grind with Kerr. The pretense of the petition was that this licensed fishing was destroying Burlington Bay's fish population.

Kerr fired back with a five-page letter that indicated,

> *It is not true, nor is it a fact that seines are used which drain the Bay of all kinds of fish. You have permitted seines to be used by the fishermen petitioned against just exactly for a distance of 1188 yards (1/7th of the Bay) and the fish caught sell very well and are prized by the community because of the scarcity of all other kinds of fish during this particular short season you have allowed them to be taken . . . The petitioners are all wrong and here endeavour to impress upon your mind that they do know everything about the Bay, while the fact is they know nothing at all about it.*

Kerr also noted that there would be salmon in the bay "if the remains of J. M. Williams and Son coal oil therein did not injure them as it has also injured other fish."

Charleton, in his letter attached to the petition, alleged the "The few fishermen who derive a very questionable benefit from the present destructive system prevent the Bay from becoming well stocked with good fish to the detriment of the whole community." Kerr noted that there were "153 persons, men, women and children who derive a major benefit from this fishing" and that "It is a willful slander, and without an appearance of truth, for a man occupying such an exalted position, to use such language, trying to injure so many peaceable, industrious people without any just cause from earning an honest and honourable living."

Pointing out that the mayor had never mentioned these concerns to Kerr, even though "he knows me well," Kerr questioned the mayor's motives and those of the others, including H. L. Bastien, who had rented out the *Empress*, which capsized in 1870, killing three children. Bastien rented boats to anglers and would presumably profit if there were more recreational fishermen: "Why did not Mayor Charleton, D. B. Chisholm and Mr. Bastien come out boldly as men and say that it was their own selfish ends they wished to accomplish?"

In regard to the other 498 signatories, Kerr snorted, "Only a few men could be got to sign the petition if they read it over, because it is to inflict an injury upon a large community of people, at the instance of Mr. Bastien and a few boat owners and anglers who have concocted the same, so as to serve their own selfish purposes... Men who sign petitions hardly ever read them."

Not to be outdone, the citizens, farmers, politicians, and others decided to send delegates to Ottawa to meet with the minister and petition in person for the end of licensed net fishing. With another petition in hand, the four delegates met with Minister Albert Smith, who then and there, without consulting Kerr, granted their request and banned net fishing. Spelling Mr. Whitcher's name wrong, the *Dundas Beaver* gleefully noted that "for the future no more favouritism in the granting of licenses can be indulged in by Mr. Fishery Inspector Kerr." The *Hamilton Times* chimed in by exclaiming, "Under the old rules equal justice was the exception and partiality the Rule." Kerr was beaten without even being allowed to fight and he was not happy.

Similarly, in Toronto, there was ongoing conflict between the fishermen and the City, the citizenry wanting recreation, and the industrialists wanting to pollute. In early March, Kerr was in Toronto meeting with Mayor Medcalf[78] and the chairman of the water works, which had damaged the fishery of poor old Mr. Patrick Gray during construction of a water intake pipe. We all know what the end result would be. Today and for many years past there has been no commercial fishing in either Hamilton or Toronto.

In March 1874, Kerr returned again to the issue of being appointed to enforce the game laws, He met with James K. Kerr (no relation), a lawyer with the Toronto law firm of Blake, Kerr, and Boyd, who he thought could help him get the position. Following the meeting he wrote to lawyer Kerr:

> *If you get me this appointment I can begin at once my active duties in connection with my position as Overseer of Fisheries. The fact is, game, of all the various kinds is being exhibited for sale*

---

78   Francis Henry Medcalf (May 10, 1803–Mar. 26, 1880) was a two-time mayor of Toronto. Like Kerr, he was an Irish Protestant and was heavily involved in the Orange Order. His nickname was "old square toes" for his foundry work boots.

> *(illegally) in all the towns and Cities of Ontario because no person is appointed by the Local Government to enforce this law. I am satisfied in my mind you have only to ask for the appointment for me to get it. When once in the harness I shall prove myself by my active exertions, worthy of your kind consideration.*

He never got the appointment, probably for political reasons, which is unfortunate because there might have been another chapter of his life to explore. No doubt, he would have been effective. It does not appear that any game wardens were appointed in Ontario until 1892. In 1898 Ontario took over enforcement of the fisheries and hired ninety-four fisheries overseers, one of whom was Kerr's son, Frederick.

Under the Mackenzie government, Kerr's district began to shrink substantially. First, he lost Norfolk and Haldimand Counties when J. A. Backhouse[79] was appointed. Then he lost the Grand River when Henry Griffith of Brantford was appointed. Replacements were rarely up to Kerr's standards, and he frequently complained about them. He often heard these complaints from fishermen, which seems to indicate they held Kerr in grudging esteem. Over his objections, his fishery guardians were dismissed, although Kerr secured their pay for an additional month. Writing to them to advise them of their dismissal, Kerr resignedly noted, "Such is life!"

Having spent a lot of time and energy redividing the stations on Turkey Point and Long Point Bay and settling most of the disputes between fishermen, Kerr was unhappy to lose Norfolk. Within a month he was writing to the minister to complain about Backhouse who, as a justice of the peace, had given Kerr trouble.[80] Kerr noted illegal

---

79 John A. Backhouse (Feb. 9, 1818–May 10, 1876) was the son of Major John Backhouse, who was the builder of Backhouse or Backus Mill near Port Rowan. Now a national historic site in Backus Heritage Village, it is one of the few mills on Lake Erie that was not torched by the Americans in the War of 1812. It's a fun place to visit with kids.

80 Malicious and false charges had been brought against Long Point fisherman before J. P. Backhouse, who convicted them and did not allow them a defence. Kerr referred to Backhouse as a "self-appointed member of this Star Chamber."

nets being used "with the sanction and connivance of the said J. A. Backhouse and William Helmer, who is represented as being appointed by Backhouse, to look after the fisheries there." The Department questioned Kerr's motives, but he innocently responded that his only object was to stop illegal fishing. Maybe, maybe not.

By 1874 there were the usual infractions by the usual offenders and the usual prosecution. There were also the usual disagreements between the usual fishermen, but there seems at least to have been a reduction in the level of threats and violence. It did spring up occasionally, such as on September 5 when Kerr was at Burlington Beach with his seven-year-old son, Edward, seizing a net. There was a standoff, and Kerr went to get help from Justice of the Peace Peter Van Wagner,[81] and the net was seized. Kerr commented afterwards, "Squire Van Wagner remarked when parting with me that if he had not been present, it appeared to him there would have been a row!" (Kerr was then sixty-two years old!) Earlier in the day, Kerr had been in Hamilton where he heard "impertinent and threatening words" from an old adversary.

Around this time, Kerr also began to send fish to his supervisor, W. F. Whitcher. Kerr would have the fish packed in boxes of ice and hay and put them on the train. He also sent Whitcher fruit, ducks, and kegs of "native wine," meaning Ontario wine.[82] Whitcher had become the commissioner of fisheries, and generally Kerr now wrote to Mr. Simon Peter Bauset, who remained with the Department for years after Kerr's death in 1888.

While Kerr's jurisdiction was shrinking, he was increasingly called on to perform "special duty," where he was assigned to go somewhere to investigate something or settle some matter on behalf of the Department. For example, in spring 1874 he was sent back to Chatham to further investigate the Thames River. Sometimes this special duty arose from complaints made to the minister from fishermen or local politicians. Other times it arose from Kerr hearing things from his numerous sources. When Kerr heard about illegal fishing in Port Frank on Lake

---

81   Van Wagner's Beach is named after Peter (1818–1906) and his brother Townsend (1825–1910) who farmed the area. Apparently, Peter also kept diaries, some of which have been abstracted in the Stoney Creek Historical Society Newsletter.

82   Niagara's first commercial winery commenced operation in 1873.

Huron, he requested authorization to deal with it, noting "If authorized, I can effectively stop this to the satisfaction of the Department."

In late fall, Kerr, likely using his railway connections, began to inspect boxcars and found barrels of freshly caught whitefish being shipped to various southern destinations from Collingwood. Since they were caught in the closed season, Kerr seized the fish and had some shipping agents charged. He wrote to warn the Department that on Georgian Bay, the fishermen paid no attention to closed season. Obviously wrangling for authority to proceed there, Kerr provided great detail to the Department and, sure enough, on December 17, he received a directive to head north and prosecute them, even though there was already a fisheries overseer at Owen Sound.

Kerr wrote to the fisheries overseer at Owen Sound to arrange a time to meet early in the New Year and to caution him not to announce his pending arrival. Stealth became an important weapon for Kerr in enforcement matters because he knew that if the fishermen were aware he was coming, the evidence would disappear, and the illegal fishing would stop. Georgian Bay became an active, if sporadic, destination for Kerr for years to come.

In the fall 1874, the minister banned spearfishing on Burlington Bay and on Dundas Marsh. Kerr was pleased and had articles placed in newspapers warning citizens and boat renters. This proved to be a short-sighted and costly decision because the population was vigorously opposed to the ban. Kerr got a first taste of their ire on December 20 when he noted he was "at Beckett's wharf where I was hooted, groaned and called an old scoundrel by several young men skating on the Bay." Knowing he was going to need some help enforcing the ban, he wrote to the Department requesting permission to hire two men.[83] [84]

....

83   Probably his two sons, Frederick, age twenty, and George, age twenty-two, who by then were frequently employed to row their father around Burlington Bay. The Department did resume spearfishing at an annual licence of one dollar.

84   By January 7, 1875, Kerr wisely changed his mind and wrote to the minister to request the ban be lifted "so as to accommodate a certain class of poor men and poor fishermen... who go round loitering at this season of the year because they can get no employment."

1875

On January 5, Kerr made the 140-mile train ride to Collingwood.[85] Recruiting local Fisheries Overseer George Miller as magistrate, he summonsed two fish dealers and had them fined ten dollars or twenty days in jail.[86] Kerr spent two busy days at Georgian Bay and sent S. P. Bauset a lengthy report. Kerr reported that about forty boats were fishing between Collingwood and Cape Rich using some 170 miles of gill nets. Kerr found problems with the Natives on Christian Island, who were cutting fishing lines, and that there was complete disobedience of the closed season and a lack of enforcement by Miller, who "never goes near them, except to collect the $5 from each boat," that there was offal being thrown into the water, and so much trouble that Kerr didn't know where to start.

To Kerr's probable disappointment, the minister immediately appointed a new fisheries overseer for Georgian Bay, from Collingwood to Point Rich. The minister asked Kerr to assist the new appointee, to which Kerr, biting his tongue, replied, "I will do so with much pleasure and will proceed to Collingwood whenever you think it expedient for me to do so."

Apparently not hearing anything, Kerr proceeded with his usual business, including his annual report for 1874, in which he bragged that he had collected $846 in licence fees and $158 in fines. As a reward, Kerr lost the Credit River as part of his district. He also lost the lower Grand River despite pleading to at least be allowed to keep the river from the Dunnville Dam to the Lake: "I hope unless there is something better in store for me, that I still be allowed to retain that portion of the Grand River below the dam at Dunnville. I urge this because I expect consideration from you and Mr. Whitcher in this matter." That wouldn't happen.

However, to pacify him, he was sent back to Collingwood at the

....

85 The Hamilton and the North Western railways did not open until 1879. Kerr would have taken the GWR to Toronto and then hopped on the Northern Railway, which ran to Collingwood.

86 It seems to me to have been exceedingly unfair to enlist one's own compatriot as the judge. Clearly, the fix was in, but that is how things were done.

end of March after obtaining information from confidential sources to assist in his investigation. Filing a long report on April 7, Kerr estimated the total value of the fish caught in the southern end of Georgian Bay to be over $100,000 and that closed season had to be enforced. The Department never seemed to carry out the recommendations of these excellent and detailed reports.

In March, James Miller, lawyer for the St. Catharines Game Club, wrote to the minister seeking to lease additional waters in Lincoln Township and also complaining that Kerr never provided them with their lease for 1874, despite being paid twenty dollars. When Kerr received a copy of the letter, he exploded with anger. One of the additional fishing stations sought was leased to Peter Nath, a.k.a. "Dutch Pete," who had been one of the defiant Niagara fishermen for years. Miller asked for Nath's station because he "has been disposed for this season—having been convicted of larceny and sentenced to 18 months, central prison."[87]

Despite Kerr's history with Nath, he went to bat for him. Commenting on Miller's opportunism, Kerr stated, "It reminds me of the old adage of 'kicking a man when he is on the ground.' The department never does this, offenders are never **persecuted**, being always treated with long suffering and kindness. And no matter what Dutch Pete's misfortunes are, he on several occasions rendered good services to me and the Department in upholding the fisheries laws."

Kerr then reported that Peter Nath's daughter had applied for the fishing licence at Port Dalhousie, "so that she may be able to support her mother and dumb[88] sister in their misfortune, besides, the people of Port Dalhousie want a resident fisherman there to supply the town." Peter Nath got his licence back in 1876. Kerr noted, "With hard times, a starving family to support, **others may pause** but I have no hesitation in making this application and I specially recommend you to be pleased to grant the licence." Kerr regretted this recommendation later.

In regard to their 1874 license, Kerr reminded the minister that one was not issued, even though paid for, because the club had declined to accept

....

87   "Larceny" is the old word for what we now simply describe as theft.
88   "Dumb" means being unable to speak.

the conditions attached to it, "Mr. Miller himself being the most active in doing so." Kerr also indicated that Miller allowed indiscriminate fishing by the farmers who then allowed club members to shoot over their farms. "Such a report is notorious... Miller has endeavoured to induce me again and again to give the Club licence of the 20 Mile Pond and thereby ruin Richard Gilbert, the present licensee and his wife and four small children, and so to accommodate the only two grumbling farmers who live on the banks of the pond. I have to tell you this is out of the question so long as the respectable poor man who now licenses it, wants a renewal."

Kerr observed that while the club had promised to stock their pond, "they have never yet been instrumental in placing a single fish of any kind therein." In conclusion, Kerr wrote, "I warmly thank you for giving me an opportunity of repelling any slur Mr. Miller might intend to cast upon me by his **direct** appeal to you, as mouth piece of the St. Catharines Game Club."[89]

Kerr was later scolded by Mr. Whitcher for the language in his letter, and he was forced to apologize: "In explanation of the same, I admit my zeal for the fisheries may have carried me too far." Kerr would learn that with the exception of the Long Point Company, most fish-and-game clubs had only their own interests at heart and not the interest of the fish, the game, the fishermen, or local citizens. There would be more battles ahead.

On a happier note, Kerr finally achieved a victory in the Court of Quarter Sessions! A jury trial appeal in front of a new judge, William Lynn Sweet, resulted in the upholding of a conviction, and Kerr was elated: "This is the first, and the only, conviction of the many that was ever sustained by the judge and jury at Hamilton Quarter sessions during my long service of ten years and six months; So that it does now really appear, to me at least, that the protection of the fisheries is at last established by this new judge and a jury's decision."[90] Kerr's happiness

---

89   Kerr hated it when people went over his head by appealing directly to the Ministry. He always commented negatively when this happened.

90   One might wonder how a new judge could influence the results of a jury, but I can assure you that juries are influenced directly and indirectly by judges—directly during the charge to the jury and indirectly on rulings made on motions or just the judge's demeanor.

was short lived, however, because just five days following this trial following a conviction before Police Magistrate Cahill, enemy lawyer C. A. Sadlier indicated his intention to appeal on behalf of another client.

The Battle of the Bay continued to flare up from time to time. Having finally had enough of the shenanigans of Daniel McGwynn and his wife, Kerr recommended the cancellation of McGwynn's fishing licence for "repeated violations and contraventions of the Fisheries Act." Noting that the other fishermen were opposed to McGwynn's "recklessness and open defiance," Kerr hoped the cancellation would "have the effect of finally stopping him in his mad, wild, and I regret to add, drunken career."

In August 1875, Kerr was horrified by a new atrocity being committed on Burlington Bay. He reported that young boys were buying "an explosive combustible called Dynamite[91] for the destruction of fish in the waters of the Bay." Describing the process, he stated, "By igniting the fuse attached and placed within the cartridge of Dynamite and dropping the same into the water, when it explodes with powerful effect, stunning the fish, so that they instantly float on the surface of the water and while labouring under the effects of the shock, can be easily caught by hand and captured." Kerr wanted instructions on how to proceed "as this is a new warfare for the destruction of our fishes."

Most of Kerr's exertions in Hamilton were centred around Burlington Bay and Burlington Beach, but he was also acutely interested in protecting Dundas Marsh or "Coote's Paradise," as it is popularly known now.[92] Dundas Marsh is about one mile wide and three miles long and is now administered by the Royal Botanical Gardens. It is dissected by the Desjardins Canal, which was built between 1826 and 1837. The connection with the bay was made through a cut excavated through Burlington Heights in 1851.

....

91 Dynamite was invented by Alfred Nobel (yeah, the Nobel Prize guy) and patented in 1867. Who the hell would sell dynamite to boys? Well, they sold firecrackers to me as a kid. Probably a bit different though.

92 Captain Thomas Coote (c. 1760–1795) was in the British Army and fought during the American Revolutionary War. While not living there, he appeared to love to visit and shoot ducks from Burlington Heights.

Dundas Marsh was an excellent fish-breeding ground and was fed by Spencer's Creek, which wound through Dundas and was the site of various mills. Never really part of the commercial fisheries, it was fished extensively by anglers and people using small nets. Partly at Kerr's behest, net fishing on the Bay and Dundas Marsh was prohibited in 1874 except for a small area near the southeastern end of the bay that Kerr was allowed to licence. Long before Kerr's time, the mills were polluting Dundas Marsh and Burlington Bay.

By late 1874, various individuals attempted to purchase Dundas Marsh from the Ontario government. Kerr always opposed these attempts because he maintained the federal government controlled the waters as part of the fisheries. Noting that Hamilton now had a population of 32,000, he stated, "whatever I can do for the citizens of Hamilton in protecting the fishery rights for the Department it is my bounden duty to do."

At Whitcher's request, Kerr had Dundas Marsh surveyed. Aware that the public were opposed to the sale he stated, "I hope the Department will never agree to the sale of… Dundas Marsh, which now becomes distasteful to the citizens and people whose farms in Ancaster, Barton, West Flamboro, Dundas and Hamilton, surround it. The public look upon the fisheries of Ontario as the vested right of the people, under your protection." Kerr returned to the issue in January 1876 when another attempt was made to get "a patent of the Marsh" from the provincial government in Toronto. A meeting was held, which Kerr attended, involving the participation of "land owners and influential persons" who were all opposed. Kerr concluded, "I hope you will consider that the time has arrived when something permanent should be done in the interest of the public and the fisheries as regards the final disposal of Dundas Marsh."[93]

A couple of curious judicial proceedings started in 1875 that caused some questions about the judicial system and the integrity of police

---

93 The motives for wanting to buy Dundas Marsh were not stated but were undoubtedly commercial. Possibilities that come to mind would be to fill it in to create usable land or to control access to it for profit.

and police magistrates. The first started with a directive from Whitcher (probably initiated by Kerr) that fisheries overseers were to prosecute railroad express agents and train conductors if they assisted in the transportation of illicit fish caught during closed season. In November, Kerr was in Galt to inspect Blaine's mill dam when he found a barrel of fish on the train. He seized the fish, brought them back to Hamilton, and sold them to a local fish vendor, John Williams, on behalf of the Department. A fish vendor in Galt (the likely intended recipient of the fish) had Williams summonsed for selling the illegal fish, and Williams was convicted and fined by J. P. Morris Lutz. Kerr was outraged.

Kerr attended the trial and gave evidence for Williams, noting that "the complainant was not examined at the trial, nor was any sale proved." Kerr's evidence "does not prove anything to convict Williams." The prosecutor had alleged that a telegram from the fisheries overseer at Collingwood had approved the transport of the fish but did not put the telegraph into evidence. Kerr argued that he had every right to confiscate the fish and have them sold but "I could hammer nothing into the magistrate's brain, who even doubted my authority to seize the barrel."

Kerr wrote to the Department asking them to hold the fine in abeyance because Miller had done nothing wrong, and they agreed to do so. Kerr concluded that this was the "strangest disposition of a case without evidence that I ever beheld before in all my experience." Ultimately, the Department paid Williams' fine.

The second case involved mill owners on Bronte Creek or 12 Mile Creek, which originates in the Beverley Swamp in Wentworth and runs into Lake Ontario at Bronte. Kerr had been there in October inspecting the mills, and he found no instance of pollution. In November, Hamilton police constable Samuel McNair (who Kerr knew) had alleged that the owners were polluting the waters and had laid charges. Kerr fired back: "These assertions are deliberate falsehoods. But in order that you may not be led astray by the imagination of Constable McNair, I have again visited the saw mills and found that they have not been sawing since I last visited on October 8th."

Nonetheless, they were convicted and fined heavily. Kerr wrote that "if they were compelled to pay the fines, over which Const. McNair is so jubilant, upon questionable testimony, it would, in my opinion, be an act of oppression." The Department noted that presumably McNair was entitled to half of the fine, to which Kerr replied, "you are perfectly right, that is McNair's sole object from first to last." Kerr also said he had a conversation with the prosecutor who acknowledged there was no evidence on which to convict.[94] The fines were ordered to be held in abeyance.

On November 24, Kerr advised the minister that he had received information from a confidential source about lawless fishing on Georgian Bay. Kerr said that if instructed he would be "in the midst of it" within twelve hours. Two days later he was there and spent two days "causing great excitement." He found out as much as he could and wanted to go to Christian Island where the "Indians have also been fishing during closed season." Unable to secure a boat because of bad weather, he had to content himself with rousing up the inefficient fisheries overseers, including James Patton, with whom "I have had some plain talk, so better things, I have reason to know will I hope follow." His hopes were dashed when he learned that Patton's own brother-in-law was fishing illegally: "[Patton has had a] complete failure to do anything I had advised him. It's just as I expected."

Trolling for more work, Kerr exclaimed, "There has been too much violating of the Fisheries Act in Georgian Bay and it is high time to put a final stop to it." On December 13, he rode the rails back to Collingwood for a good stomp around Georgian Bay for a few days.

1876

Kerr was back on Georgian Bay for a few days in early January and began his prosecutions. Eventually, after another three days there, he charged seventeen fishermen and two fish vendors. The fishermen complained that Patton gave them permission. Kerr dryly observed, "I find nothing in the Fisheries Act to Justify Mr. James Patton in the course he has thought fit to pursue in these cases, and a rigid enquiry to that end

....

94   I don't know what's more disturbing, to hear about a crooked cop motivated by greed or a prosecutor proceeding to prosecute when he knew there was no case.

will prove to you all this." On March 13, Kerr wrote for permission to go back to Meaford to "finish up these convictions." It appears he did not get it, but he would be back to Georgian Bay, although not for a few years. By not allowing Kerr to wrap up his business and put in force effective enforcement, the problems continued.

The battle for Toronto Island resumed innocently enough in March when Kerr wrote to the minister seeking permission for William Ward to build a house on the fishery reserve: "I may say on behalf of William Ward that he is deserving of this indulgence not only as a fisherman, but as a most courageous fisherman who has repeatedly, again and again, saved the lives of a great many ship wrecked mariners on Toronto Island... And for which he holds medals from the Humane Society of Great Britain and valuable presents from the citizens of Toronto for the pluck and bravery so often displayed by him in saving life."[95]

In June a meeting was held with Kerr, William Ward, and Toronto City Solicitor John Beverley Robinson regarding the house issue. The City had indicated Ward could not build his house, and Kerr went to bat for him. At the meeting they were advised to petition the City, and Kerr sought the help of the Department, writing, "I solicit your interference and protection for Mr. Ward in future from petty annoyance of the Corporation of Toronto." Kerr duly wrote the petition for Ward, which was a fawning appeal to permit the house, which had already been built, to remain where it was. Ward was allowed to stay, and he built a hotel in 1882.

Kerr illustrated the contest between the cities and the fishermen by reporting on various events on Burlington Beach that ultimately spelled the end of the commercial fisheries there.

In February 1876, Kerr wrote to the minister to report on the "Ocean House Hotel" that Birely and his partner had opened as a summer resort in 1875 at a cost of $15,000 plus $800 for the road. This was built on property formerly "owned" by Mrs. Baldry, right near the

---

95   William Ward (1847–1912) was the son of David Ward, namesake of Ward's Island. He dedicated his life to saving others after a sailing accident in 1862 cost the life of his five sisters. He was the only survivor. He is credited with saving 164 people during his lifetime.

canal, and Birely held her old fishing licences on both the beach side and the bay side.[96] Kerr had no problem with this hotel because it was seasonal use, and Birely didn't fish.[97]

Of more concern for Kerr was the plan of Benjamin Egar of Wellington Square (Burlington) to build a second canal across the beach in June 1876 to allow a "pleasure steamer running between Hamilton and Brant House Hotel." Egar had bought the remnants of the Brant land from Simcoe Kerr (remember him?), and J.W. Kerr reported Egar's plan to build the canal "by **stealth** during night." Kerr predicted hundreds of thousands of dollars of damage to navigation and implored the Department to "put a stop to this egregious folly."

A month later, Kerr learned the canal had been cut and that water was running from Lake Ontario into Burlington Bay and that a temporary bridge had been placed over the canal. I am uncertain as to what became of this. Returning in August, Kerr found that part of the bog from Brant Pond had floated out into Lake Ontario, which "has damaged and injured the fishermen by being caught in their seines while hauling at night." Kerr requested instructions on how to proceed, but apparently, none were provided. It seems like things just blew over.

At the same time, the Hamilton and North Western Railway had begun to build its line, which ran across the beach strip and across the ship canal. Kerr was concerned for the fishermen and wanted the Department "to impress upon the company, and require, that Company to construct a railway crossing over their railway to each licensed fishing ground on B. Beach." He also wanted gates at these crossings. Kerr predicted it would cause "much confusion and wrangling" if not done. It was probably done because fishing continued on Burlington Beach without apparent interruption.[98]

....

96   After Baldry was bought out, her house conveniently burned down.
97   Ocean House burned down in 1895. The Canal Amusement Park operated on the property from 1903–1978. As a kid born in 1956, I remember it as a very cheesy place.
98   The Hamilton and North Western Railway ran from its Hamilton station on Ferguson Ave (now Shakespeare's Restaurant) to Collingwood. It opened as far as Barrie in 1877 and died a slow death by the 1980s.

F. M. Carpenter, the warden of Wentworth County (and future MP for Kerr's riding of Wentworth South), wrote to the minister in August 1876 to be permitted to remove 120 yards of gravel from Burlington Beach to construct the new jail yard. Kerr had no objection: "The taking away this kind of gravel never injures nor damages the fisheries. It is the taking away the sand, leaving the deep holes, that is very injurious and objectionable." Noting that gravel and sand were being taken daily by wagon loads for building purposes, Kerr proposed that the Department establish some rules, "not to stop persons taking the sand and gravel, but that they shall take it according to some wise and fixed rules laid down for their guidance and which will at once convince the public that our fisheries rights are to some extent carefully guarded." No such rules were ever promulgated. Kerr would have been happy to draft them himself.

Another group of combatants in the Battle of the Bay were the local farmers, who held a meeting that Kerr curiously did not attend and then submitted a petition to the minister. As noted previously, net fishing in Burlington Bay and Dundas Marsh had been prohibited except for a handful of leases for a short spring season in a limited area of the bay. The farmers felt excluded and that Kerr's Burlington Beach "friends" had been preferred. The Department asked Kerr to respond.

He wrote a long letter explaining the reasons for the limited leasing and his opposition to the petition, stating, "I feel grieved at finding the petitioners, in moments of thoughtlessness, urging on your Honour to inflict an injury hurtful to individuals—fishermen, whose avocation in life is to fish for a subsistence and in a small portion of the Bay for which they annually pay, while these petitioners who spearfish are to have in future the entire run of the Bay and Marsh at their disposal."

Teeing off on the petitioners, Kerr noted, "they are mostly farmers, wealthy in land, grain, hay, fruit, horses, machinery, cows, oxen, sheep, hogs and domestic fowl while the licensed fishermen have no other means of support but by fishing for a scanty subsistence... But to ask you to inflict an injury on poor fishermen so that wealthy farmers may aggrandize themselves—This is inhuman and as such goes beyond my comprehension." The petition was not allowed, and the poor fishermen continued to fish a small portion of the bay.

Some humorous events took place in 1876. Starting at his farm house on a tromp to Winona, Kerr reported,

> Before leaving in the morning I jumped down off the wagon when a pistol in my right-hand coat pocket struck against the tire of the wagon wheel, exploded, and went back into the side of the wagon. The bullet leaving a clean hole there, also leaving another in my coat and setting the pocket on fire. Took the pistol in and locked it up in my desk. The pocket in which the pistol was in was next to the wagon and the bullet took its course through the side of the wagon.

If things had gone the other way, I might be writing "The End" at this point. I also find it amusing that he felt he had to lock up the pistol, as if it were to blame for the incident. After he locked it up, he got back on the wagon and casually proceeded on his way.

Kerr always wrote to his fisheries guardians in the fall to stir them up to protect the "noble salmon." He was frequently let down by their lack of zeal for the job. He wrote a scathing letter to Joe Black, a fisheries guardian on the Rouge River: "Are you protecting the salmon or merely deceiving me? Or are you trapping muskrats to feed your pigs or skinning weasels, that you have no time to attend to the salmon. Now just turn over a new leaf Joe, my friend. Do your duty for me like a man and then you will see what I, in return, will do for you."

In regard to James Wilcox, a fisheries overseer on the Credit River, Kerr had the following less-than-glowing comment: "James Wilcox never was a very efficient officer owing to his bodily infirmities [he only had one leg]. His tongue being at all times the only active member of his composition."

In October Kerr received a strange visit from Whitcher. Kerr took the train to Toronto to meet him at the station. On returning to Hamilton, Kerr found Whitcher had so much gear that he had to get a horse and wagon to get it to Whitcher's hotel. Whitcher mysteriously gave Kerr a cheque for fifty dollars and made Kerr return forty dollars. The next day when seeing Whitcher off to Long Point, Kerr gave him another fifty dollars, "which he ordered me to pay him and charge it as an Expenditure paid for Mr. Whitcher." Whitcher bought 500 shotgun cartridges with the money and then headed off, without Kerr, for some serious shooting on Long Point. I don't know what was going on with the money, but it sounds like some kind of a shakedown.

A week later, Whitcher telegraphed Kerr for more cartridges, and Kerr duly paid for and shipped 500 more to Port Rowan, at his own expense. Two days later the shot ducks arrived in Hamilton, and Kerr had to pay thirteen dollars to ship them to Ottawa. That was a hell of a lot of money at the time. I am not sure how many ducks 1,000 shotgun shells would get you!

Two weeks later Kerr was taking Whitcher back to Toronto and was still paying his expenses, including paying to ship his guns to Ottawa. Kerr also shipped another mess of ducks, including ducks that Kerr paid to have stuffed. It seems like Kerr was Whitcher's personal servant.

The level of threats and violence continued to subside in 1876, but hard feelings continued to abound.

In May, Kerr's boat was stolen from Gage's Inlet and presumably sunk in the bay. Kerr thought this was the act of some fishermen whom he had recently charged, but he couldn't prove it. However, turning lemons into lemonade, Kerr took the opportunity to request a new and bigger boat and a boathouse to store it. Noting that it would cost $89.40, Kerr was authorized, and he had the boat built in Toronto by Billy Ward, who shipped it to Hamilton aboard the steamship *Corsican*.

1877

This was the last full year of Alexander Mackenzie's Liberal government, and the country was in a major depression. Now known as the Long Depression, it was a worldwide economic event that began in 1873 and ended in about 1879. Mackenzie, a free trader, had no real solutions, but MacDonald's Conservatives adopted the "National Policy," which included tariffs intended to help Canada compete against cheaper US products.

Kerr was criticized for his expenses, which were noted to be about

$900 a year. The Department advised "retrenchment, as economy is the order of the day." Kerr reported that his expenses were down from prior years and that some were unavoidable, such as the cost of replacing his stolen boat. Kerr concluded, "Pay or no pay I shall continue when necessary and I find it is so, to visit B. Bay and B. Beach as I have always done heretofore."

Criticized in July for making seven trips to Niagara, Kerr set the record straight and noted it was only four trips: "My visits are only made **always** when it becomes absolutely necessary for the active performance of my duties and the welfare of the fisheries. My visits are never made trips of pleasure except it is the conscientious pleasure I always enjoy in doing my duty faithfully." In a postscript he stated that when he travelled by train he always bought a cheaper return ticket!

When the minister wanted to reduce the fish guardians' salaries from about ninety dollars to about twenty-five dollars, Kerr huffed, "No good, reliable man will watch all night under $1.50 per night and a good many men ask $2."

The year started slowly for Kerr with not a lot of action. Deciding to stir things up, he headed to Toronto and out onto a frozen Ashbridge's Bay. He found and charged twenty-four men and boys for fishing illegally, fishing on Sunday, or both and had them all brought to court. His friendly Toronto Police magistrate, Alexander MacNab, convicted most of them and fined them two dollars. Some were let off with a warning for unexplained reasons.

On December 15, 1879, Whitcher sent all the fisheries overseers a directive that they must stop enforcement of the game laws and the provincial *Sabbath Observance Act*. I don't know whether Kerr was disappointed, annoyed, or both. He thought those aspects of his career were over, but later the government amended the *Fisheries Act* to ban fishing on Sunday. So, Kerr resumed busting people for this "gotcha" offence.

In April, Kerr resumed his fight with James Miller, the secretary of the St. Catharines Game Club. Hostilities began on April 3 when Kerr met Miller to provide him with their annual licence. Miller wanted Kerr to agree to changes right then and there. Kerr refused but agreed to send the matter to Ottawa for them to decide.

Next, Peter Nath (Dutch Pete) applied for the station next to the game club's at Port Dalhousie. Nath had sent to the Department a petition signed by some local MPs and twenty-four others in support of his application. "They wish to, as the saying is, to give Peter another chance." Kerr claimed he had nothing to do with the petition but he agreed with it. Slightly misquoting the Book of Ezekiel, Kerr wrote, "God willeth not the death of a sinner, but rather that he should return from his wickedness and live."

Kerr went on to explain,

> *I am well aware that Mr. James Miller, Barrister, an active member of the St. Catharines Game and Fish Club, does not desire that Peter Nath should get a licence to fish there. But as between man and man, I cannot, and will not object against Peter Nath on that account.* "Peter Nath has been unfortunate and served some time in the Central Jail in Toronto, being convicted for theft. It is said, that he came out therefrom a new man. Hence I presume why [the Petitioners] recommended him to your consideration.

Nath got his licence, and a few days later Kerr vengefully inspected all the waters controlled by the club, noting numerous fishing infractions that the club was supposed to police. Going over Miller's head, Kerr reported the matter to the president of the club, Sheriff Woodruff, and asked the minister to reprimand Miller. Nath continued to fish at Port Dalhousie for the remainder of Kerr's career, sometimes obeying the law, sometimes not.

Probably as a result of the steady reduction of his district, in 1877 Kerr began to complain about other fisheries overseers. Sometimes these complaints were made by Kerr from firsthand observations, but more commonly Kerr received information from third parties that he would then either investigate or report to the minister. For example, in June Kerr found that two of the fishermen in his district had paid their licence fees to Henry Lawe, the fisheries overseer for the lower Grand River. Seeming to overreact, Kerr complained that Lawe "has been intruding his services in my division without any authority whatever from me."

Kerr also got a letter from Mr. Ross, a long-term fisherman in Lake Erie, off the mouth of the Grand River, who complained of being shaken down by Lawe and Charles L. Bingham, the fisheries overseer for Norfolk. Kerr sent a blistering letter to the minister: "Mr. Bingham has no business to interfere with or annoy my fishermen resident in my division and neither has Henry Lawe any right to step beyond his own fishery limit division except with my consent, or by special orders from you or to take proceedings for a contravention." Kerr noted that it was with reluctance that he drew the Department's attention "to the interference of these young fishery officers."

Rebuked by Bauset for the intemperate tone of his letter, Kerr pleaded meekly, "You appear to judge me hastily, my own real object was to see Mr. Ross get a licence." Unable to bite his tongue, Kerr continued: "The late John A. Backhouse, after his appointment and before his death carried on just in the same way as his successor, Mr. Bingham." There will be much more about Bingham later.

Kerr concluded, rather disingenuously, "Do not mix me up in the **wrangles and conflicts**…After nearly 13 years as an Overseer I have learned to attend to and mind my own business." This was plainly untrue, for Kerr was an inveterate meddler, although usually for good reason.

In September 1877, Kerr received a letter from Elora complaining about the state of the Grand River and alleging illegal fishing, sawdust, and a lack of fishways. Kerr sent the letter to the minister with his own note: "I beg to send you this letter that you may be pleased to stir up Mr. Henry Griffith. FO at Brantford." One wonders why Kerr didn't just "stir up" Griffith himself instead of tattling to the boss.

In late June 1877, Kerr received a letter from a fisherman at Waubaushene, on the southeast side of Georgian Bay, who reported, "There is considerable trouble up here between the fishermen and Inspector James Patton. The majority wishes now they had applied to government for Mr. J. W. Kerr [to be appointed]. They see their error now, as there is a great deal of favour and partiality shown James Patton to his few fishermen friends (his relations). He will find it will not continue long as there is war now declared against him."

Itching for permission to return to Georgian Bay, Kerr wrote to the minister to put him on notice: "There is too much fishing and it is unprofitable to the fishermen, except by their catching vast quantities of fish. It is excessive fishing of such an extensive character as will in a very few years (three or four) completely fish the place out if not checked by you." Kerr did return to Georgian Bay but not for a while. Meanwhile, the situation continued to decline.

In 1877 the next salvo in the simmering war of Niagara began. It occupied much of Kerr's time and caused him much consternation for years. The background was that John Bolton, Big Jim Cantwell, and Thomas Elliott had seine fishing grounds close to each other at Niagara-on-the-Lake (then simply Niagara). None of them appeared to like the other two, and there had been infractions that Kerr had prosecuted over the years.

Elliot, who was a favourite of Kerr's, ran a boarding house where Kerr would stay when he was in town on business. Kerr charged Bolton for deliberately throwing fish guts on Elliot and Cantwell's grounds, driving the pickerel out of the river. He also had a stinking pig pen, "a filthy nuisance," on his lands, which were right by the water and in close proximity to Elliott's home. He was convicted and fined five dollars or twenty days in jail. This was a triangle that did not end well for any of the participants, including Kerr.

During the summer and fall of 1877, Kerr had difficulty getting instructions from Ottawa because both Minister Albert Smith and Commissioner of Fishing W. F. Whitcher were away in Halifax attending the Halifax Fisheries Commission. The purpose of the Commission was to determine what amount, if any, the United States owed to Britain, as Canadian fishing rights in US waters had been left out of the 1871 Treaty of Washington. A joint international tribunal was struck to determine the matter and held hearings in Halifax from June until November. The tribunal consisted of a US and a British member and a third member, Belgium's ambassador to the United States, who cast the deciding vote in favour of Britain. The US was ordered to pay $5.5 million in compensation.

Also as a result of no instructions from Ottawa, the disputes at Niagara grew worse, and Bolton was openly defiant of Kerr and Police Magistrate William Kerby of St. Catharines. Trouble was also brewing on Georgian Bay as a result of it being unattended to.

1878

Kerr first turned his attention to the issue of "pound nets," which are a type of fishing net installed in relatively shallow water that guide fish into a central trap or "pot," which can be taken up every day or so to collect the fish, still alive and fresh. Pound nets had been around for a few years and were effective. They were named as such because wooden stakes were pounded into the lake bottom to create the frame for the net. Instead of seine nets or gill nets, which were licensed out for five to ten dollars a year, pound nets were licensed initially for forty dollars. They ultimately resulted in shallow lakes like Erie being largely fished out of prime fish.

Kerr was initially in favour of pound nets for the increased revenue and fish they would produce. He felt the Department should get fifty to sixty dollars from the Niagara to Port Colborne fishermen who had easy access to the lucrative Buffalo market. Kerr eventually changed his mind about pound nets, but by then it was largely too late.

He did, however, put his foot firmly down on pound nets being used in Lake Ontario. In 1879 a petition was signed by thirty-seven Lake Ontario fishermen wishing to be licensed to use pound nets, claiming the Lake Erie fishermen had an unfair advantage. Kerr was asked to respond, and he wrote back that the Ontario fishermen were not in any way adversely affected by the rights of the Lake Erie fishermen because pound nets were impractical on Lake Ontario, which was too deep. He went on to opine, "I cannot accede to nor recommend the prayer of the petition and I know that the petitioners never meant to apply for such a death like, destructive and so sweeping a privilege. Why Sir, if such a privilege was granted the name of whitefish in five years from this time, would be among the fish of the past."

Kerr also noted the vulnerability of whitefish in amusing terms: "Because of the great abundance of young whitefish, **whose giddy nature, fond of company** would lead them to congregate in pound nets by millions, and so there would be an end to them." Oh, those sociable teenage whitefish! Herd mentality!

In March the Department arbitrarily banned net fishing on the Niagara River above the falls as a result of a joint agreement with the

United States. Knowing the disastrous effect this would have on the handful of fishermen in Fort Erie, Kerr argued it should be postponed for a year. When he didn't get this concession, he asked for another month and for fishing licences to be issued between Fort Erie and Point Abino[99] on Eastern Lake Erie.

When he realized the Americans were breaking the agreement, Kerr helped the fishermen get a petition to Ottawa and rounded up local political support. In late December, under the new MacDonald government, the ban was lifted, to Kerr's elation.

On September 17, 1878, the Conservatives trounced the hapless Liberals, and MacDonald was back in power. He was sworn in on October 17, and things started to get better for Kerr.

Ice Huts on Burlington Bay by Desjardins Canal. National Archives of Canada

....
99 Point Abino is like a mini Long Point that juts out for several miles into Lake Erie. Mostly owned by Americans, it is a gated cottage community. It has a beautiful decommissioned lighthouse that I look at every summer day from my cottage patio, about ten miles away.

The Grits! (1874–1878)   123

> SEIZURE OF FISH.—This morning Fishery Inspector Kerr seized about 150 lbs. of white fish and trout in the stalls of Messrs. Morris and John Davis. Both parties were before the Magistrate and fined $1 each, the fish being confiscated and sent to the Orphans' Home and St. Joseph's Orphan Asylum. Mr. Davis knew nothing of the arrival of the fish, he being sick in bed.

Newspaper clipping from Hamilton Spectator found in Kerr diary, Fish dealer John Davis found guilty without knowledge of the fish. ROM

> FISHING IN BURLINGTON BAY.
>
> By reference to our Ottawa despatch, it will be seen that important changes are to be made in the regulations governing fishing inside of Burlington Bay. The new rules will prove satisfactory in securing "equal justice to all interested parties." Under the old rules equal justice was the exception and partiality the rule.

Newspaper clipping found in Kerr diary. Kerr was frequently criticized for favouritism. ROM

Photo of Hamilton's Crystal Palace, where Kerr exhibited his fish. Hamilton Public Library. Also shown is a newspaper clipping found in Kerr's diary, about his exhibit

Ocean House, Burlington Beach 1874-1895. Hamilton Public Library

The Grits! (1874–1878) 125

tion in East Seneca, Abington, and Caistor, for a total of thirty-one years.
Cheyne was one of two auditors for the township of Saltfleet and was the school inspector for Wentworth County. He was a member of the committee that formed the Woodburn Library Association in 1883.
Cheyne retired in 1874 and died four years later.

J.M. Bailey, *The Presbytery of Hamilton, 1836-1967* (Hamilton 1967); Burkholder, *Out of the storied past* (1960); J.E. Turner, *History of Albion Mills*. Western *Ontario Historical Notes* X, no. 3.

CHISHOLM, DAVID BLACK, lawyer, politician; b. 2 November 1832 in East Flamborough, Upper Canada; m. Addie Davis in 1864 and they had two children, but divorced in 1889; d. 1899.

David Black Chisholm, was the son of Colonel George K. Chisholm, and Barbara McKenzie. Details of his early education are not known, but from 1857 to 1859 he attended Victoria College in Cobourg. He began to study law in 1859 with Miles O'Reilly in Hamilton and was called to the bar in 1864. By 1870 he had formed a partnership in Hamilton with S.F. Lazier and had offices on James Street N. He became senior partner in the firm of Chisholm and Hazlett and was a member of other law firms at various times.

Chisholm was active in politics at the municipal and the federal levels. He served as alderman in 1869 and 1870 and mayor in 1871 and 1872. A Conservative, he sat in the House of Commons as member for Hamilton from 1872 to 1874, but he was elected for Halton as an independent in 1874-5. In his election campaigns he spoke in favour of the construction of the Canadian Pacific Railway, supported judicious protective tariffs, and approved of encouraging American investment in Canadian development.

Chisholm was involved in various businesses as well. He helped found the Bank of Hamilton in 1872 and was a member of its provisional board of directors. In 1873 he was chairman of the provisional board of directors of the Hamilton and North Western Railway, and in 1880 he was president of Standard Fire Insurance Company, Allied Insurance Company, and the Canada Loan and Banking Company. In addition he was a director of the Mutual Life Association of Canada. He was also a director of the Ontario Camp Ground Company and the Navy Island Fruit Growing Association. Although raised a Presbyterian, Chisholm became a Methodist and an active member of Centenary Church.

Excerpt showing D. B. Chisholm's biography with glaring omissions.
Dictionary of Hamilton Biography.

Chapter 10

1878–1882 – The Nation Builder is Back!

Kerr appears to have played no part in the 1878 election. In fact, he didn't even mention it in his diaries, nor did he note the October swearing-in. He was likely aware not to bite the hand that fed him. However, in the two remaining federal elections during his life, Kerr was openly and overtly political in favour of "good old Sir John A."

Just four days after the swearing-in, Kerr was summoned to Ottawa, likely to meet the new minister, James Pope, W. F. Whitcher, and his assistant, S. P. Bauset. Taking the overnight train to Ottawa, he spent the day "in the fisheries department" and returned that night to Hamilton. No mention is made of who he met or what was discussed, but it seems unlikely that he was the only overseer present. All Kerr noted in his diary was that Mr. Whitcher sent his regards to William Leary, the head keeper of the Long Point Company, and Kerr requested "a bag of choice ducks for myself." These were likely intended for Whitcher, who was back on the gravy train again.

Kerr's occasional bad judgment is reflected in an application by John Ranney of Ridgeway to secure a pound net licence near Point Abino. In December 1878 Kerr wrote a glowing letter in support of Ranney, who, like Kerr, was a staunch Conservative, having just returned home "to aid in the National Policy." Kerr highly recommended his application, noting that Ranney was "well skilled in preserving and curing fish." Ranney got the licence, but over the ensuing years proved to be a liar and a serial defaulter on his fees. Kerr wrote to him numerous times to implore him to pay up. He was a constant thorn in Kerr's side.

However, before this trouble began, Kerr again went to bat for Ranney when in August 1879 he tried to secure for him an unheard-of nine-year lease. Kerr noted that Ranney's plan required infrastructure like a wharf, fish houses, ice houses, and an ice machine and that he needed a long lease to ensure financial viability. Complimenting Ranney, Kerr stated, "I find Mr. John W. Ranney is unlike almost all other fishermen. He is law abiding and a careful man and so communicative regarding the success of his pound net fishing that I consider any privilege that the Department can legally bestow upon him will be highly esteemed and appreciated." He didn't get a nine-year licence, and none of Ranney's plans came to fruition. Kerr would learn how deceived he had been.

In 1879 Kerr was sixty-six years old, and he began to write about some health issues. Prior to this he had some rheumatism but nothing major, and he was as active as ever in his extensive travels. On January 1, he was travelling on the ice to Toronto Island when he had a bad fall, which was humorously reported in the Toronto newspapers.[100] He doesn't state if he sustained any injuries, but he likely did because he doesn't mention another road trip until January 14.

In a letter from the previous summer, he reported on another trip to Toronto: "I don't care much to tell you about the privations I encounter, and those acting with me in cases of this kind, however, after I made the seizure I started with the seines and ropes and two men in a small open boat, distance 20 miles to Leslieville,[101] encountered two thunderstorms, got wet all through and only reached there at 6:00 a.m. next morning, completely faded and worn out."

On January 24, 1979, Kerr was at Bronte collecting licence fees where he noted that he "inhaled smoke while looking at Joyce's smoked fish, which injured me very much." In February he was with John Ranney at Ridgeway when he recorded that he "took very ill during

....

100   Kerr was a pretty big guy. He told his friends he weighed 242 pounds.
101   Leslieville was a working-class neighbourhood by Lake Ontario, east of the Don River.

the night" and that he was "obliged to drink Brandy to cure my bowel complaint." Two days later he was back on the ice of the bay, making his rounds as usual.

In March, Kerr was sent a copy of a petition the minister had received requesting the return of former Fishery Guardian Joe Black's nets that Kerr had seized the previous summer in Whitby. The petition was signed by former Federal Cabinet Minister Thomas N. Gibbs,[102] a few judges and JPs, and eighty-four others. Black had tried to portray himself as an unknowledgeable man who had been hard done by. Kerr was having none of it. He wrote back to advise the minister that Black knew the law and that he had a copy of the *Fisheries Act* in his possession when he committed the offence, having studied it to try and get around it: "As to any promises Joseph Black will make of observing the Fisheries Act in the future; It will never amount to anything as he has again and again made similar promises to me and always broke them." In regard to being treated badly, Kerr noted that Black's son, who was also charged, was let off by the magistrates. Kerr concluded by noting that Black's character is "drunken and immoral" and that some who signed the petition knew that. The minister ordered the nets restored anyhow.

The Battle of Niagara heated up again in the spring when John Bolton refused to remove a boathouse he had built on Thomas Elliott's fishing grounds: "I have had to endure a great deal of bad language and domineering conduct, and my forbearance has been severely tested, I might say strained, by Mr. John Bolton." When Bolton refused to remove the building, Kerr suggested that his licence be cancelled, but the Department disagreed. There was also trouble brewing with Big Jim Cantwell, who hadn't paid but continued to fish.

Bolton maintained that he was entitled to the property by adverse

---

102   Thomas Nicholson Gibbs (Mar. 11, 1821–Apr. 7, 1883) was noted as Oshawa's chief businessman and financier. Gibbs became a confidant and fixer for John A. MacDonald after Confederation. He beat Father of Confederation George Brown in an election that was widely suspected of having been fixed. In 1873 he was appointed secretary of State and later secretary of Inland Revenue, but MacDonald's defeat in 1874 ended his Cabinet career. He was appointed to the Senate in 1880 and died three years later.

possession[103] and that the boathouse was really on the five acres owned by the Queen's Royal Hotel.[104] Kerr refuted this and stated that the boathouse was actually on the fishery reserve, which was government property. Bolton also claimed he needed the boathouse for storage because he operated the ferry between Niagara and Youngstown, NY, and that he was being singled out because there were other boathouses on the beach. Kerr reported that Bolton kept his ferry boats a half mile away at the customs dock. As far as other boathouses were concerned, they were all on private property, including that of Thomas Elliott.

With unusual dispatch, the minister ordered Bolton to remove the boathouse or he would get no licence. Kerr immediately telegraphed the news to him. Bolton partially complied but left some items on the beach. Kerr requested that he fulfil his promise to comply and ended a letter offering an olive branch: "You and I have a good many pleasant years to live in connection with the Niagara fisheries and so to accomplish that end we must endeavour to continue on terms of friendliness." Not gonna happen. Just a few days later, Kerr found Bolton and Big Jim Cantwell fishing in violation of the Sunday fishing laws, so he took their boats, nets, and fish into his possession. In the process he hurt his leg: "overreached myself, leg and thigh very sore, crippled in walking, Curtis, the constable accompanied me."

Another front opened when Peter Nath placed a net across the front of the Welland Canal at Port Dalhousie. Annoyed that Nath had betrayed his faith, Kerr wrote, "Now it does appear to me most extraordinary that you cannot be a fisherman, except you continually break the law." (So much for the "new man" who came out of jail.)

On June 2 a new aspect of Kerr's career began when Whitcher asked him to investigate an allegation of neglect against the fisheries overseer at

....

103 Adverse possession is the legal theory that if you openly occupy another person's property for more than ten years, you legally own it. The concept still exists but has been greatly restricted.

104 The Queen's Royal Hotel opened in 1869 as a world-class luxury hotel. (You can find lots of pictures of it on the Internet.) Closed in 1929, it is now a waterfront park in Niagara-on-the-Lake. The gazebo in the park was built for the 1984 movie *The Dead Zone,* starring Christopher Walken.

Brantford, Robert Watt. It was not a difficult case. Kerr learned that Watt had been absent for two months and that he was in Toronto "working his trade as a carpenter on the Parliament Buildings there."[105] Kerr also reported that as a result of his neglect of duty, many people fished the Grand River during closed season. Kerr was instructed to prosecute if he could "substantiate the charges." Employing his Irish cop skills, Kerr began to hunt down the evidence but had to admit defeat when he learned that "no person has a desire to give evidence against the persons who offended." This included the chief of police and the chief of the fire brigade! Kerr's future investigations of fisheries overseers proved to be much trickier.

The Brantford incident illustrates three points that were true throughout Kerr's career as a fisheries overseer. The first is that if people are underpaid and undervalued, as the overseers and fish guardians were, you will not get much production out of them, and without effective supervision, many people slack off. Kerr was the exception to this principle. The second point is that nobody much cared about the fishery laws, from the average Joe right up to the judiciary and politicians. Third, nobody likes a rat, and most people were not prepared to testify against their neighbours over insignificant matters like fishing laws. Most people knew each other back in that era, and retribution was easy. There are numerous incidents of people's homes or barns being burned or fishing gear stolen, and it is unlikely that many offenders were caught.

I equate fisheries laws of the nineteenth century with traffic laws today. People recognize that they are generally valuable and sensible, but they don't think they pertain to them. I mean, who doesn't speed or sometimes fail to signal or come to a full stop at a four-way? The lack of respect is probably a function of inadequate enforcement just as the fish-and-game laws were woefully under-enforced 150 years ago. In the future either self-driving vehicles or insurance company monitoring will compel compliance with traffic laws. In Kerr's day the only effective control was essentially the extinction of the fish.

....

105   He must have just been doing repairs or renovations of the Front Street Assembly because construction at Queen's Park did not begin until 1886.

The ebb and flow of fish species populations was as much as mystery during Kerr's time as it is today. Fish populations would substantially increase or decrease for no apparent reason. Although apparently lacking any scientific background, Kerr often tried to rationalize these variations with some theory or another. One of the most boring aspects of his diaries is the inordinate amount of time he spends fussing about net mesh size. As noted, gill nets catch fish by their gills and trap them. The smaller the net mesh, the smaller the fish that are caught. Smaller fish are often immature fish that have yet to breed. Needless to say, lack of breeding leads to lack of fish.

For every species, there was a mandated net mesh size, and Kerr was constantly fiddling with the size and attempting to persuade the Department to order changes that would spare the smaller fish. He even shipped fish to Ottawa to demonstrate his point, putting them in a box of sawdust and ice and sending them by train.

In 1879 there was a huge surge in the catch of whitefish in Lake Ontario and Lake Erie. In a letter to the minister, Kerr reported,

> *I feel now great pride in telling you that Lake Ontario has burst forth this year in the largest takes of magnificent whitefish that has ever been witnessed for a long series of time. Thousands of fish in a haul and selling wholesale at $2 per 100 fish, thus making whitefish plentiful and cheap to people of the neighbourhoods and communities of my division. I feel some little pride that my exertions in protecting the small whitefish from being caught in their immature state seems to me now, not to have been labour in vain.*

Maybe he was right to take some measure of credit. Then again, maybe not. However, there are certain inalienable facts about fishing. Pollution kills fish. Dams that prevent fish from reaching their spawning grounds reduce fish populations. Catching more fish means fewer fish. Kerr fully understood these principles and did what he could, but ultimately, it was to little avail.

Kerr was also aware that there was a considerable disparity between the fishing laws in the United States and Canada. In Canada, as we have seen, fishing was federally regulated while in the US the various states controlled it. In Kerr's district, Lake Ontario, Lake Erie, and Lake Huron had five states on the waters. Without any great knowledge of American fisheries laws, it seems like there was a lot less regulation than in Canada and probably even less enforcement. On closely shared waters like the Niagara or Detroit rivers, Kerr recognized it would be useless and unfair to impose rules on Canadians that did not restrict Americans. Sometimes the Department agreed and other times it did not.

The border, both on land and in the water, was a rather elastic concept in the nineteenth century. Kerr frequently reported that people would move between the two countries with no apparent restrictions, either permanently or temporarily. In the early days, if he wanted to travel to Fort Erie, he would take the GWR to the suspension bridge, cross the Niagara River, and continue on to Buffalo, where he would hop the ferry back to Canada. There is no mention of any trouble crossing the border.[106] Except during the American Civil War, hardly anybody had a passport or travel documents.[107]

Kerr frequently reported on Americans fishing in Canadian waters and vice versa, which was illegal. Although Kerr talked a good game about seizing US boats, he was rarely able to do so. It was also clear that many of the fish caught by Canadians were destined for big US markets like Buffalo, Cleveland, and Detroit.[108]

Late in 1879, Kerr scored another Court of Quarter Sessions appeal victory, this time in Brampton. Kerr had charged two men for fishing a rather elaborate trap box in the mouth of the Credit River. They appealed their convictions, and a jury trial was set to proceed on

....

106 The Peace Bridge, connecting Fort Erie to Buffalo, opened in 1927.
107 The first Canadian (British) passport was issued in 1862, but people didn't really need a passport or related travel documents to cross the border until after 9/11.
108 There is a good example of Kerr's bravado in June 1879 when he heard reports of five American boats fishing on Sunday near Queenston. He wrote, "I propose to go there with a couple of good constables and capture the entire fleet, crews and all for contraventions of the Fisheries and Sabbath Observance Act." Despite being out all night on surveillance, he was unsuccessful because the American boats did not show up.

December 12th. Kerr needed permission to retain a lawyer to prosecute, noting that the appellants had "employed the best hot **grit** counsel in Brampton." Preparing for the trial/appeal, Kerr advised, "We must not go to Brampton with our fingers in our mouths." The Department hired J. J. Foy of Toronto to prosecute.[109]

Seeing an opportunity to double down on the appellants, Kerr searched their house and seized illegally caught fish and had an encounter with a wife "who was saucy, and asked by what authority I came there to search her place." Later encountering the appellants "who used insulting and threatening language," Kerr must have felt he was right back home in Hamilton!

Kerr attended court in Brampton on December 9 together with his witness, "Mark Reynolds, an illiterate poor boy of 14 years old who saw [the appellants] make the trap" and also proved that they removed the fish. Kerr jubilantly exclaimed, "conviction **was sustained!**" Curiously, Solicitor Foy did not attend but sent an associate, John A. MacDonnell, who "discharged his duty ably, efficiently and satisfactorily."[110] Kerr had some kind words for Judge Scott, "a most excellent gentleman, deserves my highest esteem and approval for the honourable way in which he discharged his duty on the bench."[111]

This was Kerr's last prosecution in the Court of General Sessions because the government had finally taken his advice to amend the *Fisheries Act* to replace appeals with a process of petitioning the minister. Kerr wrote to Whitcher, "I am glad and rejoiced that appealing to the Court of General Sessions has at last come to an untimely end."

Kerr was still hankering to get back to Georgian Bay, and he wrote a letter to Whitcher about the Noble brothers, fishermen at Killarney, who

....

109   James Joseph Foy (Feb. 22, 1847–June 13, 1916) was a Conservative of Irish ancestry, albeit a Catholic. He was attorney general for Ontario from 1905–1914.

110   I sometimes had to send associates to court on my behalf but never for trials. I always let my clients know beforehand and assured them that they were in good hands.

111   The boy was later threatened with prosecution, and Kerr wrote to the minister to ensure he was "protected." Kerr later gave him and his father the fourteen eels he had seized. Was that a reward?

were sending fish down south in refrigerated boxcars that they claimed were not caught during closed season. Kerr claimed that $14,000 of their catch was sent to Hamilton alone and that it was also illegal to be in possession of protected fish during closed season. He also implicated the fishing overseers at Collingwood and Killarney as participating in the scheme by giving the fishermen and the shippers illegal documents. The minister did not take the bait, and Kerr remained in Hamilton.

Plan "B" was then instituted, whereby Kerr had the local fish vendors charged with being in possession of fish caught during closed season. They were only fined one dollar, but the message was sent. The event was written up in the *Hamilton Spectator*, and if correct, I find it peculiar that John Davis was convicted if he didn't know the fish had arrived, being sick in bed. However, he pled guilty, so he must have been guilty!

As usual, Kerr spent much of November frantically exhorting the fishery guardians to protect the salmon and report to him frequently. To one fishery guardian he wrote "Another week and no letter from you, have you gone over body and bones to the Enemy?"

All in all, 1879 seems to have been a pretty good year for J. W. Kerr.

1880

The year started slowly with Kerr making his rounds to complete his annual return. This was an opportunity to meet every licensed fisherman in his still-extensive division and to get to know them and their families. I suppose he used this opportunity to ingratiate himself with people, but he seemed to have a genuine affinity for the common person and often sent his regards to members of fishermen's families, sometimes by name. I think he also used this generally relaxed time of year to talk about the fisheries and to find out information about violations and violators. He clearly had a network of spies who fed him information, usually based upon personal grievances, of which there seemed to be many.

Kerr mentioned "pocket diaries" that he probably carried around with him rather than his large letter books, but unfortunately, they haven't survived. It would be interesting to see what he was scribbling in these books. As a criminal lawyer for thirty-six years, I saw a lot of police notes, and it is amazing what you can find—if you can read them!

At the end of volume seven of the diaries and letter books, Kerr attached a newspaper article about the first annual meeting of the Wentworth Fish and Game Protective Association. You would think that Kerr would be a member in light of his despair about the absence of game protection, but he was not. We shall see why shortly and embark on another fight with a familiar adversary.

In 1880 the Battle for Toronto Island resumed. Toronto Island was originally a peninsula but became an island as a result of a bad storm in 1858 that washed out part of the eastern end. The federal government deeded the island to the City of Toronto in 1867 but maintained the fishery reserve for the handful of licensed fishermen there. As we have seen, the pressure of the ever-expanding city put pressure on the fishermen.

In the winter of 1880, Edward "Ned" Hanlan proposed to build a hotel and wanted a fishery licence—not to fish but to exclude the two remaining fishermen from fishing near his hotel.[112] He wrote to the minister seeking to obtain the licence adjacent to where he proposed to build his hotel, on land given to him by the City of Toronto. Kerr was asked to comment on the petition.

Kerr noted that the fishing ground had been occupied by Patrick Gray for the last fifteen years for seine hauling, which required a foothold on the beach to reel in his nets. Kerr reported that a lawyer friend of Hanlan's had admitted to him that the real purpose of the application was to "prevent all seine hauling there." Kerr felt that Hanlon was only a one-quarter owner of the old homestead property because he had a brother and two sisters. Kerr concluded, "I cannot do otherwise, as between man and man, in Justice to all concerned, in my public capacity,

....

112 Edward "Ned" Hanlan (July 12, 1855–Jan. 4, 1908), one of four children of John Hanlan, an early resident of Toronto Island, and a native Irishman, became a world champion sculler in 1876. A huge fan favourite in Canada, he followed his father into the hotel business on Toronto Island and also became an alderman. Only 5 feet 8 inches tall and 150 lbs during his racing career, he died of pneumonia at age 52. It was estimated that 10,000 people attended his funeral. Hanlan's Point Beach, on the west end of the island, is now a clothing-optional beach.

then report against Mr. Edward Hanlan's application being granted."

The minister wrote back to Kerr wanting to know why the two licensed fishermen, Gray and David Ward,[113] had such "extensive holdings." Kerr responded that they were not actually fully fished due to Toronto's large angling community and that if Hanlan or anybody else actually wanted to fish, room could be made to accommodate them. Kerr also stated that it was necessary for Gray and Ward to be able to land on Hanlan's Point because it was closest to Queen's Wharf and the safest place to cross when the ice was breaking up.

Kerr's personal opinion of Hanlan is unclear. There had been trouble with Hanlan's father in the past, but at times he had assisted Kerr. Kerr remarked, "I would like very much to see Mr. Edward Hanlan become a genuine licensed fisherman. I feel certain it will never detract anything from his high position as 'Sculler of the World' to have a genuine fishery some place about Gibralter Point [Hanlan Point] where he could catch fish to supply the inmates of his new hotel." He may have writing facetiously, and he certainly knew Hanlan had no intent to fish. It is also curious that he described hotel guests as "inmates." The CBC nicknamed him the "scandalous sculler" and "a huge pain in the ass."

On February 7, an anonymous letter[114] was published in the *Globe* advocating for the banning of seine fishing in Toronto Harbour, Ashbridge's Bay, and the mouth of the Don River or, in other words, all around Toronto Island. The letter also alleged fish were being depleted by illegal seine fishing and being sold in Toronto during closed season. Kerr fired back by stating that the fish being sold were legally imported from Quebec. A similar article appeared in the *Toronto Evening Telegram* on February 21.

A petition to ban seine fishing signed by 242 residents of Toronto, including some police inspectors and detectives, was sent to the minister. Kerr found out it was signed at the instance of William "Billy" Lang.

....

113   David Ward (1817–1881), the namesake of Ward's Island (which is not really an island), was not a favourite of Kerr's due to Ward's difficult nature.

114   The letter was signed "Viator," which means traveler. Who might have wanted all net fishing stopped? Ned Hanlan for one. Hanlan had also travelled a bit in his career.

Kerr really unloaded on him.

> *Billy Lang, who keeps a few boats to rent out to anglers, and at present residing on Ashbridge's Bay, Leslieville, formerly a <u>thieving fisherman</u> at Port Union, and from which place he had to fly for stealing geese and fowl and for other bad conduct. His conduct was so bad, when fishing at Port Union, that the people there could stand his pilfering no longer, and so to get rid of him, he was burned out. Billy Lang pays no regard, nor respect, to the laws of God, nor man, and at present is married to his second wife, while his first wife is still living.*

Kerr reported that no net fishing was done at that time of year in Toronto: "So much for Billy Lang's **lying and slandering**." As for the 242 signatories of the petition Kerr said,

> *This is a mighty small percentage of the inhabitants of the Queen City of the west, and capital of Ontario, and even this small percentage do not comprise many wealthy and intelligent people of this Metropolis. They never saw, not one of them!!—what they assert, nor has anyone else seen it, and they all, I believe, have been misled by Billy Lang, who himself dares not sign a petition which he believes to be false and unfounded in every particular.*

Kerr noted that the thirty-five policemen who signed the petition knew nothing about the fisheries and that "Not one of the respectable boat owners or boat builders resident on the Esplanade, Toronto, signed the petition."[115] He also observed that other newspapers, like the *Mail* and the *Globe,* did not support the petition.

Kerr opined that the petition was vague and that it "is the greatest piece of effrontery that has, so far, come under my notice." As for their motives, "The only great object I see the petitioners have in view is **self**, the interest of the anglers, who have endeavoured to break the Sabbath, and having been spoken to by the licensed fishermen, have taken this

---

115 In 1880, the "Esplanade" was on Toronto's waterfront.

mode of revenging their spite and malice against good men and true."

The petitioners' request was not granted, but a compromise was made with Hanlan, who got the waters in front of his hotel but still allowed the licensed fishermen to fish in somewhat reduced waters. Kerr went to great lengths to preserve the peace by having the waters surveyed and staked out and convened a meeting of Hanlan, Ward, and Gray to make sure all understood the new arrangement, "which appeared to give satisfaction to all concerned." Hanlan then frustratingly refused to pay the thirty-dollar licence fee, trying to renegotiate with Kerr for five dollars, to which Kerr replied, "Hanlon has been offered $2,500 a year for the house and premises (rent) when completed." No reduction was granted.

Did Hanlan orchestrate the petition and enlist Billy Lang? There's no proof, but Kerr attached in his diary a curious newspaper piece about toadies "who for money or favour, praises what he detests and would lick the dust from the shoes of one in power, could he further his own ends thereby." We'll never know if Lang was Hanlan's toady. There was another toady in the chapter on Simcoe Kerr and probably a few more. The species still seems to be thriving!

In 1881 Kerr effectively gave up on Toronto Bay, acknowledging "Toronto Island, instead of being still a barren place, has now become an exceedingly smart place with nearly 100 new residences going up all over the island." He recommended a ban on all net fishing except for some limited seine fishing "to be set apart exclusively for angling for the benefit and amusement of the citizens of Toronto who will highly appreciate a boon of this kind." In a few years, Ward and Gray died, and that put an end to commercial fishing in Toronto.[116] Kerr, optimistic as always, wrote, "The anglers of Toronto will at once assist me in protecting the fish and in enforcing the law."

Probably hearing about the demise of net fishing in Toronto, the

....

116 Another Toronto fisherman was Leonard Marsh (1813–1879). In 1880, Kerr applied for Marsh's widow to get a free licence for having helped him: "Len Marsh was with me the night I seized Joe Black's seines in June 1878, and he underwent so much wet and fatigue on that occasion, along with me, that he caught cold, and a bad cold, from which poor Len never recovered." She got the free licence.

citizens of Whitby, led by Mayor Billings, signed a petition to ban net fishing in Whitby Harbour. Kerr offered a compromise that he hoped would satisfy the anglers and the two licensed long-term fishermen, whereby net fishing would stop on April 30: "I must never forget the claims of John Proudfoot and George White, both old residents of Whitby. The petition being so numerously signed by the respectable inhabitants of Whitby, I must not altogether forget them either."

An insurrection by the Burlington Beach fishermen began in the spring of 1880, led by Fred Cory (sometimes spelled "Corey"), adversary, then assistant, then returned to adversary as a result of his illegal fishing. A meeting was to be held at Dynes Tavern[117] to distribute a petition seeking Kerr's removal and to request an investigation to be conducted by the prestigious Isaac Buchanan.[118] Cory wanted Kerr to be replaced by a Barton Township farmer named S. P. Stipe, whose farm was on an inlet in the bay. Stipe was not a fisherman, but Kerr disliked him because of his difficult nature.

Kerr wrote to the minister to try and get permission to re-license the limited spring net fishing in Burlington Bay, noting that "the families are in need of something to support themselves." Kerr stated, "Some rich farmers may flare up at me for recommending you to grant this privilege, but if they do, I can't help it, there is a necessity for it, and the general public will gain the benefit."

Kerr did not attend the meeting at Dynes Tavern, but it was reported in all three Hamilton newspapers. The *Spectator* wrote, "A meeting of the fishermen was held last evening at John Dynes hotel on the Beach. Fred Cory made a speech attacking Inspector Kerr savagely, but was reminded by his brother fishermen that the most severe persecution

....

117 Dynes Tavern was opened in 1847 on Burlington Beach by sometime fisherman John Dynes (1817–1899). Then the oldest tavern in Ontario, it was controversially torn down in 2007 without a demolition permit to make way for a housing development.

118 Isaac Buchanan (July 21, 1810–Oct. 1, 1893) was a leading Hamilton businessman and politician. The builder of the Auchmar Estate on Hamilton Mountain, he had eleven children, so he was probably too busy to involve himself in the petty grievances of fishermen.

they had received was while he (Cory) was in Mr. Kerr's employ. The meeting was a stormy one, and ended about where it began."

Cory later denied the report that he convened the meeting and spoke against Kerr. This was also reported in the paper. Fake news? I don't think so. In 1880 Kerr wrote the minister and explained why he no longer used Cory to assist him. He reported that lighthouse keeper Thomas Campbell's wife, Cory's daughter, had left Campbell to take up with another man and reside in Cory's house "as man and wife." At Campbell's insistence, Kerr tried to persuade her to return when Cory's wife "spoke up in a passion and said she shall never go back to him again." Countenancing this adulterous relationship was enough to get Fred Cory fired!

Meanwhile, William Gage had applied to the minister to fish for a few pike in the waters adjacent to his farm. Gage was now a firm ally and friend of Kerr's, and Kerr supported his application, noting that Gage deserved it "in consequence of the active aid and assistance given to me from time to time, and at all times, in the protection of fish in B. Bay during the last 15 years." However, Kerr knew that the recalcitrant Simon Stipe "would bring down upon me the most vindictive and uncalled for remarks; And which he has been indulging in for quite some time, without any cause."

Kerr advised that the same right Gage was seeking should also be given to Stipe and Thomas Lottridge, another farmer with an inlet named after him. Kerr also noted that pike were "the great enemy" of salmon and trout because they devoured the fry and "it is always desirable to get rid of the pike in a legal way." He recommended a spring season at an annual fee of four dollars. When the licences arrived from Ottawa, Stipe "read it over but declined to accept it."

There was more trouble brewing in Niagara as a result of a dispute between two licensed fishermen, Joseph Gabriel and David Derror. They fished side by side in the river, and due to a dispute, Derror, who was an illiterate Black man, intentionally trespassed on Gabriel's lease, causing some damage. Kerr was asked to referee, and when he found in Gabriel's favour, Gabriel had Derror tried and convicted. Fined and ordered to pay costs—which included the police, the magistrate, and Kerr's expenses—Derror instead chose to serve twenty days in St. Catharine's jail and refused to pay the costs.

Because Derror had no assets, he could not be compelled to pay, but Kerr was ordered to revoke his licence. The Department had to pay the costs, which irked Kerr (and probably got him in trouble in Ottawa). Kerr wrote to Gabriel, saying,

> Last year you lawed away at Dave Derror and now the Department will have to pay the magistrate for trying your case. It is too bad you cannot live and let live. While I am always ready and willing to oblige you ... you must always still bear in mind that I have a perfect right _sometime_ to consider myself as _Overseer_ of fishing, not altogether for the exclusive benefit of Joseph Gabriel ... I will come down shortly and I will endeavour to fix matters for you all, but I don't expect to be able to do so.

In May, Kerr was asked to investigate allegations that the fisheries overseer for Norfolk County, Charles L. Bingham, was not doing his job. This was Kerr's first big investigation for the Department. With his own history with Bingham, he was more than happy to attend to it.

Proceeding to Norfolk, Kerr found that the fishermen who complained about Bingham had all retracted their allegations for some unknown reason. (Threats? Bribes?) However, Kerr noted lots of ill feelings between the pound-net fishermen and the seine fishermen because too many fish were being caught, thereby lowering the price. He was unable to substantiate the allegations of Bingham's drunkenness and that Bingham "is a good officer and an intelligent man, and with more experience will become still more active and efficient." This is another example of Kerr's occasional bad judgment.

In June, more allegations were leveled against Bingham by Norfolk fishermen, and Kerr was instructed to investigate again. The charges were that Bingham was licensing farmers, arbitrarily changing seine limits, and most importantly, accepting money for licences but not issuing the licences or remitting the money to Ottawa. Kerr arranged to meet Bingham in Port Dover and instructed him to bring his diary and letter book. Kerr reviewed his diaries and found that he had been padding his accounts by billing for days he did not work or spending too long on tasks and running up disbursements. Kerr noted, "it is all bosh, white lies! It would pay to keep a close eye on Mr. Bingham as matters now stand and appear." Kerr believed, "it is a regular made up and forged account."

Bingham kept his job but was probably docked pay as a result of Kerr's investigation. To sour things further, in October Kerr recommended that Bingham lose the outer bay at Long Point, which Kerr claimed he could not manage because he lived on the mainland. Kerr recommended the appointment of two Long Point friends as fish guardians. Kerr rationalized, "There will still be sufficient territory left for Mr. Bingham to oversee and protect from depredators." Kerr also noted that Bingham recently "got his boat broken up in pieces and demolished."

Kerr was asked to review Bingham's books for the last half of 1880 (which no doubt mightily pleased Bingham), and again found disparities. Kerr wrote, "From all I have seen of Mr. B. I fear there is little hope of improvement. When I am re-appointed again by Mr. Whitcher and the Department for the Norfolk & Haldimand division, and he is placed under me, he must tow the mark and earn his salary."

In March 1881, Kerr reported further falsities by Bingham. By April, Kerr had taken over Bingham's district, and Kerr was anxious to fix things on Long Point Bay. Noting Bingham's neglect, Kerr boasted, "After a little, by patience and perseverance and a little energy on my part, I will get everything all right. Believe me." That opened a whole new can of worms, and Bingham was looking for some payback. Stay tuned!

Meanwhile back in Niagara, the infighting continued. In October Joe Gabriel reported that his "fishing machine" had been maliciously destroyed.[119] David Derror and John Wadsworth (another bad dude) also had machines nearby, and Kerr had permanently cancelled their licenses, so they were early suspects. On further investigation, Kerr

....

119   This fishing "machine" was some kind of wooden contraption used only for fishing in the Niagara River. It probably used the swift flow of the river to trap fish. Thanks to Terry Boulton of Niagara-on-the-Lake for explaining it to me. By the way, Terry is related to the wicked Bolton brothers. Sorry, Terry!

concluded that the dastardly act was committed by Chester Wadsworth, John Wadsworth's son, who was also a fisherman in Queenston. Kerr noted the machine was worth about $200 plus the loss of fishing. Kerr's request that the Department offer a fifty-dollar reward for information was summarily rejected, "the Department having no funds at its disposal for such a purpose." Not having any solid proof of Wadsworth's guilt, Kerr decided to set an "ambush" to catch him fishing on a Sunday.[120]

Kerr arranged to take the 6:00 a.m. train to the suspension bridge, where he met a good fisherman, James Sheppard Jr., and then proceeded by horse and buggy to Niagara.[121] From 9:00 a.m. until 7:30 p.m., they hid in ambush to catch Wadsworth fishing. He must have been tipped off because while he was in his boat, he was not fishing, though he did taunt Kerr by whistling and singing. Frustrated, Kerr noted, "Although he did not fish he went next door to it, for he handled a spear and his fishing machine." Heading back to Elliott's boarding house, Kerr dejectedly wrote, "I was crippled and sore in legs, calves and thighs, caused by going 15' down the declivity" to the water."[122] He attempted to secure sworn evidence of Sunday fishing, but none could be found. If he could get proof, he swore to put the Wadsworths out of business by seizing their material and cancelling their licence.

1881

By 1881 Kerr was in his sixty-ninth year, and he began to experience some serious health problems. He had experienced periodic bouts of rheumatism in the past and some bowel problems but nothing that seriously affected his ability to attend to his duties. Then in March he began to mention in letters that he was "very sick" and unable to get around.

---

120   It's good to know this cop trick was in full force in the nineteenth century. "If you can't get him for this, get him for that."

121   The GWR didn't run to Niagara-on-the-Lake. People had to go to the suspension bridge near Niagara and take a separate train to get there. Probably to avoid detection, Kerr took a horse and buggy to Niagara-on-the-Lake. The train track ran right down King St. to the water's edge.

122   Elliott's boarding home was called the Whale Inn, although Kerr never referred to it as such.

Reading his diaries, I did not notice any reduction in his activity, but he was clearly not as mobile, mostly just writing from home.

In a letter dated April 11, Kerr wrote, "I have been very sick, part of the time in bed, not able to turn in it, nor able to eat, my principle diet being powders and the contents of medicine bottles! Thank God!!! I am now recovering again and I expect will soon be able to fly around again. In two weeks I was reduced 17 lbs in my weight and size." Obviously feeling better, Kerr reported a bit of derring-do on Burlington Bay in mid-April when he caught three teenagers fishing illegally with their father's net. On his way to see Andrew Gage, "my own son, Fred Kerr, overtook me, our plans were at once made! And Fred and myself were soon after amongst the boys, before they were made aware that I was no longer sick."

Meanwhile, trouble was brewing on Lake Erie as a result of Bingham's failure to fix the fishing ranges, as he had been instructed to do. In April, Kerr visited Port Dover and Turkey Point to try and settle things down, without much success. After one acrimonious session, he noted, "David Moore used threats. Dr. James W. Stuart even came up to my bed room to talk with me." This dispute had a political element; there seemed to be a very bad relationship between some Liberals and some Conservatives. Dr. Stuart, for example, was noted to be "such an enemy of William Wallace, the Conservative M.P. for Norfolk."[123]

Moore and Stuart had their knickers in a knot because Kerr wanted a licence to go to Frank Jackson, who had applied for it first and paid one hundred dollars more than they were offering, and he had paid it upfront. They were not amused. Contrary to Kerr's recommendations, the Department gave Moore and Stuart the grounds they wanted, and Kerr was told to find somewhere else for Jackson. He was not amused.

Noting that Jackson had his ice house at Port Dover, Kerr made a temporary arrangement for Jackson but wrote to the Department, saying, "But next year, please God, if I am alive and well, I hope to be

....

123   William Wallace (Feb. 4, 1820–Aug. 28, 1887) was the MP for Norfolk, from 1872–1882. He also owned the Simcoe newspaper, the *British Canadian*. It later became the *Simcoe Reformer*, which is still published today.

able to provide him with better grounds, near a good market, somewhere near Port Colborne." Jackson's grounds had been previously fished unsuccessfully, but Kerr wrote that he was willing to try it again, saying, "I hope he will succeed." As Jackson's grounds were about one and a half miles from those of Moore and Stuart's, Kerr hoped "no fears may be now apprehended from that quarter."

To prevent the squabbling on Lake Erie over trespassing, Kerr proposed that fishing limits be staked off or marked by buoys. By then everything seemed to be in order, and Kerr hoped everyone would calm down and just fish.

Meanwhile in Toronto, Kerr reported on numerous small fish, shad or alewives, washing up dead on the shore. He had reported similar events for several years, but in 1881 the Toronto newspapers incorrectly blamed the few licensed fishermen for the deaths. Kerr took the opportunity to make some comments: "The clamour of newspaper scribblers, so notoriously false, should never be relied upon. So much for the false, lying, damnable lies and falsehoods of some of the Toronto newspapers." Fake news, 1881 style!

In Niagara, Kerr attempted to referee a dispute between John Bolton and Big Jim Cantwell. Kerr apparently took Cantwell's side and even ordered some fish from him: "Have you got Mrs. Cantwell to smoke the whitefish for me? I want about 4 dozen to send to Ottawa. Keep every thing about you! As a North of Ireland man would say to yourself and with best wishes for your success." Spreading the goodwill around, Kerr also requested four dozen from Thomas Elliott but none from Bolton.

By June, Kerr heard that Bingham was trying to stir things up by making allegations against him. Kerr wrote, "I don't care a fig for anything Bingham has said or may say about me. I am perfectly independent of him, in all things and so I will say no more." Kerr declined to take any further steps against Bingham, noting to Whitcher, "I don't think it would look well for either you or I to go back and rake up Mr. Bingham's shortcomings. I was not appointed to do that!! And so that matter so far as Mr. B is concerned had better be dropped." In addition to not doing his job generally, Kerr proved that Bingham had failed to remit licence money, which would be fraudulent and the subject of criminal prosecution today. However, in 1881 it was swept under the carpet.

In June, Kerr heard that Pat Gray had died, "Drowned in Toronto Bay." He visited with Mrs. Gray to offer his condolences and to see if she still wanted the fishing licence. No mention is made as to whether the death was an accident, a murder, or a suicide. The Department wanted Kerr to explain why there should be any net fishing permitted in Toronto Bay, so Kerr sent a long, detailed report arguing that it was so limited that it would have no impact on angling. However, just a week or so before Gray's death, Kerr warned Gray that he didn't think the Department would permit any net fishing. As we have seen, Patrick Gray suffered a lot of abuse during his career as a Toronto fisherman.

Things were about to heat up again on Lake Erie, and Charles Bingham would be back to try and exact revenge on Kerr. It started when a friend of Kerr's at Port Dover wrote to him about Dr. James W. Stuart. The friend reported, "Stuart said to me the other day that you were a God damned old Scoundrel and that he would do his best to get you bounced." Kerr observed to the minister, "I am in no way alarmed by Dr. Stuart's bad language nor threats." But he did "want to know what I should do in a case of this kind."

Kerr heard that Bingham's boathouse was being sold for a mortgage default, and Kerr wanted to know if it was built with lumber paid for by the government. Kerr also wanted Fishery Guardian Owen Bowers of St. Williams to get him proof that Bingham didn't remit all the licence money to Ottawa, "and I will end all this **humbugging and rascality**. It is time to put a stop to it for all time." Kerr was later advised that the Department did not pay for the boathouse and to drop the matter. Get out the broom again!

The problem at Long Point Bay continued when Bingham helped a fisherwoman, Aspha Ferris, raise a complaint about William Snook, who she accused of fishing on her station. Kerr wanted Snook's version, so Snook wrote a long letter explaining how former Fisheries Overseer John A. Backhouse had displaced him and gave the station to Ferris and William Helmer. Snook had been leasing another station, and Ferris and Helmer wanted him off because a family feud was occurring. Kerr stated that Ferris' complaint was "made up of falsehoods and lies, one lie exceeding the other in wickedness, spite and malice."

Kerr blamed it all on Backhouse "who obtained his position as a fisheries overseer by his efforts to calumniate [slander] Sir John A. MacDonald in a speech he made at Waterford on the Pacific Scandal, and for other dirty acts."[124] Kerr thought he had settled all this the year before with a new survey of the stations. Acting as referee, MP Wallace advised Kerr to support Snook's position.

Bingham then ghost wrote a letter on behalf of William Helmer slandering Kerr for favouring his friends and arbitrarily reassigning fishing stations. Kerr dryly responded, "I am glad to learn I have friends, **but no favourites.**" Helmer (through Bingham) alleged that Kerr was removed from office for his "arbitrary and ungenerous acts." Helmer threatened to sue Kerr, and he told people that "he has put me away from here before and he would do so again!" Kerr recommended that the new licences be issued immediately, "then all this fuss and threats will be ended." Kerr also accused Fishery Guardian McColl of being complicit with Bingham in defrauding the Department. Kerr then summarily dismissed McColl. Another day, another enemy.

In Niagara, Kerr continued his love/hate relationship with Big Jim Cantwell. On hearing that Cantwell has been unwell, Kerr wrote, "I am told that if you drink porter and eat vegetables you will get all right again—shall I send you six or a dozen bottles? Just say the word." In September 1881, Kerr again reported that he had been feeling unwell, presumably with the same complaint: "On Sunday morning last I took the chill again! Just imagine the hot day Sunday was. I got so chilly and cold that woman like, I had to get hot bricks to my feet and scalding hot flannel to my belly before warm circulation was restored and I remained in great agony and pain all day until relieved by Dr. White. I am at the bottles, the pills and the powders again. I am nearly well again, and God willing, I will come down next week."

In a letter to Thomas Elliott, his best Niagara friend, Kerr wrote, "I

....

124   Backhouse replaced Kerr at Norfolk after the Alexander Mackenzie government took over.

was so pained this last sickness that morphine was put in my arm to assuage the pain which it did in about one minute or less. After it was forced into my arm, I fell asleep for about 5 minutes and when I awoke, I was able to say I was better... I am now confined to 3 pills a day and some black stuff in a bottle." So much for nineteenth-century medicine!

By mid-December Kerr seemed to be fully recovered, and he again wrote to Elliott.

> *I am sure you will be all glad to hear that I am now perfectly recovered and in good health again and I feel so well and happy over it. My life, I believe, is prolonged for some years to come... Glory be to God on high. Peace and good will to all mankind, particularly fishermen, their wives and bairn. Powders, pills, injections of poison into my blood and system to kill the disease has cured me most effectively. Besides, I must not leave out all the brandy I had to take.*

Kerr became noticeably more religious in his later years, often giving praise and thanks. Always Church of England, he was a member of the Church of Ascension, which is still located at the corner of John St. and Charleton Ave. in downtown Hamilton. It would have been a relatively easy ride there, but I can find no record of him ever having attended church services! In fact, he was frequently on the hop on Sundays enforcing the Sabbath prohibitions, which was a bit hypocritical.

Kerr alluded to his curious relationship with Whitcher in August. Whitcher was heading to Manitoba on official business, and Kerr wrote, "When you leave Ottawa for Manitoba let me know and I will meet you in Toronto. Perhaps you may want me to do something for you." Was Kerr looking for an invite to tag along, or was some financial chicanery going on with money being exchanged between the two? Maybe he just wanted to carry Whitcher's canoe![125]

---

125 Manitoba entered Confederation in 1870. In 1885 it was the site of Riel's North-West Rebellion, which was of considerable interest to Kerr. I believe Whitcher might have settled briefly in Manitoba after he left the Department of Marine and Fisheries.

The battle between Kerr and Bingham simmered through the fall, with each man trying to achieve his objective. Kerr's objective was to prove Bingham's fraud and settle the Lake Erie disputes. Bingham's objective was to get his old job back or, if not, to exact revenge on Kerr. Receiving information that the government boat that Bingham claimed was smashed up off Long Point, was, in fact, in perfectly sound condition, Kerr sent his fishery guardian to find it. Bingham recruited Dr. Stuart of Port Dover as his willing ally in his campaign against Kerr and had him circulate the story that as soon as Bingham repaid the Department one hundred dollars, he would be reinstated.

In November, Kerr's fish guardian had an encounter with Bingham, who claimed he had been reinstated. He reported to Kerr, "Bingham claimed you and I were not fit but only to be ready to hold the pot for the Tory Commissioner [Whitcher] to deposit his night soil in. He said you and I had done our damnedest to hoist him but we could not do it."[126] There are other occasional references to Bingham's misdeeds in Kerr's diaries, but by May 1882, Kerr reported that Bingham, his wife, and his mother had moved to Michigan to enter the lumber business. Kerr mused, "What a pity—whiskey done it all." As for the Long Point fishermen, "Serenity a common event now."

In 1881 Kerr got mixed up in a lawsuit involving John Bolton of Niagara. Bolton was sued by Adam Crooks, then Ontario's Minister of Education,[127] regarding his use of the beach to fish his seine lines. Crooks claimed to own the land and sued Bolton to secure his ownership. Kerr found that Crooks was not on title to the land in question and had never paid municipal taxes. More importantly, the suit put into question the Fisheries Department's claim that it had exclusive ownership of all shorelines for fishing.

Bolton was no favourite of Kerr's, but Kerr found him a lawyer[128] and gathered evidence on his behalf. The suit was brought in the Court of

---

126 In case it's unclear, this means to "carry his shit."
127 Adam Crooks (Dec. 11, 1827–Dec. 28, 1885) was a Liberal MPP from 1871–1883. His bio notes that he suffered from physical and mental problems toward the end of his life.
128 Bolton used Kerr's own lawyer, R. R. Waddell.

Chancery[129] in Toronto, which would be expensive for a poor fisherman, so Kerr attempted to get the Department to fund his defence by trying to get them to see the important legal principle that was in play.[130] Kerr enlisted the political support of Niagara MP J. B. Plumb and offered him support in return, not just from himself but also from the fishermen and Kerr's own sons, for as property owners in Niagara they were able to vote there. Kerr asserted, "Have I not already pledged myself to you, to vote and do all in my power for you. But no inducement on Earth can change me: all my family for ages past have always been conservative, and neither by word, act or deed shall I do anything to mar your position as Member at present and candidate for re-election in 1882." Kerr never went back on his conservative friends: "I cannot be bought and I am never for sale!"

On December 15, Kerr reported that the case of *Crooks v. Bolton* was settled, by which, it appears, Crooks was granted title to the land provided he agreed not to interfere with seine hauling in front of his property. It was a compromise that worked for the benefit of all concerned, including the Fisheries Department.

As Kerr sat in his house on Christmas Day writing letters, he must have been relieved that the year was over and that he was back in good health. To the fishery guardian at Long Point he wrote, "I wish you the compliments of the season and many happy returns. Let nothing trouble you, leave all your affairs in the hands of God, the great architect and geometrician of the Universe, who alone cares for us, and who, as friend and father, protects us." Things must have seemed pretty good to Kerr. Lake Erie and Niagara had calmed down, Toronto was pretty well done, and Hamilton was quiet. Unfortunately, clouds were on the horizon, both personal and professional.

1882

An amusing incident took place in Niagara toward the end of 1881. Kerr had Thomas Elliott manage his property in Niagara, and Elliott

----

129 The Court of Chancery is a court of equity or natural justice instead of a court of common law. First-year law school nonsense.

130 To no one's surprise, the Department refused to pay.

was supervising the building of a fence for him when he was threatened by a butcher named Best. Elliott wrote to Kerr to complain, and Kerr wrote back, "I don't understand what Best the butcher has to do with the place. I will have him taken up and punished for threatening. In England a Butcher is not allowed on a jury.[131] Butchers are always opposed to fishermen, for the sale of fish hurts the butcher's market. Let Best pull my fence down at his peril. The Town of Niagara has always a number of obstructionists in it and I don't wonder at this threat." Was Bolton behind this? Or Cantwell or the Wadsworths? Who knows? There were a number of possible suspects!

On hearing of the death of David Ward, Kerr wrote, "There is now only one licensed fisherman on Toronto Island whom I met there in the year 1865, others, dead and gone. May they rest in peace and with due respects." Regarding Ward himself, Kerr reminisced, "Mr. Ward, although apparently rough at first sight in outward appearance, was a very kindly, warm hearted good natured man, most civil and obliging to every man."

In 1882, commercial sturgeon fishing in the Great Lakes became popular. They had always been caught but were not considered a desirable species and were often thrown back or used as fertilizer. Suddenly, they became valuable both for their meat and for their roe or caviar. Worldwide, there are about twenty-seven species of sturgeon, and they are generally long-lived, deep-water bottom feeders. In the Great Lakes, male sturgeon can live for 50–60 years and females up to 150 years, and they weigh up to 240 pounds. They are the oldest and largest species in the Great Lakes.

In the Niagara River, they were generally caught on long lines baited with minnows. In other areas they were caught in nets, particularly pound nets. The commercial sturgeon fishery collapsed by about 1900 due to over-harvesting. In Niagara the sturgeon were often shipped by train to Buffalo. From Lake Erie the destinations were Buffalo, Cleveland, Toledo, and Detroit. Naturally, Kerr was tasked with licensing these fishermen, who often also fished with seines or gill nets. In

....

131 Surprisingly, that was probably true because it was thought that butchers, being too used to blood and gore, could not appreciate the gravity of violent crime!

Niagara, where the river does not freeze due to the current of about four miles per hour, the annual fee was five dollars.

Kerr noted that Big Jim Cantwell had initiated commercial sturgeon fishing and that once caught, their heads and skin were cut off, and the meat was smoked. Kerr found it delicious and wrote that they sold for five cents a pound in Buffalo. Kerr painted an amusing picture of 132-pound Bob Taylor fishing in his 16-foot skiff and catching an 8-foot long 150-pound sturgeon and cutting off its 31-pound head before selling the rest for $3.90. How did he manage to land such a giant fish? Well, at least the Niagara fishermen had something new to squabble over.

One such grievance was that Kerr had licensed two Americans working with Cantwell. Jack Bolton lost his temper, as usual, and threatened them. Kerr wrote to advise them that they were fishing legally "in British waters and our laws will protect you. Stand your ground, fast and firmly." By the end of March 1882, Kerr noted that sturgeon fishing "has brought about $3,000 into the poor little Town of Niagara."

Sturgeon lines were left in the water and taken up later, usually within a day or two. There were reports of lines being cut and fish being stolen and fish heads and offal being left on the beach. Kerr had a notice posted that "Roguery of this kind must be instantly stopped." In a private letter to Elliott, he vowed "A stop must be finally placed on Jack's {Bolton] domineering, overbearing conduct."

To promote the sturgeon fishery, Kerr obtained about thirty pounds of sturgeon, which he gave to various prominent Hamiltonians, including businessmen, politicians, and newspaper reporters. Kerr also wanted to send twenty pounds to Ottawa! Despite the ongoing hostilities between the Niagara fishermen, Kerr tranquilly noted, "I am writing this letter occasionally looking out of a window [from his house], south aspect, just 4 p.m. Sunday afternoon with no reason whatever for commencing a quarrel, with either man, woman or child. I am at peace with everyone from Big Jim and Jack Bolton on down to Henry Podkins." Not for long.

Kerr sent the sturgeon to S. P. Bauset, who wrote him a thank-you note: "That smoked sturgeon is simply utter[like out of this world]. I had some for breakfast this morning and both myself and my brother in law, Senator Dumouchel, pronounced it too too!! [like too much]"

Although the case of Adam Crooks and Jack Bolton had been settled, there was a related case of Crooks v. Dr. Pyne of Niagara. Pyne had bought the Secord farm on the lake, which included the "Old Indian Encampment," and Crooks was claiming part of this land. Kerr had learned that the Department had evidence from a former fisheries overseer, John McCuaig, that supported Crooks' claim, and he had notified the lawyers. Accordingly, Kerr was subpoenaed to testify in Toronto at the Court of Chancery.

Kerr duly appeared at Osgoode Hall[132] on February 6 and gave his evidence before Vice Chancellor J. H. Ferguson and won the case for Crooks. Commenting on the previous case of *Crooks v. Bolton,* Kerr noted, "Jack Bolton has had a fortunate escape from being put in [jail] for the costs of the Court in his suit. It should do him some good, but it won't."

A major dispute between certain fishermen in Niagara and Kerr heated up in February 1882. Kerr had slightly realigned the fishing stations to the satisfaction of no one and to the particular consternation of Big Jim Cantwell and Edward Wooten, who had complained to MP J. B. Plumb. Attempting to explain his reasons to Plumb, Kerr said, "I pity any gentleman, an MP like you, who has to depend upon such flimsy supporters as Big Jim and Wooten."

To the Long Point fishermen and fisherwoman, Mrs. Aspha Ferris, Kerr wrote, "In order to prevent all disputes and quarreling in future amongst you people, who are nearly all blood relations, the ranges must be fixed on shore by placing high poles firmly in the ground." Poles were placed but sometimes surreptitiously relocated, causing more disputes.

Gerrymandering is the practice of redistributing an electoral district to produce a more favourable result for one candidate or party.[133] It still happens in the United States, which is shameful and usually based along

---

132   I argued a few cases in the Court of Appeal at Osgoode Hall. I'm pretty sure I lost every one of them.

133   "Gerrymandering" is a word made up from "gerry," named for Gerry Elbridge, US vice president from 1813– 1814, plus "mander," as in "salamander," named for the slimy amphibian.

racial lines. Prior to the June 1882 federal election, it was happening in Canada to a considerable extent and was just as disgraceful then as it is now. As noted by Richard Gwyn in his bio of Sir John A. MacDonald, *Nation Maker,* the purpose was to "hive the Grits."

Kerr's own riding of Wentworth South was itself rigged to secure a Conservative victory for R. R. Waddell by adding Grimsby and Caistor to its boundaries.[134] Plumb's riding of Lincoln was also altered, and it was expected that Plumb would lose, which he did. Kerr had attended Waddell's nomination meeting and was aware of the gerrymandering. In February he wrote to Plumb to advise him that the fix was in: "Waddell says you are to be shelved by an appointment as Bank Inspector and so Niagara is to go into the arrangement."[135]

In a later note to Plumb, Kerr stated, "I may mention for your own information and for Sir John's and the Conservatives generally, that this boundary question is the only thing upon which adverse opinions are expressed as regards Sir John A. and his administration. I mean as amongst some Conservatives. Of course, as regards Grits, they are all down on Sir John." So, it seems even Kerr was uncomfortable with this despicable gerrymandering.

It wasn't all partisan politics with Kerr, and he did have Liberal friends, such as James Wynne of Queenston, who worked in the customs department there. On learning that Wynne had died, he wrote to Plumb to see if he could secure a position for Wynne's son to help the widow with "her position in life, with a large family." To Fanny Wynne he wrote, "I received your sorrowful letter conveying to me the sad intelligence of your husband's death and burial, which I deplore as a friend and sympathize with you in your bereavement." He also said he would try and get Plumb to have her appointed as postmistress. I don't know if he succeeded, but Wynne's son turned out to be a bad guy, and Kerr regretted helping him.

Meanwhile, some fresh skirmishes developed in Ashbridge's Bay, part of the fallout from the banning of net fishing. One of the Leslieville fishermen

---

134   It did not work. Liberal Lewis Springer defeated Waddell by forty-eight votes.
135   In fact, he got a better reward. He was appointed to the Senate in January 1883. He later became speaker of the Senate.

who had lost the ability to fish was John Gunsell, a good fisherman who had been paralyzed on one side, presumably from a stroke. Kerr tried to get him a new licence at Presquille but was refused by the Department, and Kerr felt sorry for him. So, Gunsell made some money by running Kerr around Ashbridge's Bay looking for the inevitable illegal fishing.

Kerr wrote to the minister to report that people were shooting pike in the water, which Kerr called not only illegal but also "unsportsmanlike," and he wanted to put a stop to it, together with net and longline fishing. Kerr hired Gunsell to help him patrol Ashbridge's Bay, and they found nets and a long line with 113 hooks, which Kerr thought belonged to Billy and George Lang. They seized the nets and line, and the next day a newspaper article appeared in the *Mail* implying that Kerr was not doing his job.

The Langs were bad guys who had burned another fisherman's house down and used the iron of his stove for net anchors. Kerr wanted justice. To set the record straight, he advised the paper of the real story, and they published a second article, naming Kerr and giving him credit.

Another flare-up occurred at Long Point involving William Snook, whom Kerr had previously taken pity on and helped out with his lease. Now Snook was the problem. He hadn't paid his lease because he thought he was paying too much. He was also causing vexation with the other fishermen by moving the marker stakes and trespassing on their waters. Kerr wanted Whitcher to "**give him a reprimand**" as "all the fishermen here are doing well, and peace and plenty reigns there, except with Snook." Kerr also noted, "I always treat him with much consideration from the fact that he is lame."

Snook took matters into his own hands by having the grounds resurveyed without Kerr's knowledge or consent. It became clear that old adversary William Helmer had been moving the stakes but that Snook wanted his grounds back and more. He wanted compensation from the Department and to be reimbursed for the surveying costs. Kerr went to Long Point to make it clear that Snook was only getting what was his as originally surveyed and that if he wanted compensation he could sue Helmer himself. Kerr also told him to: "live at peace with his neighbours—all brother fishermen."

The Niagara front opened up a new round of hostilities when Big Jim Cantwell and Wooten asked Kerr to settle their dispute. Reporting on the meeting he arranged, Kerr wrote, "I believe that if Ontario was searched from end to end, two more arbitrary, overbearing individuals could not be found amongst our fishermen. Such insults and threats and bad language as I was obliged to put up with. I was only too glad to escape from a scene of blasphemy." However, the dispute seems to have been settled.

By 1882 it was clear that Kerr had become the clean-up man for the Department in Southern Ontario. He was asked to investigate the fisheries overseer for the lower Grand River, W. Allan McCrea, and promptly proceeded there to have a look around. He was quite familiar with the river, so he had no trouble getting to the root of the problem. Knowing illegal fishing was occurring, Kerr asked McCrea why he hadn't acted. "His reply was he had no funds to employ a man to assist him, and he did not feel like going alone!"

Apparently, McCrea had inherited the job from his brother-in-law, Henry Lawe, who had moved to Manitoba.[136] In addition to neglect of duty, he had also failed to remit fifty dollars he had collected. Kerr made an interesting observation: "Everything has been managed loosely, he is a young man of about 20 and he is a brother to Miss McCrea, who was seduced by a married man in Chatham and who was tried last fall in Buffalo for murder. Miss McCrea, having gone to Buffalo to hide her shame, died there in the hands of an abortionist."

McCrea's father, a man of about Kerr's age, wanted Kerr to visit his house to discuss matters, but Kerr had to "politely decline, as I was tired, wet and covered with mud after a 44 mile drive and a five mile boat ride." Kerr requested permission to "smarten up" young McCrea. Shortly thereafter the McCreas paid about half the money owing to the Department, and Kerr recommended that he receive his pay.

Despite Kerr's expressed concerns and young McCrea's probable fraudulent conduct, young McCrea was appointed by the Department as the fisheries overseer for the lower Grand. Kerr wrote him a letter of

....

136   I don't know what the big attraction was in Manitoba in 1880, but it seems that a number of people Kerr knew were moving there. Maybe to get away from him!

congratulations, which was really just an epistle on how he should act and behave: "Be active and industrious and intelligent in the discharge of your public duties as Overseer. Be firm and determined for at your age 23, your career in life should be fixed and established. You can do a great deal by kindliness to the fishermen and avoid being tyrannical."

Kerr was perplexed when young McCrea wrote back to advise that it was his father who had gotten the appointment, not him. Kerr sought clarification from Bauset who angrily wrote to McCrea Jr. to advise that he had the appointment and that he "must never deceive the fisheries department." Bauset wrote, "You had better take the oath of office and obey the instructions." I find it curious that the Department didn't just sack him for pulling this stunt on top of what Kerr had told them.

Ultimately, however, it was McCrea Sr. who was reappointed, and Kerr was not happy because McCrea was already receiving a $500 annual gratuity from a previous government job. Kerr considered this double dipping and that his fisheries salary should be reduced to take this into consideration. Despite McCrea Jr.'s obvious deficiencies, Kerr expressed disappointment that he himself did not get the job, which is a sorry reflection on McCrea Sr. At Kerr's instance, McCrea Sr. later received a letter of reprimand from Whitcher for dereliction of duty: "I think it should straighten him up, but then! In his own opinion and estimate of himself, he knows more (too too much) than all the rest of the human family."

Seemingly never satisfied with the enormous amount of work on his hands, Kerr wanted even more. He wrote to advise that undersized fish were being sold in Hamilton from Georgian Bay and Southampton and that illegal fishing was taking place at Port Burwell on Lake Erie. He wanted to go have a look around, but when he didn't get permission, he sulked in a letter to a fishery guardian: "You and I must be satisfied where our lot is at present cast—and so mote it be."

Kerr was excited about the forthcoming election and on May 15 noted, "House will rise on Tuesday!! Election will soon follow!!!" By then he was overtly political, even in his official correspondence with Whitcher and Bauset, where he frequently noted which members he would help and how many votes he thought he could get for them. It is startling to see this open politicizing of his position considering how risky it could have been to his career if the Conservatives lost.

Writing to his friend and MP at Simcoe, William Wallace, Kerr requested a copy of the voters list in order to help Wallace get re-elected: "I will assist you all I can in your election." Kerr even instructed his fishery guardian at Norfolk to get out the vote for Wallace. Can you imagine the clamour it would create today if federal employees were told to do this? It is almost Trump-like in its outrageousness. I can't help noting the parallel between America today with its two-party system and Canada in 1882 with only two parties. The effect is polarization and division.

Due to the gerrymandering of MacDonald's Conservatives, Plumb's riding in Niagara was abolished and became part of the Lincoln riding held by J. C. Rykert.[137] By agreement, Plumb ran in Wellington, where he lost. Awarded the consolation prize of a Senate posting, Plumb remained somewhat useful, but Kerr began corresponding with Rykert and offering to help him get elected.

The winter of 1882 was mild with little snow and no substantial ice on Burlington Bay. Kerr reported that he hadn't had a sleigh ride and that there was no ice fishing. Hoping for an early start to fishing season, Kerr was disappointed with a wet and wild spring that even by early June was tempestuous. A severe storm did a lot of damage, ripping out seine and pound nets all over his district. The water was three feet higher than normal, and Kerr observed that Toronto Island was now four separate islands.

The election was in full swing, and on June 8 Kerr wrote in a letter to Elliott, "The Right Honourable Sir John A. MacDonald is to be at Dundurn this evening, where no doubt there will be at least 10,000 to hear him speak. I am going down to the train to be at the reception… Electioneering is the all engrossing question of the day!! May God protect our Right and Just Cause, and Queen and Country." In the days leading up to the June 20 election, Kerr wrote to many of his fishermen to get out the vote.

On June 15, Kerr reported being "flung out of my buggy on last Thursday afternoon into a muddy drain and except a few bad scratches,

---

137 John Charles Rykert (Mar. 10, 1832–Dec. 28, 1913) was a Conservative politician and lawyer from St. Catharines who was an MP from 1878–1891.

all wet and dirty, clothes and face. I came off better than I expected." Kerr was on Barton Street heading east to round up voters when the accident occurred, rendering him "flat as a flounder" in the ditch. So badly was he muddied that when he got home, "I had to take all off." He later wrote, "You may imagine what it is for 232-pounds to come with full force as I did into that mud creek." He would be seventy years old in eight days.

Heading to Niagara on June 19, Kerr voted early there before taking the train home to Hamilton, where he voted a second time in Wentworth. I presume that was legal at the time. Referencing MacDonald's resounding victory, Kerr wrote, "I am glad and feel happy now that the excitement is all over."

Writing to Whitcher on the day before his birthday, Kerr said, "On tomorrow, with God's blessing I hope the sun will go down on my 70th year. I feel so thankful that God has been pleased to allow me to live out the allotted life of man."[138] As for the mare that "flung me into the drain," he said, "I bought her just recently for $100; I will never ride behind her again; she is treacherous, besides, I have three other better steady horses." Kerr would need steady horses for the years to come.

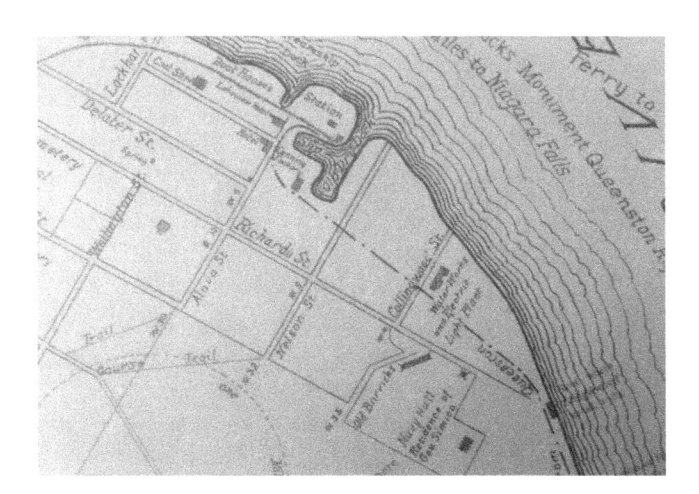

Detail of Niagara on the Lake map, showing shoreline, 1894.
Niagara Historical Society and Museum

....

138 "Our days may come to seventy years, or eighty if our strength endures." (Psalm 90:10)

Caught!

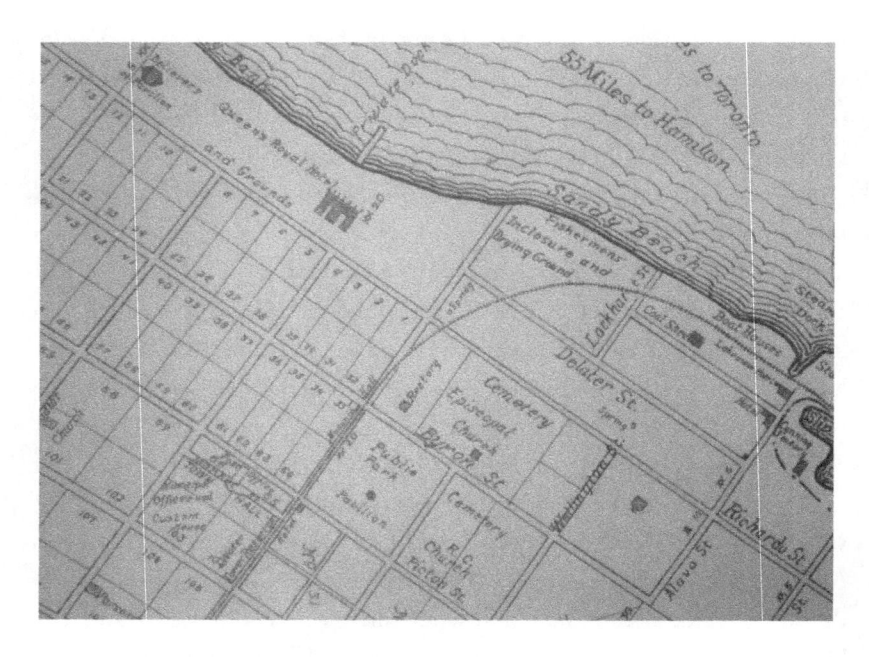

Another detail of Niagara on the Lake map, showing fishing area, 1894. Niagara Historical Society and Museum.

THE BEACH FISHERMEN.

Stormy Meeting at John Dynes'.

For some days past word was sent around amongst the fishermen of Burlington Beach to rally at Mr. John Dynes' hotel, and last evening a considerable number of them had assembled. Mr. Frederick N. Corey having been chiefly instrumental in calling the meeting, was asked by a brother fisherman what business was to be brought forward. Corey arose and made a speech, attacking the Inspector, Mr. J. W. Kerr, in the most savage manner, declaring that he should be dismissed from the position, as he (Corey) had plenty of charges to bring against him.

Another fisherman present said he had plenty of grievances, too, and that Fred. Corey had been the cause of most of them. At the time he (Corey) was in the employ of Mr. Kerr there was nothing too mean for him to be engaged in both as regards the persecution of his brother fishermen, and illegal fishing as well, and now that his services were not required any longer by Mr. Kerr, he turned Turk on one who not long ago he had pronounced the "best and only man in Canada." Mr. Corey would neither move nor second a resolution to have the grievances spoken of investigated. He said he would rather keep quiet and let some of the others do it.

The meeting was a pretty stormy one, and the instigator of the gathering seemed to have let loose a hornets' nest at his ears.

FISHERMEN.

A meeting of the fishermen was held last evening at John Dyne's hotel, on the Beach. Fred. Corey made a speech attacking Inspector Kerr savagely, but was reminded by his brother fishermen that the most severe persecution they had received was while he (Corey) was in Mr. Kerr's employ. The meeting was a stormy one, and ended about where it began.

Frederick N. Corey, a Burlington Beach fisherman, called a meeting of his brethren at Corey's Hotel yesterday, for the purpose, ostensibly, of condemning the conduct of Inspector Kerr. After Corey had concluded his vituperative remarks, other fishermen plainly stated that Corey had had some spite against Mr. Kerr, whose employ he was formerly in, and the meeting ended in a censure upon the convener. N. Corey was recently before the Magistrate for an attempt to throw a train off the Hamilton and North-Western Railway track, but, owing to a breach in the chain of evidence against him, he escaped punishment.

Newspaper clippings found in Kerr diary, about Fred Corey's attempted revolt. ROM

Toadies.

One of the meanest things on earth is a toady. The bluntest, roughest creature that independence ever made is preferable to a fawning, cringing toady, who for the sake of money or favor praises what he detests, flatters without admiring, changes his opinions at a nod, and would lick the dust from the shoes of one in power could he further his own ends thereby.

With some people the toady passes for an amiable soul who likes to please, but could they see him with those from whom he can gain nothing, they would discover their mistake. How he snubs such people! What bitter things he can say; how well he can give the cold shoulder. All the venom he hides when it is his interest to do so, he vents upon those who have neither money nor influence. His very face changes; his smiles are gone; he is cold and snappish; he scowls and frowns.

Wretched toady! Happily, those on whom he fawns are seldom taken in by him, and more happily still, he is a rare specimen of human nature.

The days of kings and courtiers are well nigh over, and republics do not foster the toady. He is dying out, and when at last he shall be but a memory, who will not be glad?

Newspaper clipping found in Kerr diary. Kerr did not like "toadies". ROM

Ned Hanlan, the Sculler of the World, c.1878. Library and Archives Canada

Thomas Elliot's Whale Inn, at Niagara. Niagara Historical Society and Museum.

How He Fell.—The other day Mr. J. W. Kerr, Fishery Overseer for Ontario, visited Toronto in order to receive the returns necessary to be made by fishermen at this season of the year. After crossing to the Island, and seeing that all was right about Gibralter Point, Mr. Kerr thought, as the day was fine, and the ice was inviting, that he would walk across to the city, but herein he forgot that years had deprived him of that suppleness which is the salvation of youth on such dangerous footing. He had proceeded about a hundred yards from the shore when both feet passed from under him and he landed on his back on the ice, seeing more stars in a few moments than he supposed could possibly be stowed away in the firmament. Simultaneously with his tumble the ice cracked for a distance of about half a mile, the reports resembling very much the discharge of a park of artillery, the water gushing up in considerable quantity, and causing those who were disposed to laugh at the Overseer's mishap to slide for the shore at their best speed. A boy, however, remained in the vicinity and to him Mr. K. appealed to signal an ice-boat so that that he could secure a passage across. The boy looked at Mr. K. for a moment, and then replied, "I guess not, Mister, there's too much water and cracking round yer for this chicken to go there." Mr. Kerr managed to recover his hat, walking-cane, muffler and other "dunnage," and hoisting his scarf on the end of his stick brought those in the ice-boat to his assistance, when he reached the metropolis without further mishap.

Newspaper clipping found in Kerr diary.
Account of Kerr's fall through the ice in Ashbridge's Bay. ROM

1878–1882 – The Nation Builder is Back! 165

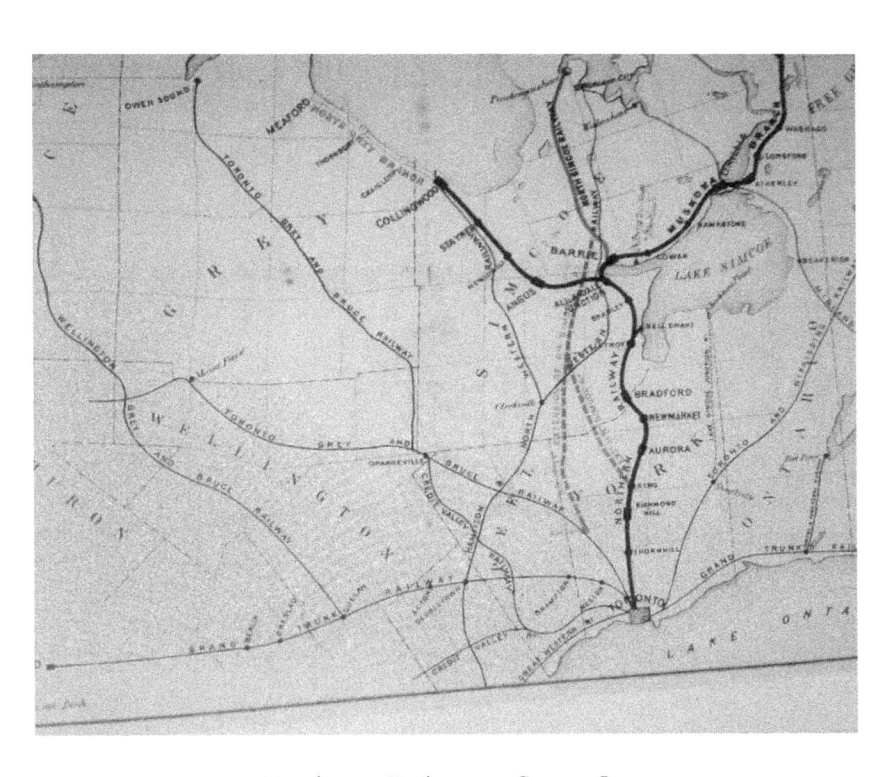

Map showing Kerr's route to Georgian Bay.

Wardell's farmhouse near Selkirk, Ontario on Lake Erie. Photo by Joel Kerr, 2019.

Chapter 11
1882–1886 – England Expects Every Man to Do His Duty

Not only did Plumb and Waddell lose the election, so did Kerr's friend at Simcoe, William Wallace. He had been an important ally in Kerr's squabbles with the Long Point and Port Dover fishermen, and he would be missed. By July, Kerr learned that large parties of men were taking steamers to Long Point to fish on Sundays "under the nose organ of Alfred Marsh, Overseer of Long Point." Kerr humorously noted, "It may be that he will attend to it but I think he is too slow on the march." Of the forty men fishing, Kerr learned the names of eleven and passed the information on to John I. Mackenzie of the Long Point Company.

Disappointed that he did not have all forty names, Kerr decided prosecuting the eleven "is too trifling to take hold of. Besides, we might not succeed in convicting them! From what I have heard, Mr. Alfred Marsh knows nothing whatever about it." Kerr decided instead to chew out March and post notices warning of dire consequences for Sunday fishing: "It is time to stop it and stopped it will be. And so mote it be!!!"

In October 1882, Kerr attended the Conservative Party convention held in Shaftesbury Hall in Toronto as a delegate from Niagara. Holding 1,700 people, Shaftesbury Hall was the largest auditorium in Toronto. It was built as part of the YMCA in 1872. Kerr proudly noted, "I was in the big crowd in Shaftesbury Hall & I heard the Grand Man of Canada address the great audience."[139]

After returning from Toronto, Kerr learned that Jack Bolton had built a fence at Niagara that prevented Thomas Elliott from accessing his seine fishing grounds. This was the opening salvo in a long and bitter dispute amongst the Niagara fishermen that led to Elliott losing his mind and becoming a permanent invalid, much to the dismay and the expense of Kerr.

One of the fishermen in Niagara was Joseph Masters, who also operated the ferry between Niagara and Youngstown, NY. His son, Joseph E. Masters, was born in 1871[140] and was a very active man in Niagara, holding numerous official positions including reeve and mayor. Assisting his father in fishing from an early age, he knew everyone involved in this saga, including Kerr, Elliott, and Bolton. Masters wrote extensively on Niagara people, events, homes, and businesses. His writings, under the title *Niagara Reminiscences*, have been put online by the Niagara Historical Society. This 717-page opus is magnificent in its description of Niagara and is mandatory reading for anyone interested in the area's history. It is also well indexed, and the Historical Society deserves a great deal of credit for this project.[141]

Growing up on King Street near the lake, the Masters' family were next-door neighbours with the Elliotts, and Joseph Masters had high praise for them. They were "next door neighbours for 14 years and could not have been better ones. Kindly and generous, God rest them." Jack Bolton was described as a "stout, portly figure" whose nickname was "Fluffy." He was reported to have been involved in a rescue on the lake. How could a cad like Bolton have had a nickname like "Fluffy"?

Masters would have been eleven years old in 1882, and he was aware of Bolton's fence. He reported, "The last time I saw Tommy Elliott in his right mind he was standing looking sadly at the wire fence Jack Bolton had put up and which put an end to his [seine] hauling." Describing

---

139 Built at the corner of Queen and James Streets, it was demolished in 1901 after having been renamed the Bijou Theatre.
140 Joseph E. Masters (Aug. 14, 1871–Aug. 7, 1955).
141 The Niagara Historical Society Museum is definitely worth a visit. Interesting buildings, interesting displays, and friendly, helpful staff.

Elliott, Masters noted, "Poor Tommy Elliot lost his mind when he was growing old, and for years he might be seen staring from a window, near the rear of the house, a pathetic figure with a long white beard and hair."[142]

Elliott wrote to Kerr on September 18 to advise him about the fence and to request that something be done about it. He had spoken to Plumb, the defeated Conservative MP, who had told him the fence had to be removed. Kerr immediately wrote to the minister to seek instructions: "I recommend that you will be pleased to stop Mr. John Bolton, in this domineering, overbearing way of his towards his brother fishermen." Kerr noted that Elliott and his father had fished the space for twenty years and that for fifty years it had been a public place.

Kerr consulted his lawyer, R. R. Waddell, who had curiously advised that they should take the law into their own hands and tear the fence down, but Kerr advised caution and recommended they wait until the Department instructed him: "I do really think, when a man like Bolton continues to give so much annoyance, he should be told his licenses in future will not be renewed." Apparently throwing caution to the wind, a few days later, Kerr wrote to Jim Cantwell, who was also affected by Bolton's fence: "Have you pulled down Jack Bolton's fence yet! I laid every particular as you and Elliott gave them to me, before the Fisheries Department; so, we may be expecting **squalls** from there soon!"

Kerr was on good terms with Cantwell or was at least trying to stay on good terms by writing him chatty letters. On September 24, Kerr wrote, "We are all well and since the present natural weather set in I have got to be myself again, just 230-pounds. No use in my challenging you to run now! For after we started I would leave you so far behind! You would never catch me again!" Masters described Cantwell as "a big hearty man, a typical son of the Old Sod" [Ireland] and that his wife Kate "was a character too." As a Catholic and self-professed Fenian, there was not a lot of natural affinity between Kerr and Big Jim.

Waiting for an answer from Ottawa, Kerr proceeded to pick another

....

142   Thomas Elliott, born in 1824 in New York State, lived on in madness until his death on Feb. 4, 1899. He had three daughters, Adelaide (1866), Emily (1868), and Sarah (1870), who were friends with Kerr's youngest daughters.

fight with McCrea on the Grand River, admonishing him again for not doing his job. McCrea wrote to Whitcher alleging that Kerr had failed to remit licence fees to Ottawa. Not surprisingly, Kerr responded vigorously to this falsehood, indicating that McCrea was motivated by a desire for revenge. Kerr stated, "This made old McCrea mad and it appears by his report… that a bad feeling is still boiling up in his miserable mind and disposition about the matter."

In his usual thorough manner, Kerr dismantled McCrea's allegation by alluding to previous correspondence and enlisted the man whose money he supposedly did not remit to assist him: "You will perceive McCrea, through his ignorance and revenge, misstates facts and attempts to mislead the Commissioner, and cast a slur on you and I… We must and shall defend our reputation and let the consequences befall McCrea." McCrea received a letter of reprimand from Whitcher, to Kerr's glee.

Still not having heard anything by early October, Kerr wrote to Elliott again, hoping to hear that the police had pulled Bolton's fence down. No such luck. Apparently, Whitcher was heading to Long Point for another duck shooting marathon, so Kerr hoped he would get instructions in person and maybe even get him to visit Niagara. In a follow-up letter to Cantwell, Kerr noted, "My object is to live on peaceably for the rest of my days, hoping, in the end, God will through the redemption of his blessed son, save and protect my soul from Hell."

Not content to wait any longer for instructions from Ottawa, Kerr decided to take matters into his own hands and implored Elliott to go ahead and tear down the fence: "You must not be too soft any longer. You must fight for your rights. Pull the fence down and let Bolton take you up [to court] if he dares." Kerr sent Elliott ten dollars to assist with legal expenses and promised more if required: "As J. W. Kerr, a fishery officer, I am guided by my instructions… and I cannot be a partisan, but as J. W. Kerr, your private friend 18 years, I say clear the fence out of your way. It is a duty you owe your wife and family that you now stand firm and act the man, and defend your own lawful rights against Jack Bolton, a **Bully**."

Kerr noted that on his first visit to Niagara in May 1865, Bolton had taken advantage of an earlier bout of Elliott's mental illness to get a hold of his grounds but that Kerr had stopped him, "but from that day to this, Bolton's applications for the grounds is periodical, so that the time has arrived when you must finally put a settler for his encroachments on your rights." Kerr also noted, "you have Big Jim and every fisherman in Niagara on your side and to prove to you that I am with you, heart and hand, you will find $10 enclosed."

Kerr went to Niagara to inspect the fence and found that Bolton had also put a square wooden box five feet out in the water that prevented any seine hauling on the beach. The Niagara Town Council had "empowered the Mayor of Niagara to remove the fence put up by Bolton," but this fresh outrage still prevented Elliot or anyone else from fishing from the beach. Kerr disingenuously wrote to Bauset, "Without instructions to myself personally, I have no desire to act on either one side or the other, even though it is clearly illegal under the Fisheries Act."

For unknown reasons (maybe he wore out his welcome), Whitcher was not asked to visit Long Point, and Kerr had to write to him on October 16 to advise him of this, thus eliminating an opportunity to settle the Bolton and Elliott matter face to face. Not to be denied, Kerr later found out that Whitcher was shooting ducks in Campbell's Bay, Quebec.

On a Sunday night near the end of October, Kerr was "lying in ambush on the bank of the Niagara River… in company with police constable Curtis" when he found Chester Wadsworth, son of John Wadsworth (remember him?), using his "machine" to fish in the river. Kerr arrested him and had him hauled before J. P. Kerby in St. Catharines, where he was fined one dollar plus five dollars for expenses, thereby exacting some measure of revenge for the damage Wadsworth Sr. had caused years before to Joseph Gabriel. Kerr had a long memory. Wadsworth later blamed Gabriel for tipping Kerr off, which Kerr denied.

Things got kind of ominous when Kerr offered to obtain four pounds of dynamite with fuses and caps for Jim Cantwell, but no mention was made of the intended use. It appears that Bolton's fences were taken down (not blown up) because Elliott had resumed fishing by the end of October.

Bolton's next move was to have a fisherman named Edward Wooten trespass on Elliott's grounds. Elliott frantically cabled Kerr to get to Niagara, and Kerr attended, summonsing Wooten to court at which time Wooten was "very humble and very willing to remove his reel and so that ended the case." Kerr observed that "John Bolton is always ready to breed contention amongst fishermen… I have told these disagreeable people… that unless they get along more harmoniously, I will not recommend them for a renewal of their licenses."

In a letter to Wilmot, Kerr recounted the Sunday night arrest and proudly observed, "It was just at the place where General Sir Isaac Brock, with British and British Canadians, made that glorious bayonet charge and drove the Yankees over Queenston Heights in 1812—the year I was born."

In mid-October, 480 yards of gill nets were stolen out of the water that belonged to Cantwell. Kerr suspected a member of Cantwell's crew, William Patterson, but couldn't prove it and put up a notice offering a twenty-dollar reward to "any person who will prosecute the thief and thieves to conviction. $10 to any person, except the thief, who will give me private information that will lead to the recovery of the gill nets and $5 to any person who will give me private information about who owned the boat the thieves used." Was Bolton behind this? The thief was never found.

In 1882 a bit of a personal relationship developed between Kerr and his immediate supervisor, S. P. Bauset, who was apparently quite deaf. Kerr sent him a #3 horn or ear trumpet, which was an early hearing aid like you might see in an old movie. In return, Bauset inquired if Kerr was fond of reading, to which he replied, "I like Dickens! Thackeray, I know only by report. Mr. Whitcher has given me a good number of books… and those I have read them over again and again. I frequently read in the middle of the night, and always with candle light when home! When from home, with lamp light." Very considerate to Mrs. Kerr!

Kerr continued,

> *After nearly 18 years as Fishery Overseer, accustomed at home and abroad as I am, to get up in the middle of the night to watch and capture offenders… so that I almost invariably waken up at those particular hours now nightly, read a while, blow out the light, drop over, and go sleep again. When from home stopping at*

> any hotel, and I wish to waken up at any particular hour, invariably I can do so, without being called up! Such has custom made me! And still, if I desire to sleep all night, God is very good and enables me to do so.

Kerr requested books on "Natural History of Canadian fish and on fish breeding and anything else after that you please." Shortly thereafter, Kerr received eleven books. Thanking Bauset, he said, "I have got a most pleasant winter's reading before me." Referring to William Thackeray's book *Irish Sketches,* Kerr advised that, "I was personally familiar with many of the dear old places and persons referred to."[143]

The troubles in Niagara seem to have abated by the end of 1882, but Kerr anticipated a return engagement in the future. He had heard that Bolton intended to fish for sturgeon in Elliott's licensed grounds and that Bolton intended to apply to lease Elliott's grounds from under him. As a pre-emptive strike, Kerr had Elliott apply for 1883 before the end of 1882 so there would be no gap affording Bolton an opportunity to commit further annoyance: "We must keep the Bolton's off your seine hauling grounds from sturgeon hook and line fishing."

To curtail costs and possibly because Kerr was now seventy years old, he stopped making his district tour to create his annual return and began writing to the fishermen seeking the information. He had various degrees of success, but he was persistent and eventually got the details. Still ambitious, he was trying to get the Lake Erie district as far west as Port Stanley, as if he needed more trouble!

At the end of the year, the Department received a request from Benjamin Meade Gifford, who was unknown to the Department, and Kerr was asked to find out who he was. It turned out that Kerr's friend and fish guardian, Owen Bowers, knew him well, so Kerr asked for a report. Bowers' report is as follows.

> *His letter to the Ministry is a kind of mystery, however! So far as he is individually concerned, there is no hidden mystery about him in the neighbouring counties of Norfolk and Haldimand!!!*

---

143   *Irish Sketches* is William Thackeray's 1863 book about his travels in Ireland.

1*st* He was a school master
2*nd* He was a merchant
3*rd* He was a watch tinker and jeweler
4*th* He was a billiard saloon keeper
5*th* He was a hotel keeper
6*th* He is an agent for fruit trees
7*th* Kept an improper house in York and Dunnville at one time[144]
8*th* Was 3 years in the penitentiary for horse stealing
9*th* Is not worth 50 cents
10*th* He has a wooden leg."

Kerr didn't reference him again, and I have no idea what he wanted from the Department. Maybe a better reference? And what did Bowers have against wooden legs?

After a trip to Niagara just before Christmas, Kerr received some disturbing news about his friend, Thomas Elliott, which he reported to Bauset: "Mr. Thomas Elliott is very sick, he is a little out of his mind, and I deeply regret to tell you that this is the 3*rd* time he has been similarly burdened since I became acquainted with him on the 5*th* of May, 1865." This time, however, he did not recover and became progressively worse.

Just before Christmas, Kerr was informed that he was losing Norfolk County and that a new fisheries overseer was being appointed in his place. He seemed a little wistful as he wrote to the fishermen: "I bid you all a kindly farewell. This will be about the end of it." He was also extremely proud that he had cleaned up the mess left by C. L. Bingham: "I hope Bingham's successor, Mr. David Sharp of Port Ryerse… will succeed as well as I have for the last 21 months up there. I leave him a clean foundation in all things."

On finding out that his friend and fishery guardian, Owen Bowers, was being let go, Kerr was angry and bitterly wrote to him: "I think my course in the future will be to attend to my own affairs, and let the fisheries go to ____. And then the Department will find out that no novice can do what we have done. I did all that I could to get it in shape and

....

144   A house of ill repute, I presume.

then to hand someone else to enjoy the fruits of our labours. Let it go to ____. I must live and move and let Sharp manage it. Maybe he will want me. God only knows." There would be more about Sharp in the future.

1883

Kerr quickly learned that David Sharp knew virtually nothing about the fisheries and that he was a political appointment as a faithful Conservative. Kerr took him under his wing and spent the winter tutoring him about his responsibilities. Sharp remained an underperformer for years who picked strange fights with the fishermen. Every year Kerr had to help him with his annual returns because, despite his name, he didn't seem that sharp!

Kerr was surprised to learn that Owen Bowers had fled to Michigan on account of financial problems on his large farm. Having a $5,000 mortgage at 8 percent, he was unable to make the payments and lost everything. Kerr noted, "Bowers had never talked of himself but he certainly seemed to know a lot about everyone else's personal business."

Thomas Elliott was still unwell, and Kerr was trying to find a way to preserve his seine-hauling grounds for the benefit of his wife and daughters. This was a recurring theme for years, and the person to be concerned about was John Bolton. On March 12, Kerr wrote to Whitcher to update him about Elliott and to plead for a free licence for Mrs. Jane Elliott to support herself and her three daughters: "Thomas Elliott has been very ill and confined to his bed and to his house for the past 5 months. And, I may add, his mind is afflicted. He is out of his mind and incapable of managing his affairs." Kerr promised to obtain a seine net for her and a "steady crew" when fishing commenced.

Elliott's partner, Tom Moir, had bought Elliott's nets and immediately went to John Bolton to cook up some plan to destroy the Elliotts. Bolton's intention was to "ruin Mrs. Elliott and her family." Kerr was not going to let that happen, and he wrote Jim Cantwell to advise him of the plan. Kerr wanted to "do some good kind, beneficent act for the family of an afflicted fellow being. More especially as God has always been very good and kind to us." Testing this theory, Kerr's oldest son,

George, died suddenly and unexpectedly exactly fourteen days later.[145]

Kerr described Elliott as "raving" and only eating apples and grapes and drinking lukewarm water but provided no other details of his symptoms. As a lawyer, I worked with psychiatric patients for thirty-six years at the Consent and Capacity Board and the Ontario Review Board.[146] The major symptoms of mental illness are depression and psychosis, which is where one becomes delusional and loses touch with reality. People can suffer from both, and that may have been true of Elliott. Other than for people with substance-abuse problems, it always amazed me how random mental illness was. Even today, psychiatrists struggle with causation.

Kerr was elated when the Department granted the leases gratis and planned to buy out Elliott lock, stock, and barrel in order to continue fishing on the family's behalf. He let Cantwell in on the news and swore him to secrecy, not wanting Bolton to find out. Determined to avoid an apprehension of bias, Kerr decided he could no longer board with the Elliotts when in Niagara. He also surreptitiously obtained a new net and boat to fish Elliott's limits, in cahoots with Cantwell.

Just prior to George Kerr's unexpected death on March 28, 1883, Kerr received a petition from the Fish and Game Protection Club of Wentworth seeking that net and seine fishing be prohibited in Burlington Bay. Kerr noted, "I was solicited to become a member. I was willing to do so! And subscribe my annual dollar fee, thereto, when I found out it was to interfere with legal, legitimate net fishing and vested right established by you for the benefit of fishermen resident on B. Beach. I then declined to connect myself or be a tool of the so-called club."

....

145 According to his death certificate, thirty-four-year-old George died of pneumonitis. See chapter 16 for more details.

146 The Consent and Capacity Board provides for the determination of many issues, such as involuntary admission to a hospital and capacity to consent to treatment. The Ontario Review Board is mandated under the Criminal Code to deal with people accused of crimes who have been found not criminally responsible or not fit to stand trial due to mental illness. It is tough work for a lawyer to represent clients at these tribunals and frequently unrewarding, both financially and professionally. I did hundreds of these hearings during my career.

As usual, Kerr quickly learned that the club had no intention of protecting fish or game but rather wanted to monopolize the fishing and shooting of game for their exclusive membership. They even wanted the right to trespass on private property to do so, all to the exclusion of the licensed fishermen of Burlington Bay who had been previously assailed on several occasions.

Kerr recommended a refusal of the petition. In retaliation, the club had Kerr's friend and fellow Irishman, Patrick Hand, charged with illegally catching ducks in his seine net and fined five dollars before Magistrate Cahill when Kerr was absent and unable to attend court. Outraged, Kerr wrote to Ottawa to advise that it was impossible to avoid catching a few ducks in a seine net and that the Act should be amended to allow this. The saga of this fish-and-game club continued over the next few years and ultimately resulted in the early death of an innocent mill owner as we shall see.

The Elliott family were not the only recipients of Kerr's charitable deeds. In late May he went to bat for an old friend and fisherman in Fort Erie, Chester A. Harris. Kerr had known Harris for nineteen years and liked him, even though he had prosecuted him a few times for fishing infractions, which was not uncommon. Harris had paid thirty dollars per year for his seine-hauling ground, but in 1883 two novice fishermen came along and offered seventy dollars, which Kerr was grudgingly obliged to recommend because Harris had not yet paid.

Knowing this would ruin Harris and feeling deep moral regret, Kerr engineered a scheme in which he had the new guys appear before Welland MP Thompson, who talked them into withdrawing their application, freeing the way for Harris to regain his grounds. Unfortunately, the Department smelled a fish and would not reinstate Harris, and Kerr was instructed to refund Harris's money and advise him and his wife that he would not be allowed to fish.

Kerr reported on that conversation: "Both Mr. Harris and his wife were **thunder struck** when I made known to them your instructions. I may here inform you that Mr. Harris will do everything that is possible to have the fishing ground given back to him. His own personal support! And you and the Acting Minister may soon expect a personal visit at Ottawa from Mrs. Harris and then she will no doubt tell her own side of this unfortunate case." Having already risked his own position, Kerr doubled down and assisted Harris on the sly with sending a petition to Ottawa.

Rather than face the wrath of Mrs. Harris, within two weeks the Department reinstated her husband. Kerr jubilantly supplied them with the news "With a hip, hip hurray!" To make it right with the Department, Kerr got a further ten dollars from Harris for his licence.

By July 1883 the Fish and Game Club of Hamilton was at it again, having charged mill owner William Campbell of Progreston for having allowed sawmill dust to enter 12 Mile Creek. Winding its way up from Lake Ontario, the creek starts near Carlisle and was then a bit of an industrial hub due to its twenty-two-foot waterfall, which fed several mills. Appearing before Police Magistrate Cahill, who seemed to have been acting a bit strangely of late, Campbell was convicted and fined the outrageous sum of fifty dollars plus costs. Had not lawyer, politician, and sometime moneylender D. B. Chisholm been present, it seemed that Cahill would have committed Campbell to jail right then and there. Instead, proceedings were adjourned to appeal to Whitcher, and Kerr went to work.[147]

First of all, Kerr noted that the prosecution had been initiated by a dirty cop, Samuel McNair, who had a history with Kerr and was himself a member of the club. Then Kerr advised Whitcher that Campbell had been summonsed while he was on duty out of town, which certainly seemed prearranged. Kerr also noted that the minister had previously warned McNair to keep his hands off fisheries matters.

Citing the prevailing policy that one half of any fine levied went to the complainant, McNair, Kerr noted, "It is all done for to make money." To buoy up Campbell, Kerr wrote him a letter of support indicating they had known each other since 1858 and that "I have always found you honest, sober and upright." Kerr had previously prosecuted

---

147 William Campbell and his brother, Sam, established a sawmill and a grist mill in Progreston in 1869. If Kerr knew him in 1858, it would have been a couple of years after he moved into his Hamilton Mountain home and a couple of years before the Wentworth Society for the Protection of Game and Fish.

him for "trivial offences under the Fisheries Act... But I have tried you and found you loyal and true."

Assisting Campbell in appealing to the minister, Kerr indicated that the charges were brought without notice to him and that they were brought in Hamilton, which was fourteen miles from where the alleged offences were committed, having passed over three local jurisdictional magistrates, which illustrates the age-old concept of "judge shopping."[148]

Kerr reported at length on the sleazy nature of the proceedings, including that witnesses had been stirred by promises of half the fine and that members of the club had attempted to influence Cahill, who had promised Campbell a small fine in exchange for a guilty plea and then imposed a massive fine. Kerr also noted the lack of evidence of mill waste and that any fish were impacted. Naturally, Kerr's nemesis, C. A. Sadlier, was involved in the prosecution. He lied in court, saying the stream was stocked with fish when he knew full well it was not. One wonders what was going on in Cahill's head. Up to this point, he had been a pretty steady, reliable justice.

Perhaps worst of all was Kerr's gut feeling that he had been the cause of the prosecution because he had failed to join the club and actively opposed its policies. He also surmised political motivation because both Kerr and Campbell were firm Conservatives while James Edwin O'Reilly, three-time mayor of Hamilton and a club member, was a Liberal. Kerr laid into the "illegal, unconstitutional" club, assuring the minister that "there is no Irish imagination in this!! Put your foot on the viper!" By "Irish imagination" Kerr meant he was not inventing his concerns.

On September 17, Kerr received instructions to report to Killarney on special duty. Taking the overnight train to Collingwood, he boarded an open sailboat for the 120-mile trip north to Killarney, a small fishing

....

148   Judge shopping is the process of having a case appear before a favourable judge, either favourable to the lawyer or to the client, or to avoid an unfavourable judge. Trial time is scheduled by a trial coordinator. In the old days, one used to be able to use the trial coordinator to find the right judge and secure the best result. If lawyers didn't judge shop, it was almost negligence. Now it is more difficult but not impossible to do.

town on the mainland adjacent to Manitoulin Island. Never having been there, Kerr described it as follows: "It is a village of about 30 houses and 300 inhabitants, chiefly French, Scottish and Irish. It is a prosperous fishing town with a Roman Catholic unfinished church, a post office, two wharves and a public school where the teacher is paid $400 a year." Having known the teacher, who taught in Niagara some years earlier, Kerr commented that "he is a steady sober man."

The nature of the inquiry was with respect to some suspiciously high accounts submitted by Fisheries Overseer James Patton, whom Kerr had suspected of wrongdoing five years before, though he still held his job. Smelling a rat's nest of illegal fishing, improper licensing, and monopolistic dealings, Kerr requested all the fishery records, so he could conduct a thorough investigation. It revealed a state of insurrection between the fishermen and Patton that was on the verge of boiling over.

Georgian Bay comprises about 5,800 square miles at the eastern end of Lake Huron and is entirely within Ontario. By the 1880s, large commercial fishing fleets were operating out of Collingwood, Owen Sound, Meaford, and a number of other fishing communities, including Killarney and various seasonal island stations. Because of the railway system, fish dealers were able to buy the fish and move them south to cities like Toronto, Hamilton, and Buffalo, where they were sold at public markets. There seemed to have been too many fish overseers doing too little protection of the fisheries. The linchpins of the entire sleazy operation were the brothers James and Charles Noble and their brother-in-law, James Patton.

Kerr began to accumulate witness statements from the Collingwood fishermen that revealed a pattern of extortion and intimidation to benefit the Nobles' monopoly, with Patton as the official company goon acting under his authority as overseer. Throw in a scattering of Natives with their own grievances, and it was an explosive mix. Opposed to them were the twenty-four boatloads of Collingwood fishermen, being fifty-six in number, most of whom were prepared to give sworn statements. They alleged a litany of offences, including fishing during closed season, Sunday fishing, using undersized nets, selective enforcement against enemies, and distribution of fish offal over the waters fished by those opposed to the Nobles.

Kerr's recommendations were multiple in nature, starting with the cancellation of the Noble brothers' licences and that Patton be fired. He also recommended strict enforcement of net mesh sizes and a much more vigorous and lawful enforcement of the *Fisheries Act*. Not included was a recommendation to prosecute Patton, who was a Liberal appointee. The pattern of sweeping such matters under the carpet was long established, and clearly the Department did not want to have to deal with the political ramifications of such an ignominious event. Greed and corruption being what they are, the ultimate responsibility rested with an ineffective Ministry, under the direction of Whitcher, the Commissioner of Fisheries. Few of the recommendations were implemented, and the problems continued to smoulder.

By the end of 1883, Kerr was quite insistent about a pay raise and a promotion. He wanted to be promoted to fisheries superintendent for Georgian Bay and Lake Huron in light of the near disaster he had temporarily prevented. Promising to restore "peace and harmony," Kerr suggested that his son Frederick be appointed as overseer for Lake Ontario and the Niagara Hatchery and that "I will supervise all." Kerr believed Whitcher had been "superannuated" (fired?), and his friend, S. P. Bauset, could help him achieve these objectives. He didn't or couldn't.

Just before Christmas, the Department made its orders about the Georgian Bay-Killarney fiasco. The decision was to discharge Patton but to allow the Noble brothers to maintain their licences. Kerr was shocked. He initially sought to publish his report and full recommendations, predicting that if things didn't change, "the fishery is doomed to desolation.... in about 5 years' time ... I can do nothing now except bear with the ignominy that is sure to be heaped upon me. My disappointments are so many that this one won't affect me any!"

The Georgian Bay fishermen were outraged that the Nobles' monopoly had been left intact and predictably blamed Kerr, who suggested they obtain a copy of the full report and talk to their local MPs about trying to change the minister's mind.

Meanwhile back in Niagara, Kerr continued his efforts to prevent John Bolton from getting his hands on Elliott's lease by proposing that the lease be shared with Jim Cantwell and that they fish alternate days and share the rent. Thomas Elliott, who was out of his mind, never fished again, and Kerr needed Cantwell as an ally to fend off Bolton. Kerr had been carefully cultivating a friendship with Cantwell and his wife, Kate, in the hope that this would deter Cantwell's designs on the Elliott lease. Cantwell was well known for his prickly nature and had to be handled carefully.

On January 3, 1884, Kerr wrote a long letter to Cantwell that included the following passage:

> *I don't know anything about you having made a damn fool of yourself! When you get to Heaven and Peter and Andrew, his brother fishermen ask you where you come from, and where you fished! Just tell them you fished in the Niagara River, between Rousseaux's wharf and Kennedy Hollow!!! And you can! Whereas you are so damned particular, refer them to me, Jim!" Now then, what is your next objection! I am coming down on Monday for to vote for Garrett. Any objection to that! Then again, I suppose I can remain over in Niagara until Tuesday and go up by train to Fort Erie! Any objection to that!!*

1884

On January 4, James Patton was notified that his services were being dispensed with and that Kerr had been instructed to wind up the business of his division. Kerr was back in Collingwood in early February, noting, "in my return in a cutter for the Globe Hotel, wet to the knees, for I got into the water out about 4 miles. Patton looked at me and passed by on the other side. I never heard a fisherman regret him. They say he ought to have been dismissed long ago."[149]

Kerr was forced to complete Patton's returns for 1883 and made every effort to get an accurate picture. He ultimately found the total value of Georgian Bay fishing to have been $102,000, of which the

---

149 The Globe Hotel was built in 1865. Later renamed as part of the Mountainview Hotel, it closed its doors in May of 2009 and was torn down.

Noble brothers' catch exceeded $36,000. He found there were 246 men fishing from 119 boats and tugs including "Indians and half-breeds" who often fished in return for whisky, to which Kerr was adamantly opposed. Kerr's returns were delayed by his having no response from J. W. Ranney of Ridgeway, who had fished at Killarney as part of the Nobles' cartel. Kerr's monumental bad judgment in befriending Ranney was evidenced by Ranney consistently abusing him by refusing to pay or comply in any way with Kerr's requests and by lying to his face.

On March 31, Kerr heard a rumour that Patton was to be reinstated based on his political support, including another brother-in-law, ex-MPP Thomas Lang.[150] Kerr wrote to Bauset to express his thoughts: "unlikelier things have come to pass. My own impression is that there will be a bigger row if he is re-instated!! Patton is very indiscreet, for even before he left Collingwood... he made threats what he would do when he got restored." Kerr went on to observe, "Georgian Bay fishermen are like the Jews of old! A favoured but dissatisfied people!"

Another one of Kerr's charity cases was John Gunsall of Toronto who had been licensed to fish in Ashbridge's Bay until the City put a stop to net fishing in the inner harbour for the benefit of anglers and trollers. Gunsall, who was paralyzed in one leg, was still able to fish, and Kerr had tried to get him a licence near Belleville, without success. Then Kerr proposed that he be licensed to fish on the Lake Ontario side of Toronto Island near the gap at the eastern end. Gunsall was blamed for killing young fish in the bay when, in fact, it was the pollution from the Gooderham distillery's cow byres that was doing the damage.

To top things off, Gunsall's wife left him, and he was disconsolate with grief. Kerr offered to write to his wife and did so on February 5.

> *I was perfectly surprised on Saturday last when I called at your husband's to find that you had left him. Whoever advised you as to this course is no friend of yours, nor your husband's. My advice to you is to return home as soon as you receive this! Don't leave your poor husband any longer disconsolate and in misery. I told*

---

150 Thomas Lang (Oct. 7, 1836–Oct. 9, 1920) was the Conservative MPP for Simcoe West from 1875–1883. He married Ann Patton in 1861.

> *him if I could find out where you were I would prevail upon you to return home! I advise you as a friend to return home at once! He can never get along without you.*

As a former twenty-first-century family law lawyer, I have a few concerns about this letter. First, it seems to have little to do with her and is mainly concerned with him. He asked no reasons as to why she left and what could be done to promote reconciliation. She, of course, had no property or support rights because she had left his house. There must have been some valid reason for her leaving in an era when separation was a shameful event. They did reconcile though and remained together until Mr. Gunsall died. Then Kerr had to try and help her.

The Toronto Gun Club had opposed Gunsall getting a licence to fish in Ashbridge's Bay. In addition, in St. Catharines the local club was gunning to have Richard Gilbert, an unwell man with a wife and five children, stripped of his licence. Kerr had had enough. In a letter to Bauset he expressed his frustration: "I wish to God you would put your foot down! And tell Gun Clubs, Game Clubs, and their solicitors and municipal councils, who are all under the direction of Oliver Mowat's[151] local government, to mind their own business!! I am getting heartily tired of their annoyances."

Before the end of the winter, Kerr had another dust-up with the Wentworth Fish and Game Club. The minister had wiped out the outrageous fine imposed upon Campbell, and Hamilton MP and club member Thomas Robertson had tried to bribe Kerr by offering to recommend a promotion if Kerr would support the club. Kerr responded as follows: "His pimping after me settles the salary question for ever, for I would starve before I shall ever ask a favor from such a person. No surrender, Never!" 12 Mile Creek is not in his constituency. I don't live in his constituency! And this is the second time he has been trying to find out some dirt at my door!! I am prepared for him, and if either he

---

151 Oliver Mowat (July 22, 1820–Apr. 19, 1903) was a lawyer and a Liberal politician. He was one of the thirty-six Fathers of Confederation and served nearly twenty-four years as Premier of Ontario, from 1872–1896.

or his Game Club attack me, I am ready for them!"[152]

Kerr fought one last battle for the fishermen of Toronto in the spring of 1884 when the minister proposed not to renew the licences for William Ward, Mrs. Jane Gray, and Edward "Ned" Hanlan. Writing a passionate letter about William Ward's exemplary character, Mrs. Gray's extreme deprivations, and Hanlan's achievements, Kerr felt it would never do to have them ousted from the island just for the benefit of the recreation of Toronto citizens. But, of course, this battle had long since been lost.

Shortly thereafter, a portion of Gunsall's net was stolen to prevent him from fishing, and Kerr suspected members of the gun club, who were shooting thousands of fish in Toronto Bay. Outraged, Kerr offered to post a reward of thirty dollars to arrest these "unsportsmanlike and illegal people who seek to put a poor man out of work." Nobody was arrested.

On April 10, Kerr received a poorly written death threat: "Mr. Carr, Sir—If you value your life, keep from Toronto watters! And save your family from going into mourning. Sworn to by 11 men." Kerr laughed it off. "**How silly:** I spent nearly all last night in Ashbridge's Bay. I am, I hope, no coward! A threatening letter never alarms me! … I will laugh at their calamity, mock when their fear cometh and take care of and protect the fisheries and myself in the meantime."

The Wentworth Fish and Game Protection Association petitioned the minister to "set aside" Waterdown Creek for "our use and benefit for sporting purposes only," and Kerr was asked to respond. He impatiently noted that a body of water could only be set aside for "natural or artificial propagation of fish" and that he was not even going to respond to this "selfish and illegal request."

Kerr did respond to the petition of the Toronto Gun Club, which wanted all licensed fishing banned so its members could protect the fish and game. Kerr snorted about this assertion, noting that in his nineteen years he had never known any member of a gun club to protect fish and

....

152   Thomas Robertson (Jan. 25, 1827–Sept. 6, 1905) was the Liberal MP for Hamilton from 1878–1887.

game or enforce the law.

Anticipating trouble, Kerr was itching to get back to Killarney as soon as the ice cleared. He had sought to be appointed superintendent for Lake Huron and Georgian Bay or to at least to retain Patton's district, but he got neither, and he was disappointed but wrote to Bauset, saying, "I am contented–a few years more and the struggles of this life will be over… I shall still continue to labour under your kind and prudent management." Patton's replacement was Captain Joseph Wilson, and Kerr arranged to meet him: "I am told Captain Wilson is a decent red haired Scotchman! Not an Englishman!" He proved to be another lackluster overseer.

Kerr planned a military-like mission to get to Killarney on the first boat out of Collingwood and sneak attack the Nobles, whom he hoped would be found fishing out of season. Then he would break up the monopoly, whether the Department liked it or not. His plans were partially compromised when he learned cartel member and former friend J. W. Ranney planned to be on the same train hauling new nets to Killarney. Kerr's revised plan had him evading Ranney on the train and getting on the steamer, *Pacific*, together but without permitting Ranney an opportunity to alert his friends.[153] What could go wrong?

At Killarney, Captain Wilson inexplicably failed to show up, but Kerr achieved one objective: "I was in Killarney on Saturday morning at 10:00 a.m. to the surprise and astonishment of J. & C. Nobles, **at least**." The Nobles tried to involve Kerr in their affairs, but Kerr would have none of it because it was no longer his jurisdiction. He made use of his time by having the usual poke around on a trip to the French River and the Squaw Islands, gathering information for future use.

Unable to keep Richard Gilbert's lease on 20 Mile Pond in Niagara out of the greedy hands of the Township of Louth, Kerr secured him a position as a boat captain at Killarney, working for fish dealer W. A. Clarke. Another good deed for another deserving fisherman. Having

----

153   Kerr recited an amusing limerick about Killarney, Ireland: "Have you not heard of Kate Carney? She lives on the banks of Killarney! From the glance of whose eyes, shewn danger and fly! For sweet are the smiles of Kate Carney."

finally made arrangements with F. O. Wilson, Kerr travelled the 350 miles to Killarney.

Spending a week at Killarney, Kerr handed off the territory to Joseph Wilson, with whom he initially seemed to have had a good relationship: "For now, I hope my mission may end altogether at Killarney. Wilson has now taken the Nobles in hand and made them pay up for all their boat fishermen, Indians, half breeds, French and Whites."

Kerr had a curious encounter with an Aboriginal chief, the Reverend Solomon James,[154] that may or may not show a racial bias on Kerr's part. Apparently, Chief James was a fisheries overseer for Shawanaga, an area near Parry Sound. Kerr observed,

> *This <u>noble red man</u> came to me on the morning of the 29th of May at Killarney, when he said he was appointed on the recommendation of Mr. O'Brien, MP for Muskoka.*[155] *To place an Indian as Overseer over white fishermen is objectionable! Personally, Mr. Wilson and I have no feelings in this case! However, fishermen have expressed themselves in language that we deem it expedient to apprise you of. Mr. James might be appointed to collect fees from the Indians and watch over them . . .*

Was this racial prejudice or was it merely a perception of racial bias on the part of local white fishermen? I suspect both.

At the end of this trip, Kerr became quite ill and was laid up for about two weeks with some kind of bowel and kidney ailment. He reported a violent bowel complaint on the boat back to Collingwood and that Wilson had provided a bottle of gin, which produced "immediate relief" but not a cure. Compounding matters, there was a violent storm on the way to Collingwood, and pretty much everyone aboard was seasick. To add insult to injury, as he disembarked, Charlie Noble shouted, "Here comes the old fellow up again to take our lease from us!"

---

154 Chief James had advocated for exclusive Native fishing rights from Shawanaga to Parry Sound, without success.

155 William Edward O'Brien (Mar. 10, 1831–Dec. 21, 1914) was Conservative MP for Muskoka from 1882–1896.

Fortunately, another fisherman came to Kerr's defence, saying, "Charley, we will all receive equal justice from J. W. Kerr. All will eat the porridge out of the same pot in future!"

Wilson and Kerr submitted a long, thoughtful report to Bauset on June 11 in regard to Georgian Bay and made numerous recommendations that included the cancellation of the Nobles' leases because they were still fishing illegally. They also warned about the excessive use of pound nets and how they were often left out unchecked until the fish rotted and polluted the waters.

Kerr was over the moon when he learned that the Nobles' leases had been cancelled. He immediately wrote to his friends at Killarney: "Prepare for a great surprise! The die is cast **and down goes the Big Monopoly! Stand to your arms! Don't yield an inch! Your battle is won and not a drop of blood shed!** For England shall many a day, tell of the bloody fray. When the blue bonnets came over the borders!"[156] On July 20, Kerr received a letter from Killarney advising him that the Nobles "have placed their buoys around the consecrated water again and are on the war path. They had notices posted that they would fish up all nets found fishing on the same." The writer implored Kerr and Bauset to pay a visit, but it was not to be. Kerr did return to Georgian Bay again but not for a few years. All his hard work and deprivations appeared to have been futile.

D. B. Chisholm was a lawyer, a politician, and a moneylender of some renown in Hamilton. Kerr had hired him as a lawyer and borrowed money from him. Chisholm had done some good things in Hamilton, but by the summer of 1884, he fled Hamilton for the United States because he "became embarrassed while carrying on lumbering near Stokes Bay on Lake Huron... He fled the country taking considerable money with him," including $2,200 from Mrs. Sherbenell, the eight-three-year-old widow of a fisherman at Burlington Beach. Thousands of dollars were stolen from widows, orphans, ministers, temperance people, and so forth. He also left his wife and son behind to fend for

....

156   From "Border Ballad" by Sir Walter Scott, a Scottish poet (1771–1832). The blue bonnets or the blue hounds were the Scots.

themselves. Mrs. Chisholm tracked him down in Illinois and obtained a divorce, which was somewhat controversial for the time.

I have known a number of lawyers who have stolen from their clients, and most eventually get caught. The reasons for theft are multiple, and nowadays the Law Society makes good on misappropriations from a fund into which all lawyers pay. People give lawyers money to invest because they appear trustworthy. Don't be fooled! Anybody can steal, and some will. If you read Chisholm's biography in the *Dictionary of Hamilton Biography*, there is no mention of these shameful events, for reasons that are unknown to me.

As a follow-up to the Georgian Bay fiasco, Kerr began to agitate for some action on Lake Huron where everyone from Goderich to Southampton was fishing undersized nets under the nose of Fisheries Overseer Muir. Kerr heard this from his reliable sources in Owen Sound and Wiarton, and obviously, he wanted to be involved. He would get his chance soon enough.

By mid-July there was a shakeup in the Fisheries Department, and John Tilton became the deputy minister over S. P. Bauset, who was commissioner of fisheries. Kerr wrote to both men, and for the life of me I cannot determine why he wrote sometimes to one and sometimes to the other. Tilton had been the department accountant, so Bauset was the guy who knew the fisheries. Kerr commented, "We have a new deputy minister of fisheries now! To reign over me! He is a right good man!" Kerr, however, always had a much better personal relationship with Bauset.

In August 1884, Kerr had a meeting with Bauset and his son, a young lawyer, in Toronto. Bauset was on his way to Detroit and then up to Lake Huron to meet Fisheries Overseer Wilson in Sault St. Marie and then accompany him back to Killarney. By prior arrangement, Kerr met the Bausets at the train station en route from Montreal, where they had breakfast in the railway saloon. Kerr hired a cab, and they proceeded to somewhere in Yorkville, where they continued their discussions about the fisheries.

This may have been the first time they met face to face because Kerr describes Bauset Sr. as a "Jolly good fellow" who was "quite deaf."

Curiously, Kerr had to "do a little banking for Mr. Bauset," which he did not want divulged. This is reminiscent of when Whitcher rolled into town years before. I am not going to speculate as to what this was about except to hope it was on the level! Bauset paid Kerr the ultimate compliment by stating, "You are the only man in the service I can depend upon!" Kerr must have been walking on clouds when he left that meeting!

On Bauset's return trip, Kerr met him in Toronto and spent an evening with him discussing fishing matters.[157] The following morning, they had a couple of hours together while Bauset waited for the train to Ottawa. "What a good time I had!" Kerr recalled. Curiously, when Bauset got to Sault St. Marie to meet Fisheries Overseer Wilson, Wilson was not there, having gone to Lake Superior, which resulted in Bauset returning earlier than anticipated through Southampton. I don't know what Bauset thought, but I would have been angry about being stiffed, and this was not the first time Wilson pulled a no-show. Kerr learned that his "next scene of operations will be Lake Huron."

Kerr reported two buggy accidents in August, the first one being when a rear axle broke while he was driving with Mrs. Kerr, though neither of them were injured. However, a few days later, he had a second accident while driving down the Jolley Cut of the Escarpment with his eldest daughter, Annie, who was then thirty-eight years old. He reported: "The fore axle, right under me snapped and I was pitched out on my right side, a finger was cut and my elbow was bruised. It was very wet and raining at the time! My clothes were covered with mud! And had to be all washed." He reported they ended up hanging over the edge of the road, only inches from falling to his death down the mountainside.[158]

Having all the fishing records in his possession from Ottawa, at the end of August, Kerr hopped the train to Southampton, where he took

....

157 Frustratingly, I can find only a few details about Bauset. I do not know his date of birth or death, but I know he survived Kerr because there are departmental references to him until at least 1892. In 1884 if he had a young lawyer son, he was probably in his forties. So, he was considerably younger than Kerr, who was then 72.

158 If you travel down the Jolley Cut today, you will know what a steep precipice it is.

a room at Busby's Hotel[159] and for the next week wreaked havoc on the Saugeen Fishery District of Fisheries Overseer James Muir.[160] Fifty-eight-year-old Muir was a busy man. Aside from his post as fisheries overseer, he was also a tavern and licence inspector, earning $500 a year. He owned a hearse, ran a furniture manufacturer and store, and was a local politician. Worst of all for Kerr, "he is a notorious politician opposed to the Right Honourable Sir John A. MacDonald's government and stumped for the riding with the Liberal candidate in the last election."

Kerr quickly determined that Muir was way too busy to do his fisheries overseer job and that he "was remiss in his duty." That was an understatement; the Saugeen was a complete mess. First observing the tannery on the Saugeen, Kerr found it was polluting the river by discharging "acids, deleterious substances, poisonous matter and chemicals" into the river "abounding with black bass." He hauled the proprietors before the local magistrate, and they pleaded guilty and were fined five dollars plus two dollars in costs. Kerr recommended that the fines be held in abeyance based upon their promise to observe the law. Kerr blamed Muir because this had been done right under his nose for the past three years.

Proceeding next to Sauble Beach, Kerr found that Muir had never been there and that none of the commercial fishermen were paying rent. This was inexcusable because Sauble was an easy six-mile ride from Southampton. Kerr obtained several statements to prove this. Then he found that Muir had not been remitting the little money he had collected to Ottawa. Muir was openly allowing fishermen to dump fish guts and offal into the river, "stinking up the locality" to the point where citizens had petitioned to have something done. Visiting the nearby town of Paisley again, Kerr found that sawmills there were dumping sawdust in

....

159   Busby's Hotel on High Street, Southampton, was destroyed in the great fire of Nov. 4, 1886, that consumed over fifty buildings.

160   James Muir (Oct. 5, 1826–Oct. 5, 1909) was born in Scotland and trained as a carpenter. Muir arrived in Port Elgin in 1857, where he first employed his carpentry skills to build coffins. Later, he served as president of the Undertakers Association of Ontario. The funeral home he started is still there, known today as T. A. Brown Funeral Home.

the Teaswater and Saugeen Rivers and that fishways were broken and useless as a result of Muir's obvious neglect. Meanwhile, on the lake, undersized nets were being used by unlicensed fishermen fishing on Sundays and during closed season. It was truly the trifecta of fuck-ups, and Kerr wanted Muir discharged for his "willful neglect of duty… It is about time to ship Overseer Muir, who is a humbug."[161]

Like the marshal riding into town to clean it up, Kerr got to work with some of the easy stuff, like collecting licence fees and threatening mill owners. He also began to plan an elaborate fishway at a grist mill owned by George Gordon and John Denny in Southampton. Based upon a model designed in New Brunswick, it was considered state of the art, but it was also expensive, with an estimated cost of $370. The question now became one of who was to pay. The dam owner felt the government should pay because of Muir's neglect. Kerr wisely put it to the government to decide. Meanwhile, the project was put on hold.

By late September, Gordon had agreed to pay, and work got underway based upon the New Brunswick model. Kerr was involved in the planning, and when it was completed, he crowed, "I have succeeded far beyond my expectations with this fishway! It can now be put down as a grand success." Not everyone agreed, as we will see in chapter 20.

In early October Kerr saw an opportunity to stitch up John Bolton in Niagara, but he was thwarted by a legal loophole. On receiving information that Bolton and his crew had been setting nets in American waters on Sundays, Kerr proceeded to Niagara to investigate and determined it was true and that Bolton took up the nets on Mondays to legally sell the fish locally, as reported by Joseph Masters. However, after consulting with the customs collectors, he was advised not to lay charges because a previous case had been dismissed based upon the fish being caught in US waters and, therefore, not in violation of Canadian laws. Kerr reported,

> Last year, John Bolton got into a row with the customs authorities of the United States, Youngstown, NY, for setting sturgeon

---

161 Mostly known to us now from Dickens' 1843 novella, *A Christmas Carol*, the word "humbug" dates back to the 1740s as a description for a dishonest swindler.

gill nets in forbidden American waters, since which time Bolton has become a proscribed individual in Youngstown where he dare not since show himself, nor make his appearance. I may report for your information that since General Penrose,[162] *at present commanding officer in Niagara Fort, was placed in command there, the American fishermen who have been in the habit of gill net fishing on Sunday, have been stopped fishing on Sabbath Day! General Penrose has taken some gill nets and he has notified the U.S. fishermen he would seize all their gill nets there altogether on Sundays . . .*

It is a very unseemly thing now! For to see John Bolton violating the Sabbath law, while our fisheries laws cannot lay hold of him, because the fishing was done in America, where American citizens are debarred from fishing on Sundays. There is no occasion for any such desecration of the Sabbath. I would respectfully recommend you apply to the Hon. Minister of Her Majesty's Customs—to instruct the collector of customs to enforce the law in this case if it should happen again and a letter to this effect, written to me by you, to be read to the Niagara Fishermen, as a warning will do much good . . . Besides, John Bolton's Sabbath breaking is not fair play—to our own Sabbath observing law abiding fishermen of the Town of Niagara.

On October 31, Big Jim Cantwell wrote to Kerr wanting to lay charges against the Boltons "for fishing on my grounds and all around it." Kerr wrote back: "I may here tell you that if John Bolton, Fred Bolton or Charles Bolton have been fishing gill nets within the limits described in your seine license, except by your permission, they are liable to a fine of $100 and costs and the forfeiture of fishing apparatus so used and all fish taken or caught by them!" Kerr advised that because it was closed season, he was too busy to come down but encouraged

....
162 William Henry Penrose (Mar. 3, 1832–Aug. 29, 1903) served during the American Civil War and later commanded Fort Niagara and others before his death. He is buried in Arlington Cemetery.

Cantwell to see JP William Kerby and make a "severe example" of violators of the fisheries law. Cantwell was probably not happy that Kerr did not have time for him.

Despite how busy Kerr was, as evidenced by his third-quarter records, he was still angling for more work at age seventy-two. Staying in contact with his Georgian Bay sources, he fretted about the upcoming closed season and said he would have been happy to have been ordered back, but that did not happen. On finding that Fisheries Overseer Sharp of Norfolk had sustained multiple fractures of his leg as a result of a threshing machine falling on it, Kerr stepped in to help but recommended that Sharp still be paid.

Meanwhile, Thomas Elliott "is a raving mad man, locked up in a room, savage in every act of his. God pity him and protect his wife and children! For he can do nothing for them!" A month earlier Kerr had tried to get Elliott admitted to the Hamilton Institute for the Insane, which had commenced operations in 1876. Kerr had difficulty getting him admitted because it was very full, and women were first on the list. He succeeded eventually, only to have his hopes dashed a few weeks later when a determination was made that they could not assist Elliott, and he had to be escorted back to his Niagara Home. Century Manor on the West 5th grounds of what is now known as St. Joseph Centre for Mountain Health Care is badly in need of renovations and has been closed since 1995. It would be a wise idea for Mohawk College, which is right across the street, to agree to fix this beautiful old building in return for some land! Apparently an agreement to this effect was recently scuttled by Ontario P.C. Premier, Doug Ford.

Hearing that Elliott was in the asylum, John Bolton resumed his attempt to get his licence by approaching Senator Plumb and MP Rykert, purporting to be a Conservative supporter. However, Kerr was onto him and annoyed by his gall. Writing to Bauset, Kerr stated,

> *Jack Bolton and Charles Bolton's politics, I wrote Mr. Plumb and I told J.C. Rykert, is always cash down! First tried Plumb and failing! Then tried Rykert–I was proof for both! Take away the living from a poor afflicted wife and her 3 children! Her husband*

is a <u>raving lunatic</u>! How thoughtless we find our great men sometimes! I did not and have not yielded an inch to either of these applicants... Thank heavens I was good for both! No weakness in my knees! I never in my life saw any poor man so afflicted as Elliott is! Now my friend, don't you think I done right in refusing these great men to become a tool in their hands to inflict a grievous injury by taking from a poor family under affliction—A fishing ground occupied by the family for upwards of 50 years. And not getting nor receiving a cent for giving it up! You can now judge the predicament I escaped. Except the fishery and keeping boarders in season, they have no other means of living.

While Haldimand-Norfolk was his district, Kerr had repeated trouble with the Wardell family of Rainham Township, first father Elijah and later his son, Peter. They were licensed pound-net fishermen but frequently did not pay their lease, and they were notorious for fishing on Sundays and during closed season. When Fisheries Overseer Sharp broke his leg, and Kerr temporarily took over his district, Kerr determined to pounce. His plan was to take the evening train to Port Dover and then rent a buggy to travel the twenty-six miles to what was known as Wardell's Bay, catch them in the act, and arrest them. His point was to let them know that even if Mr. Sharp was disabled, the Department was still on the job.

Leaving Port Dover at 3:30 a.m. in mid-November, Kerr drove by buggy in total darkness until about 5:00 a.m. when he found them fishing. On threats of charges, he was able to secure $11.50 in licence fees and hopefully teach them a memorable lesson.

This was an insignificant event in Kerr's history, but I include it to illustrate two points. First is the incredible grit this seventy-two-year-old guy had for performing his job. Second, I know something of the Wardells because we once had a cottage in his bay, and we "toured" the abandoned Wardell home in the early 2000s before it was bought and renovated. Like most rural fishermen, they also farmed.

The fishway at Southampton was almost completed, and Kerr planned to inspect it. He had also heard about substantial unlicensed fishing on Bruce Peninsula up toward Tobermory and devastating amounts of sawdust washing through the Sauble River into Lake Huron. Naturally, he wanted to investigate but did not get permission because he only spent November 26 in Southampton. He had nothing but glowing things to say about the fishway, concluding, "I must report to you that I feel a pride in being the first fishery officer in Ontario permitted to superintend the erection of a fishway that must always reflect honour and respect on the intelligent inventor, Mr. William Henry Rogers of Amherst, Nova Scotia." The final cost? $482.72.[163]

Meanwhile back in Niagara, Kerr had given Charles Bolton permission to fish sturgeon lines in the river provided it did not affect Mrs. Elliott's seine fishing. Predictably, it did, so Kerr wrote him a polite letter asking him to refrain, appealing his humanity: "In consequence of the sad affliction in Mrs. Elliott's family, by the sad illness of her husband, Mr. Thomas Elliott, and for whom we all feel and grieve, I am satisfied that you will at once as a friend and well-wisher for Mrs. Elliott and family, remove the line at once." I think he did because most of the rest of this saga involved his bad boy brother, John (Jack) Bolton.

In Kerr's absence, other Niagara fishermen had begun to fish on Mrs. Elliott's territory, and she wrote to him for help. He reassured her that no one had the right to fish on her lease and that the law was on her side: "Except yourself, no person can legally fish a gill net between Rousseau's wharf and Dr. Stevenson's point, and still they all do it. However, next year will tell the tale!" Who knows what he had in mind?

Kerr ended 1884 sitting in his big house banging out letters to the Department complaining about the neglect, if not illegal conduct, of Fisheries Overseer Muir in Southampton, the unlicensed fishing on Lake Huron, the uncontrolled pollution, overfishing, and illegal net fishing by Lake Huron fishermen, even during closed season. Was anybody listening?

....

163   On his way home from Southampton, Kerr got a taste of lake-effect snow off Lake Huron to the point where only one other passenger accompanied him in the railroad car. It was not his last experience with this amazing meteorological phenomenon.

1885

This was a year of discontent and disappointment for Kerr, who expected and was promised a promotion to supervisor of the western Lake Ontario, Lake Erie, and Lake Huron district. His discontent was primarily directed at the excessive fishing and lack of adequate enforcement. For good measure, also thrown into the mix was the province's attempt to secure control of the fisheries and the North-West Rebellion, which put other government business on ice. It was also a year of great personal achievement for Kerr who was at the height of his powers. Having brought Lake Ontario under control, he spent a good portion of the year cleaning up Lake Erie, at which he was largely successful.

Kerr began the year by continuing his rant about fish matters in general and closed season in particular. He wrote to Bauset, "You know and God knows closed season has been a farce and the laughing stock of the Province of Ontario." It had dwindled down to just ten days in November for whitefish and salmon, both of which were in serious decline, never to return to former levels. Reporting sales in his district from Whitby to Moulton Bay in Lake Erie of $60,044 in 1883, an increase of $17,143 over the prior year, Kerr noted it was mainly because of the increase in herring and sturgeon, and he morosely noted not a single salmon had been caught by commercial fishermen.

On January 12, Kerr wrote directly to Minister McLelan to request a promotion, setting out in detail his services to the Department and how Whitcher had promised this to him. On January 16, Kerr wrote to Bauset to seek a promotion to overseer for Georgian Bay and Lake Huron, but not at the cost of his other districts, which he insisted on keeping. On January 21, he again wrote to Bauset, exhorting the Department to promote him to inspector for Ontario: "I will relieve you and the Deputy Minister of some of your troubles; and by activity and example make Ontario Officers what they should be! In protecting the fish and fisheries! An active and efficient corp.!!" Then he proceeded to give a two-page biography of his service, starting with the Royal Irish Constabulary.

Returning to the topic, Kerr advised that he didn't care about the label of his promotion.

198   Caught!

The rose will smell as sweet if you call it by some other name . . . The salary of Inspector will be quite as acceptable under any other name you may feel disposed to dust me with! Give me plenty to do, I don't want, nor do I wish, to eat the bread of idleness!"

Somehow, he was advised that the promotion would go through more quickly if he got the backing of Hamilton MP, F. E Kilvert[164] who I presume was the bag man for Hamilton. Kerr immediately wrote to him to solicit his support. Kilvert met with the minister and reported back to Kerr that he "urged your claims with all my might."

On January 27, Kerr reported, "My arm pains me" despite boasting to Bauset that he was "Hale and hearty." He later described a fall on the ice at Ridgeway: "I got a bad fall on the ice, landed on my left shoulder, hurted the muscles of my left arm... It is now getting better. Lucky for me it is not my right arm or I might not be able to write to you!" In a later letter he elaborated: "I imagined my left arm and shoulder were broken; it was not so bad however! Altho bad enough. The muscles of my arm caught it and it is in them the pain lies." Kerr later disclosed that "the fall shook me badly." He described hurting his left knee and kidneys as well.

He reported further health problems in February when he caught a chill on a trip to Lake Erie: "took a stitch [a sudden sharp pain] in my right side at Niagara. All day in bed; Mustard plasters, turpentine, bottles of medicine. I am getting all OK again!" He also developed a serious lung condition from a cold he thought he picked up in Point Edward, near Sarnia: "My right lung was so bad for 3 or 4 days I could not get out of my bed without help. Except on last Saturday, I have not been out of the house for 11 days!" That was a hell of a long time for the habitually restless seventy-two-year-old.

Kerr was still obsessed about Lake Huron and astounded that Muir had not been sacked. He wrote to Bauset: "If Overseer James Muir continues much longer to disregard your letters to him for explanations, with the proofs in your hands! If I was in your place I would make him

---

164   Francis Edwin Kilvert (Dec. 17, 1838–Aug. 21, 1910) was a Conservative Hamilton lawyer who was mayor from 1877–1878 and an MP from 1878–1887. He was not always on good terms with Kerr.

sweat! Send him up for trial! If you or I were in Muir's political power! He would handle us! And make no mistake! But then your kindly disposition is always on the side of mercy!"

Why had they not discharged Muir with all the ammunition Kerr had provided? Aside from his Grit political cover, it would likely have been an embarrassment to the government to have this scandal made public and the gross negligence of the Department exposed. Unfortunately, the result of delay was ongoing turmoil and chaos, ultimately affecting the well-being of the fisheries, a pattern that repeated itself time and again. They must have taken some proceedings against Muir because Kerr noted on February 20 that he had sought a "respite of judgment."

On February 9, Kerr was off on his first special duty of the year, making a trip to Sarnia and the Point Edward fisheries on instructions from Bauset. The problem seems to have been a lack of engagement on the part of Overseer D. McMaster, and Kerr quickly straightened him out. There was no allegation of misappropriation but rather only neglect on the part of McMaster, who was a bookseller from Belfast: "I had a long chat with Overseer McMaster. He will answer the Deputy Ministers letter! In doing this I advised him to be frank, open and truthful in doing so. And he promised me he would make out the returns you required." Case closed. Kerr actually got a thank-you letter from the Department!

On February 19, Kerr was ordered to go to St. Thomas and meet Overseer Alexander McBride regarding some irregularity, and he quickly ascertained that McBride had misappropriated $850 from the Department! McBride also managed the Hutchinson Hotel in St. Thomas, and apparently, all the stolen money was used to fund this establishment.[165] Kerr sought to temporarily superintend Elgin County and sniff around for any other improprieties, even though he held to the foolhardy belief that McBride "is honest and will pay it back."

Bauset wrote to Kerr that he "had better give McBride a further hint to square up as soon as possible by remitting the balance by draft

---

165 Kerr later told of his affinity for Hutchinson House because it was the first place he and his wife stayed on their arrival in Port Stanley on August 26, 1846. Although Kerr had an uncle in the vicinity, it doesn't appear that he stayed with him.

certificates and not by cash or cheques. And not to do it again! If a thing of this kind was known to his enemies, that would soon settle him." What if it was known to the government enemies? It seemed to be in everybody's interest to keep it under wraps. Transparency? Not so much.

Meanwhile in Niagara, another skirmish developed in the Elliott saga when Jim Cantwell interfered with Mrs. Elliott's designated fisherman, R. J. Allan. On Kerr's orders: "As a matter of consequence, Mrs. Elliott will not permit Cantwell to fish there! This year!" Kerr later explained, "Last season, Mrs. Jane Elliott allowed James Cantwell under licence for $10 to seine haul, expecting as he promised he would aid and assist her in many ways! But this he never done. But on the contrary, gave her much mental annoyance and had Robert J. Allan, a licensed fisherman, whom she permitted to fish within her licensed limits, fined to the extent of $5.25." Kerr also noted, "From the sad and grievous affliction which has happened to Thomas Elliott for the past three years! Her husband, he being silly, out of his mind and not able to do anything, nor take care of himself."

In March, Kerr was refused the promotion, and he was annoyed, though he tried not to show it. In a letter to Bauset, he whined,

> I told a few of my intimate friends that I expected the Promotion! They will be disappointed! I will not–for a thing so frequently promised since 1868, by Mr. Whitcher up to the year before he left, did not disappoint me! Major Tilton got a chance of doing the graceful act, but even then he would not agree with you, who knows me so well. My promotion would be popular amongst fishermen, conservatives and many of the Reform MP's and benefit the majority. However, as the troubling of the waters has come and nearly abated, I shall still continue to do my duty and praise my friends as I find them.

This was like a Victorian "Fuck you!"

McBride had promised to pay when his patron, MP Dr. Wilson,[166] paid him for his services to the Hutchinson House Hotel but had failed to do so, and Kerr determined to pay McBride a visit. First, Kerr wrote to Bauset: "Now that Dr. Wilson MP, has been home to St. Thomas during Easter recess, and gone back to Ottawa again, and nothing done, although faithfully promised! I have now no more confidence in anything Overseer McBride may say about the $1,041 collected by him and not paid in to you. Shamefull!!! I am now done for present with County of Elgin."

But in fact he was not, for he soon discovered that McBride had licensed fifty-four pound nets in his district, far too many for the fish stocks to bear. Kerr was now faced with the dilemma of how to retract these licences without promoting an insurrection amongst the fishermen. On April 15, Kerr wrote, "5:00 a.m.; Since 2:00 a.m. I have never closed an eye, thinking over since how I can shape my course and render unto you ample satisfaction." After agonizing over the matter, Kerr recommended the number be reduced to thirty-eight licenses and tried to be fair to all concerned.

Reduced further to thirty-one licenses by the Department, Kerr planned a mission to Elgin to do the redistribution. Meanwhile he reflected a bit: "I am always so suspicious of such people as McBride, Bingham, Patton and Muir! Is it any wonder! All Grits, why I should not keep my eyes open!" By the way, Muir was discharged, and Patton, in Collingwood, applied for a lighthouse keeper's position on Georgian Bay. McBride stayed on as the manager of Hutchinson House but not the owner.

McBride revealed that he had been encouraged to buy Hutchinson House and renovate it and that his friends would assist him financially, but he had not done so. Kerr observed that the "prospect of getting the money appears to be slim! McBride's spirit appears to be willing but the flesh is weak." Ultimately, Bauset threatened to act within a week, and miraculously, $800 was paid to Kerr, with McBride wanting credit for

....

166   John Henry Wilson (Feb. 14, 1834–July 3, 1912) was a medical doctor and Liberal politician. Wilson was MP for Elgin East from 1882–1891. He was later appointed to the Senate by Wilfred Laurier.

the balance based on expenses not submitted. Kerr was ecstatic. Where had this sizable amount of money come from? Kerr didn't care.

In March 1885, Louis Riel returned to Canada from exile and set up a provisional government in Saskatchewan, which prompted the North-West Rebellion that gripped the country because it was widely covered in the press. Bauset's son had joined the militia, and Kerr wrote to him to wish him well: "Such are the men I glory in! To leave wife, father and mother when duty calls." Kerr, an avid newspaper reader, followed Bauset's son's outfit with interest. On April 16, the 65th Regiment arrived in Winnipeg, and Kerr wrote, "May God protect our Canadian forces who have gone very nobly forward to fight for their Queen, Country and British Constitution."

On May 17, Kerr wrote to Bauset Sr.

> *The Troops in the North West have achieved wonders! And deserve well wishes from their Country and the Government of Canada, Riel, after all is a poltroon [wretched] cowardly murderer. I hope the Troops will do nothing to him to tarnish their laurels. Give him a fair trial and if found guilty–Hang him! And may God have mercy on his soul . . . Our troops have been well handled by General Middleton,[167] and his distinguished officers! The Grits and Blake[168] can now ask more silly questions! Sir John, the Franchise Bill and our friends forever!! Hurrah!*[169]

On May 30, Kerr again wrote to Bauset about the North-West Rebellion: "Our troops in the N. West have immortalized themselves!

---

167   Frederick Dobson Middleton (Nov. 4, 1825–Jan. 25, 1898) was a British military general. Middleton was appointed head of the Canadian Militia in 1884 and led the troops to victory over Riel in 1885. Described by Desmond Morton as a man who mixed common sense and pomposity in equal measure, he was knighted by Queen Victoria and paid $20,000 by the Canadian government.

168   Dominick "Edward" Blake (Oct. 13, 1833–Mar. 1, 1912) was a former premier of Ontario who led the Liberal Party of Canada from 1880–1887. In 1892 he entered the British House of Commons as an Irish nationalist.

169   The Franchise Bill (1885) amended Canada's election laws and gave some indigenous people the right to vote.

And General Middleton has proved himself to be a prudent officer, endowed with all the abilities of a great commander! For I may tell you, it is often a hard matter to find an officer from the Regulars, who can command the Militia as General Middleton has done. Instance his predecessor, General Luard."[170]

Poor old John Gunsall continued to have no luck in Toronto. He lost his fishing grounds in Humber Bay, his boathouse was burned down, and he was destitute. Kerr tried to get him the lighthouse keeper position in Whitby on the basis that the current keeper was up on criminal charges for being in possession of $3,000 worth of goods stolen from Grand Trunk boxcars. Unfortunately, he was out on bail, so Kerr had to bide his time. "Be prudent!" he advised Gunsall. "Talk no more about it—when proper time arrives, I will advise you! Lie low Jack, and keep very cool! You are all right."

Unfortunately, it was not to be alright because the lighthouse keeper, Lane, paid a witness to get out of town and accordingly, the GTR had to drop the case for lack of evidence. Kerr continued to advocate for his friend on the basis that Lane was a Grit appointed by the Mackenzie government, but it was not to be. As a last act of support, Kerr agreed to buy Gunsall's boat.[171]

In Niagara, Mrs. Elliott got her usual seine fishing stations, and Cantwell

....

170   Richard George Luard (July 29, 1827–July 24, 1891) a British Army officer, was appointed head of the Canadian Militia in 1880. His lack of tact and fearsome temper alienated the militia.

171   I can tell you from long experience in criminal court that one of a defendant's best hopes is that a material witness will fail to show up for trial because if there is no evidence, there is no case. Generally, when an accused is released on bail, it is a condition that he have no direct or indirect communication with witnesses. If the defendant breaches that, his or her bail is usually revoked. Nonetheless, witnesses frequently fail to show up for trials, and if a subpoena has not been personally served on them, there is not much the Crown can do but drop the charges or make a bad deal. If a witness is served personally, the Crown can request, and will generally get, a material witness warrant, whereby the witness can be arrested and transported to court. The other big trick of witnesses is to claim memory loss, but usually their statements these days are on videotape, so that rarely helps the accused.

was, as usual, unhappy. He asked Kerr if it was true, and he was told that it was. Kerr also reminded him of his own stations, some of which were not in use. In an unusual act of compassion, Bolton was persuaded not to apply for Elliott's grounds, and Kerr also tried to sweet-talk Cantwell.

> *You had better see Mrs. Elliott, she is a woman who never talks about her neighbours affairs. And she holds your wife, Mrs. Cantwell, in high esteem. As for me, I am getting up in years and I desire to live and die at peace with you all. See Mrs. Elliott and arrange with her the privilege of fishing. Mrs. Elliott is obliging. But God has been pleased to afflict her very severely in the sad affliction of her husband. I hope that God will never afflict Mrs. Elliott, or any of us, beyond what we are able to bear.*

Cantwell refused to accept Kerr's advice and fired back with a wild allegation that Kerr was having an affair with Mrs. Elliott. Kerr responded with a threat of criminal libel. Then Cantwell had the Reverend P. J. Harold, the Roman Catholic Rector of Niagara, write a petition full of lies. Kerr retorted angrily.

> *James Cantwell is no cripple. He did fish last year within Mrs. Jane Elliott's limits with her consent... No sooner had Cantwell got his licence last year than he turns around and abuses Mrs. Elliott, under whose consent he got there! He declined to fish on that particular station on the Niagara River in front of John Bolton's property, crowded Mrs. Elliott, tampered with her fishing crew, made them discontented and everyone else also unhappy, an insulted me because I refused to apply for a licence for him to fish a <u>Drift net</u> over every other fisherman's seine hauling grounds in the Niagara River.*

The rector also alleged that Cantwell was the only Catholic fisherman in Niagara. Kerr went ballistic, explaining there were several other Catholics fishing "and although this may have escaped the Reverend's mind! He knows it and he also knows these fishermen personally and their families! I can assure you that there has never been the slightest disposition on the part of any of the fishermen about Niagara to raise an objection to Catholics. I have none!!!" A man of God lying? It seems inconceivable, but if Cantwell fed him these lies, it may not have been the rector's fault.

In regard to the allegation of a relationship between Mrs. Elliott and Kerr, he wrote,

> *Cantwell judges people as he lives his own life, which appears to imply a slur on Mrs. Jane Elliott's character, if not immoral as between Mrs. Elliott and myself. It is a criminal libel! Mrs. Jane Elliot, whose name and fame as a wife and mother is above reproach . . .*
>
> *Cantwell has no sympathy for the afflicted, is bereft of all the tender feelings of humanity for poor Thomas Elliott and is purposed for self, to sacrifice everyone, even me, his friend, an old friend at that, for his own greed. Cantwell's motives, wanton feelings towards his afflicted neighbour, is known all over the community. Begging under false representations for sympathy, but has not a spark of it to give away . . . It is all folly for him to try this grab game!*

This is perhaps the worst example of knavish activity in Kerr's life as a fisheries overseer. It seems to point to today when people will enlist some talking head to spew a stream of lies without any concern for the consequences—or the truth, for that matter. Greed has always been a part of human nature and may someday result in the extinction of this species unless goodness and common sense prevail. I, for one, am not optimistic. This entire letter is worth a read and can be found on page twenty-six of volume thirteen. In a postscript, Kerr wrote, "in my travel through life, it is those persons for whom I do the most! Who treat me and serve me worst."

Ultimately, Cantwell was restricted to his existing limits, and Kerr was relieved that the matter had been brought under control. He wrote to Mrs. Elliott on May 9 to advise her of the result and referred to the Jimmy Hutchinson altercation, as reported by Joseph Masters: "I think you as well as myself have offended Mr. Hutchinson! He will doubtless tell you what transpired between us this morning; he is too meddlesome and cranky, I will say no more!" Kerr also reported John Bolton being up to his old tricks by fishing three boats instead of two in the river, presumably annoying the other fishermen as well as Kerr.

As if expecting imminent repercussions from Cantwell, Bolton, or both, Kerr sent urgent instructions to his handyman to secure his property in Niagara. He instructed John Thornton to pull down the cottage on the ferry lot and board up the windows and doors of the ferry house and the old barracks [Navy Hall]: "Now with regards the bricks, have them placed at the west end of the Ferry House, all built up in a row. Examine the wire fence on the side next the River and repair it."

Cantwell was apparently chastised by the rector for lying to him, but he doubled down in a further attempt to get Kerr in trouble and to get a hold of Mrs. Elliott's lease. He sent a further slanderous and malicious letter to the minister, and Kerr unloaded again. He began by giving the full details of the arrangement between Cantwell and Mrs. Elliott to let him fish in 1884. He then noted, "James Cantwell and his wife are not the only fishermen who have attempted to force themselves on Mrs. Elliott's fisheries [John Bolton?], and this has all happened since the sad affliction has befallen her husband, Thomas Elliott."

Referring to Cantwell seeking to enlist the support of Senator Plumb and MP Rykert, Kerr observed,

> *this will convince you what unusual efforts were then made by these thoughtless people to take away from Mrs. Elliott and her three children their birthright. Send any man you like to interview Thomas Elliott, I wish you could see him yourself and then I am sure you would applaud me for not becoming the supple tool of a Plumb, a Rykert, a Cantwell no! not even Mrs. Kate his wife . . . I may here tell you that James Cantwell refused and did not, and would not fish opposite John Bolton's property and I am sure he would not fish there this year if he had a chance!"*

He probably knew that Bolton would not tolerate his BS.

This year, for good reasons, Mrs. Elliott declined to admit him on her seine ground–then he commenced slandering me for a just and proper act exercised by Mrs. Elliott. Her own family needs all she can make on the fisheries... Now about Morals! It is only 3 years ago Cantwell's wife would have left him in consequence of the immoral life he was then leading, only Mrs. Elliott prevented her! Last Sunday, John Bolton told me Cantwell was slandering me about his wife and wished me to have him taken up and punished. My reply was there is no cause for slandering me! And I heard nothing more about it...

I can honestly and truthfully tell you that during the 20 years and 5 months I have served in the fishery department, although I have heard many people talk of the drunken bad conduct of fisherman's wives! I am prepared to affirm and swear upon my solemn oath! That not a single case of this kind has ever come under my personal observation."

Remarkably, on June 24, Kerr wrote to John Bolton requesting his seine licence fee and concluded, "You have proved to me a true friend." I didn't see that coming! Was he just trying to recruit allies like he once had with Cantwell? Historically, nothing could have been further from the truth.

By August, Kerr wrote that Mrs. Elliott was doing well because she had paid back a $157 loan and bought a cow. As for her husband, "she told me he still gets worse! And now he curses and blasphemes at an awful rate. I did not see him. He is kept shut up in a room all the time. God pity him." Probably as a result of Cantwell's slanderous allegations, and as a result of his obvious interventions on behalf of the Elliotts, Kerr noted that he no longer boarded at the Elliotts but stayed at the Doyle Hotel. In a further effort to help the Elliotts, Kerr planned to evict his non-paying tenant from the ferry lot and allow Mrs. Elliott to use it for a vegetable garden and one apple tree to provide red apples for her husband.

In May 1885 Kerr assumed responsibility for the waters off Port Burwell, on Lake Erie, between Long Point and Port Stanley, and struck up a curious relationship with a merchant and fisherman named William

Y. Emery. He doesn't appear to have met him before but remarked he "seems to be a respectable man." There was a connection, however, as Emery seemed to have known of Kerr's uncle, also John William Kerr, who was now dead. In 1847 our Kerr was adjutant to Thomas Dobbie of the 3rd Middlesex Militia, and there was mention of a dinner in 1837 with Uncle John Kerr. Kerr explained to Emery that it was not him because he was in the RIC at the time and didn't arrive in Canada until August 26, 1846.

Next, it was off to the small town of Blenheim to straighten up Kent County on Lake Erie, then under Fisheries Overseer John McMichael, "a good Irishman" who was not so good at collecting or remitting fees, being $390 in arrears. Kerr also seemed to have no trouble collecting and settling matters. For once, this fisheries overseer had not pocketed the money!

As if all this turmoil were not enough, in late May, the Wentworth Fish and Game Club once again started to stir up trouble against Mr. Campbell of Progreston (Carlisle) on 12 Mile Creek. The club had written Kerr a registered letter making inquiries of him. Kerr huffed to Bauset, "I have not replied to these questions! Because I don't see by what authority I am asked to become the pliant, servile tool of such an assumed authority. I attend to my duties on 12 Mile Creek on which there is at present only 2 saw mills, one at Progreston, the property of Mr. William Campbell, who these people are so desirous of persecuting, as you are already aware."

Kerr was then shocked to get a letter from Conservative Hamilton MP Kilvert in support of the Club. Kerr responded to Bauset: "I want to know in the name of common sense, what has induced Mr. F. E. Kilvert to make himself so conspicuous for Dr. Malloch–Grit–John Hall–Grit, Tinsley-Grit, Fish and Game Club, as against old Mr. Campbell. He is 75 years old and he does not care to be annoyed any longer."

Kerr met with Campbell and reported,

> Mr. Campbell had no hesitation in telling me, that because he is a Conservative... he has been persecuted by an illegal combined assembly of people being in the City of Hamilton and

> *styling themselves as the Fish & Game Protective Association of the County of Wentworth! With no stake nor personal or individual interest in the County [Halton]... Campbell could not understand why these Hamilton people, including two MP's were putting him to "expense, loss and damage.*
>
> *Mr. William Campbell saws about 400,000 feet, board measure annually. He burns up all the sawdust in his mill which is a considerable quantity."*

Kerr noted the two other mills were equally as careful. "The Club is more destructive to speckled trout than sawdust. I give you my experience."

Kerr observed that the creek often went dry in the summer and that as a result of twelve shuttered mills, it had not been a fish stream for a long time. He had also ensured that Campbell was properly disposing of his sawdust and reminded the minister that Campbell, a good Scotch Conservative, had been fined years before and learned his lesson. Finally, he noted that the fish and game club "celebrated only for hunting for money and annoying a respectable, industrious man, a supporter of Sir John A., on his own private property" repeatedly trespassed upon him. Unfortunately, the persecution would continue.

On the eve of his seventy-third birthday, Kerr wrote to Bauset to express his gratitude to God for giving him a long life. "I may tell you, I never felt happier in my life than I do now!" Kerr also opined on the present debate in Ottawa regarding Irish nationalism: "As an Irishman by birth, I condemn Blake for his unpatriotic, silly conduct, in putting questions, imbecilic in nature, leads me very often to think that there is something wrong in his upper story. His questions to Sir John A. MacDonald were most disgraceful!" Edward Blake, the second premier of Ontario, was leader of the Liberal Party of Canada and a fervent Irish nationalist. He later sat as such in the British House of Commons. Needless to say, Kerr was not a fan.

On finally wrapping up McBride's mess in Elgin, Kerr wrote an amusing note to Bauset citing an old Scottish drinking song: "And here's a hand to Catholic! And Protestant gie us thine! We'll drink and say 'God save the Queen! And auld lang syne! Scotland forever!!! Well, God bless you anyhow.'" Unfortunately, the Department could not decide what to do with McBride. Should they dismiss him and risk it becoming a public scandal or sweep in under the carpet and maintain him under Kerr's supervision?

Later in the year, Kerr found evidence of further misappropriation by McBride, and he set out to prove his case. To gain some cover, McBride attempted to change his political allegiances to the Conservatives, to which Kerr huffed, "Can the Ethiopian change his skin, or the leopard his spots. McBride was at first Conservative. Then he turned Grit. I suppose he will go back one of these days to his first love, a conservative. I may as well tell you that I don't admire turncoats. Neither in religion nor politics."

During the summer of 1885, Kerr received applications from American fishermen in Cleveland to fish in Canadian waters in Lake Erie. Based upon Kerr's views that the lake was being overfished, you think he would have been opposed, but in fact he was in favour because he knew they were fishing illegally anyway, and he might as well licence them. From time to time Kerr had asked permission to hire a tug to stop such illegal fishing, but the Department was never prepared to authorize payment. The Department refused to licence the Cleveland fishermen, so Kerr requested his fishermen to "keep an eye out for the Yankees." What they were to do about trespassers, however, was unclear. Pelee Island, the southernmost point in Lake Erie, is thirty kilometers south of Leamington, a big area to patrol.

Kerr had been agitating for years for the Department to strictly enforce the closed season for whitefish throughout the Great Lakes in November, and in 1885 it seemed like they were determined to do so. Kerr's limits were extended to Leamington, and he was "authorized to employ any necessary assistance you may deem necessary to a rigid enforcement of the closed season" by Deputy Minister John Tilton. Kerr was very excited and began to plan his campaign, writing to Bauset, "All! Every Mother's son! Must toe the line this time!! We must be all ready and, in our places, when the 1st of November arrives" (the beginning of closed season).

Kerr was now at the height of his powers and the pinnacle of his career, and he was feeling great. Writing to a friend at Killarney, he attributed his success to his venture on Georgian Bay: "From the moment you routed me up to go to Horse Island **my career has been upward! Upward!! And successful.** I am, thank God, in good health and spirits."

In preparation for closed season, Kerr returned to Essex County for the first time since 1872 when he fondly remembered being driven twenty miles on the ice to Pelee Island by Doc Wilkinson, who had since passed away. Having once taken the comfortable ferry to Pelee Island, I can only imagine what a twenty-mile trip on the rough ice of Lake Erie must have been like! Kerr was concerned about tugs from Cleveland and Sandusky taking fish directly from pound nets to their US markets during closed season.

The problem was that closed season had been extended to cover the entire month of November rather than just the first ten days. This was largely due to the constant nagging by Kerr that ten days was too short. However, for pound net owners, it was too long because pound nets were driven into the lake bottom and fished 24/7. They had to be emptied every day or two, or the caught fish would rot. The fishermen were supposed to "liberate" the whitefish or trout during closed season, but there was a lot of temptation to bring in the illegal fish as well or let American tugs and steamers load them directly from the pots onto the boats for sale in Sandusky or Cleveland. With 117 pound nets fishing in Lake Erie, Kerr noted with good reason that he was "nervous."

Just as closed season was about to start, Kerr had another problem on his hands when he gained information that caused him to believe that Fisheries Overseer McCrea of Grand River had his hands in the cookie jar by not remitting funds. Considering their longstanding feud, it is not surprising that Kerr had "lost confidence in McCrea" and supported his discharge. Whether McCrea was discharged, I don't know.

On November 21, Kerr planned and executed another mission to catch Dan Wardell in the act of illegal fishing at Rainham. Taking the evening train to Port Dover, he was up at 2:00 a.m. for the twenty-six-mile buggy ride on terrible roads to Rainham, where he arrived at 7:00

a.m. "just in the nick of time" to seize 1,200 yards of all new gill nets. Wardell and his crew just didn't seem to get the message! Kerr proposed a twenty-dollar fine and confiscation of all nets and boats. Ouch!

Despite all of his best efforts and those of his other fisheries overseers on Lake Erie, there were still numerous infractions of closed season, and Kerr was determined to prosecute. Unfortunately, he ran into another recalcitrant JP in the small Essex town of Duarte who determined that some accused could not be convicted because the local constable had some kind of improper motive. Kerr doubled down and had the Department lay the charges, and he was told to seek the maximum fine. Kerr somehow got the cases moved to another town and succeeded in front of a different justice of the peace.

The remarkable rehabilitation in the relationship between Kerr and John Bolton is again demonstrated in a December 4 letter to Bolton.

> *My dear Friend John Bolton: James Cantwell, you may rely upon, will never fish in Mrs. Jane Elliott's seine hauling grounds. <u>The scoundrel, he slandered Mrs. Elliott and he slandered his wife.</u> His aim and object was to hurt me, but he failed and everything went home to him and his lovely Kate. I propose next year to recommend you, Allen's and Mrs. Elliott for seine licenses on your respective grounds, and no one else! About Big Jim and Jack Raynard, I am always ready for such scheming fellows. No danger about shooting, as two can play at that game. One is privileged to carry arms, the other can do so only under a penalty of $40.*

Fortunately, gunplay did not result.

In December, Kerr learned that Minister McLelan had been appointed Finance Minister, and Kerr wrote to Bauset in the hope that his promotion would come through before he changed ministries. Despite his herculean efforts, it was not to be. The new minister was "Professor Foster of Nova Scotia, the Great Temperance Orator."

Kerr described the prosecution in Duarte that was orchestrated by an American named Wilkinson, who appeared to be only motivated by what he could get out of the case. Kerr had nothing but contempt for him: "I don't think it is either right, just or proper to receive a complaint from a speculating Yankee against a British born subject, for the purpose of blackmailing." Wilkinson alleged that Kerr had promised him money for assisting him. Kerr fired back: "I wonder what rights does a speculating, blackmailing, drunken, Squaw hunting, Yankee informer expect to receive. We discarded him." Tell us how you really feel, John!

Apparently, Wilkinson had been hired on as a crew member for C.W. Gauthier of Sandwich, and trouble soon ensued: "J.S. Wilkinson had two Squaws at the fishing grounds last summer, when he and they got drunk and a gun being fired off, a fatal accident nearly happened." Wilkinson was fired, and, swearing revenge, initiated a prosecution against the only Canadian member of the crew. When Kerr intervened, Wilkinson's motives were revealed, and his evidence was not heard: "Wilkinson's statements about me are all imaginary. I never employed him! I never promised him anything."

And so the year ended, with Kerr creating his annual returns and, like the control freak he was, the returns for all his other fisheries overseers, contemplating a year of triumph and disappointment.

1886

This was a year of strife for Kerr, who got into fights with the Hamilton Fish and Game Club and his former friend, Samuel Wilmot, amongst others. The federal election of February 22, 1887, meant stirring up the electorate in support of Good Old Sir John A., and Kerr suffered a health crisis that presaged the end of his lengthy career.

The year started quietly, as usual, with Kerr doing his annual returns until he turned his sights on fisheries overseers McBride and McCrea. Noting their misappropriations Kerr, commented, "in my early life they would be transported as thieves for committing such depredations!!"[172] Noting that they were both Masons, Kerr observed that his obligations ceased toward them upon them committing their crimes: "A fig for

---

172   The process of transporting criminals to colonies like Australia began to wind down by 1857 and pretty well came to an end by 1868. Had Kerr been convicted while in the Royal Irish Constabulary, he could well have been transported.

such A. F. & A. M. Masons."[173]

Suddenly, and without any warning, Kerr received two letters from MP F. E. Kilvert and Samuel Wilmot regarding 12 Mile Creek and the Hamilton Fish and Game Club. The club had tried repeatedly to recruit Kerr to act as their tool to secure hunting rights over private property for club members, and Kerr had refused based upon his belief in the inviolate rights of property owners to be free from trespass. Kilvert, a Conservative MP and friend of Kerr's, had been induced by the Grit members of the club to write a letter of complaint about Kerr's attitude toward the club.

It seems the club was aware of Kerr's report on 12 Mile Creek that there was no major pollution and that old Mr. Campbell was a favourite of Kerr's, so somehow they convinced Wilmot to inspect the creek and order that Campbell install a fishway in his dam. Kerr was livid and wrote to Bauset, "I never imagined before that Kilvert was a two-faced animal!" Regarding Wilmot: "I shall handle the traitor and betrayer of his best friend as he deserves! Just you mark my words if I don't!" Kerr was particularly incensed that Wilmot had proceeded behind his back and then attended the game club's annual meeting, where they slagged Kerr in the press.

Kerr railed on: "I will not stand this!! And now just say what I am to do and I am prepared to fire away." Unbelievably, the Department sided with Wilmot and ordered the construction of a fishway at Campbell's dam. Kerr had to serve him with the order. He wrote to Bauset, "Mr. William Campbell feels indignant at being selected by Samuel Wilmot, an expert, and members of the Game Club to build a fishway in his dam [while others were not]. It is suspicious."

In regard to the club, Kerr continued: "Except Ned O'Reilly,[174] I believe they are every man jack of them Grits **of the worst stripe!** Combined and conspired together!! To damage, injure and control the minister, deputy, and your honoured self! But me, never! Death to me is welcome anytime, before dishonor!" Campbell wrote to Kerr to express

---

173 A. F. and A. M. stand for "Ancient Free" and "Accepted Masons."
174 James Edwin "Ned" O'Reilly (1833–1907) was mayor of Hamilton twice in 1869 and 1871.

his anguish about being singled out for no purpose because during the thirty to forty years he had been there he had never seen a single fish and wanted Kerr to write to the newspapers. However, Kerr refused to do so as a matter of policy: "I never write in newspapers, for as you say, if my Irish got up, I might play the devil."

Kerr did write again to Bauset on Campbell's behalf: "The proceedings of Sam Wilmot, F. E. Kilvert [and members of the Game Club], although intended for me, has placed Mr. William Campbell of Progreston, as a marked man on 12 Mile Creek." Kerr also wanted some support from the Department in regard to Wilmot's slanderous report that Kerr had misled the Ministry: "I can bear more wanton slanderous attacks than any other fishery overseer but I think in justice to me that report should not be allowed to remain uncontradicted by the deputy minister." Bauset did send a letter to Kilvert, for which Kerr was grateful.

Kerr railed on: "For nearly 54 years I have faithfully served my Queen and Country and her two illustrious predecessors in one capacity or another, and I should not now allow Sam Wilmot to tarnish my name! by stating in his report that I deceived the Department." Kerr again referred to being sworn in to the Royal Irish Constabulary by Sir John Harvey, the British general at the battle of Stoney Creek, on September 1, 1832: "Every day of my life that I go out through the gate in front of my house I can see Stoney Creek and the Battleground! Where the late Sir John Harvey defeated the Yankees in 1813. He was the first person before whom I ever took an oath."

The game club's next audacious move was to try and get exclusive rights to fish in Burlington Bay. Predictably, Kerr went apoplectic. Pointing out to the Department that all of the bay, except for private inlets and Kerr's Pond, were navigable waters, Kerr made it clear that it was public domain and not for sale. Noting the game club's object, Kerr stated it was to "get a hold of Dundas Marsh and Burlington Bay, by hook or by crook, for a monopoly, and then farewell to every other one… If they knew me, they would keep far away from me! I may compel them to do it most effectively still!" Apparently, Kerr wasn't the only one opposed to the club's nefarious objects, as he wrote in a March letter: "I heard today that people are up in arms against the notorious

Game Club! Meetings are called to oppose them!" They did not get their exclusive rights.

In April, Kerr again attempted to get his now nineteen-year-old son, Edward, appointed as a fish guardian for $150 a year and invited Bauset to seek references from Senator Plumb and MPs Rykert and Ferguson[175] but not Kilvert: "It is out of the question for me to ask Kilvert anymore. I want no favours from a man whom has been in league with a pack of humbugs trying to injure!" The appointment wasn't destined to be for poor Ned, who became a house painter.

The game club's next move was to send a petition to the Governor General to stop all net fishing in Burlington Bay so that it would not impede their shooting of pike. Kerr was annoyed that they had bypassed the Ministry and that the only people net fishing were local farmers, like Andrew Gage, whose property fronted onto the bay. Kerr's view was that

> ... fishermen who have paid licence fees for 21 years should never be set aside for such an illegal grab all! So that they might have the sport of shooting pike! Which they have been doing to the extent of at least 10,000. Of course, 1,000 may be said to escape wounded and will linger, die and pollute the waters of the Bay, contaminated already by the filthy sewage of the City of Hamilton. No true sportsman would shoot pike; they are created to be angled for and netted.

While Kerr was away at Lake Erie, the game club played their next card by having several Saltfleet Township farmers charged for netting suckers, or catfish, in what is now known as Red Hill Creek, adjacent to their farms. Kerr was outraged that the club had requested County Attorney John Crerar[176] to lay the charges against farmers who for years had had the right to fish for these non-protected fish on their farms. This also involved crooked cop McNair who was, once again, interested

---

175   Dr. Charles Frederick Ferguson (July 20, 1834–Sept. 29, 1909) was a Conservative MP from Leeds Grenville from 1874–1896. I have no idea how Kerr knew him.
176   John Crerar was born in Scotland in 1836 and eventually emigrated to Canada. He opened his law practice in 1871 and became county crown attorney in 1881.

in the costs awarded if convictions were entered. Kerr immediately wrote to Bauset: "I consider it very perplexing and annoying that respectable farmers should be molested by persons calling themselves 'The Hamilton Game Club.' It is going too far! Stop it! If you please."

Kerr was summoned to court as a witness. It is unclear what happened, but Kerr later wrote to Police Magistrate Cahill to protest that Crown Attorney Crerar had misled the court by alleging false statements by Kerr and that the whole proceedings were a sham "in order to have me turned out of my situation and another person appointed in my place." The farmers were convicted and fined five dollars plus four dollars in costs. The allegation took place the day after Kerr and his sons seized 600 yards of nets from Burlington Bay, apparently set on behalf of the gun club.

The next salvo in this protracted war was fired when Provincial Constable Samuel McNair proceeded to Progreston and purported to inspect William Campbell's sawmill for sawdust being allowed into the creek. Despite never being closer than fifteen yards to the mill, charges were laid, and Magistrate Cahill convicted poor Campbell and fined him fifty dollars plus eight dollars in costs.

Kerr, who was not in attendance, went berserk. Proceeding immediately to Progreston, he carefully examined the mill and wrote a long description of how Campbell disposed of his sawdust by burning it in a furnace. McNair, whom Kerr said was a "Provincial Officer" having been "dismissed from the County of Wentworth" had refused to visit the mill with Kerr, who believed that Campbell got railroaded.

Kerr observed that the fine and costs "are enormous as compared with the trifling offence committed!" and that the mill was likely to close as a result. He and Campbell's lawyer wrote to the Department asking for the fine to be withdrawn, but John Tilton, bureaucrat and deputy minister, refused. Kerr was astonished that the Department had permitted this persecution, noting nine other mills on the same creek had not been inspected.

Less than six weeks later, seventy-five-year-old William Campbell was dead, thrown from his buggy by a runaway horse. Kerr attended his funeral and noted it was the largest he had ever seen in Canada, with about 300 carriages and buggies "with respectable ladies and gentlemen" from Wentworth, Halton and Cardwell."[177] Kerr wrote to Bauset: "The proceedings carried on by Constable McNair and the Hamilton Game Club are disapproved of! And they are despised for persecuting the late William Campbell. I am not afraid to tell you the plain honest truth."

By late October, Kerr observed "About the Hamilton Game Club, I never hear a word about them." When the *Hamilton Spectator* published lies about him at the behest of the Club, Kerr "saw the editor and I gave him a bit of my mind about the Grit Game Club. The wanton newspaper attack made on me, hurt them! For no man believed them, besides the Grit newspaper, the *Hamilton Times!* Although repeatedly asked! Refused to write anything against me!"

That year the minister received a petition from the Southampton fishermen to allow smaller net mesh sizes, and Kerr was asked to comment.

> *It is the same old story over again!! The Highlanders from the Lowland Islands of Scotland at Southampton are entirely too selfish. However, I may tell you there are some very decent good fellows amongst them. They don't all come from the Isle of Skye. Nonetheless, they are all fishermen at home in Scotland, and now here in Canada! All hardy good fellows only too selfish! Full or empty, never satisfied seems to be the motto with some of these Scotch crofters. Take all and leave nothing behind would be their way of doing up the fisheries!! Well, they can never do this as long as you [Bauset] are at the helm."*

I am always amused by Kerr's attitude toward the Scots. He was consistently condescending toward them, and they were always "difficult" or "impossible to please." The irony is that Kerr could not have been more than a couple of generations removed from his Scottish cousins, and his family probably left Scotland because they could not make a go of it there!

On April 6, Kerr reported a strong northeast gale that dumped a foot

---

177   Cardwell was a federal electoral district that included the towns of Bolton and Caledon.

of snow on his farm. Kerr sat in his big house and wrote letter after letter to occupy his time. The storm caused substantial damage, as he later learned and reported. In Niagara, Kerr found his fences blown down and Mrs. Elliott's boathouse destroyed. The newspapers reported extensive damage from Toronto to Niagara as a result of the "violent raging storm."

On April 14, Kerr visited Burlington Beach and reported extensive damage, such as roads carved up, fences down, gardens demolished, and sand everywhere. He witnessed more than one mile of the beach submerged under several feet of water and John Dynes' ballroom "blown down." The Hamilton and North Western Railway tracks were "carried away in two places and traffic was stopped for 3 or 4 days." His boat in the Elliotts' boathouse was also damaged, and he had to get it repaired by boat builder John Redhead.

As fishing season started, things began to heat up again in Niagara. Mrs. Elliott and another fisherman reported to Kerr that at least 10,000 feet of gill nets were set in the lake by the Boltons and others emboldened by them. They were also taunting Mrs. Elliott's crew. Kerr promised to deal with it. The next Sunday he took the evening train to Niagara where he partnered with the chief constable and fished up about 900 yards of net belonging to John Bolton. Kerr had him summonsed to court in St. Catharines. After pleading guilty, Bolton was fined five dollars, and his nets were confiscated. The war was back on.

In May, Kerr reported an ugly incident on the Niagara River, near Fort Erie, where two men, armed with a double-barrel shotgun, in small boats from Buffalo or Black Rock, entered a creek and began to fish a trammel net. When the local farmers "remonstrated," the man carrying the gun "cocked it and pointed it in the direction of the farmers." As they left the creek, the man with the gun was captured and his gun, boat, and nets were seized. Kerr got down there as soon as he could to take possession of the seized objects in what could have been an international incident. Fortunately, such events were rare.

In the fall, Kerr began to bang the drum for the upcoming federal election. Riel was hanged in November 1885 after a controversial trial, and the Conservatives were struggling in Quebec as a result. Kerr stated to his friend Emery, "It will require every effort in our power, and in the power of every good loyal Conservative, to keep Sir John A. MacDonald in power. All must work!! Work! Work!! And get our friends to the polls." He said people must not condemn MacDonald "because it became necessary to hang Riel, a double and treble murderer, put down by our brave militia, most worthy and brave soldiers!!"

On October 14, Kerr reported the second major storm of the year, this time on Lake Erie. As on Lake Ontario, the damage was extensive, especially to the pound-net fishermen, who lost almost all their nets and stakes during the best part of the season. There was also significant damage on land, caused by the seventy-five-mile-an-hour winds, such as to the Fraser House Hotel in Port Stanley. Kerr wanted a complete inventory of the loss, which he planned to submit to Ottawa in the hope that licence fees for 1887 would be reduced. It wasn't to be, but the deadline for payment was extended.

Kerr had not heard from Bauset for some time despite sending numerous urgent letters about Georgian Bay and Lake Huron. At the end of October, he learned that Bauset had been unwell and wrote to express his sympathy.

> *I am sorry indeed to hear of your illness. For Heaven's sake, keep away from the opium! It is a treacherous commodity. Exercise, exercise; run around and a little fatigue will soon enable you to obtain your natural sleep again!. . . Let the opium alone! I do not wish that you should leave the fisheries department until after I go first! And I have not made up my mind on this subject yet!. . . On two occasions a half dozen bottles of Guinness porter cured me. That was 15 years ago! You must take good care of yourself for good men are few.*

In December Kerr sent Bauset some wine and wrote again to expostulate on the sleep benefits of alcohol: "I am really glad to hear that the wine has helped you sleep. Guinness's XX porter I believe would help you better still. It is of a drowsy nature, just drink a tumbler full every day at your dinner and I am sure it will help to sleep."

Also in October, Kerr received a typed letter from Deputy Minister

John Tilton. First invented in 1874, the typewriter did not become common until the mid-1880s, so this was a real novelty. If you want to see a letter typed in 1886, it's on page 227 of volume thirteen.

Meanwhile, John Bolton continued to covet Mrs. Elliott's seine-fishing grounds, but this time he was prepared to pay for it. Kerr wrote to Mrs. Elliott to see if she would consider this, noting that she was "all powerful, the power behind the throne in the case." It doesn't seem like she trusted Bolton because she had once trusted Jim Cantwell, to her dismay.

Using his network of informants in the Toronto fish market, in Southampton, and in Owen Sound, Kerr had been warning of vast quantities of fish being caught in closed season, frozen, and shipped by rail car to the southern markets. His theory was that if he stopped the fish buyers, he would stop the illegal fishers, and he was itching to get back up north. Finally, he was permitted to go. Taking the train to Collingwood, he picked up Fisheries Overseer George Miller and proceeded to Meaford, where he found his prey with eight tons of freshly caught salmon and trout.

The matter appeared in court, and the accused pled guilty to buying one ton caught during closed season, and the matter was remanded for sentencing to ascertain the Department's position. Kerr recommended leniency because he had to admit that the entire month of November as closed season was too long and that men were going to succumb to temptation and perhaps financial need to fish. The accused was fined five dollars or eight days in jail. As for the seized fish, they were sold for twenty-five dollars. To Kerr's chagrin, it was now December, and closed season was over, and so was his chance to nab any more offenders! He would get back to Georgian Bay for one more special duty.

On making his rounds in Niagara, Kerr again visited his old friend, Thomas Elliott. He observed: "Thomas Elliott, a complete imbecile! I never thought any man could be so reduced to the state of an idiot as he is! All his manhood has vanished. I never witnessed the like before in all my life." He noted that he had first met Elliott on May 5, 1865, and that he was

> *a good husband and father, admired and respected ... suddenly his mind gave way, April 1883 ... Mr. Elliott was for a short time in the Hamilton Asylum for the Insane, but as his disease did not*

> come under the head of *afflicted persons maintained there*, Mrs. Elliott had to fetch him home from there and care for him and her three daughters herself. I saw him and such a wreck of the man he is at present. Only a remnant of the once intelligent man of 22 years ago.

Perhaps knowing that his days were numbered and that Cantwell and Bolton were still out there, Kerr tried to get Mrs. Elliott a nine-year lease, which would have been extraordinary for the Department to grant. He didn't tell Bolton about this application, and the Department did not allow it. Kerr ruefully observed, "I have done all that ever lay in my power for Mrs. Elliott and her family."

Kerr was unhappy that Mrs. Elliott wanted the entire licence in her name alone rather than jointly with her fishing partner, Dick Allan, and felt that she was "screwing or attempting to screw" Allan. Kerr felt this was illegal and noted "I cannot mix myself up in any arrangement between Dick Allan and Mrs. Elliott, for if John Bolton comes to hear it, he **will raise Cain,** for I believe John Bolton will be an applicant himself for the fishery next year, he thinks he is entitled to that part in front of his property."

Feeling uncharacteristically sorry for himself, Kerr stated,

> Got reported by the <u>Roman Catholic Priest, Big Jim Cantwell! And by that Scotchman, Jimmy Hutchinson</u>, all on Mrs. Elliott's account. I think I guard my reputation as well as I possibly can, but whatever scandal has been circulated by the above persons, because I declined cutting up Mrs. Elliott's fishing grounds, I alone became the sufferer, for I had to move off from a comfortable Boarding House and go to a tavern, the last place of all I care to stop at. Mrs. Elliott displayed cowardice in not meeting me at the Murray House.[178]

---

178   The Murray House was a sixty-room, four-storey hotel located at the corner of King and James in St. Catharines. It opened in 1864 and closed in 1972. Kerr clearly wanted to meet Mrs. Elliott in a clandestine location to discuss her situation away from prying eyes and ears.

Kerr was concerned that if the Department learned of Mrs. Elliott's plan, it "could take the fishing grounds from her altogether...And I fear Jack Bolton knows about the arrangement. Now I swear Bolton will bring all his forces to aid him in capturing from Mrs. Elliott a portion of her grounds."

On Christmas Day, Kerr was preparing for dinner when he decided to look out his front door and promptly lost his footing on his icy front porch, badly injuring his right leg: "Just immediately before dinner, the turkey on the table, I walked to the front door, and the moment I got on the upper step, away my feet went from under me and I was dashed down 5 steps to the ground. I was so badly hurt I could not get up! My right leg and foot lay on the walk, helpless. I sent for a doctor who bandaged up my knee and thigh, which I had to keep stretched on a sofa or bed to avoid being a cripple."

Now seventy-four years old, this injury was a life-changing event for Kerr and was truly the beginning of the end, although he soldiered on for another seventeen months. As 1886 ended, Kerr sat in his house writing letters as if it was business as usual.

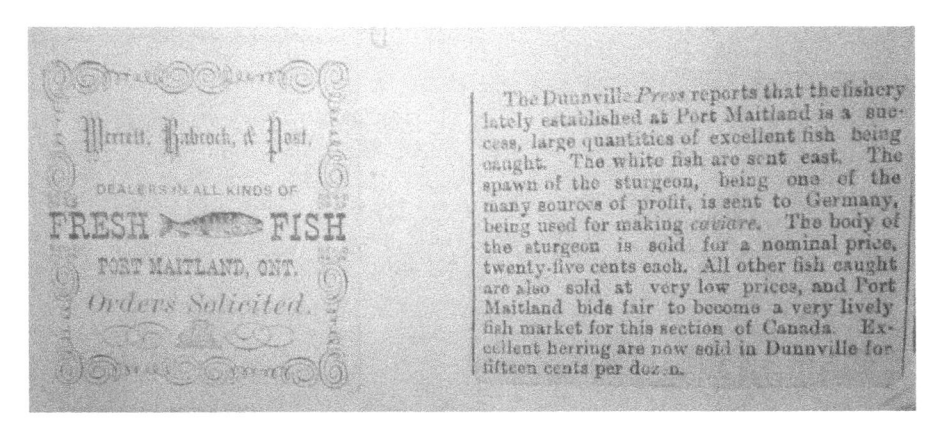

Newspaper clippings found in Kerr diary, about fishing on the lower Grand River. ROM

Burlington Bay Fisheries.

The following letter has been received by the city and county members:

GENTLEMEN,—The Minister desires me to inform you, that, in accordance with your request, net licenses will be discontinued in Burlington Bay after the termination of those already issued for the current season. The usual privileges of angling, trolling and spearing (the latter under special licenses for specific periods) will continue. Instructions to the Fishery Officers have been issued to such effect.

I have the honor to be, gentlemen,
Your obedient servant,
W. I. WITCHER,
For the Hon. Minister of
Marine and Fisheries.

Messrs. Thos. Bain, Jos. Rymal and A. T. Wood.

From the foregoing it will be seen that this question has now been effectually and satisfactorily settled, and we presume all parties interested will be gratified to know that their efforts to secure proper protection for the fish in Burlington Bay and the Dundas Marsh have at last been fully recognized by the Fishery Department, and that for the future no more favoritism in the granting of licenses can be indulged in by Mr. Fishery Inspector Kerr.—*Dundas Banner.*

Newspaper clipping found in Kerr diary. The Ministry eventually banned net fishing in Burlington Bay, to Kerr's chagrin. ROM

*Front door of Kerr's house, from where he fell on Christmas Day 1886.
Photo by Kristen Kerr, 2020*

SPEARING IN BURLINGTON BAY.—Mr. J. W. Kerr, Overseer of Fisheries, captured a boat last night with speared fish therein and light wood. The spearers, who are farmers, resident in Saltfleet, fled, with the spear and light jack. It is a shame for the farmers to employ their time in catching such small pike, besides running the risk of being fined $20 and costs. They have been warned repeatedly by this journal that if they are caught breaking the law they will have only themselves to blame hereafter.

SPEARING IN THE BAY.—Last night about 10:30 p.m., Mr. J. W. Kerr, Fishery Overseer, being on the bay in a boat with his crew, observed a jack-light in front of Record's Inlet. He gave chase and on approaching the spearers the light was put out by the offenders, who ran their boat to Elisha Harris's inlet, closely pursued by Mr. Kerr, and landed on Mr. Thomas Jones' side of the inlet. Although the spears and jack-light were not found in the boat, sufficient speared fish and lightwood were found therein to warrant the seizure and confiscation of the boat. The offenders, who made good their escape, are known. The boat is one of Mr. Aaron Fletcher's make, of Burlington Beach.

Newspaper clipping found in Kerr diary. Typical newspaper accounts of Kerr's exploits. ROM

A FISHERY CASE.—Patrick Hand, licensed fisherman, was charged before the Police Magistrate, this morning, by Mrs. Scott, with obstructing a side line running from the road to the lake, near her farm, by building a shanty, thereby preventing free access to the water. Mrs. Scott's evidence supported the above. Mr. J. W. Wilson deposed that the shanty was on the road, and within 140 feet of his warehouse, and 200 feet from the water; that it stood between lots 4 and 5 of the broken front, and damaged Mrs. Scott's property to the value of one thousand dollars. For the defence Mr. J. W. Kerr, license issuer, deposed that Hand's house was built upon the open beach, in no one's way, and at the end of the road; that he, Kerr, had seen several of the township councillors, and they had assured him that if Hand presented a petition to them they would grant his wish to build there. At the request of Mr. Barr, the case was adjourned until the 8th, to allow consultation with the Council and Government.

Newspaper clipping found in Kerr diary. Kerr went to bat for his Irish friend Patty Hand when he was charged with obstructing access to the waterfront. ROM

HAMILTON.

HAMILTON, Nov. 23.

This morning Mr. Broughton, the General Manager of the G. W. R., has given instructions to the employees of the road not to carry white fish for any person over the road, during the close season, under a penalty of dismissal.

The American Express Company has also forbidden their agents from carrying fish during the close season.

A conductor, named Daney, on the W. G. & B. R., had a barrel of fish at Galt, on the 18th inst. Mr. Kerr, Inspector of fisheries, has received instructions to prosecute him and the shipper, and also the N. R., and G. T. R., for carrying the fish over their roads.

Newspaper clipping found in Kerr diary.
Kerr warned the railways against transporting illegal fish. ROM

Chapter 12

And So Mote It Be! 1887–1888

1887

Despite his fall on Christmas Day, it was another busy year for Kerr, including his last visit to Ottawa and a couple of special duty events. There was a major escalation in the war with Samuel Wilmot, and Kerr was made a big promise by Deputy Minister John Tilton that would not be kept. Overall, Kerr travelled about 10,000 miles by his various means of transportation, which was a little above average.

With his badly injured right leg, Kerr sat in his house writing letters and writing up his annual returns, as usual, but he was clearly worried about his future mobility. He reported extensive bruising and swelling but was happy not to have broken anything, and by January 4 he was able to get up steps one at a time. By January 8, Kerr was out and about but clearly struggling.

The previous November, the Department had agreed to allow spearfishing in Burlington Bay during winter but only for herring and pike, not bass. Kerr knew this made no sense because fishermen couldn't see what they were catching when spearing through the ice or in the muddy water of the bay. MP F. E. Kilvert circulated a petition to amend this bizarre rule, and Kerr met with him to support it, even though he still considered him a "double dealer."

As Kerr predicted, in Niagara, John Bolton applied for a portion of Mrs. Elliott's lease, so Kerr wrote Bauset a private memorandum opposed to the application.

> *Mr. John Bolton, not having the fear of God before his eyes, and not a particle of the milk of human kindness in his heart, nor no sympathy for Elliott, the maniac, has applied for a portion of Mrs. Jane Elliott's fishing ground. I believe you should stamp Bolton out–just as you have done with Cantwell, who got so angry and enraged with his clergyman, because he did not get me reprimanded, that he never went to mass nor meeting since.*

Kerr also wrote to the deputy minister.

> *I cannot recommend the application of John Bolton for the simple reason that I have already recommended that Mrs. Jane Elliott receive a license, from the fact that for upwards of 50 years the Elliott family has been in continual possession of the ground now applied for by Bolton ... Mrs. Jane Elliott's husband is a raving maniac. Herself and her family have the kind sympathy of the public except a couple of heartless people who covet their fishing ground.*

Privately, Kerr wrote to Mrs. Elliott that he already had her license, but she was not to tell anyone. "I fight your battles and protect you from two men who made a wanton, untruthful and malicious attack against me, simply because I would not be a party to assist them to rob you and your children of their birth right."

On January 17, Kerr wrote to his physician, Dr. James White, to advise that he could not easily walk, being unable to put any pressure on his right leg: "I'd fall. I speak from experience having had one fall already. I want something to strengthen me up! I sleep well and can eat my grub. For all the rest, my son can tell you." By the end of January, Kerr was once again deeply involved in his business—election business, that is!

Kerr's plan was to vote for J. C. Rykert in Niagara, assist him in getting others to the polls, and then return to Hamilton to vote for Carpenter in South Wentworth. He was also busy assisting Colonel Tisdale in Norfolk, Dr. Ferguson in Welland, and McCullagh in Peel as well as the Hamilton candidates. He did all this on the government dime! Kerr wrote a friend to outline all his electioneering efforts and to ask him to write to Sir John A. MacDonald to get credit for these exploits. Kerr claimed he was "personally known" to MacDonald. Although they may have met, I doubt very much that he was "known" to MacDonald as anything other than a faithful supporter. Kerr wrote shamelessly to most of his fishermen in support of the Conservatives.

The election was held on February 22, and there was another Conservative majority victory, albeit smaller than in 1882. Kerr was elated that most of the Conservatives in his district were elected, including Carpenter in his home riding of South Wentworth, which had gone Conservative for the first time in thirty-three years. Rykert also won in Niagara, where Kerr also voted due to him owning property there. Kerr recited the campaign slogan in a letter to Emery: "Confound their politics! Frustrate their knavish tricks!! On thee our hearts we fix: God save the Queen!!!" Apparently, F. E. Kilvert chose not to run.

Kerr had been requesting for several years that he be invited back to Ottawa for talks at the Department. Just after the election, he got the call to come up, all expenses paid. Kerr was instructed to catch the 8:00 p.m. CPR express to Ottawa, which arrived about 6:00 a.m. the next morning, and then proceed to Bauset's office for a 9:45 meeting. He would spend the day at the Department, have lunch and dinner with Bauset, and then catch the 11:30 p.m. train to Toronto. "Come along John, and help us to put down bribery and corruption!" Tilton wrote. Kerr was excited because he was also going to meet the deputy minister for the first time (and the only time!).

On his return from his whirlwind trip to Ottawa (hadn't these guys heard of hotels?) Kerr reported gratefully to Bauset, who had also introduced him to the minister, George Foster, "For the kindly and courteous manner in which the Deputy Minister received me and talked with me! And introduced me to the minister, I have to thank you! Always kind to me... I do so from the bottom of my conservative heart. I felt and I feel as if fresh vigour has been imported to me and that I have been made more good and useful to the Department for the next 5 years!"

Naturally, Kerr wrote a similar thank-you to Tilton: "It was kind and considerate of you to invite me to come and see you at Ottawa and have a chat. For you to take notice of me is more gratifying than I can express. It is pleasant for me to know that my humble exertions are favourably noticed by you."

Kerr was also made a promise at Ottawa, and it was a secret he could not keep from his best friends. To Emery, he wrote, "The Deputy Minister has come to the conclusion to appoint me Inspector of Fisheries, at an increased salary." But there was a catch: Kerr had to submit some reference letters from his powerful friends. Kerr ultimately obtained ten testimonials from all the political allies he had supported in the election who referred to him in terms like "indefatigable, zealous and efficient, with great energy and ability." Kerr bragged that he could get 150 more if he had the time.

Kerr made several more attempts to get the promotion, but by August it was clear that his hopes had been dashed. He wrote to Bauset regarding Tilton: "I had no faith in his sincerity—I have less now." Kerr noted later that he had "done his duty in the greatest pain, never asked for a holiday and that if promoted Inspector not a single MP would object." This was a bitter disappointment for Kerr, even though he claimed he was "happy and content." Kerr's age and bum leg may have been the deciding factors for his change in fortune, or they might have just been lying sons of bitches! We'll never know.

Kerr's MP and friend, F. M. Carpenter, had approached Minister Foster on Kerr's behalf in Ottawa regarding his delayed promotion and was told flat out that "it was out of the question." He did offer Kerr "superannuation" but did not think he would consent. Damned right he wouldn't. Kerr wrote Bauset a letter, finally telling the truth about his leg: "In the greatest pain and agony I have done my duty during the last half year, and done my duty I hope, to the satisfaction of the Department. I always earn my pay, and I have never, sick or well, asked for a holiday. I always worked hard, having in view such an appointment, and God at the same time has been pleased to prolong my days for this some other purpose of his own."

Meanwhile in Niagara, the strange saga of Kerr and John Bolton continued. In 1881, Bolton had been sued by Adam Crooks, a prominent lawyer and Ontario cabinet minister, over the old Secord farm that Crooks had purchased in Niagara. Bolton was a squatter on two acres at Two-Mile Pond and had no legal title to his seine-hauling grounds, and Crooks wanted him off the property. Kerr had obtained a lawyer for Bolton and testified in court in Toronto on his behalf. The case was settled by an out-of-court agreement whereby Crooks would allow Bolton to use the property as long as he wanted to without being disturbed.

In 1887 a subsequent owner, lawyer Thomas Gordon of Toronto, brought a suit in the Court of Chancery to have Bolton ejected, and again Kerr came to his assistance, travelling with him to Toronto to meet his lawyer and assist in the preparation of an affidavit. Kerr noted that Bolton had been in possession of the land for over twenty-five years, and the legal opinion was that he could not be removed. Kerr was concerned that if Bolton forfeited this land, the Fisheries Department could be asked by Gordon for all the fees Bolton had paid over the years. He urged Bolton to be firm and not surrender. Kerr was also of the view that the land in question had been washed away by storms over his twenty-two years. The result of this law suit was not stated before Kerr's death the following year.

A curious event occurred in Niagara in the spring that seems completely ridiculous and may be another example of Kerr's occasional bad judgment about people. He had rented his ferry property to a fish vendor named Aldridge, who was instructed to keep up Kerr's fences and protect his newly planted fruit trees. Kerr received information that Aldridge had removed a piece of the fence and burned it and that someone had taken an axe to about thirty-five trees. Kerr was annoyed and determined to prosecute Aldridge: "I planted $65 worth of fruit trees on the property last year, and I hold Aldridge accountable to me for the loss and serious damage I have sustained, through his negligence."

Kerr clearly blamed Aldridge for stealing and burning his fence, but it is less clear whether he was guilty for the wanton destruction of the trees. If Aldridge did it, had he acted alone? Also, what was his motivation? There is nothing in the diaries to suggest any grievance with Aldridge, although Kerr did occasionally prosecute fish vendors for selling undersized fish or fish caught during closed season. This must have been connected to the Bolton/Cantwell feud, though it was probably not Bolton, who needed Kerr's help in his lawsuit. So, the likely culprit was Cantwell, who had lots of motivation to harm Kerr. It is hard to believe no one witnessed someone taking an axe to thirty-five trees, although they were apparently not cut down, just destroyed. We will never know.

In April, Kerr was again sent on special duty to the Thames River, from London to Lake St. Clair, to report on how the three fisheries overseers were performing their duties and to examine the dams and mills. He spent five days on the Thames, starting on the north branch at St. Mary's and proceeding to the mouth of the river at Lighthouse Cove, on Lake St. Clair. There were nine mills and dams, and Kerr examined them all, noting generally the need for fishways and complaining about the City of London emptying its sewers into the river.[179]

In mid-May Kerr headed back to London to rendezvous with Fisheries Overseer Peter McCann, whom he had known since 1847, and proceeded up the south branch of the Thames as far as Woodstock. Reporting on London, Kerr observed, "I saw a good deal of the City of London and its surroundings. What a difference 40 years makes. In May 1847, London had a population of 2,500 inhabitants and today it numbers nearly 40,000… I had a pleasant trip over the Thames and oh! The country looks splendid, beautiful! A pleasure trip it might fairly be called."

Kerr also wanted the Department to buy a boat for forty dollars for the fisheries overseer at Cashmere . The boat in question belonged to poor old John Gunsall of Toronto, who had died in 1886. His widow

....

179   One of the towns he visited was Cashmere. When I couldn't find it on my trusty Province of Ontario map, I Googled it, only to learn that it is a ghost town! In the mid-nineteenth century, it was a thriving little town of about one hundred people, with mills, a hotel, and light industry. Bypassed by the railway and prone to flooding, it began to shrink until it disappeared. Now it's part of a cornfield. There is a legend that a Black man tried to find a room in Cashmere, only to be repeatedly refused until he was finally taken in by the owner of a white house. He supposedly placed a curse on the town that it would all disappear, except for the white house. Today, the white house is apparently still standing…

was being evicted. Kerr didn't get permission to buy the boat, but he tried to prevent her eviction by getting a legal opinion that the landlord had trespassed on her by closing off her boathouse and causing her about $800 in damages. What a persistent guy!

In virtually every letter Kerr wrote in 1887, he reported that his leg was getting better, as if to convince himself that it was. He also noted he had lost twenty-two pounds, which although he had been a big guy, is never good if not explained.[180] Despite his gimpy leg, Kerr travelled over 5,000 miles in the first half of 1887. That summer was very hot and dry, and Kerr complained that the heat was affecting his health. That had never been the case before and was indicative of something to come. By August Kerr noted a "bowel complaint" and that he had lost a further ten pounds.

A petition was received from Fort Erie to stop the seine-net fishing on the upper Niagara River. It was circulated by Mrs. Sherman who owned the Sherman House Hotel. Mrs. Sherman, "a brawling woman," made her living selling whisky to Americans who would travel across from Black Rock to angle for fish off the wharf by her bar. She alleged the three Fort Erie seine fishermen were interfering with her American anglers/whisky drinkers, and Kerr was asked to investigate.

He first noted that none of the seine fishermen fished anywhere near the wharf and that they fished at night, which would not interfere with the daytime drinkers. He also noted that all the American anglers were fishing illegally. He also observed that sewage from Buffalo and barge loads of "filth" were damaging fishing in the river generally and that seine fishing ceased by the end of June. He duly filed his report opposing the petition, which was not granted, to his relief, because the three Fort Erie fishermen were all old friends.

In July Kerr was ordered to go to Southampton and examine the fishway built on George Gordon's dam. Kerr was happy to oblige. He found the fishway was working well and that fish were slowly but

---

180 I lost eighty pounds while going through chemotherapy and haven't put any back on because I have no sense of smell and little taste. That combination results in minimal appetite. I don't even eat chips anymore!

steadily restocking the Saugeen River system. He recommended that fry be placed in the river from Walkerton to Gordon's dam to hasten the process.

In November Kerr was stunned to learn that Sam Wilmot had been asked by a local MP to go to Southampton to inspect the fishway and that he had found it deficient and defective. Kerr responded with a detailed rebuttal that included the fact that Wilmot had mismeasured the fishway and that Wilmot "is a damned idiot." Kerr also spewed a lot of invective at Wilmot, so much that he was rebuked for his "intemperate language." For a full report, see chapter 20.

By 1887, fishing in Toronto harbour had been lost for several years, to Kerr's annoyance, but there was a sudden resurgence in net fishing for herring on the Lake Ontario side of Toronto Island. Kerr wrote to Bauset to get boat licences for William Ward, William Montgomery, and George Durnan Jr., son of lighthouse keeper George Durnan Sr. By this time the island was quite developed with hotels and attractions, including a bowling alley, for Toronto tourists.[181] Kerr was in favour of these applications, but foreseeing the future he observed, "These three, and no more, for evermore. Amen…"

To his amazement, Kerr learned that garbage from Toronto Island was being dumped into Lake Ontario about two miles off the island by George Durnan! On August 27, Kerr wrote Durnan a nasty letter threatening to prosecute him: "You must instantly stop putting the filthy poisonous stuff into the waters of Lake Ontario, and on your own licensed fishing ground. Can you not bury it in some place on the island and stop at once polluting the waters?"

Having been refused the promotion he was promised, Kerr was offered the consolation prize of a trip back to Georgian Bay. All the usual suspects were up to their old tricks, and, as usual, enforcement was nonexistent. Having recovered from his summer illness and regained five pounds, Kerr was itching to go.

....

181   The Gibraltar Point Lighthouse was built in 1808 and is the oldest on the Great Lakes. James Durnan, from Belfast, Ireland, was the third keeper from 1832 to 1854 when his son, George Durnan, took over until 1905. Champion rower Ned Hanlan married a Durnan.

In September he headed north, visiting Killarney, French River, Wiarton, Owen Sound, Meaford, and Collingwood, taking statements and musing about the many problems he had found. Taking twenty statements and accumulating 160 pages of evidence, Kerr submitted his report in October. He estimated that between 500 and 600 tons of fish were caught in Georgian Bay by seven tugs and 131 boats packing 1,060 miles of gill nets: "It is wonderful, exorbitant, superfluous fishing to excess, it must be stopped. If you don't stop them in their Mad, wild career of fishing to excess, you may depend upon my word, the end is nigh at hand."

Laying blame for all the fuss squarely at the feet of the Noble brothers, who had acquired a monopoly with their nine-year lease, thereby irritating all the other fishermen to the point of bloodshed, Kerr made a number of recommendations:

1. Don't renew the Nobles' lease beyond its expiry of December 31, 1887.
2. Don't allow any syndicate or monopoly to control any aspect of fishing.
3. Don't allow any "Yankee" fishing: "I do not think it advisable to offer inducements to Yankees who have exhausted their own fishing grounds in Lake Michigan, to come help destroy our own."
4. Limit the quantities of nets on boats.
5. Enforce legal gill net sizes.
6. Increase boat and tug licence fees.
7. All fees to be payable in advance before fishing commences.
8. Better enforcement, including appointment of fish guardians.
9. Some areas to be set aside for fish propagation.
10. Don't make any changes to closed season.

Kerr wanted to go to Ottawa to present his report in person (and to renew his efforts at promotion), but Bauset said he was too busy to see him. Kerr also wanted to go back to Georgian Bay to enforce closed season, but Bauset declined to authorize that, feeling the local fisheries overseers could handle the job. So, despite all his hard work, which Kerr crowed was the "greatest report that ever passed through my hands," he appears to have been largely ignored again.

After warning the Department repeatedly about closed-season infractions on Georgian Bay, Kerr wrote to Bauset: "I would not have hurried up and made my special report on Georgian Bay, only being under expectation of seeing my recommendations regarding the closed season carried out at this present November, as the wish and desire of prominent Georgian Bay fishermen. You might show this to the Deputy Minister, and you may say to him, that I am still ready, willing and able to do my duty to my Queen and Country, on Georgian Bay." However, it was not to be and Kerr never returned to Georgian Bay.

Edward Joyce of Bronte had been arbitrarily denied a licence by the Department, so Kerr went to bat for him, writing an emotional appeal to Bauset.

> *Edward Joyce is a loyal subject and an old fisherman of 40 years standing. He is 53 years old. I applied for and I recommended the licence to be granted which you now refuse to give him for reasons assigned. Edward Joyce has not been successful in fishing. He has a wife and 7 children. His oldest daughter was married within the last 18 months but her husband recently died in the City of Hamilton and she had to return to her father and mind her 4 younger brothers and sisters. She is likely soon to become a mother. Edward Joyce has rented a small house at Port Credit for $2 per month, whilst his wife with the other two children rent a room in the City and works out for a living and to help her husband support the family. I felt badly myself seeing his poor half-clothed children, the poor furniture and little of it, with the prospect of fishing put off signified cold comfort for small children commencing housekeeping at this inclement season of the year...*
>
> *I candidly told him I would lay his case before the Department and recommend that you will be pleased to grant him a license, free—gratis. His poverty entitles him to it. I will provide 1000 yards of gill net.*

I don't know if he got the licence, but it would be hard to refuse this appeal. It was an illustration of how hard life could be in Ontario in 1887.

In December, Kerr attended to his last special duty of 1887 when he was instructed to proceed to Sarnia and investigate Fishery Overseer D. McMaster, who was suspected of not remitting licence money to the Department. McMaster's district included the St. Clair River and part way up Lake Huron as far as Kettle Point, so Kerr did a tour and confirmed the Department's suspicions. Apart from being a thief, McMaster had also committed the cardinal sin of "vilifying and opposing the Government." Apparently, he had also made some enemies in the persons of Hamilton MP Adam Brown and John Carling of London, who both wanted McMaster to be "gotten rid of."

In addition, Kerr also found that McMaster had turned a blind eye to the capture of undersized whitefish, which were then pickled and sold in jars as "Breakfast White Fish." Upon investigation, Kerr found the fish were herring and that it was "a Yankee trick, a fraud and swindle and should not be tolerated to exist any longer, deceiving the public." Kerr also reported that the local fishermen "were perfectly astonished that the Department would keep a man in office, paying him $200 salary a year for doing nothing." Whether McMaster was kept on is not known.

Kerr spent Christmas Day writing to all his friends to convince them (and himself) that his leg had recovered and that he was not in any pain. He also took another swing at Wilmot who had "swindled" someone in Quebec, noting that he was "not done with him over the fishway."

1888 – THE END

The year started off slowly, as usual, with Kerr writing his returns and squeezing money out of fishermen for the coming season. On January 10, he wrote to Mrs. Gunsall: "Glad to hear you have beaten the inhuman, immoral man who has done you and your business so much damage, loss and injury. I will come and see you. I won't forget you." Perhaps she had a happy ending, but she was never mentioned again.

As usual, many of the fishermen and overseers were late in providing Kerr with the required information, so he had to write numerous cajoling letters and make several trips to prepare his report. He also had to create the report on Haldimand-Norfolk for Sharp, who seemed incapable of putting pencil to paper.

On January 30, he wrote that he became unwell when arriving at the Hamilton train station: "lost my hearing for two hours and got so weak that I had to be helped on and out of the train! and the same way to sleighs. I have been taking pills and bottles to cure me ever since!" Two days later, Kerr wrote to remind Tilton of his promise from 1887 to appoint Kerr's youngest son, Edward Thomas, to assist him at $250 a year: "My long and faithful services will I hope entitle me to this indulgence." It didn't.[182]

Travelling to Toronto to scare up statistics, Kerr noted that he got his "right ear badly frozen" travelling from his home to the train station. That's not likely going to help your hearing!

In 1887 a man named W. B. Woollard had applied for an exclusive licence to fish all the waters in the Port Credit area, which would dispossess some of the Bronte fishermen, of whom Kerr was very fond. He fought vehemently against this application, which would create a monopoly, one of Kerr's biggest bugaboos. So, using his police skills, he dug up the dirt on Woollard and duly reported it to the Department.

Woollard had been fishing on Lake Superior with the backing of net merchant John Leckie of Toronto.[183] On his return to Port Credit, Woollard bought a house, a horse and wagon, two new fishing boats, and a large supply of nets. "Mr. Leckie has informed me that everything Woollard has, or pretends to have, is in his wife's name and so they have defrauded Leckie and all his creditors." Preferring the Bronte fishermen who had fished for eighteen years, Kerr thundered, "Woollard has no right nor title to them!!! [the fishing grounds]." Woollard did not get the licence, at least while Kerr was alive.

Before Kerr could complete his returns, he was ordered to Goderich, where he predicted he would have a "hard road to travel. I have been

....

182   "Ned" Kerr remained a house painter.
183   John Leckie immigrated from Scotland in 1861 and began selling Scottish-made fishing nets, the finest in the world, made from Irish linen.

there before and I know the place well." Kerr was sent to investigate concerns about Fisheries Overseer Alexander C. McKinnon. The Department thought he resided at Goderich, but, in fact, he lived on his farm near the town of Tiverton. After arriving by train in Goderich, Kerr was forced to take a horse and buggy or sleigh for the forty-five-mile drive to find him.

Kerr noted, "The weather was excessively cold, the snow mountains high, during my drive from Goderich to the residence of Overseer McKinnon, and then back to the village of Tiverton, where I found him at Mrs. Turner's Hotel." He later reported the temperature as -16°F and that the snow was so high, he had to leave the road and drive in the fields where, looking down, he could see the tops of the fence posts.

Meeting McKinnon in a private room in the hotel, Kerr questioned him about the allegations. They had never met, and Kerr learned that he was first appointed in 1872. Then and there McKinnon confessed to misappropriating $740 "to spend it for his own use and his family use… Mr. McKinnon said, 'I feel keenly the degrading position in which I have placed myself'. That for some time he was expecting some one up, expected it would be me as I generally looked after such things for the Department." Then Kerr slogged back through the snow to hop the train and to seek instructions from Ottawa.

While at home, Kerr received a letter from McKinnon, noting that he "pleads hard his poverty, sickness of himself and in his family and relies on you [Bauset] to help him out of the trouble." Kerr, however, had heard reports about McKinnon's drinking during the last two years. Kerr was instructed to go back to Lake Huron and make further inquiries, which he did, again in the bitter cold of February. He ended up spending almost two weeks at Lake Huron because he had to examine McKinnon's district to determine the extent of the loss. He noted four days of sleigh driving, averaging over thirty miles a day.

This time McKinnon spun a different story, which Kerr quoted verbatim: "When I made my collection of the pound net money and was returning home, I went into a hotel near Grand Bend, and had a drink of liquor, a thing that I am not in the habit of taking. The liquor was drugged and when I recovered from its effects about $400 had been taken from my pocket and I could do nothing in recovering it."

Needless to say, Kerr was having none of this: "It is strange he never made any fuss when he lost the $400… I pity the man if poverty has compelled him to steal. Death before dishonor!" As Kerr noted no prospects of a recovery, Bauset wrote to suggest getting a mortgage from McKinnon for $500 secured against his three acres, his house, and his fruit trees. Kerr felt they were maybe worth $300.

Kerr could not understand what McKinnon had done with the stolen $750, but he did mention his drinking problem: "He asked me twice to drink, once at Tiverton and once at Kincardine. When engaged in cases of this kind I have invariably made it a rule of my life, never to drink. It is a sad disgrace he inflicted on the Department. I'll do my part to get it all OK again."

Kerr also mentioned some of the other thieving overseers he had dealt with over the years, such as Patton and Bingham, and optimistically reported, "By degrees we are getting rid of all the **scallywags.** Just give me full power and I will make such an example of McKinnon and those people to whom he paid your money and another cent will never be stolen from your fisheries department again."

As March commenced, Kerr seemed happy and content, and he was making plans for the summer. His writing was still strong, and the tone of his letters was still pleasant and friendly. In submitting Mrs. Elliott's application, he noted that her "husband is still alive but he is become a complete imbecile, incurable! She maintains and keeps her family by carrying on fishing and keeping boarders." There were no apparent problems with Big Jim Cantwell, but Kerr wrote John Bolton a letter warning him against fishing on Sunday, which his network of spies had tipped him off about.

Kerr heard from Bauset that Whitcher "was dying so I sent him a 5-gallon keg of native wine to cure him, and so mote it be. I am 34 pounds lighter than I was when I got that bad fall. I am 208 pounds now. We are all very well. Sometimes I get weakly, but when good weather arrives, I am off to Port Burwell and Port Bruce, to see my friends and drink some of Mrs. Emery's nice tea."

While waiting for McKinnon to see his lawyer about signing the mortgage, Kerr mused about McKinnon's improbable tale of woe: "It is surprising to me if he really thinks you, the Deputy and I are green—if he does, he will slip up. I met hundreds of such people as McKinnon during 13 years and 8 months of my lifetime—such people make no impression on me." That was the time he spent in the Royal Irish Constabulary.

In mid-March, Kerr took the train again to Kincardine to meet with McKinnon and his lawyer, where McKinnon signed a mortgage for $400 in favour of Kerr on behalf of the Department. After allowing for McKinnon's expenses, this was just about enough to cover what McKinnon had stolen. Kerr wrote, "I hope to see everything wound up and settled amicably so that no one can be blamed." This was another example of the Department keeping matters under wraps to insulate themselves from the criticism that could have entailed.

One of McKinnon's excuses for the theft was that Whitcher had promised him a promotion. Kerr scoffed: "I soon disposed of this by telling McKinnon Mr. Whitcher had promised me 50 things he never fulfilled." Kerr was more receptive to McKinnon's claim that he had been stiffed by Wilmot regarding the exhibition debacle. Unsure if McKinnon was going to be kept on, Kerr got him to sign over his pay to make up the loss.

Kerr was still mystified about where the stolen money went and asked to go back to Lake Huron "when the weather moderates" and that he "would soon find out what became of your $775. I hope I have saved the Deputy's bacon."

Kerr then availed himself of an opportunity to take another whack at Sam Wilmot and his son, Charlie, complaining that while they were paid $2,000 and $1,000 respectively, and he was only paid $600 after nearly twenty-four years' service. Good point. He also candidly admitted that the trips to Lake Huron were a "terrible hardship" and that he had got through "by the skin of his teeth." In the first quarter 1888, Kerr had travelled 1,852.5 miles!

On April 9, Kerr crowed that he and two of his sons fished about 1,400 yards of gill nets out of Burlington Bay: "Last Saturday was a very rough day—stormy! With the ice breaking up. Just such a time as fishermen don't expect me or my people. Rough weather. Ice breaking up, damaging and injuring my boat. This duty, I can assure you, was honestly and fearlessly done to the surprise of the fishermen! Who did not expect we could or would venture out in a storm. Such is life!"

By April 12, something must have been seriously wrong with Kerr's health because he sent his son to the bank on his behalf, apparently for the first time in nearly twenty-four years. There is also a noticeable deterioration in his handwriting in his letters and diary entries at around this time. In an April 19 letter to Emery, he reported that he "has not been very well" but gave no details.

By April, Kerr noted a number of deaths. His friend, Senator J. B. Plumb, had died suddenly, and so had Whitcher. Kerr regretted not being able to attend Plumb's funeral because Kerr was away in Kincardine. MP Thomas White, whose father Kerr had known in Ireland, had died, as had the widow of his colonel in the 3rd Middlesex Militia, Andrew Dobbie, whom he had first met in 1846.

In the week before Kerr's death, he made a trip to Toronto to settle an issue about a man illegally fishing off Toronto Island. Three days before his death, Kerr and his son, Fred, made a trip to Sarnia to settle an issue about Aboriginals fishing at Kettle Point and not paying licence fees. On May 7, he sent a bank draft to the Department for $250. The next day, he was dead, just six weeks short of his seventy-sixth birthday.

I have stated that Kerr worked himself to death in service to the Ministry of Marine and Fisheries and I do not think I am overstating this conclusion. Was it worth it?

244   Caught!

Relocated train station at Goderich. Photo by Joel Kerr, September 2019.

Excerpt from Kerr Diary. Kerr's final travel entry, compiled after his death. ROM

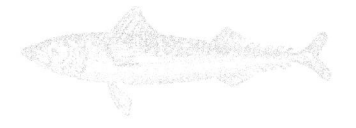

Chapter 13

Pollution

By May 1870, Kerr began to express concern about industrial pollution and its effect upon fish and wildlife. In Hamilton, several factories were producing coal oil, a type of oil distilled from coal and shale that was used primarily for outdoor lighting. Chemically similar to kerosene, it was replaced by cleaner-burning oil distilled from petroleum.

Kerr reported, "A large number of speckled bass and sunfish have been destroyed by this fluid and the effects of it. The fish of these kinds may be seen dead all over the shores of B. Bay. And even muskrat, oiled all over have been found dead from its effects. Even wild and tame ducks have had their feathers injured as to prevent the former rising on the wing and the latter to be seriously injured." Kerr observed that even if fish were not killed outright, they became "unpalatable food."

On April 3, 1871, Kerr summonsed James Williams, "for putting deleterious stuff in the Bay from his oil refinery." He had made a detailed inspection of the "black vitriol" coming from the Carbon Oil Company and took a sample. He also had witnesses who testified in court. The case was later dismissed "because the chemical substance was not analyzed nor shown to be a chemical substance." Kerr complained, "In another place and before another magistrate any other person charged would, I suppose be convicted and fined." He did not name the magistrate, but it was probably James Cahill, who Kerr could generally rely upon.

There was a positive aspect to this, as Kerr noted that "Mr. J.M. Williams and his son have put up a large tank filled with water through which they pass the refuse I complained of." Kerr was told that "this water neutralizes the power of the refuse, which is carbonic acid, and makes it harmless so that as they say, it will not injure or destroy the fish in the Bay." So, at least some attempt was made to rectify the problem.

However, Kerr had his doubts and continued to attempt to prove that the fish still tasted of coal oil. He found one convert to the cause in John I. Mackenzie, local business magnate, and the secretary of the Long Point Company, who lived in Hamilton, and would, "if necessary, witness in future for me—as a pike bought and cooked in his house, tasted of coal oil when brought to the table." Kerr was not finished with this matter.

In the summer of 1871, Kerr spent a good portion of his time inspecting and reporting on the various mills on streams in his district. There were three types of mills: sawmills, grist mills, and shingle mills. Sawmills used the force of flowing water to turn saw blades to create lumber for building purposes. Needless to say, the by-product of sawmills was sawdust, which had no value and was frequently allowed to fall into the open water, polluting the entire downstream area. Grist mills ground corn and grain to make flour and feed, and the waste products were chaff or husks, which were also allowed to fall into the stream. Shingle mills sawed wood into roofing shingles, which was the most common roofing material at the time. Again, sawdust was the by-product.

All such waste had an effect on the fish and frequently rendered streams devoid of fish, which could not survive or breed in the murky water. Interference with the fish was an infraction under the *Fisheries Act,* and there were a lot of mills. Kerr would generally notify mill owners to stop polluting and then prosecute them if they didn't comply. He was particularly vigorous about major fish streams such as the Grand and Credit Rivers, but he also visited many mills on smaller streams, such as Big Creek in Norfolk County.

The *Fisheries Act* gave him the authority to be completely arbitrary in his enforcement, but he generally attempted to balance the interest of mill owners and the resulting economic benefits against the preservation of fish. However, if mill owners were repeat offenders or reluctant to comply, he could be very strict. The justice system of the day permitted him to make quick work of things. When he found infractions, he could have mill owners summonsed before local magistrates and complete the matter within a few days, usually with a conviction and a fine.

He was often sent to various streams because of complaints from local citizens who would speak to their MP and have him write to the Minister of Fisheries. They would often blame Kerr for not doing his job, which would quickly get his attention because he was acutely reactive to criticism.

After finally paying James Blaine the agreed-upon half share for creating the fishway at Galt, it was washed out by a "freshet"[184] in the spring of 1871. Blaine blamed Kerr for a shoddy design, and the citizenry blamed Kerr for not insisting it be fixed immediately. Finding in favour of the fish, Kerr ordered Blaine to fix it, at his own expense.

Visiting the headwaters of the Credit River in July 1872, Kerr found that most of the mill owners had complied with the notice served on them the prior year not to allow sawdust into the river. However, those who didn't comply were prosecuted, and those found guilty were fined twenty dollars or thirty days in jail.[185] He recommended that the fines "be held in abeyance" as a guarantee of future good behaviour. This became a common thing for Kerr to request from the Department.

In July 1872, Kerr observed coal oil from a refinery and lime from a glue factory flowing into Dundas Creek. Despite his earlier defeat, Kerr had the offenders summonsed, and they pleaded guilty. They were each fined one dollar plus costs. An easy victory for once.

Kerr was asked to respond to a complaint from William Cowan on behalf of the Galt Fish and Game Association that he had failed to stop the pollution of the Grand River from various mills and factories in Galt. Never one to back down from a fight, Kerr proceeded to Galt, where he found, first, that the Galt Fish and Game Association had ceased to exist, and second, that none of Cowan's allegations were true.

....

184   A "freshet" is the word Kerr always used to describe a surge of water in a river. I had to look it up in my 1979 *Random House Dictionary*. Thanks, Mom and Dad!

185   Curiously, Kerr sat as one of the two required justices of the peace on these cases even though he had investigated and laid the charges. To do this with at least the appearance of neutrality, he would recruit other witnesses to testify in court, if necessary.

Describing Cowan as "a small specimen of humanity," a "contemptible person," and a "malicious vile slanderer," Kerr concluded by noting that "this is the position in which he is held by the respectable community of Galt." Gee, tell us what you really think!

By the spring of 1873, Kerr was back on the offensive against industrial pollution on Burlington Bay. Visiting William Gage on Gage Inlet, Kerr found "black, oily, tar coloured stuff running down toward the inlet" from a wooden pipe of a refinery owned by the Parson brothers. Finding bass in the water, Kerr had them cleaned and cooked but noted that "no person could eat them because they were impregnated with oil."[186]

Kerr returned to Sherman's Inlet in May and did a more thorough inspection. He found two coal oil refineries and "oil and vitriol running into the inlet in more than half a dozen different places without let or hindrance." He noted "the smell was overpowering." The next day he began to recruit witnesses, and one "complained about the fish tasting of coal oil, also of the injury done to the legs of the cows when they walk into the water where the oil is."[187]

Kerr had the Carbon Oil company charged, and they were in court on May 30, but the case was adjourned because the superintendent was planning to get tanks from London "to use in stopping everything injurious from entering the water and thereby, for all time to come, prevent a like occurrence happening."

On June 4, Kerr was back at Sherman's Inlet inspecting a pork slaughterhouse. He stated that he "went around the premises outside and saw a good deal of filth such as offal, guts and blood." Kerr was then given a tour of the slaughterhouse. Kerr wrote, "I observed the pork going through different processes of curing—even up to the packing and seasoning in white loaf sugar when put into boxes."

Returning to court in the coal oil cases, several witnesses were heard, but it was adjourned again because Kerr wanted to have the water and oil analyzed to determine "what chemicals or deleterious matter is contained therein." Not taking any chances this time, he secured twenty-five

....

186 The Parson brothers also had a refinery in Toronto.
187 Can you imagine seeing a cow in Burlington Bay today?

witnesses, including Dr. Mackintosh, who was to analyze the oil.

Meanwhile in the pork factory case, Isaac Atkinson was convicted by Magistrate Cahill and fined fifty dollars plus costs. Atkinson appealed to the Court of Quarter Sessions, which annoyed Kerr, who believed he would continue to offend until the case reached court in September. Kerr fumed, "The pork, after being cured, is shipped to England. The hogs are all bought in the Western States and slaughtered and cured here, and, except the benefits derived therefrom to the people of this place, all and every other benefit derived from this pork factory accrue to persons not resident here."

Kerr then passionately stated, "The damage done to the fish and fishing of B. Bay has been immense, more especially when this filthy accumulated filth and putrid polluted water become impregnated with saltpeter, lime and sulfuric acid, and coal oil." Noting how the pollution had filled up the head of the inlet to a depth of 9 feet and 150 yards out, Kerr couldn't even imagine how much had escaped into the bay.

Kerr implored the Department to take action: "I believe that unless the most stringent measures are carried into effect at once against this pork factory, that the destruction of fish... will be so immense that I cannot calculate the damage and injury. It is only a question of time to accomplish their complete destruction if immediate action is delayed."

Kerr also noted public sentiment: "The public, besides all the fishermen, are roused and become now deeply interested in this case and the coal oil cases... and they cry out vehemently that this pork factory nuisance should be stamped out at once. Because of its unbearable filthy state and the fear that it may spread contagion, I believe, but for the sulfuric acid used as a disinfectant, this would have happened ere this."

Kerr concluded by thanking the more than thirty witnesses, his lawyer, Mr. Lazier,[188] and James Cahill who "held on so patiently through

....

188   Stephen Franklin Lazier (1841–1916) was the patriarch of the Lazier legal dynasty in Hamilton. He lived in a large house at 67 Charles Street, which is still there. I acted for Patricia Wallace and her then husband, Alan Cooper, (both lawyers) who bought the house in the 1990s. They fixed it up, and it became their offices until they were both appointed judges. S. F. Lazier's grandson, Colin Simpson Lazier, was a stern county court judge during the early years of my practice.

a long tedious inquiry, he never flagged or faltered from the beginning to the end." The case was settled with a guilty plea and a fine of ten dollars plus sixty dollars in costs.

In celebrating what was probably the most important pollution prosecution of his career, Kerr wrote the following.

> *18 July 1873*
>
> *I have the honour to report for your information that I have just succeeded after a protracted enquiry in convicting Messrs. James M and Charles Williams owners and occupants of the oil refinery works situated at the head of Sherman Inlet, an inlet of Burlington Bay, for allowing coal oil, sulfuric acid, chemicals or drugs, poisonous matter or deleterious substances to pass into ... the waters ... frequented by the kinds of fish mentioned in the Fisheries Act.*
>
> *This case was frequently adjourned until Wednesday last, when C.A. Sadlier, solicitor for the Messrs. Williams, caved in, pleading guilty for the mitigated fine of ten dollars and costs inflicted by James Cahill, the Police Magistrate. This was done with the distinct understanding that due care and attention is to be taken in future to keep off the stuff and from out of the waters altogether.*
>
> *The neighbouring farmers, the vegetable gardeners, the fishermen, who have been injured by this coal oil mixture and the merchants, John Brown and John I. Mackenzie, who purchased fish, after being cooked could not eat them, stand by me gallantly! And assisted me most nobly in getting this conviction.*
>
> *Then there is Dr. Macintosh, whose report clinched the case, and who has put the deleterious effects of the coal oil mixture beyond all question and for all time to come.*
>
> *Mr. Lazier done his duty well in this and the other cases and he deserves my warmest consideration, and to the Doctor, whose report tells volumes, and to the other witnesses, not forgetting the two merchants: to all of them I am infinitely indebted.*

I must, however, pay occasional visits to the William's establishment weekly, when it is in operation. So that you can please judge there is no difficulty whatever to comply with the requirements of the Fisheries Act.

Mr. Charles Williams informed me that the establishment pays about $6,000 revenue duties annually... while the carbon oil works adjacent pay not a cent.[189] Mr. James Williams[190] is the local member of Parliament for Hamilton.

In conclusion, I may here state, that the Magistrate from the commencement to the end of this case done everything well and gave it his undivided attention.

John W. Kerr

In regard to the Parsons brothers and their Carbon Oil Company, the case was adjourned to allow the construction of a large holding tank for the sulfuric acid to be stored and shipped by train to London "where it is re-distilled and made fit for use again." The company pleaded guilty, and a fine of fifty dollars was imposed, but Kerr recommended it be held in abeyance in consequence of their efforts to rectify the problem. This seems to be an early example of recycling and corporate responsibility, if only as a result of prosecution.

In his annual report for 1873, Kerr noted the pork company appealed, but I could find no further reference to its outcome. Kerr confidently reported, "The cases were very glaring so that I have no fears for the result."

In September 1876, Kerr returned to Dundas to examine the sheepskin tanneries of William Mason and Charles Lawry. After consulting with Police Magistrate Cahill, he had them charged for discharging lime into Dundas Creek (Morden's Creek, now Spencer Creek). Kerr

---

189   That would change. See chapter 22.
190   James Miller Williams (Sept. 4, 1818–Nov. 25, 1890) was a businessman and politician and is noted as the father of the petroleum industry in Canada, producing the first oil well in North America at Oil Springs in Lambton County. He set up his refinery in Hamilton in 1860, and he was the father of Charles Williams. You can read more about him in the *Dictionary of Canadian Biography*.

achieved another easy victory; they were convicted and fined twenty dollars and ten dollars respectively.

Kerr was told that cows were dying from drinking contaminated water in Dundas Creek from the paper mill and the glue factory. Returning to Dundas in August 1877, Kerr inspected the paper mill, the cotton factory dye works, and the gas works and glue works on reports of "large quantities of dead fish caused by the chemicals and deadly poisons emptied therefrom." He had the manager of each charged. Two pleaded guilty and were fined twenty dollars, but the other two requested an adjournment to apply to the minister to have the creek exempted, meaning not subject to the provisions of the *Fisheries Act* pertaining to pollution. A petition was sent to Ottawa by the owners and by local politicians for the exemption. As Ontario industrialized, this became an increasingly common event and illustrated the dichotomy between protecting fish and water versus industry, jobs, and money. Guess who won? The Department directed Kerr to stay the proceedings!

Always tenacious, Kerr argued that non-enforcement was effectively legalizing pollution. He went on to argue that this pollution could be stopped without shutting down factories and mills. Asked to comment on the petition, Kerr wrote a long and passionate report outlining the specific chemicals polluting the water, what fish were being killed, and the destruction to surrounding lands. He also offered specific alternatives that each owner might utilize to avoid polluting.

Kerr also asked how it was fair, or even possible, for him to prosecute polluters on Burlington Bay and yet ignore the Dundas atrocities. He also pointed out that these chemicals and other poisons would find their way into Dundas Marsh, Burlington Bay, and ultimately, Lake Ontario. He concluded with the following: "These Dundas people, the defendants, have no real grievances to complain of. I have treated them in every respect with kindness, and they have never yet paid one cent for the offences they have been committing…The public would have taken hold of the cases if I had not done so."[191]

---

191   This eloquent and prescient letter can be found in vol. 7 on p. 426. It is worth reading in full.

Kerr was ordered to stop all proceedings, and the creek was exempted. Kerr warned, "I am led to believe that so soon as the fisheries department abandon and exempt such places, others will take it up." How right he was.

Kerr wrote to the minister requesting the $34.75 he had expended for witness and lawyer's fees for these cases. He boldly stated, "These would have been paid only for the interference of persons who retard my active operations in discharging my legitimate duties." The minister immediately shot back: "Who do you mean interfered?", to which Kerr smartly replied, "the solicitors." Nice save! Kerr was not done with industrial polluters.

Curiously, the Department had no apparent problem with the continued prosecution of mill owners for "sawdust and other mill rubbish," as Kerr invariably described it. Maybe it was just a lot easier to stop. Or maybe the government foresaw the coming virtual extinction of water-driven mills. Or maybe it was politics because mills were usually in the country where there were not a lot of voters.

In early November 1876, Kerr's boss W. F. Whitcher asked Kerr to investigate the Saugeen River system, which flows into Lake Huron at Southampton.[192] He asked Kerr to determine the state of the salmon in the river and whether attempts by Samuel Wilmot to place fry there on two occasions had been successful.

Kerr duly tramped all over the river and reported seeing only a few salmon, mostly around the Town of Paisley. He did find other fish species in other area and stated, "It is in every respect well adopted and suitable for the reproduction of salmon, and, in my opinion, it is well worth experimenting further on stocking it with a large quantity of adult salmon as well as young fish of that species… But then as regards sawdust & mill rubbish of all kinds it pains me to tell you that I never witnessed anything so bad or like it before."

Kerr indicated that because of the many branches of the Saugeen,[193]

....

192   The Saugeen River system is the third-largest river system in Southern Ontario. It runs 198 km from the Dundalk Highlands to Southampton. From its headwaters it falls 353 m.

193   The Saugeen is a convoluted river system that can be best understood if you look at a Province of Ontario map. You can get them at Tourism Ontario outlets for free! (For now.)

he would have to make a more thorough examination before he could advise what specifically could be done to enhance the salmon's prospects. Kerr predicted that within three years the salmon could be restored "to what they were only a few years ago, and I may add that although many persons will rejoice to see it, no man more than I will myself."

Having spent only two days there, Kerr visited about twenty mills, mostly sawmills and shingle mills, and virtually all of them were polluting the water. He recommended that "prompt measures should be taken at once to keep out the sawdust and mill rubbish, and if necessary, impose some fines." He would return.

Kerr returned to the Silver Star Oil Company on Sherman's Inlet in March 1877 and, on finding "considerable coal oil refuse," laid charges against the plant manager, Maurice Franks. When Franks appeared in court the next day, he requested time to rectify the problem by getting tanks from Petrolia to contain the chemicals. Kerr noted he "acceded to the proposition, for the present."[194] Ultimately, the matter proceeded in court, and a large fine of twenty dollars was imposed when Franks failed to deliver. Kerr was making some progress on stopping pollution in Burlington Bay but this was long before large scale industrialization began.

In April 1877 the Toronto Fish and Game Club had a number of mill owners charged for allowing sawdust to fall into the Don River. The owners wrote to the minister to exempt the river, and Kerr was asked to investigate. In May he did a thorough examination as far up as Richmond Hill. He filed a detailed report on the mills and predicted that the sawmills would all close within five years due to a lack of logs. However, he recommended the exemption, ruefully noting, "History tells us it was once a tolerable trout stream but the erection of machinery, more particularly saw mills, has nearly exterminated the fish."[195] The

---

194 The Silver Star Oil Company was owned by American, Jacob Englehart. It opened in Hamilton in 1875 and moved to Petrolia in 1879. It was a finishing refinery, and the raw material was shipped by the GWR from Lambton County.

195 In 1958 the *Globe and Mail* described the Don River as "heavily polluted and laden with scum, its bank littered with all varieties of filth, and the whole sending up foul odours."

charges were ordered stayed.

Kerr was more optimistic about the Credit River when he spent a few days there in May 1877. He observed, "The west and north branch of the River Credit is polluted with sawdust and mill rubbish, still I am able to report there are abundance of speckled trout therein. How much more numerous, when the sawdust will be completely kept out." He proceeded to prosecute a number of mill owners at Caledon and urged action: "My best and most active exertions will have to be brought into operation, at once, as regards the enforcement of the Fisheries Act in the River Credit."

In June, Kerr was back on the Credit giving notices to the mills that they had to install fishways. As part of the plan for the Credit, Kerr wanted to help Wellington Hull get a fish-breeding operation going at Erin. Wanting to expand his jurisdiction to include the Credit, Kerr noted he could get to Erin in three hours by train. Kerr had known Hull for some time some and highly recommended him: "He has let out annually thousands of speckled trout fry into the west branch of the Credit, and has been using his best efforts to breed and to hatch out, and to act in a praiseworthy manner, on behalf of the fisheries and for the good of the community."

Noting the former fishery guardian had departed three years before for Bracebridge, Kerr also wanted to secure the position for Hull, at fifty dollars a year. Hull got the post in October.

Kerr was back on the Credit in July serving more fishway notices on the east branch. He noted "Out at 6:00 a.m. came in at 9:00 p.m.—sick all day."

On receiving a report that the Williams Coal Oil factory was discharging oil into Gage's Inlet, Kerr got in his buggy with C. J. Kerr (my great-grandfather) and rode down for a look. He found nothing wrong, and the manager "pledged to obey the law." So, it seemed that Kerr's activities were having some positive effect.

Next it was on to Toronto to investigate the numerous small dead shad or alewives on the shore. Kerr pointed the finger of blame at the Gooderham distillery at the foot of the Don River. The by-product of grain distilling is a sort of mash that can be fed to cattle and pigs. The

Gooderhams kept their own livestock, and by 1880 there were 7 sheds or byres housing as many as 4,000 head of cattle. What the cows didn't eat was sold to local farmers, and up to 650 wagon loads a day were leaving the facility. About 80,000 gallons of cattle manure flowed into Ashbridge's Bay each day.

Kerr observed that a mile-long square wooden pipe discharged the manure into the marshy water and that this was what was killing the fish. Kerr disappointingly observed, "I don't suppose there is any remedy in this case because should I bring Gooderham up before the Police Magistrate, no doubt great efforts will be resorted to, to prevent a conviction." He was essentially admitting they were too big and rich to prosecute.[196]

He returned again in 1883 to report on the dead fish poisoned by Gooderham's cow byres: "About 10,000 cattle were fattened and sold from Mr. Gooderham's byres during this season, say up until the end of June last." After the cattle were shipped out, the "extensive premises" got a "general overhauling and were cleaned out and in doing so, I have been told, chemical, disinfectants and chloride of lime were extensively used. When all this destructive stuff combined, was pumped into Ashbridge's Bay that its water became so impure and poisonous that no fish can live in its immediate vicinity. Its destructive properties kill every living fish that it comes in contact with and it even kills the marsh grass, flays, bullrushes and water lilies."

Kerr sought the minister's advice, noting that "this is an industry bringing annually hundreds of thousands of dollars into the City of Toronto, whilst at the same time it is also destroying the great fish food of its inhabitants. I consider it high time that proceedings should be commenced against the owners of these cow byres for polluting that water of Ashbridge's Bay." I think we know what Kerr's answer was going to be even though he had proposed a completely obvious solution by shipping the manure by train to farms.

---

196   Founded in 1831 by William Gooderham and his brother-in-law, James Worts, by the end of the century, it was Canada's largest distillery. During prohibition from 1918–1927, Gooderhams sold whisky to Kerr's grandson, John Bensley Kerr, who became the "King of the Rumrunners." J.B. Kerr was my father's uncle, and having the same initials, I have his engraved gold cufflinks!

In May 1882, Kerr turned his sights again upon Burlington Bay polluters by bringing up the manager of the Cotton Works on James St. N., Mr. W. C. Snow, for allowing "dye stuffs" to pass into the bay. Noting that this was the same man he had tried to prosecute in Dundas, Kerr hauled him up before Cahill, but the case was adjourned to have "the stuff analyzed and so establish its deadly injurious effects on the fish." After being refused permission to analyze the stuff, Kerr bitterly wrote, "I suppose the Department will have to let him off."

Kerr reported that a "very black, thick stuff" discoloured the bay for a distance of about 150 yards flowing through a wooden pipe running about 200 yards from the factory to the bay, killing "large quantities of young fry." The company petitioned the minister to be exempted from the *Fisheries Act* provisions, and Kerr was asked to comment. He was obviously conflicted, noting it was a new industry and would employ 400 people and deserved to be treated "tenderly" but that as things stood, fish were dying from the effluent. He suggested a compromise whereby it may be exempted but only if it guaranteed that it would "destroy the deleterious properties of all dye stuffs, acids and other pernicious poisonous matter used for colouring before it is allowed to pass" into the bay. He also wanted them to pay the costs of the prosecution, noting the directors "are all, every one of them, wealthy."

Kerr was irked that the lawyers for the cotton company had lied in their petition by alleging that it wasn't the company polluting but rather the city sewer. After a careful examination, Kerr stated without reservation that this was untrue. They had also argued that other companies like the Hamilton Gas Company and the GWR were polluting without restriction, which Kerr also painstakingly disproved.

However, Kerr continued to mull the issue over in his mind and decided to investigate further, particularly after a letter to the editor of the *Hamilton Times* claimed that the dye was killing fish. Kerr observed, "There is a great diversity of opinion, in the mind of the public, about those dye stuffs flowing from the Ontario Cotton Mills of Hamilton and daily entering the waters of Burlington Bay, and its poisonous effects on the Bay fish." Kerr spoke to the dyer of the company, Mr. H. Chambers, a man who had forty-five years' experience. He advised that the dye was not discharged until it had been totally used up and thus, although it discoloured the water, was not poisonous. This became one of Kerr's blind spots because he believed this malarkey.

He also observed boys fishing from the wharves and that they were catching live, healthy fish, and he spoke to boat builder William Massie, whose boathouses were right near the point of discharge, and reported that he had no concerns. He also spoke to police detective Ian Mackenzie, who shared this opinion. Lastly, he noted the company employed 320 persons, paying $8,000 a month in wages.

In conclusion, he recommended an exemption, noting, "personally, I feel a deep interest in the success and prosperity of our valuable fisheries, but on public and National Policy grounds, the clear course I find laid down in this case before me, to recommend that the Cotton Mill be exempt from the Fisheries Act." Sell-out or pragmatic realist? Who can say? He did the best he could to balance the competing interests. He should have been allowed to have the discharge analyzed, but the government was either too cheap or too disinterested to learn the scientific truth. The fix was in.

After trying to wrap up the tawdry state of the fisheries and mills on the Saugeen River system in 1884, Kerr was requested to proceed up the Grand River to examine the fishway at Galt that had been washed out and to inspect Seagram's Distillery[197] and the woolen mills as a follow-up from his last visit in 1879. On a drenching September 24th, Kerr headed by train to Preston and began his one-day tour.

Kerr headed to the woolen mill first and found a vastly enlarged operation with $150,000 worth of new equipment and buildings[198] and 185–188 people employed, compared to just 24 in 1879. Kerr noted that

....

197 Seagram's Distillery opened in 1857 in Waterloo as a partnership between Joseph Emm Seagram (Apr. 15, 1841–Aug. 18, 1919) and three others. By 1883 Seagram had bought out his partners, and by 1907 its marquis product, Seagram's VO, was the largest-selling Canadian whisky in the world. After his death the company merged with Samuel Bronfman's Distillers Corporation. Since then it has had many incarnations. Seagram himself was elected Conservative MP for Waterloo North.

198 One of the woolen mill owners was John Randall, a former partner in Seagram's.

they produced about $250,000 worth of product and paid a monthly payroll of about $3,200.00. After an examination he concluded,

> *I am satisfied they use every effort to comply with the Fisheries Laws... From long personal experience and observation of woolen mills of this class... I can now safely report to you, that so long as a particle of vitality remains in the dye stuff, they are still kept on for future use and housed up in the vats! It is only when all the good and vital parts are used up and extracted therefrom, the balance, if any, is made harmless by repeated use of water before discharged into the creek.*

In regard to the distillery, Kerr also noted "vast improvements to the premises," which have been "enlarged, and are now valued by Mr. Seagram at $75,000 with all modern improvements and expensive machinery for distilling." Noting about 200 head of cattle and 400 hogs in the byres, Kerr said,

> *Mr. Seagram told me he sells the manure, every particle of it, to the farmers of the surrounding country, nothing escapes into the creek and I am satisfied he told me the truth...Mr. Seagram buys hay, straw and grain in the neighbourhood! Employs 45–50 men daily in the distillery and all are heads of families... Farmers are so desirous of securing the manure for their farms, so highly prized as a fertilizer, as farmers who have succeeded in procuring it can prove by the vast increase and improvement to their crops. There is no cause of complaint so far as my humble judgment leads me to know and believe, this time against the distillery.*

In July 1884, Kerr was advised that complaints were being made about the Beardmore Tannery Mill of Acton and other local mills. The complaint came from a local fish-and-game club, so Kerr was automatically suspicious, but he sent local fisheries overseer Wellington Hull to have a look.[199] Hull fined Beardmore and two other mill owners twenty dollars each. The local politicians and the *Acton Free Press* were in an uproar, seeking that the stream be made exempt, and accused Hull of only being interested in the half of the fine that they thought went to him. Naturally, Kerr was asked to intervene. He started off by letting the paper know that the fine went to the Department, not to Hull. Then he proceeded to Acton, where he did a thorough investigation.

I am going to give Kerr's results in full because I think they paint a good picture of Acton at the time and describe the mill in interesting terms, and it is also reflective of a typical Kerr report.

> *The Town of Acton, is a smart enterprising place of 1,200 inhabitants. The Grand Trunk runs through and intersects the north part of the Village on its course west. It is situated in the County of Halton.*
>
> *Mr. George Beardsmore's tannery here was burned down some years ago but has been recently rebuilt by him at a cost of about $20,000, and is equipped and rigged out with all modern improvements introduced by the National Policy art in tanning. I went through and all over the building and premises accompanied by the foreman who took pains in showing and explaining everything to me.*
>
> *The present capacity of this tannery is 250 hides a week. When in full production it will be more. There is a foreman and thirty men employed daily in this tannery and the pay is $1.25 per man, per day. In getting out the tan bark twice this number of men are employed each year! While this is going on.[200] The hides are all purchased in South America and shipped by New York & Boston,*

---

199   George L. Beardmore (Feb. 16, 1818–1893) bought the original tannery, founded in 1844, in 1865 and substantially enlarged its operations into a one-million-square foot facility that by the turn of the century was the largest tannery in the British Empire. It is now known as the Olde Hyde House. Is it worth the drive to Acton? Don't know; I haven't yet been there!

200   Western hemlock bark is used to tan and colour leather.

consigned to George Beardmore in Toronto and taken to Acton by GT Railway. Converted and manufactured all into sole leather and when this is done re-shipped to the warehouse Toronto, sold and distributed to persons engaged in trade all over Canada.

Since the fine was imposed, the small creek has been bridged over, near the Tannery so that tan bark will not in future escape from the extensive heap alongside the same. This heap of tanbark, essential in tanning, is being daily burned up in the furnace of the tannery, making steam to set its machinery in operation and hot air pipes placed on the lofts for drying the leather in winter! Smart results. Hoists, presses, horse power engines, boilers, besides a variety of implements all put in motion.

The only material burned in the furnace is the tan bark that has done its duty already in tanning–is a second time used and burned in the extensive furnaces of the tannery- two men being employed daily wheeling it in and keeping the furnaces fed and going. The furnaces are fed from above.

In this tannery are compartments in which the hides are placed, when the hair is removed off them. No lime or horse dung is used to do this. There are 100 vats filled with hides in preparation besides 20 hook nets in this tannery.

The trade appears to be extensive and flourishing, and is well and carefully carried on so as to reflect great credit on the proprietors, Mr. George Beardmore and his son, a young man who appears all business at Acton, civil, courteous and obliging towards me. Whilst his father attends to the warehouse trade in Toronto.

The mounds of tanbark, corded up at the railway station, Acton, for this tannery, strikes the beholder with admiration.

You will perceive Overseer Hull, of Erin, whose duty it is to attend to the protection of these speckled trout streams was in ignorance of a fact that tan bark, old, used up, had got into this trout creek through the negligence of a Mr. Wilson, then foreman, but whose

> *place is now occupied by a much more careful person.*
>
> *Satisfied as I am that the facts contained in the letter and the petition of the Reeve are correct, from enquiries I made, and from the assurances given to me by Mr. George Beardmore and foreman, who has just come there, that no more contraventions of the Fisheries Act will again happen and buoyed up as I acknowledge by this extensive tannery industry! I have from the facts herein quoted been induced to recommend that the minister will be pleased to exempt a portion of this stream from the provisions of the Fisheries Act. And I would also recommend that the fine be remitted.*

Was Kerr just selling out to corporate power and public pressure, or was he really ensuring that there was no pollution killing the fish? He concluded: "I never wish to say a word against an officer for actively doing his duty, Hull is a good fellow but acted too precipitate in the case. The creek is free from tan bark so far as Beardmore and Co. are concerned! And nothing from their premises will affect the trout anymore!" That was a bold prediction that probably did not hold true. Kerr had applied his observational and analytical skills, as usual, to produce the best report in his power for the Department.

In 1885 the Department received an anonymous petition about mills and dams on Big Creek, which runs from Port Rowan on Lake Erie up to Delhi and beyond. Kerr had last visited the area in 1871. The petition claimed that fish were being prevented from going up or down the creek because of the dams and that there was substantial pollution.

Kerr hopped the train to Delhi to meet with a group of about fifteen disgruntled citizens. However, it turned out they were not really interested in the fish or the pollution but were rather seeking to retaliate against the mill and dam owners who had voted for the *Scott Act*. This federal legislation allowed each county to determine whether to outlaw the sale of alcohol by the "local option." The group Kerr met with were primarily Grit ex-tavern owners and others who had been put out of work by the invocation of the Act in Norfolk. They wanted revenge, but Kerr would have none of it. He duly drove his horse and buggy the fourteen miles to Port Rowan and inspected all the facilities mentioned in the complaint. However, unimpressed by the complainants' motives, he refused to make any recommendations for enforcement.

In September 1886, Kerr was asked to investigate concerns made by Welland MP Dr. Ferguson[201] regarding pollution coming from Buffalo into the Niagara River. He confirmed that barges from Buffalo were dumping "excrement and objectionable stuff from privies" on the Canadian side of the Niagara River. Kerr also reported that Buffalo had a trunk sewer large enough to "admit a team with a load of hay" discharging into the Niagara River near the Erie Canal. Noting that the river flowed at six miles an hour, Kerr was uncertain if it was damaging the fisheries but suggested the Department communicate with the Mayor of Buffalo to deal with the barges.

In 1887, Kerr returned to the topic and revisited Fort Erie, noting twenty-five to thirty scows and barges "are at work depositing from privies and all kinds of filth, garbage, including the sweepings of the street of Buffalo [horse shit] in the waters of the Niagara River." Kerr reported that "the American people themselves at Black Rock and Tonawanda, had stopped these people dumping this objectionable stuff into the Niagara River on the American side, hence they dump all the filthy stuff on the Canadian side of the River." He wanted instructions from the Department to "stamp out this great nuisance." It doesn't seem that he got any.

With his death in 1888, Kerr's attempts to curtail pollution came to an end. His successor, son Frederick Kerr, did some enforcement, but I have not fully read his accounts. Industrialization was just getting started in Canada, and by the early twentieth century it was massive. Did Kerr's efforts have any impact on pollution, or was he just whistling in the dark? It's hard to say, but at least he made an effort in an era when nobody else seemed to give a damn. I am sure lots of papers have been written about industrial pollution in early Canada, and I think Kerr, at least, deserves a footnote in environmental protection history.

....

201   Dr. John Ferguson (Apr. 27, 1839–Sept. 22, 1896) was the Conservative MP for Welland from 1882–1891.

AN INTERESTING QUESTION.—Last week we noted the fact that Mr. Lawry and Mr. Mason, tanners, of Dundas, had been fined $10 and costs by the Police Magistrate of Hamilton, on complaint of Mr. Kerr, Fishery Inspector, for allowing the refuse from their tanneries to be emptied into the creek, and now we learn that the Cotton Works Co. have been summoned to answer to a similar charge, the question being meanwhile referred to the Minister of Fisheries at Ottawa. With regard to this subject, we can only say that the complaint is a most frivolous one, and we trust the head of the Fishery Department will view it in this light. That there are some little cat fish and suckers in the creek we will not deny, but that they could possibly be injured by any of the dyes or other refuse which is allowed to go into the creek from the Cotton Mills and Tanneries is simply ridiculous, as long before the fish are reached the injurious properties of the refuse must be completely destroyed. This is the view which any man of common sense would take of the subject, and it is simply nothing more nor less than a species of petty persecution which has dictated the action we have spoken of. If our manufacturing establishments are to be thus annoyed by those who have a little brief authority the sooner the Government gets rid of such over-anxious servants the better will it be for the public interests.

Newspaper clipping found in Kerr diary, from the Dundas Beaver. The Dundas Beaver always took the side of the Industrialists. ROM

Pollution   265

Dundas Cotton Mill, Hamilton Public Library.

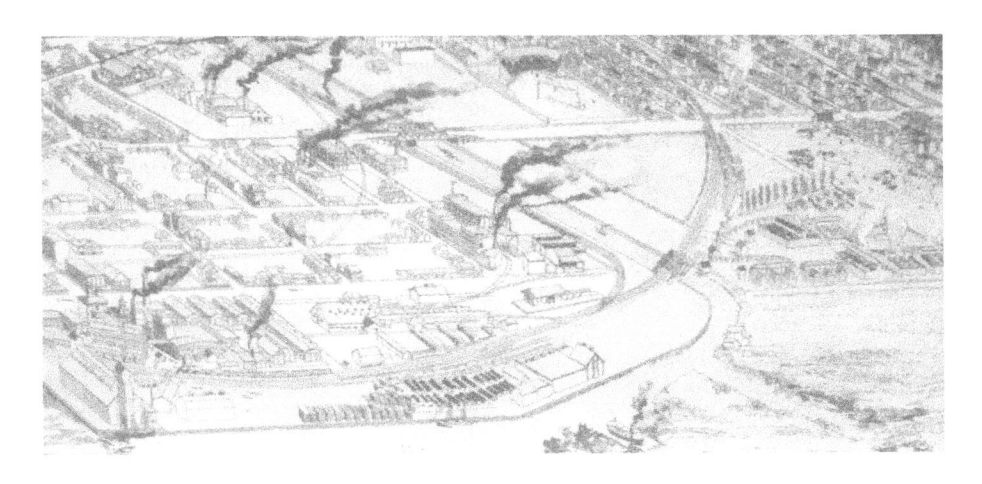

Section of Illustration of the Gooderham and Worts Distillery, Toronto 1892.

Chapter 14

Kerr and the Long Point Company

When Kerr became fisheries overseer for Long Point Bay on Lake Erie, he was in regular contact with members of the Long Point Company, including its solicitor, Colonel David Tisdale, a Simcoe lawyer, and its secretary, Hamilton businessman John I. MacKenzie.

Long Point in the 1850s was Crown land and was being heavily exploited for its forests, game, and fish by local residents and Americans crossing from Erie, Pennsylvania. On May 4, 1866, a group of seven businessmen from Hamilton and St. Catharines purchased most of the point (14,934 acres) from the Commissioner of Crown Lands to stop the rampant exploitation and for their own sporting activities.

On August 15, 1866, the Long Point Company was established by an act of the legislature with one of its purposes being to protect fish and game. One of the seven original members was Thomas Cockburn Kerr of Hamilton.

T. C. Kerr was from Scotland and thus not directly related to J. W. Kerr, but they probably knew each other. Together with his brother, Archibald Kerr, they formed A. & T. C. Kerr and Company, and they constructed the "Kerr Building," which was a notable stone structure on King St. E in downtown Hamilton (long gone now).

J. W. Kerr probably also knew T. C. Kerr as the owner of the Caledonia Mill, which he had bought as the Balmoral Mill in 1867.

T. C. Kerr resided in a grand home at the corner of MacNab St and Herkimer St. that was sold to Frederick Broughton, the manager of the

Great West Railway. Thomas Kerr named the residence "Merksworth" after his birthplace in Scotland. After his death, for seventy years until 1953, it was the home of the Crerar Family until it was sold and demolished to make way for the Merksworth Apartments.

The patriarch of the Crerar family was General Harry Crerar, who rose to command the First Canadian Army in World War II.

When the Hamilton and Port Dover Railway was completed in 1878, J. W. Kerr began to use this line frequently on his travels to Lake Erie (it had been completed as far as Jarvis in 1873). The line climbed the escarpment along the mountainside just below Kerr's Barton Township home. Prior to the completion of the line, the trip to Lake Erie was a difficult and probably exhausting stagecoach ride along Caledonia Plank Road. The railway was a project of Sir Allan MacNab starting in 1855 after he was dumped as the chairman of the GWR. It stalled over expenses, particularly building the line up the side of the escarpment. When it was finally completed, its mountain station was on Dartnall Road, near Rymal, at the site of the co-op building (which became Home Hardware but recently closed).

Kerr seemed to respect and have affinity for the Long Point Company, probably because they shared his conservationist views and possibly because he knew the wealthy Hamilton businessman, Thomas Cockburn Kerr, or some of the other Hamilton members. Peter Price, Colonel Tisdale's uncle, became one of Kerr's local fishery guardians.

In 1870, Kerr leased all the fishing at Long Point to Thomas C. Kerr and John I. Mackenzie. He noted: "I consider no person more worthy of a license of this description than those gentlemen composing the Long Point Company. They protect the fish, have never fished themselves, - In fact, I consider Long Point a good nursery for protection. And my last year's returns show the profitable advantages the licensed fishermen in the neighbouring fisheries have derived from this nursery."

In 1874 the Long Point Company proposed that they begin to use their fishing lease for commercial purposes. The lease extended five miles into Lake Erie and ran for twenty miles from the lighthouse at the point to the Old Cut near the mainland. The minister wrote to David Tisdale to express approval for this proposal and Kerr was shown a copy of the letter by John I. MacKenzie, the secretary of the company. One wonders why Kerr wasn't consulted by the ministry about this, but on May 11, 1874, he wrote to the minister to advise him that he had seen the letter.

Contrary to his position in 1879, Kerr had no concerns about the plan because he trusted the integrity of the LPC and, in fact, Kerr reminded the minister that there was another fifteen miles of Lake Erie before the US border. Somewhat remarkably, Kerr suggested that the government, together with the LPC, should "lease to the American Capitalists this large expanse of Lake Erie." He went on to propose that the matter be brought before the LPC at their annual meeting. He commented on the "immense body of whitefish in the summer before they migrate up the Detroit River in October and November."

Kerr reported that the Canadian fishers at Turkey Point and other areas "are now fully provided for," and it would, therefore, be acceptable, even to them, if the additional waters were leased to the "American Capitalists." He even suggested that his supervisor, Mr. Whitcher, attend the LPC meeting. As a postscript to his letter, he noted, "by Mr. W. attending to this the American Capitalists won't have the best of the bargain." As far as I know, Whitcher did not attend, and the waters were not leased to the Americans, which was probably a good thing.

In November 1872, Kerr spent three days at Long Point. There are no diary notes for these days. However, when Kerr returned home, he went to the railway station and "Dispatched a box and four bags of wild ducks to Ottawa for Mr. W. F. Whitcher, in weight 400 "(pounds presumably). Clearly, Kerr was with his friends in the Long Point Company shooting ducks. He also "expressed Dr. Ryerson's bag[202] and

....

202   Dr. Adolphus Egerton Ryerson (Mar. 24, 1803–Feb. 19, 1882) was a Methodist minister, politician, and early proponent of public education (for boys, at least). His father received a substantial land grant in Vittoria, Norfolk County, and Ryerson spent his boyhood years on Long Point. He owned property there and was instrumental in launching the LPC, although he was not a member. Wikipedia says that Ryerson died trying to invent shampoo, to which he added too much lead, which got into his eyes and caused lead poisoning. Sounds like BS to me.

delivered John I. Mackenzie's box at his house and three bags at George H. Gillespie's house."[203]

Kerr also brought home seven bags "four of them for present's to Mr. Whitcher's friends," which he delivered the next day. The other three bags, containing an unknown quantity of ducks, Kerr presumably kept for himself.

In an October 1874 letter to Samuel Wilmot, a fish breeder from Newcastle, Kerr excitedly wrote, "Mr. Whitcher has been invited by the Long Point Company to duck shoot there this fall (so have I!!!)." I can't find any record of either of them going.

By 1874 Kerr had lost the Long Point district to J. A. Backhouse of Port Rowan, whom, apparently, he did not like. However, he was still friends with John I. Mackenzie, who consulted him from time to time. Kerr wrote to the minister in October 1875 in regard to an issue and had some complimentary things to say about the LPC "Because the Long Point Company from the protection they afforded me at all times heretofore to preserve the fish and fisheries in and about their property at Long Point—So highly merited my approval that I had much pleasure always in reporting the same to you annually in furnishing my report for each season."

The LPC rewarded Kerr during an October visit by Whitcher, which was probably one of the proudest moments of his life. This amusing story began on October 11 when Kerr trotted down to Burlington Bay to meet a steamer bringing Whitcher's gear from Ottawa, which consisted of a canoe, four trunks, and a basket. Kerr had to lug this stuff to the station of the Hamilton and North Western Railway, which was on Ferguson Ave. in downtown Hamilton. Putting the gear on the train for Port Dover, Kerr returned home eleven and a half hours after setting out and having travelled twenty miles. He also paid the freight charges and "gave a dollar to treat the crew of the steamer."

The next day, Kerr was at the GWR station getting a "free pass for

---

203 George Hamilton Gillespie (Aug. 10, 1827–Aug. 24, 1900) was a Hamilton Mountain resident and wealthy local merchant. It is said he left an estate of $80,000. Gillespie was a shareholder and officer of the LPC (Harry. B. Barrett. *Lore and Legends of Long Point*. Toronto: Burns & MacEachern Ltd.: 1979, 212)

Mr. Whitcher from Toronto to Hamilton." Kerr took the train to Union Station to pick up Whitcher and his eleven other pieces of luggage and deposited him at the Royal Hotel in Hamilton, where Whitcher hit Kerr up for a twenty-dollar loan. The next day Kerr was up early at the train station to ensure that Whitcher's stuff was placed on board the train for Port Dover and then had to pay Whitcher's fare.

Three days later, Kerr was off to Port Dover and then to Turkey Point on Whitcher's orders, to "settle ranges off the outer bay at Turkey Point." When Norfolk Fisheries Overseer C .L. Bingham failed to meet him at Turkey Point, as arranged, Kerr had to hire a horse and buggy back to Port Dover. The next day he returned to Turkey Point and somehow got across Long Point Bay to the LPC headquarters, where he met Whitcher and Bingham. I don't know if it was planned, but Kerr was greeted as the guest of honour. Here is what he recorded about the meeting.

> On my arrival I was well treated, treated like a Prince, made the guest of the Company, dined with the sporting gentlemen there at the time and had the Post of Honour conferred on me, being placed on the right of the chairman, Mr. John I. Mackenzie, the LPC's secretary.
>
> Mr. Whitcher, Commissioner of Fishing, sat on my right. There was present Mr. Lord, tea merchant New York and three other New York gentlemen, a Mr. Walker was one, I forget the names of the other two, although I was introduced to them.
>
> Mr. William Hunter, tea merchant of New York, Col. Walker of London with who I became acquainted while crossing over on the Steamer Annie Craig of Port Burwell [in 1846]. Col. Allan Gilmour, Ottawa [Whitcher's travelling companion], Col. Tisdale of Simcoe, all enjoyed themselves immensely. The dinner was roast mutton, whitefish and wild ducks, punkin pie and rice pudding–All of which I partook, except the punkins—plenty of ale and champaign. I had two cups of tea.

After this great honour, it was back to being Whitcher's servant. Whitcher stuck Kerr with a pile of ducks and got him to take them back to Hamilton and distribute them to a bunch of friends. Kerr made another trip to Port Dover to retrieve three more boxes of ducks destined for Ottawa and Montreal. After about twenty days of shooting and drinking on Long Point, Whitcher was ready to come home, so Kerr took the train to Port Dover (apparently Whitcher had managed to get that far by himself) and loaded all his luggage, his canoe, and "two large boxes of ducks" on the train for Hamilton and then the steamer *Corsican* for Prescott. Apparently, Kerr did get a dinner out of Whitcher at the Royal Hotel, the best hotel in Hamilton. Keep in mind that Kerr was then sixty-eight years old!

As a postscript to the Whitcher visit, Whitcher asked Kerr to lend the LPC his hoop net, which was a rather complicated hand-held net. Kerr was also asked to give a free fishing licence to William Leary, an employee of the LPC and good friend of Kerr's. Kerr went one better: "Since I began to write this note, something is urging me all the time, Kerr, Kerr! Give the LPC the hoop net altogether, so that they may have always on hand an abundance of good fish."

Kerr asked Leary to present the net to John I. Mackenzie "as a small token of my warm regard and esteem, and may every success attend them, and you, in all their undertakings." Giving detailed and totally confusing instructions on how to use the hoop, Kerr ended with, "And now Bill, my dear fellow and Brother Mason, keep steady and live a sober life." He wouldn't.

In 1884, after being "superannuated," Whitcher wrote to MacKenzie to see if he could get a return invite to hunt at Long Point. Mackenzie wrote to Kerr, saying, "Mr. Whitcher, in office would be no doubt invited, but out of office, after all that he had done for the Long Point Company, we will not send him an invitation to shoot there anymore!" He likely wore out his welcome with his twenty days of shooting and his entitled attitude.

In 1885, Edward Harris was elected the third president of the LPC. Born in 1831 and related to the Ryerse-Ryerson families, he was a younger member of the company and somewhat abrasive. As we have seen, the LPC acknowledged the federal government's primacy over the waters of Long Point Bay and the one-chain (sixty-six-foot) fishery reserve. They had licensed the fishing from the Department and had sublet it with Kerr's permission to two local fishermen. However, by 1885 they wanted control of the water by allowance from the provincial government but Kerr adamantly opposed it on jurisdictional grounds.

Draft legislation had been sent to Toronto, and Kerr obtained a copy and wrote an urgent letter to Bauset.

> *I respectfully recommend that you will be pleased to stop this at once! And stop such an invasion of the fisheries at once. It is about time to do away with this Long Point Monopoly, especially when they show a desire to acquire illegal rights over Lake Erie fisheries by a Provincial Act of Parliament, Toronto. The intention, I believe, is to sell out. I would cancel the fishery lease! And let fishermen fish direct by licence from the fisheries Department. I would recommend this with all my heart and mind!*

Kerr's concern was for the province taking over the inland fisheries, which ultimately did happen but not until after his death. It was a constitutional matter, and he hypothesized that MacDonald would quash the bill, and it would be sent to the Privy Council:[204] "I suppose it will be a grit squabble of some years, however, if the miserable crew in the majority in Toronto succeed, I am perfectly satisfied if as you say 'your occupation and mine will be gone.'" Was that his only concern, or was he concerned having seen how woefully inadequate the province had been in enforcing the game laws?

He later wrote the following to Bauset: "Things look squally for the Ontario fishermen and fisheries right now! It is your bounden duty and mine to stand firm and firmly by them and the Fisheries Department, Ottawa. The Right Honourable Sir John A. MacDonald, Canada's Greatest Statesman! Will fix things for the benefit of the people! Legal, right and proper!" To which Bauset replied, "We must not get into a

---

204 After 1867 Canada was not in complete control of its constitution or its laws. The *BNA Act* provided for appeals from the Supreme Court of Canada to the Judicial Committee of the Privy Council at London which, until 1949, was the final Court of Appeal.

scrape with the Ontario Government, further than we are now, if we can avoid it, and we must look to our officers to assist us in that direction."

Kerr thundered back: "My advice has been, **is and shall be to stand firm!!** Stand fast by the Fisheries Department, Ottawa. One comfort, we are in possession and can not be kicked out nor put out by a Local Statute!! And Grit at that, of a hostile nature!!! God save the Queen! No surrender!!" Throughout his career, Kerr was always dismissive of the Ontario government, which was usually Liberal during his working life.

After Whitcher was superannuated, Kerr's relationship with the Long Point Company changed. John I. Mackenzie was still the secretary, but he had taken up with the fish-and-game club in Hamilton, which Kerr abhorred, and Kerr was no longer in favour of the LPC's monopoly over 200 square miles of Lake Erie, which they got for a song and were then allowed to sublet to Port Dover fishermen. The Department decided to disallow the subletting, which Kerr applauded. Mackenzie asked him to write to the Department about the matter, but he flat out refused. Kerr exclaimed: "**Thank Heaven!** I am now at this present time in such an independent position altogether apart from the Long Point Company, that I can distinctly and without hesitation, answer **No!!!**"

On April 11, Kerr jubilantly reported that the LPC had caved and agreed to preserve Long Point Bay for angling only. "Another Glorious victory won! Ten pound nets gone, never to return. You [Bauset] are one of the greatest men of the age we now live in. May you always conquer!"

In October, Kerr noted that Sheriff Samuel Woodruff of St. Catharines had died and that as a shareholder in the LPC he had sold his share for $5,000. That was the equivalent of over thirteen years' pay for the average workman. Replacing Woodruff as president, London lawyer Edward Harris was elected in 1886. By that time most of the shareholders were wealthy Americans who apparently loved to drink and shoot ducks! I mean, who doesn't?

By December 1886 the federal election was on Kerr's mind, and he noted that Colonel David Tisdale had gotten the Conservative nomination for South Norfolk. Despite not having always seen eye to eye with

Tisdale, Kerr promised to get out the vote for him.[205] Tisdale won the election, along with ten other Conservatives in Kerr's district, allowing Sir John A. MacDonald to maintain his parliamentary majority.

In 1887 Kerr got involved in a dispute between Edward Harris and Long Point Fisheries Overseer Peter Price, whose sister was the mother of Col. Tisdale. Price wanted to continue to allow sport fishing at Long Point, of which he was a financial beneficiary, whereas Harris wanted Long Point Bay preserved as a natural fish hatchery. It is no surprise that Kerr supported Harris. He observed that Price could not serve "two masters."

Kerr had taken the steamer to Long Point. Edward Harris's brother, George, and his family were on board. Naturally, George supported his brother's position. Kerr told a curious story about Edward and George Harris, whom he had apparently known in London: "I have known Edward and George Harris for 40 years [1847], since they were school boys. Edward Harris paddled me in a dugout canoe up to a she bear 38 years ago [1849] in the River Thames at London when I killed the bear with the blow of an axe in the head." This is such a weird story that I can only presume it is true. This might have been the last bear to ever swim in the Thames in London!

Kerr met with Edward Harris in London on July 27 to discuss the future of Long Point Bay, for which the LPC had a nine-year lease for exclusive fishing purposes. The two men agreed that the bay should be set aside for fish breeding purposes, meaning no commercial or recreational fishing. Kerr wrote a long, passionate letter to the deputy minister exhorting the Department to adopt this position: "The vastness of these fisheries [200 sq. miles] require that your special attention should be given and bestowed on a place so valuable… A breeding place of unsurpassed wealth, with bright prospects ahead, should make the place entitled to your kind consideration."

Shortly before his death in 1888, Kerr was elated to hear that both the Long Point Company and the Turkey Point Company had agreed

---

205   David Tisdale (Sept. 8, 1835–Mar. 31, 1911) was elected MP in 1887 and four times thereafter. He was appointed Minister of Militia and Defence in 1896.

to set aside the waters exclusively for fish breeding. The members would thereafter devote themselves to hard drinking and duck shooting. However, after Kerr was dead, they allegedly gave up drinking and resumed fishing and shooting. It's fun to shoot when you're drunk but not so much fun to fish, I guess.

The Long Point Company continues to exist as a private club and maintains exclusive access to the almost twenty-five-mile-long sand spit. It remains rather secretive and is still controlled by an amalgam of wealthy Canadians and Americans who use it, as always, for their shooting and drinking pleasure.

Members of the Long Point Company, J. I. McKenzie is second from right. From "Lore and Legends of Long Point".

Chapter 15

Farming and Family

Kerr made occasional reference to his farm and farming activities, but I don't think he had much interest in it. He had four sons. The oldest, George, died in 1883. My great-grandfather, Charles John Kerr, lived in Hamilton at 428 Mary Street, and I believe he became a machinist and then a fisheries overseer after his older brother, Frederick, gave up the post. Kerr's youngest son, Edward or Ned, became a house painter. So, the only son who likely stayed on the farm after Kerr's death in 1888 was Frederick. There are some references in his diaries to farming activities. J. W. Kerr's wife, Mary, lived on until 1903 and was probably somewhat involved with the farm, although there is little mention of her in the diaries. Kerr also had five daughters, none of whom ever married. (What's up with that?) I believe they all lived on the farm until the last one died in 1930.[206] Thus it seems that if any of the family were farmers, it was the girls, and possibly Fred.

The first mention of the farm is in May 1867 when Kerr noted rather ruefully that after a run on Lake Ontario "I must then farm for a few days."

On July 4, 1871, Kerr wrote to J. W. Dunne of Mount Hope: "Will you be pleased to furnish the combined reaper and mower with self

---

206   Two daughters died the same day, on January 5, 1929. My father, who was seven years old at the time, remembered attending the house where they were laid out in their coffins together!

raker[207] attached at the rate and upon the terms you propose. You may order it at once—to be delivered to the Great Western Railway station at Hamilton. My son George will be down with you, pay the freight charges and take it up home, when I expect you will come here, set it up and show him how to work it." George, however, was not destined to be a farmer but rather a railway man.

In Toronto in 1872, Kerr bought four beehives for his farm, which was the first mention of beekeeping. He seemed to take a lot of pleasure in it and returned to the topic several times over the remainder of his life.

In 1873, Kerr noted the crops he had grown: spring wheat, fall wheat, barley, oats, and straw, for a total value of $200.58.

In the summer of 1874, there was a first mention of some of Kerr's daughters. He made a trip to Burlington Beach to meet some affluent Hamilton men to discuss the Beach Hotel project. He noted "Louisa, Eveline and Clara with me." When I read this, I thought he was looking to marry them off to Hamilton businessmen until I realized they were only fourteen, twelve, and ten at the time!

On January 12, 1876, Kerr paid Mr. W. R. Gray of Dundas thirty-two dollars for a cultivator.[208] A cultivator is a pretty important piece of farm equipment, so that seemed like a pretty good price, being about what a working man could expect to earn in a month.

It seems that Kerr had a typical mixed farm that had a little bit of everything. Back in that era, it was good not to put all your eggs in one basket by specializing in only one aspect of farming. In January 1879, Kerr wrote to a man at Cashmere[209] to request a live wild turkey, noting "I have 5 hens but no gobbler."[210]

When Kerr got paid, which was usually quarterly, and often months late, he sometimes recorded how he disbursed the funds. For example,

....

207 A combine, as the name implies, is a versatile farming machine capable of reaping, threshing, and separating grain. Originally pulled by horses or oxen, it later became a steam operated and then gas operated implement.
208 A cultivator is a pronged machine used for secondary tillage to prepare ground for planting or for weeding between rows.
209 Cashmere was a small town near Chatham. It no longer exists.
210 A gobbler is a male turkey, named for the vocal sounds it makes.

he noted "Mrs. Kerr – $30." As far as I can see, he never referred to his wife by her first name anywhere in the 10,000 pages of his diaries. He often paid the boys for assisting him, and there was a curious entry in May 1880 when he noted that he gave Emily J. Kerr $1.25. A few days later he gave her twenty dollars. She turned twelve two weeks later, so maybe it was for her birthday or maybe for a church confirmation. We will never know, but this was a substantial amount for a gift.[211]

In 1880 Kerr tried to get his son, George, a promotion. He wrote to the mechanical superintendent of the GWR, whom he probably knew from his days with the railroad (1851–1858). George was a fireman with the Wellington, Grey, and Bruce Railway, and Kerr wanted to see him promoted to engine driver. Kerr noted that George had been with the north end of the WG & B Railroad for four years on the run up to Palmerston and that he had previously been with the GWR since 1869 when he was twenty. Kerr reported, "There are no black marks, not even a reprimand against George." George got the promotion, and he was still an engineer with the railroad when he died at age thirty-four in 1884.

In 1880, Kerr mentioned that his daughter, Louisa, then twenty years old, drove him down to the train station. Later, he remarked that he took her on a Sunday fishing mission to Burlington Beach, which is, I think, the only time he mentioned taking one of his five daughters on active duty. She must have been quite a girl. She lived until 1930, probably never having moved off the farm or held any formal job.

Aside from all his other employment, in 1881 Kerr noted he was working as an auditor in the Standard Insurance office on the corner of Vine and James in downtown Hamilton. He seemed to work this job for several years and reported earning $100 for what was likely only a few weeks' work. That was good money for the time when the average daily wage was only about $1.

From time to time in his correspondence, Kerr remarked on farming or family matters and, typical of all farmers, the weather. In one August

....

211   According to the Church of England website, there is no fixed age for confirmation, but typically it is ten years of age or older.

1881 letter he wrote, "Hardly any apples this season, peaches too are scarce, and I have no bees and no honey."

The mixed nature of Kerr's farm is further confirmed in a letter he wrote to Big Jim Cantwell in November 1881. Apparently thanking Cantwell for sending his daughter two ducks, he wrote, "My little daughter, Emily Jane [age 13] desires me to return you her sincere thanks for Mr. & Mrs. Browne [the ducks' names]. She fed them with corn until they got used to the house and place, and got to be good friends with the other ducks. Now they take pot luck and are fed along with the other fowl, three times a day."

In an August 1, 1882, letter to friend/foe Cantwell, Kerr noted, "Splendid rain here all day today. A good deal of wheat out, only it would be better in the barn. The boys got in 14 loads yesterday. A good many loads out still! And 6 acres of fall wheat to cut yet. Spring wheat, barley, pears and oats ripening fast. It is a nice sight to see the old duck and 19 young ones parading around, besides 17 half-grown and feathering in another flock."

Noting the abundant 1882 harvest, Kerr stated, "We have 477 bushels of wheat, 320 bushels of barley, and 185 bushels of oats, besides good potatoes, corn, mangles,[212] turnips, squashes and the prettiest peach orchard you ever beheld." Kerr also must have had a smokehouse on the farm because he noted having received a sturgeon from Thomas Elliott that it "is now in the smoke house, being smoked with corn cobs."

Owen Bowers was of German ancestry and was a fishery guardian at Long Point. He was also a farmer in Port Royal. As such, Kerr often sent him letters mentioning farm matters and typical farm topics like the weather. He was a favourite of Kerr's. Kerr bought seed from him. In a September 1882 letter, Kerr mentioned that he had planted twenty-one acres of fall wheat and commented on the "splendid rain" and that it was "a grand thing for farmers and the farming community… If you come to the Hamilton fair, you had better come and stop with us!!"

Bowers did attend the fair, and Kerr took him on a tour of Niagara to show him around. However, there was a secret side to Bowers, who

....

212 Mangles were a type of beet used to feed livestock.

was highly in debt and who eventually lost his farm.

Winter came early in 1882, and Kerr observed, "The snow on the Mountain road between my place and the Jolley Cut, where we go down into Hamilton, is mountain high. The avenue from the house out to the high road is so completely filled up with snow that at present we can't get in nor out by that way. The biggest snow drifts I ever saw on the Mountain since the winter 1855 are seen here at present."[213]

Kerr also made a rare mention of his daughters, noting, "Two of my daughters, Louisa, and Emily Jane, were both sick when I got home, but are now getting better again. Neuralgia, I believe, was the ailment."[214]

In terms of other livestock on the farm, he mentioned pigeons, which were sometimes kept as food, but I can't confirm if Kerr kept them or not. He definitely raised turkeys because there is a November 10, 1882, reference to Thanksgiving when "Mrs. Kerr sold 5 turkeys yesterday at $1 a piece at the house. Thanksgiving dinner turkeys."[215]

There is no mention of any pets in the house except for canaries, which Kerr had apparently obtained from John Hand, a fisherman in Grimsby, for his daughters. Kerr seems not to have been a dog lover. He was offered a puppy by a friend in Toronto, to which he replied, "I don't care for a pup of any kind out of the bitch you refer to." He was rarely that blunt in any of his letters except about enemies, of which he had a few. As mentioned, Kerr kept bees, and in 1883 he wrote to obtain "a skip of Italian bees."[216] There are occasional references to his bees and the quantity of honey produced. As a nineteenth-century farmer, he had to be diversified and able to withstand the vicissitudes of the weather.

Demonstrating the precarious nature of life in nineteenth-century Canada, Kerr's oldest son, George, died suddenly on March 28, 1883. Single and just thirty-four years old, George had gotten a job as an

---

213 The Kerr family moved to their Hamilton Mountain home in October 1855.
214 Neuralgia is a stabbing, burning pain caused by a damaged nerve.
215 Thanksgiving in Canada was not always on the second Monday in October. It became an annual event in Canada on November 6, 1879, but the date was changed yearly, sometimes being as late as December 6.
216 First imported into England in 1859, Italian bees are the most widely distributed of all honeybees.

engineer on the Wellington, Grey and Bruce Railway that ran between Guelph and Southampton. George's death certificate listed the cause of death as pneumonitis or pneumonia, and it was signed in Hamilton, so he must have died at home, even though he was apparently staying at a hotel in Palmerston on the railway line.

Kerr's letter book for the days leading up to George's death are unreadable, so I don't know how sudden his death was, but Kerr announced it in a letter dated March 31: "I deeply regret to inform you that I lost my eldest son and best boy." The whole family must have been shocked at the death of the eldest son. In a letter, Kerr wrote, "Mrs. Kerr feels keenly the loss of our son George." Having been a Mason like his father, George was buried with Masonic rites in Hamilton Cemetery after a service in the house.

There were a few monetary matters to conclude, such as paying George's bill for room and board at the Queen's Hotel in Palmerston and settling his estate. Kerr wrote, "He had no will, knowing all his property would pass to his father. I am determined to divide it equally with his mother, sisters and brothers." To Whitcher, Kerr lamented the loss of his son: "He was a good boy, and he was very good natured to all. I have taken the liberty of sending you his likeness" (a portrait). Within a few days, Kerr went back to business as usual.

On June 30, Kerr wrote to the deputy minister to request $120 for a new buggy, noting the wear and tear on his buggies and wagons "used by me during the last 18 years, 5 months and 14 days, during that period in driving thousands of miles in the protection of fish and fisheries." Before he got his letter press in 1881, Kerr meticulously recorded all of his mileage and his various methods of travel. Rail was most common, followed by horse and buggy, and the total for his 23.5-year career was about 225,000 miles, or approximately the distance to the moon. At an estimated approximate speed of 10 miles per hour, that would be about 22,500 hours of travel time or 937.5 days of 24-hour-per day travel. Perhaps exceeded only by professional travelers like railway men or sailors, that is about ten times the circumference of the earth!

On Christmas Day, 1883, Kerr wrote a letter to a friend that painted a poignant vignette of his life.

> We are all well here today and happy. Some of the girls are out having a sleigh ride; some at Church; one boy home! Two gone off shooting. Mrs. Kerr, Charley's wife and son and Emily in the kitchen; and I am writing this all alone, except 4 canaries in the dining room; May you all live long and be happy. I sent your daughter, Emily, a book of piano music and some sheets of music! A list made out for me by Jennie and herself. I sent or had them sent to you care of Emily C. Elliott. Kindly remember me to Mr. Hutchinson. And believe me, as ever, your friend.

Mr. Hutchinson, who has been previously mentioned, was Jimmy Hutchinson, who boarded with the Elliott family and was probably part of his fishing crew. At the time of this letter, in 1883, Kerr and Hutchinson were apparently on good terms, but that changed in the future for reasons that I can only guess at. Later, they had a physical altercation of a somewhat humorous nature.

Joseph Masters Sr. was one of Kerr's licensed fishermen in Niagara. His son, Joseph Masters Jr., was born in 1871 and lived next door to the Elliotts at the foot of King Street. Masters' *Niagara Reminiscences* were put online and comprise a 717-page opus about life in Niagara from the 1880s until his death in 1955. He knew all the fishing characters in Niagara, including Kerr and Hutchinson. Some grudge had developed between the two, and Masters told the story.

> *Jimmy was very scotch. He was a short dumpy man, a ship carpenter by trade. Jimmy boarded at Elliott's for a long time and he took a great dislike to the Fishery Overseer from Hamilton. One day he met the Overseer and at the sight of the man he hated, he went for him and bowled him over. If you could have seen a stout man rolling down the hill with Jimmy prodding at him with his garden fork it would have given you a thrill. No serious harm was done, however, but Jimmy left his boarding house and moved. Jimmy said afterwards "I ha narna dirrk with me, or I'd a fenished him." [Dirk is a Scottish word for a knife] Masters later recalls being asked by Hutchinson "Did Kerr no come to see ya before he went to Hell?"*

Kerr made a vague reference to this event in a letter to Mrs. Elliott in May 1885, just prior to his seventy-third birthday! Apparently, things got so bad between Kerr and Hutchinson that Kerr stopped boarding with the Elliotts partly to avoid the curses and taunts of the small Scotsman. What became of him is anybody's guess.

In 1884 Kerr reported a good harvest and that by the end of July his boys had put in forty tons of hay. That seems like a lot of hay from a one-hundred-acre farm that also produced other crops, so I assume the farm was able to support a significant amount of livestock. Cows are supposed to consume about 24 pounds of hay per day, so if someone had 80,000 pounds of hay to feed cows for half the year, that would only support about 20 cows. I have no idea if that is even close. I do know that Kerr had cows though because he noted buying a pair of calves and having them shipped from Port Credit to Hamilton.

Suddenly, in early December 1884, Kerr's wife took seriously ill, as he reported in a letter to Bauset, his new immediate boss: "My wife took seriously ill at 11:00 p.m. on Tuesday night, I very much regret telling you, with heart disease and she is still far from better, although able to be up in her room and out of bed. One of my sons, with horse and buggy, flew to Hamilton for the doctor. I am in hope she will soon be right again." By Christmas she was still ill but improving slowly. Perhaps hoping for some sympathy from Bauset, his immediate boss, Kerr took the opportunity to try to get his 15-year-old son appointed as his assistant at $150 per year. I don't think it happened, and Edward later became a house painter. The boys did all get paid for assisting Kerr, usually by rowing him around Burlington Bay.

In 1885 Kerr established a warm relationship with William Y. Emery and his family in Port Burwell. Kerr must have stayed with Emery because he repeatedly thanked him and his family for the hospitality. Emery, or at least his wife, must have been Irish, and they invited Kerr and his wife to visit. Kerr wondered if Mrs. Emery knew some of Mrs. Kerr's family, mentioning a visit to Blackrock, which was either a suburb of Dublin or a seaside town just south of Dundalk in County Louth, where Mrs. Kerr and her mother visited with her aunt, who was married to Mr. William Thomas Mulvany. At the time he was the Commissioner of Board of Works for Ireland and the Commissioner of Fishing.[217]

For some reason, Kerr refused the invitation, possibly related to his wife because he said he could not explain in a letter but would explain when next they met. Was it Mrs. Kerr's health or some other reason that precluded the trip? She was only fifty-seven at the time, but she had a health scare in 1884, so who knows. In 1886 Kerr and his wife were invited to spend a week at the Fraser House Hotel by his friend, John Ellison. Opened in 1871, Fraser House was on the bluffs above Port Stanley and was an elegant 62-room hotel with a dining room that could seat 200. Sir John A. MacDonald would stay there when in the area. Kerr said he could not accept the invitation "for obvious reasons which I will explain to you." The mystery continued.

In November, Kerr and his family received a gift of eggs from the Emery family. He wrote in thanks, "My wife said when your kind present of eggs arrived, she felt grateful to you, but observed it was such a strange thing to get a present of eggs where there were 60 hens. Besides eggs packed away for use during winter! Packed in the dust taken off the road in front of my house. With my warm and kind regards." Unknown to me, apparently chickens do not lay eggs in the winter months unless under artificial lighting. So, people had to preserve eggs for winter. There were various ways to do this, and I guess one was to pack them in dust and put them in a dark place. Apparently, they will last for a long time. Who knew?

Planning to trade a duck for some bees, Kerr planned a trip in December to meet Francis Reid in Clarkson: "You might send David up there to meet me with the sleigh. I propose to bring another duck with me." It was not unusual during Kerr's era to ship live fish and fowl

....

217 William Thomas Mulvany (Mar. 11, 1806–Oct. 30, 1885) was born a Catholic in Dublin but converted to the Church of England due to the limited educational prospects for Catholics. He became an engineer and was responsible for planning waterways in Ireland and modernizing fishing. His wife was Alicia Winslow, the daughter of a wealthy landowner in County Fermanagh. They married in 1832 and had four children, a son and three daughters, who would have been Mrs. Kerr's cousins. He moved to Germany to assist in the commencement of coal mining in the Ruhr Valley. He became quite famous in Germany.

by train. Kerr often sent fish, ducks, and fruit to Ottawa.

Emery had a fishing licence, and he was also a businessman. Kerr had stayed at his home while on duty at Lake Erie. He became quite attached to Emery's children, and the letters Kerr sent were quite affectionate. In May 1886, Emery sent Kerr a letter in which he stated, "the heart of man is never satisfied," to which Kerr responded, "But the old song says against that: 'When the heart of man is oppressed with care! The mist is dispersed when a woman appears' These old ditties of a long time ago, come up in my mind occasionally."

In October, not having heard from Emery in a while, Kerr wrote to him to observe that his letters were "like the Angel's visits, are far between." He went on to talk about the Irish robin, which "when hard pressed with hunger, enter the houses in hard and severe weather, so to be fed." He recounted the following Irish ditty: "Oh where are you going sweet robin! What makes you so proud and so shy! I once saw the day little robin, my friendship you would not deny."[218]

Kerr's relationship with Emery and his family is a little weird. In another letter he wrote of how a cousin of his, Ellen Brock, age sixty, would sing this song "They say I have a heart that's so small, it can't be divided in two! But Johnny then shalt have it all, for I am always thinking of you." Not sure what to make of that!

Although not really about farming or family, a curious event in 1886 doesn't really fit anywhere else in this narrative, so I am going to mention it here as an example of the kind of man Kerr was. There was a Black barber, Andrew Provo, in Hamilton, who had been born a British subject at Holland Landing and who had enlisted in the Union Army in 1865 as a member of the 38th Maryland coloured troops. When one enlisted in the Union Army, he received "bounty money" as an inducement. The amount a person received depended upon how long he enlisted. Apparently, Provo was cheated out of his money, around $500, by Major Lucius H. Warren, as the 38th was travelling to Texas.

In 1886, 21 years after the American Civil War ended, Kerr took up Provo's case and wrote a petition for him to President Grover Cleveland

....

218 This is an 1815 English song about fickle, fair-weather friends.

seeking compensation. Kerr, as we know, was a good and experienced writer and may have just been ghostwriting for his barber. The petition read, "Your Petitioner went into the American Army to do his duty to the Republic, and having done so, is in justice entitled to fair treatment and honourable consideration." Kerr also wrote a personal letter to the president on behalf of Provo and got Hamilton Mayor McKay and Provo's clergyman to do the same.

It is unknown if any result was ever achieved, but this illustrates Kerr's constant concern for fair play and justice. This seems to have been deeply ingrained in him as a result of his upbringing as a British citizen of Irish birth, and he frequently refers to his need for "British fair play."

In August 1886 Kerr reported that his youngest son, Edward, age nineteen, had a serious fall off a scaffold while working as a painter. He and another young man had fallen twenty-eight feet to the ground, sustaining serious injuries that apparently required hospitalization and rendered him "insensible for some time." By September he was beginning to recover. He must not have been too badly injured because he got married in 1894 and went on to have twelve children!

On August 26, Kerr noted the fortieth anniversary of he and his wife arriving at Port Stanley aboard the steamship *New London,* plying the waters between Buffalo and Amherstburg. He was particularly proud that although he knew no one on his arrival, he was now the fisheries overseer for Port Stanley and had lots of friends there. He seemed quite sentimental, talking about his service in the RIC and his militia service in Canada with the 3rd Middlesex under Colonel Burwell and later with the 1st Wentworth, as adjutant and captain to Sir Allan MacNab, the "Great Man of Gore." He concluded by stating, "I have commenced another year in this Canada of ours and the prospects are bright."

William Emery's daughter had found five dollars, and they wondered if it belonged to Kerr, so he wrote back: "That $5 bill that your honest girl picked up is not mine! I never lose any money except once I lost a half sovereign and I think over that loss to this day. Why I suppose it fairly belongs to your honest girl. I once found 30 pounds, if there if anything to be admired so much, it is honesty. To find money and keep it is stealing!"

Writing again to Emery just before Christmas, Kerr included another bucolic note on his home life: "I may tell you I am well and in good health, and how can it be otherwise, for in the parlour Clara, my 4th daughter is playing *My love is but a lassie yet!* because she knows it is one of my favourite tunes."[219] As recounted earlier in this narrative, Kerr's life was about to undergo a big change just six days later as a result of a serious fall off his front steps.

Of all his farming activities, beekeeping seems to have been his favourite. He obtained his bees and equipment from Alex Robertson of Progreston (near Carlisle), and he occasionally wrote to describe things. In 1887 he wrote requesting "6 swarms" and reported that "my 5 swarms are very strong, working well and I expect to have swarms this month, perhaps during the fruit blow." Now I associate the word "swarm" with a bad thing, like an out-of-control hive of bees, but when you look it up, swarm just means a hive of bees.

Later, Kerr sent honey to Bauset and wrote, "I never eat honey myself but still I love and like it and I am so fond of bees. And Canada may properly be called 'the land flowing with milk and honey.'"[220] Schools of fish—hives of bees. I guess I see a parallel in that they are both large groups working together for a common cause. Kerr also offered up a curious folk remedy: "Honey sickens some people, but if they will drink a cup of new milk after eating the honey, they will never be sick." On the arrival of his bees, Kerr observed: "They are the most docile and pleasant bees to handle I have ever seen! Not a sting, although I have been amongst them with bare hands, my coat off and no covering over my face."

In the summer 1887, Kerr wrote to Robertson to happily report on the progress of his "swarms" and noted that honey "will be plentiful." Kerr also wanted to purchase an extractor, which is a device used to

....

219 This song is based on a Robbie Burns poem from 1787.
220 Full confession: My mother's father, William Muirhead, kept bees, as did my Uncle Bill. I used to help him when I was a kid and remember it well. I love honey and usually buy it wherever I travel. I also have one of the largest honey tin collections in Canada, at about seventy-five. Weird thing to collect. Peanut Butter tins are more popular. I've got about fifty of those. For some reason, my kids don't want this inheritance! Ingrates!

separate honey from the frames by using centrifugal force.[221]

In another letter to Emery, Kerr recited an old Irish song: "Let the farmer praise his grounds. Let the huntsman praise his hounds! Let them boast of the deeds they have done, done done! But we will go to Killalee, without stocking or a shoe! And we'll take our little cruiskeen lawn, lawn! [a little jug]." An ode to leisure and pleasure, Kerr noted, "These things come in to my mind since I commenced to write, and so I send them to you and spin them out as they come!" If you Google the first line, you can hear a version of this Irish drinking song!

Kerr would occasionally rail about Irish nationalism to friends, particularly when it was imported into Canadian politics. As an Irish Protestant, Kerr was fiercely loyal to Britain and particularly to the four monarchs he had served. However, he observed that he was not an Orangeman, as his father and grandfather had been, and it did not seem to affect how he performed his duties. That is about all I know about his father and grandfather! Noting Queen Victoria's Golden Jubilee on June 20, 1887, Kerr wrote in very large print, "God save the Queen."

Kerr's good friend Emery, of Port Stanley, wrote to invite Kerr and his wife to attend the picnic of the Irish Benevolent Society of London, and Kerr wrote back with some flimsy excuse that he was too busy. Kerr remarked in passing that when he had lived in London, (1847–1851), he was a member of the society. So, I Googled the society and learned that it had been started in 1877. Kerr had not lived in London since 1851! Was he lying, or was there some earlier similar organization?

For some reason, Kerr had an affinity for wild turkeys, and in 1887 he obtained a pair for three dollars from a friend on the Thames River: "About the gobbler I got last summer, I gave it to my friend, Mr. Andrew Gage, who lives down at Burlington Bay. He let it out with his other wild turkeys, they commenced to beat him and he flew away. He has never seen that Gobbler since. Mr. Gage has about 70 wild turkeys tamed, splendid birds. He has a good large farm to keep them on." If

....

221   My uncle had an extractor in the basement of his house. The frames were set in the cylindrical drum and spun at high speed, dislodging the honey into a collector. It was a chaotic place with a large number of pissed-off bees hovering around.

you tame a wild turkey, isn't it just a turkey?

The farm house continued to be occupied by the Kerr family until the last of Kerr's daughters died in 1930 when it may have been leased or left vacant because by the war years it was in very poor repair. The property began to get subdivided for housing by the 1950s. My grandfather, Gordon Kerr, built his house at 401 Upper Gage during WWII, and my father built our house at 431 Upper Gage just after the war. My youngest daughter now lives in my grandparents' house, which means 165 years of continuous ownership by a member of the Kerr family. Can anybody else in Hamilton beat that? I don't think so!

As the farm was being developed for housing in the 1950s, the streets were laid out and named. The developer must not have thought much of the Kerr family because "Kerr Street" is a tiny one-hundred-yard-long street with only two houses. It is right behind my old elementary school, Highview. The big house has been totally renovated over the years and is currently owned by Alan and Leslie Hurman. They graciously gave my daughter and me a tour of their beautiful home.

Inkerman Cottage, Kerr's home built 1855. Photograph by Steve Burditt, 2020.

Historical plaque in Mountain Drive Park across from Kerr Home.
Photograph by Steve Burditt, 2020

Kerr Road looking East, with Flock Mountain Road, behind. Source unknown.

Farming and Family   291

Kerr's four surviving daughters, c.1902. From "Mountain Memories"

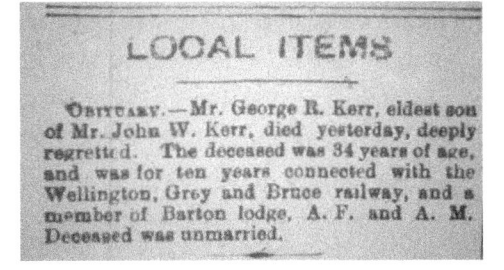

LOCAL ITEMS

OBITUARY.—Mr. George R. Kerr, eldest son of Mr. John W. Kerr, died yesterday, deeply regretted. The deceased was 34 years of age, and was for ten years connected with the Wellington, Grey and Bruce railway, and a member of Barton lodge, A. F. and A. M. Deceased was unmarried.

Obituary of George Kerr from Hamilton Spectator. Hamilton Public Library.

CHAPTER 16

Revenge is a Dish Best Served Cold

At several points in his diaries, Kerr noted that in May 1858, he and about forty other employees of the GWR were fired for supporting Isaac Buchanan, who was one of the railway's directors and a major Hamilton businessman.

Kerr started working as the chief clerk in GWR's engineering office on May 1, 1851. Since 1847 he had been living in London, ON, and when he took the GWR job he moved his wife and two oldest children to Hamilton. As far as I know, Kerr knew nothing about railways, but he was well educated, very organized, and good with numbers.

In 1851, the railroad, running from Windsor to Niagara was just under construction, and the engineering office would have been very busy. They would have been responsible for bringing into existence the working railway from the survey of the line, which was completed in 1847. The ground-breaking ceremony was held in London on October 23, 1847, and undoubtedly Kerr was present, as was almost everybody else in London.

Sir Allan MacNab was the driving force behind the construction of the line and had gone to London, England, to secure financing. Robert William Harris,[222] a partner of Isaac Buchanan, was elected president

---

222 Robert William Harris (1805–Mar. 22, 1861) was born in County Antrim, Northern Ireland. Harris worked himself into a partnership with the Buchanan brothers due to his integrity and expertise in the dry goods trade. He was elected president of the GWR in 1849 and resigned in 1856. Described in the *Dictionary of Canadian Biography* as a "shy man who made few friends and never married," he got caught up in the Buchanan/Canada Southern fiasco.

of the GWR in 1849, and it was possibly him who hired fellow Irishman Kerr.

The engineering office was likely responsible for planning and construction, and the chief clerk would have had a very busy job lining up materials and men and making day-to-day arrangements. The main materials required to build a railway are stone for road ballast, wood for bridges, and ties and fencing to keep livestock off the track, together with the rails and all related hardware. Kerr's job was likely to keep track of the expenses because he was always a meticulous detail guy, maintaining books and keeping receipts.

A railway makes no money until it is completed, so there was an urgency to get it done as quickly as possible at the lowest cost. When Kerr was hired, the chief engineer was Charles B. Stuart, an American, and the assistant chief engineer was Roswell Gardinier Benedict. Benedict was also an American. He was a good friend and business associate of Samuel Zimmerman, the great railway contractor, whom he had met during the construction of the Welland Canal. Benedict became the chief engineer just after Kerr was hired in 1851, and he was highly influential in getting Zimmerman the primary construction contract.

Because of huge cost overruns, the English board of directors appointed Charles John Brydges[223] as managing director, and he moved to Canada to take over supervision of the railway construction. Roswell Benedict was fired in 1853 because of the cost overruns and was replaced as chief engineer by John T. Clark, another American. Kerr described Clark as a "prudent man of a most judicious character, with long and known experience." He said nothing about the character or experience of his two previous bosses.

Clark had been employed as a commissioner with the GWR at the behest of the equally concerned US shareholders. As Kerr said, he was

---

223 Charles John Brydges (Feb. 1827–Feb. 16, 1889) was born in London and was employed since his youth in railways. He became the managing director of the GWR in 1852. Described by the *Dictionary of Canadian Biography* as possessing a "driving ambition and an extraordinary capacity for hard work," he was also "authoritarian" and "headstrong." The town of Mount Brydges, west of London, is named for him.

"perfectly conversant with all the works on the line, his duty being to examine all works of construction, which he did by personal examination." On October 17, 1853, Clark submitted his cost estimate, which was almost $1.5 million more than the initial estimate of $1.9 million.

The problems seem to have been that Managing Director Brydges was acting in such haste that bribes and extortionate accounts were being paid to sleazy guys like Zimmerman and that corners were being cut to get the line open. In November 1853, the 229-mile line did open, under protest from Chief Engineer Clark, who maintained the line was unsafe and unready. He was absolutely right. There were nineteen major accidents and fifty-two fatalities in the first year of operation. Clark quickly took another job, but Kerr stayed on.

It is highly likely that Kerr saw all this and sided with Clark. Everybody knows that a secretary or clerk knows where all the bodies are buried, and Kerr, a deeply moral man, was likely horrified by what he knew. He would have been a marked man in the eyes of C. J. Brydges. It soon became clear that the line would have to undergo a huge additional expense to rehabilitate the shoddy construction.

The GWR was in competition with its northern neighbour, the Grand Trunk Railway, and Samuel Zimmerman, who was sometimes described as the richest man in Canada West, began to advocate a plan that would aid the Grand Trunk at the expense of the GWR. There was a proposal to build a Canada Southern Railway that would travel between Detroit and Buffalo on a shorter, more direct route than the GWR. By this time the GWR was complete, and Zimmerman's only interest was in securing more railway contracts, most of which he subcontracted. The GWR would be caught between the Grand Trunk and Canada Southern and squeezed out of business.

Sir Allan MacNab was dumped by the GWR and was also thought to be acting in support of the Grand Trunk. When Isaac Buchanan learned in 1857 that Zimmerman was buying up stock in what would become Canada Southern, he moved to thwart Zimmerman by beating him to the punch, which included paying a $25,000 bribe to get a Canada Southern director to resign. By this resignation, Buchanan was able to arrange a friendly appointment to the board, tipping it in his favour.

Brydges, who later worked for the Grand Trunk, was also opposed to Buchanan's plan.

Zimmerman had great political connections and was known to lavish money on his friends and politicians, especially in Toronto. In any event, Zimmerman and Brydges prevailed, and soon thereafter Brydges lowered the boom on Kerr and others who had supported Chief Engineer Clark and Isaac Buchanan plan to control the Canada Southern.

Kerr, who noted in his diaries that he earned $1,200 a year while at the GWR, had just two years previously built a big house on Hamilton Mountain, and the loss of this job could not have come at a worse time. I always wondered how Kerr, a clerk, could buy a one-hundred-acre farm and build an elegant and unique home. Maybe it was possible on his salary, which was about four times what an average laboring man earned. I hope, and feel pretty certain, that there were no nefarious sources of money that built the Kerr farm.

By 1860 the English shareholders in the GWR were howling for heads because of a deep recession and were still annoyed about the huge cost overruns. C. J. Brydges was called upon to account for why the construction of the GWR had cost so much more than the cost of constructing the Grand Trunk. There were also rumours about his personal integrity involving kickbacks.

Here is where the story gets interesting. Kerr offered to provide the London directors with the dirt they would need to get rid of Brydges! A series of letters in 1860 make it clear that Kerr had the information and that he was prepared to use it against Brydges, a man he described as "acting wrong, injudicious and improper." Kerr said he "will the tale unfold, and believe me. Deny it who can! Confute it who dare!! It is a living monument of the true facts which I here assert!!!"

On October 12, 1859, the *Hamilton Spectator* published a report about Brydges that sounded a lot like the information Kerr was willing to provide. Reporting on Brydges' inexperience when he arrived in Canada, the story stated, "Surrounded as he was by greedy and unscrupulous contractors who are said to have acquired rapid and almost fabulous fortunes, through, as has been alleged, the connivance or complicity with professional men then, and for some time after, in the Company's employ." Did Kerr tip the newspaper off? I don't know, but I would not be surprised.

The problem was that Kerr only wanted to get Brydges and did not wish to impair his relationship with the GWR, with whom he had hopes of regaining employment. He was confident of success.

> *I shall have to bear the brunt of the battle, when we arrange that I am to do so, still I apprehend the charges once made, Mr. Brydges and his confederates will yield. I say so because I know him to be a coward, besides, our weapons are pure, and not stained. Won't he tremble before the men he has attempted to ruin—and why! Because of their fidelity to the shareholders, as time and an investigation will unfold, for the GWR is not the property of a single individual, but of a large number of influential shareholders, and when I see their property, once so prosperous, now in danger from bad management, I consider it my duty to speak out if required to do so.*

Kerr had clearly kept copies of the accounts and had consulted a local lawyer because he knew that revealing this information could result in him being sued for breach of trust. He also consulted with former engineer John T. Clark, who had returned to the US and was quite ill. Without mentioning what he wanted, Kerr sought to obtain a "distinct understanding" from the London directors as to how his evidence would be used and what the consequences would be for him and others.

Indicating that his motives were not "mercenary," Kerr seemed upset about the incompetence and unscrupulous dealings that resulted in the many deaths and the financial harm to the shareholders. Ironically, Samuel Zimmerman was killed in the Desjardins Canal disaster, which resulted in the deaths of fifty-nine people when a GWR train returning to Hamilton from Toronto broke an axle and took out the bridge, plunging into the canal on March 12, 1857. Even though an inquiry determined it was an accident, Kerr had some thoughts on this, ominously writing, "I shall say a few words on the Desjardins Canal accident after a little, and its cause." Some of the dead were railway men who Kerr would have known, and he probably attended their funerals. Unfortunately, Kerr never told his tale, at least not in writing.

Kerr was also annoyed that Brydges had been taken advantage of by American contractors like Zimmerman, who was born poor in Pennsylvania in 1815. Brydges had sidelined Chief Engineer Clark, which was a big mistake "for the contractors, being American by birth, and being an American himself, he was acquainted with the American character, with which Mr. C. J. Brydges then was not." I presume the "American character" to which Kerr referred was of an unscrupulous, extortionate nature.

Kerr was writing to H. B. Wilson, a member of the "Corresponding Committee" of the London, England, board of directors of the GWR. There was also a board of directors in Canada, but it was the London board that was raising the fuss and wanted Kerr's help. Kerr warned Wilson that the Canadian board was trying to extinguish the flames by declaring a dividend to placate the shareholders, which included the City of Hamilton, which owned 37,500 British pounds worth of stock.[224] Kerr promised to use his "exertions to get the Mayor and Council to act," meaning to support his efforts to unseat Brydges.

Kerr wanted to attend the meeting in London as a shareholder, so he cooked up a scheme whereby shares would be temporarily placed in his name, thereby allowing him a vote. He wrote, "Make all your other arrangements for the attack and you may rely upon me. My reserve battalion will be up in time to win the day." The meeting was scheduled to be held in April 1860, so Kerr needed to know his position because he had "an immense amount of labour" to prepare his report. Kerr had met with Wilson in Hamilton, but no agreement was reached, and he was reluctant to participate for fear of consequences to himself and his friends at the GWR. After "much anxiety of mind," Kerr was prepared to strike. He never mentioned who the members of his battalion were.

....

224   It was not unusual for cities to own stock in railways, usually to ensure the line passed through their lands. If a community was bypassed by a railroad, it was doomed to economic extinction.

Kerr continued: "You may not fully comprehend the magnitude of what you ask me to embark on, but I have given it my entire attention and I know it well. Why! It will turn out to be the degradation of a great many persons who at present occupy a respectable position in society, I should consider well what I do and how I do it. Don't you think so?" Kerr wanted to testify publicly, and "I shall so express it, do everything independent and above board, give Mr. Brydges and the other directors an opportunity of knowing who it is that assails them. A discerning public will have to be the judges between us."

Despite the breach of trust, Kerr wrote that "the stockholders have a right to know what has been wrongfully done, and attempted to be done with their property" and that the information he would provide "they can never get at through any other source but me." Part of the "distinct understanding" that Kerr wanted was to know "the consequences that may result to the individuals whom we assail." Kerr clearly did not want to ruin everybody, just Brydges.

Kerr proceeded to give a taste of his evidence, which would include "a general statement as to the manner in which Mr. Brydges or other directors may have administered the Company's funds, such as expenditure of large sums of money without the sanction of the Engineer, payments made to contractors in order to have the line opened before it was in a fit state and before the conditions of the contracts were in any manner fulfilled."

Kerr continued to lay out his case.

> *Should a Board of Enquiry be appointed and I am summonsed before that Board, I will go there and answer every question put to me touching the Estimates, final estimates, contracts, appropriation of accounts, pay rolls etc. for the period of 7 years and upwards I was employed in the Engineering Department of the GWR as chief clerk. The bridges, given up as finished and finally estimated to the contractors, had to be overhauled thereby proving the incomplete manner in which Mr. C. J. Brydges thought proper to accept them on behalf of the Company.*

Aside from the shady dealings of Brydges and Zimmerman, Kerr noted that another reason why the GWR cost so much more than the Grand Trunk was that the Grand Trunk was contracted at so much per mile whereas the GWR was contracted at so much per cubic yard of excavation, which gave the contractors an incentive to cut corners. "The result followed—the ballasting and considerable of the grading had to be relet at advanced prices, above the original contract then followed the serious accidents entailing enormous expenses."

Then Kerr lowered the boom on Brydges.

> *I am able to prove Mr. C. J. Brydges' want of knowledge, his complicity and connivance with the contractors by raising the rates per cubic yard from the original contract has made the rate per mile so much higher . . . The fact is that the GWR was well known to be nothing more than a most excellent contractors road–and it is now very questionable if it can ever, under the present management, become a valuable investment for the original shareholders.*

Kerr concluded:

> *By examining the Minutes of the proceedings of the Board of Directors presided over by Mr. C. J. Brydges, pending the final settlement with the original contractors, it will be found that the interest of the contractors was always a first <u>consideration</u>, that of the shareholders an <u>afterthought</u>. And thus it is that this property over which Mr. C. J Brydges presided has deprived in its value, for confidence once lost, can never be regained, for the men who first aided in the project are not now in the employment of that Company for they have been nearly all supplanted by more favoured individuals of less abilities, to the disgust and disapproval of the resident gentlemen of Canada and who felt always a deep interest in the prosperity of this Railway.*

For whatever reason, Kerr did not go to London and did not give his evidence to the committee meeting, which was widely reported in the *Hamilton Spectator*, including Brydges' lengthy defence of his actions.

The *Dictionary of Canadian Biography* says that "By attempting to lay all the faults of the line at Brydges feet, the Committee created a backlash in his favour." Brydges and the directors received a firm vote of confidence from the stockholders on April 11, 1861. On his return to Hamilton, Brydges was celebrated at a large dinner at the Crystal Palace on May 19.

What if the committee had heard Kerr's evidence? Would the decision have been the same? Having been a courtroom lawyer for thirty-six years, I know that without the evidence, you don't have a case. You cannot baffle intelligent people with bullshit! Despite his faults and his enemies, Brydges prevailed, no doubt to the eternal consternation of Kerr. The *Dictionary of Hamilton Biography* notes that despite the nature of Brydges' management, "the railway had proved an enormous economic boost to the City." As for those fifty-two people who died in the first year and the fifty-nine others who died in the Desjardins Canal disaster? Well, they were just the cost of doing business.

Brydges went on to work for the hated Grand Trunk Railroad, which eventually swallowed up the GWR. He was noted for the same management style, "jeopardizing the safety of the trains by buying inferior equipment for exorbitant prices." Amazingly, he was appointed government inspector of railways in 1872 until he lost that job due to his authoritarian acts. He ended up in Winnipeg as commissioner of lands for the Hudson's Bay Company until he lost that job in a fight with the Canadian Pacific Railroad (CPR). In Pierre Berton's book, *The Last Spike,* Brydges is reported to have earned substantial amounts of money from buying and selling land based upon inside information about the CPR route. George Stephen, president of the CPR, commented on the "meanness of the man's character" and that his "time is coming." Brydges died of a stroke in 1889, the year after Kerr's death, and is buried in Winnipeg.

These curious letters from 1860 are found inserted in Kerr's diary for December 1866. None of the letters from the Corresponding Committee in London are preserved, and Kerr never returned to the topic for the balance of his life. Why were these letters retained? I can only think that Kerr wanted this information known someday, maybe as a record that he was prepared to stand up to the "coward" C. J. Brydges, if given the chance. Kerr maintained a cordial relationship with the management of the GWR, and we know that his oldest son, George, was employed by a subsidiary of the railway, but Kerr never worked there again.

CN Yard, formerly Great Western Railway. Photo by Joel Kerr, 2020.

*Great Western Railway yards, illustration from inside cover,
Dictionary of Hamilton Biography 1981. Hamilton Public Library.*

Brydges

(New York 1971). B.G. Trigger, *The children of Aataentsic* (Montreal 1976). W.S. Wallace, *The Macmillan dictionary of Canadian biography* (Toronto 1963).

BRYDGES, CHARLES JOHN, railway director; b. February 1827 in London, England; m. (1) Letitia Grace Henderson, and they had two sons and one daughter, and (2) Martha —; d. 16 February 1889 in Winnipeg, Manitoba.

Charles John Brydges spent his youth in railway work. By age twenty-five he was secretary of the London and Southwestern Railway, and when the London directors of the Canadian Great Western Railway required a representative to act as managing director, Brydges was chosen. He came to Hamilton in 1853 and immediately assumed control of the company.

The Great Western Railway had its beginnings in 1834, with a government charter allowing the construction of a line from London to Burlington Bay. In 1845 Sir Allan MacNab travelled to England to secure financial support for the railway, and although this support provided funding for expansion, it led to difficulties as decisions were often delayed for months because confirmation from England was necessary. It was hoped that the arrival of Brydges from England would solve these problems.

The Great Western Railway was opened in January 1854, and a year later a Toronto-Hamilton line was completed. In 1856 Brydges organized the purchase of stock in the Detroit and Milwaukee Railroad in order to provide the company with a connecting line to the United States. The vast amounts of money being expended worried the English directors, however, and Brydges was called to London in 1860 to account for his actions. According to a report filed by G.L. Reid, an engineer sent to investigate the situation, the railway had been seriously mismanaged and Brydges and his Hamilton officers had been involved in illicit business dealings, particularly in the form of kickbacks from contracts granted. On his return to Hamilton, however, Brydges was fêted with a dinner at the Crystal Palace on 19 May 1861; despite the nature of his management, the railway had proved an enormous economic boost to the city.

Brydges remained managing director of the Great Western Railway and about 1862 he assumed the same position with its greatest rival, the Grand Trunk Railway. He had been pressing for amalgamation of the two lines in the late 1850s, and when an 1862 bill failed to unite them, Brydges chose to stay with the Grand Trunk Railway. The same problems followed in his management of this railway, and he was accused of jeopardizing the safety of the trains by buying inferior equipment for exorbitant prices. During this period he also supervised the construction of the Intercolonial Railway, a government-run enterprise plagued by mismanagement. Ironically, Brydges informed Prime Minister Alexander Mackenzie of the activities of several commissioners, which led to their dismissal. A conflict of interest forced him to resign from the Intercolonial in December 1873, and in April 1874 he was forced to leave the Grand Trunk when it was discovered that the company's capital requirements had been underestimated by a substantial amount.

Despite his problems at the Grand Trunk, Brydges was appointed government inspector of railways in 1874. He fired several officers and decreased expenditures by approximately one quarter. In his role as inspector, he clashed with the Conservative Charles Tupper, who had been supplying railway orders at 50 per cent above the cost of other suppliers. Not surprisingly, when the Conservatives defeated Mackenzie and the Liberals in 1878, Brydges was removed from his post.

Brydges went to Winnipeg in 1879, where he became a Hudson's Bay Company land commissioner. He was also the president of the Manitoba Board of Agriculture and managing director of the Winnipeg General Hospital.

Brydges died of a stroke in the board room of the General Hospital.

HPL, CF. Hamilton railway disasters, Desjardins Canal. *Hamilton City Directory*, 1853-63. T.M. Bailey, *The laird of Dundurn* (Hamilton 1968). Campbell, *A mountain and a city* (1966). C.W. Currie, *The Grand Trunk Railway of Canada* (Toronto 1957). *Encyclopedia Canadiana* (1977). Evans, *Hamilton, the story of a city* (1970). M. Pennington, *Railway and other ways* (Toronto 1894). G.R. Stevens, *History of the Canadian National Railways* (Toronto 1973). F.D. McDowell, 'One hundred years of the Great Western Railway,' *Wentworth Bygones* 9 (1971). *Evening Times*, 20 May 1861. *Globe*, 18 Feb. 1889. *Hamilton Spectator*, 19 Feb. 1889.

BUCHAN, JOHN MILNE, educator; b. 16 March 1841 or 1842 at Lockport, New York; m. Miss Thorton of Dundas and they had three children; d. 9 July 1885 at Toronto, Ontario, buried there in Mount Pleasant Cemetery.

John Buchan came to Canada at a young age with his parents. He attended Central School in Hamilton under headmaster J.H. Sangster; he acted as head boy and became the school's first graduate in 1858. He entered the University of Toronto, earning his BA in 1862 and receiving the silver medal for modern languages. In 1865 he received his MA and accepted the position of headmaster at the Hamilton grammar school.

The Hamilton grammar school resulted from the establishment of classical and modern language departments at Central School in 1854 and its amalgamation with the Gore grammar school in 1856. Ten years later the Hamilton grammar

Excerpt from biography of Kerr's enemy, C. J. Brydges. Dictionary of Hamilton Biography.

CHAPTER 17

Indigenous People

There is not a lot of mention of Native people in Kerr's diaries, but they crop up from time to time, and Kerr seemed to have had a generally dismissive and condescending view of them, which was probably typical for the time.

On July 6, 1867, Kerr noted visiting Lake Erie "to see old John Jackson an old savage. He paid me–grumbled and growled a good deal." At Mount Healy in the Grand River that same month Kerr wrote, "Indians and half-breeds fishing off the dam at Mount Healy—more than 60 wagon loads of rough fish."[225]

In August 1867, Kerr reported the rather unlikely event of "certain Indians from the State of Maine come into our Dominion early in the fall before mink and muskrat trapping time commences and kill off everything in this line to our fishermen's injury." Maine to Toronto is about 600 miles!

When he was overseer of the Grand River, Kerr would likely have had contact with members of the Six Nations, but there is little if any mention of them. They seemed to have been just bunched in with other non-Indigenous illegal fishers.

When he got to Georgian Bay in 1880, he had some contact with

---

225   Rough fish were species of less desirable fish like carp, mullets and eel that were not designated under the *Fisheries Act*. Even the yummy perch were considered "rough fish" as they were too small to bother catching. That would change as other species went into decline.

the natives of Christian Island, Manitoulin Island, Cape Croker, and the Shawanaga reserve near Parry Sound. He found that, like everyone else, they were fishing without licences and often fishing for the cartel run by the Noble brothers. He was upset to find that they were often paid in whisky by these unscrupulous men. There was also a reference to a Reverend Solomon James, who was a fisheries overseer for the French River area. Kerr repeatedly warned how this "Noble red man's appointment was obnoxious to our white fishermen and that appointing an Indian over Scotch, Irish, English and Canadian fishermen is very unpopular and causes feelings and expressions of displeasure and even threats." As earlier discussed, it is not clear if these were Kerr's views or whether he was merely parroting the opinions of others.

In his diaries Kerr kept a rather lurid account from the Collingwood newspaper outlining Native "depredations" on Georgian Bay. The undated article is provocative and universally stereotypical about "the Indians'" conduct. Did Kerr keep this article because he agreed with the tone and content, or did he keep it because he knew the "victims," such as James Noble? I would like to think the latter, but I don't know.

In 1884 Kerr oversaw the creation of a fishway at Indian Rapids Mill on the Saugeen River at Southampton. Before the creation of the fishway, he reported the mill owner having to hire "lazy Indians" to dip net the fish over the dam. Kerr also noted that a local merchant would take advantage of the Natives by ensuring that when they received "their gratuity, to bring them all into his debt. The last haul I heard Denny made on the Noble Red Man was $9,000." This was an astronomical sum at the time. It was like the company store charging extortionate amounts.

In 1885 Kerr was trying to understand the mystery of how certain species bred in Georgian Bay, and he had a theory that the Native population was involved. He had some rather condescending thoughts on the matter: "Of course, I never for the moment gave the Noble Red Man Indian a thought. But now that you allude to it you of course know that the Indian of 20 years ago! Is not the Indian of today! They are now a civilized people, as easily taught as some of our white fishermen to obey the law and live and fish according to the fishery laws, rules and regulations."

Kerr also regularly referred to mixed-race Natives as "half breeds," which is surely a derogatory name. He also generally referred to native women as "squaws." And, of course, there was Kerr's epic battle with Simcoe Kerr, Joseph Brant's grandson, who tried to apply his "Indian cunning" on J. W. Kerr. (See chapter 24.)

So, Kerr did not leave us with a good legacy in regard to his relations with Natives, but he was probably par for the course at the time. I have no indication that Kerr ever set foot on a reserve, but he probably did on Georgian Bay and maybe on the Credit River,[226] the Grand River, or at Walpole Island. If he did, he never made reference to it and never described the living conditions of Native persons. It seemed like it was "out of sight, out of mind."

---

226   The Mississauga of the Credit were from a reserve on the Credit River, near Port Credit, that moved to just south of the Six Nations Reserve in Tuscarora County. In 2010 they settled a lawsuit with the government of Canada for $145 million. Each of the 1,700 members received $20,000, and the remainder was put into trust for the future.

INDIAN OUTRAGES.—Owing to either the connivance or carelessness of those in authority, the fishermen on the Georgian Bay and North Shores of Lake Huron are being continually annoyed by having their nets stolen and fish destroyed by the Indians. During the month of October last, Mr. James Noble, of this town, had about eight miles of nets and fifty packages of fish taken from him by the Indians at Wequimikon. Again, a short time ago, the Indians on the Christian Islands, emboldened by the action of their Manitoulin friends, carried off Mr. Shooter's nets and fish ; and now we have to record yet another glaring outrage of the same kind—Mr. Malory having had all his nets taken from him by the Cape Crocker Indians. We would draw the attention of the Government and their agents to this state of things, and would point out to them the necessity of taking active measures to have the thieves brought to justice. And whoever counsels the Indians in the depredations, for it is clear they are working their little game under some master hand, should be promptly taught that it is as criminal to be an accessory as a principal in dishonesty. The Indians have no exclusive privilege with regard to fishing, and have no exclusive right to fish without licences, the same as any other of her Majesty's subjects, and manifestly they can have no right to steal, for it amounts to that, the property of any fisherman who has taken out a licence to follow his calling on these waters, even should they encroach a little too close to one of the Islands occupied by the Indians.—*Colling-*

Newspaper clipping found in Kerr diary. Collingwood report of "Indian Outrages". ROM

CHAPTER 18

Americans

Kerr had quite a bit of contact with Americans over the years, so I thought I would speculate a bit about what he thought of them generally. I will try to give my evidentiary basis for these conclusions, but I may be totally wrong because the record is slim and contradictory.

When Kerr and his wife landed in North America, it was in New York City, but not at Ellis Island. That famous immigration facility did not open until 1892. Neither did they land at Castle Garden, the previous immigration station, because that opened in 1855. They would have just debarked in the dock lands without government restriction and been free to go. It was often at the docks where immigrants were swindled or robbed by the locals. That probably didn't happen to the Kerrs, but stories were likely well known and would have created an initial bad impression for weary travelers. There was no formal immigration process until the latter half of the century.

Kerr would have then spent, by my estimate, another week or so getting to Buffalo and on the steamer to Port Stanley. He made no mention of this time in America, but he was likely taken aback by the bold, brash, and crass persona of Americans.

For a timely impression of what the British thought of Americans, read Charles Dickens. *American Notes* is his account of a visit to the USA between January and June 1842 just four years before Kerr arrived. Dickens was highly critical of slavery and the sanitary conditions, including the obscene habit of spitting tobacco into spittoons. He was also critical of the deep suspicions and distrust held by many Americans and the sharp practice of their commercial dealings. Dickens also sailed on Lakes Erie and Ontario, having travelled by land to Sandusky, where he caught a steamer heading east to Buffalo by way of Cleveland and Erie. Dickens visited Niagara Falls and tells an amusing tale about a shop selling tourist "relics" that had a number of visitor books on display with comments. Opening a few, Dickens found them "scrawled all over with the vilest and the filthiest ribaldry that ever human hogs delighted in." Presumably many of these were by Americans.

Dickens caught a steamer for Toronto at Queenston and noted the closeness of Fort Niagara to Fort George where "the sentinels in either Fort can often hear the watch word of the other country given." That was clearly an exaggeration as the two forts are at least a mile apart. Dickens described Lake Ontario as an "inland sea" and had a favourable impression of Toronto, although he described it as "bare of scenic interest."[227]

On Kerr's trip up the Erie Canal, he was most likely travelling with immigrants like himself, and he recorded no impression of the Americans he encountered or his fellow immigrants. It doesn't seem like people needed permission to travel through the States, and, of course, as a British subject, he had every right to immigrate to Canada.

For the seven years that Kerr worked for the GWR, he would have had lots of contact with Americans. I believe at least four of his chief engineers were American born, as was primary contractor Samuel Zimmerman. My impression from what he wrote about Managing Director, C. J. Brydges, is that he found the American contractors unscrupulous and dishonest and that they took advantage of the naïve Brydges. If you read Zimmerman's bio on the Internet, you will get a pretty good impression of the kind of guy he was, and it was generally not good.

....

227   When I was much younger, I decided to read every book that Dickens published, and I did, except for the unfinished *Mystery of Edwin Drood*. It came in handy to reread what Dickens thought of Americans and Canadians. He noted, "Canada has held, and always will retain, a foremost place in my remembrance." That probably summed up Kerr's attitude.

For the twenty-three years that he was fisheries overseer, Kerr also had a fair bit of contact with Americans, whom he invariably called "Yankees," a common and somewhat derogatory term. The Canada-US border was pretty much nonexistent at the time, and people travelled freely between the two countries, often relocating between countries at the drop of a hat. Some of the "Canadian" fishermen were Americans, and Kerr licensed Americans to fish in Canadian waters, sometimes to the criticism of locals.

Kerr often complained about Americans fishing illegally in Canadian waters, but the reverse was also true, particularly on the Niagara River. Several times he promised to arrest American boats on Lake Erie, but he never did because the Department was too cheap to allow him to rent a boat. His son, Frederick, who succeeded him, did arrest a boat off Port Colborne for which he was highly praised. It might have been the highlight of his career.

I don't think Kerr thought much about American enforcement of their own fishing laws, if any, and they were more guilty than even the Canadians of overfishing. A lot of Canadian-caught fish were shipped by train or boat to major cities like Buffalo, Cleveland, Toledo, and Detroit. Sometimes this was done legally, such as by a highly regarded fish importer named Treble out of Buffalo, but more often it was done illegally with the connivance of Canadians.

Kerr also noted Buffalo polluting the waters of the Niagara River and mills at Tonawanda discharging sawdust and mill debris into the lake and river, but, of course, this was equally true of Canadians, as you can see chapter 14, which covers pollution. The only difference seems to have been the Buffalo discharge of street sweepings (horse shit) and toilet waste by barge in the Niagara River.

So, I have to think that Kerr, like most British people, had a slightly condescending and somewhat contemptuous view of Americans but not to a rabid extent. When Kerr first arrived in Canada, the War of 1812 was still within memory of old soldiers like Sir Allan MacNab and the fishing and farming communities that had their houses and farms burned. Bitterness, resentment, and suspicion toward Americans was probably prevalent.

LORD LOVELL AND HIS VELOCIPEDE

A NEW VERSION.

Lord Lovell he stood by the garden gate
   With his shining velocipede,
And whispered farewell to his Lady Bell,
   Who wished for his Lordship good speed.

"When will you be back, Lord Lovell?" she said
   But he gave to her question no heed—
Placed his feet in his stirrups, and galloped away
   On his famous velocipede.

Then Lady Bell cried, in frantic alarm,
   "What a monster my Lord is, indeed,
To ride thus away, from his loving young wife,
   On that horrid velocipede?"

Lord Lovell returned, broken-hearted and sore,
   Broken-armed, and, alas! broken-kneed;
For he struck on a post, nearly gave up the ghost,
   And smashed his velocipede!

MORAL.

Remember the fate Lord Lovell has met,
   Let this be your warning and creed;
Stay at home with your wife for the rest of your life,
   And beware the velocipede.

Clipping found in Kerr diary. A curious poem about Lord Lovell and his bicycle. ROM

Chapter 19

Samuel Wilmot and the Fish Hatcheries

According to the *Dictionary of Canadian Biography*, Samuel Wilmot was born on August 22, 1822, on the family farm near Newcastle, Ontario. His family were prosperous people both in New Brunswick and Ontario. Sam was educated at Upper Canada College from 1830–1834, which even then was probably a snooty private school. When his father died in 1856, he took over management of the farm, which was located on a salmon creek.

Noting a decline in the salmon population, Wilmot built an experimental hatchery in his house and began the artificial propagation of salmon. In 1868 he was appointed by the Department of Marine and Fisheries as a fisheries overseer, with responsibility for fish hatcheries, which were then new to Canada. In 1876 he was appointed superintendent of fish culture, a position he held until he retired in 1895.

Like Kerr, his immediate boss was W. F. Whitcher, and Wilmot may have had a role in getting Whitcher fired in 1883 because Whitcher had publicly questioned the efficacy of Wilmot's fish hatcheries. In a 2018 *Toronto Star* article, Wilmot was described as an "inveterate self-promoter." Wilmot died on May 17, 1899.[228]

....

228 Wilmot became something of an international celebrity which apparently went straight to his head and he applied to be appointed as a baronet, a British nobility ranking above a knight but below a baron.

Kerr first met Wilmot on July 21, 1868, when he took the train to meet him at the fish hatchery he had established adjacent to his home on the Wilmot family farm. Wilmot had been appointed fisheries overseer on July 1 with special duty to breed fish and for two years before had been developing his hatchery on a stream that ran through his farm at Newcastle.

Kerr was immediately smitten with the idea of breeding salmon, and he was probably impressed with Wilmot, who was a confident and well-educated man ten years younger than Kerr. Kerr's initial affinity for Wilmot slowly turned to acrimony and perhaps jealousy years later in what was one of the strangest relationship reversals in his life. It eventually devolved into mutual hatred and acts of revenge.

At Wilmot's request, in August 1868 Kerr sent him a detailed listing of the then fifty or so men fishing under him in his district including where they fished and what nets they used. Kerr must have received some instruction from Wilmot because he immediately began to plan to create fish ponds stocked with Wilmot's fry.

In July 1869, Kerr inspected a trout pond at Galt that was proposed to be used for the "artificial and natural breeding of trout." Kerr was very impressed and noted "they have good facilities to begin the work, splendid springs and plenty of good water, a house with 500 trout therein. The house is 110 feet long with a pond of spring water therein continually running." Thus began, for Kerr, an important but ultimately unrewarding history in the fish-stocking business.

Returning to Galt in February 1870, Kerr reported, "About 4,000 young have now made their exit into life" and that it is "most pleasing to behold." He went on to observe, "I am satisfied that the nearer nature can be approached in hatching fish, the greater the success," meaning they should be hatched under natural conditions.

In September 1869, Kerr wrote to the minister seeking to purchase three acres of ordnance lands in Niagara "for the purpose of breeding salmon by artificial means." Hearing nothing, he wrote again in December to be more descriptive, noting, "A spring of pure water, several thousand gallons of water, run daily into the Niagara River." It was there that he wanted to place a hatching house on a pond for breeding salmon: "I want no other aid from the Department but this land and permission to get salmon eggs when I have a place prepared for them."

In November Kerr was back at Wilmot's facility and stated that he was "highly pleased and gratified." In his annual report for 1868, Kerr applauded Wilmot, saying, "His exertions in the cause of pisciculture entitle him to my warmest regard and esteem."

In August 1870 Kerr wrote to the reeve of Barton Township seeking permission to "erect a fish breeding establishment" near the Hamilton waterworks reservoir, which was just below his farm. It did not get built for unknown reasons, but cost was probably a factor for the always hard-up townships.

In October 1870 there was a bit of a dust-up between Kerr and Wilmot. In response to complaints from licensed Whitby fishermen, Kerr was on Lake Ontario at 3:00 a.m. when he seized about 3,600 yards of salmon net set by an unlicensed fisherman who later claimed he had received permission to fish from Wilmot. Kerr was annoyed with Wilmot intruding in his jurisdiction and sent Wilmot a terse note: "I am going to seize Allan Scott's net for fishing on other licensed fishermen's limits. Consult me next time before you lead him into difficulties. Answer."

Kerr and Wilmot met, and Whitcher ordered Kerr to return the net to Scott. Licking his wounds, Kerr wrote Whitcher, saying, "I did not mean to use any harsh word that might irritate the feelings of my valuable colleague Mr. Wilmot, and Mr. Wilmot did not attribute to me anything of the kind…The best feelings exist between Mr. Samuel Wilmot and myself, whom I look up to in consequence of the proud position he occupies at Newcastle." In regard to their meeting, Kerr noted, "Mr. Wilmot and myself jointly agreed that in order to palliate and remove anything that might be construed into severity or injustice we determined to deliver up the nets." However, to get in the last word, Kerr indicated he was justified in seizing the nets.

In June 1871 Wilmot planned to deposit salmon fry in the Credit River, about ten miles up from the lake, and telegrammed Kerr to meet him in Toronto. They travelled by train to Port Credit and then hired a team and wagon to take them up the Credit River. Kerr reported they deposited "about 6,000 salmon fry, of one month old, which he brought with him from Newcastle in 8 tin pails adopted for the business."

Volume six of Kerr's diaries starts with some newspaper articles he cut out and glued into the book. One is a fawning description of Samuel Wilmot's Newcastle establishment from "a Correspondent," who was obviously Kerr, writing anonymously. This is probably because it also contains a glowing reference to Kerr's own work on Duffin's Creek! After reading thousands of pages of Kerr's writing, I recognize his style and the many buzzwords he uses, such as the "noble salmon." It also contains details only Kerr could know. His purpose? Unclear. They are worth a read to understand the business of fish breeding and the mutual admiration that existed between these two men. The clippings also contain two amusing poems. "Lord Lovell and his Velocipede" is a humorous ditty about a guy who is injured on his bicycle. It ends with the following stanza:

Moral
Remember the fate Lord Lovell has met,
Let this be your warning and creed,
Stay at home with your wife for the rest of your life
And beware the velocipede.

Curious, ain't it? I doubt very much Kerr was ever on a "velocipede"! As for staying home, that didn't seem to be his preference. This poem is followed by the even stranger "Faithless," which seems to be an epistle to unrequited love. The combined moral of these two poems seems to be, if you want a happy wife, stay home, but she may still not love you. The true nature of their marriage is lost in the haze of time, although they did have nine kids!

By August 1873 Kerr began to hear complaints about the lack of salmon for sale in the public markets and wondered why there were not more "if the flattering accounts (about Wilmot) they have read from time to time in the Toronto Globe and other newspapers be true…As the people say! Where are the salmon bred at Newcastle?"

Unable to get his own fish hatchery, Kerr began to consider other methods to restock fish. He proposed to capture fry and transport them to other areas where fish were not found in abundance. In Sept. 1874, he wrote to Wilmot to get one of the special pails Wilmot had developed for transporting fish. They began a periodic correspondence about various fishing issues.

In June 1874, Kerr met Wilmot's assistant in Toronto and received salmon fry from him, some of which he brought home to Hamilton and which he temporarily "put in the pond at Court House Square." I presume they were later placed in Burlington Bay or surrounding streams. By the fall he was busy planning an exhibition of whitefish in the Crystal Palace in Hamilton.[229]

In early October he obtained twenty-two large whitefish from his friend, Paddy Hand, in Winona, and on October 7 he took them to the Crystal Palace, together with some other fish he bought from a local fish dealer. "I hope the fishermen who caught the fish for me, will get a Special Prize for them," he wrote. "It is promised at all events!"

On October 10, Kerr wrote to the minister to report on the exhibition of his whitefish, which averaged about eight pounds: "Many persons, farmers etc, from the country asserted that they never saw such large white fish before." Lamenting the lack of an award, Kerr wrote, "The fish were well and favourably received at the fair, but as no prize was set apart for fish, we received none. Will you be pleased to offer a prize to be competed for next year at the Provincial Fair in Ottawa." Kerr attached articles from the newspapers, but only one has survived.

Writing to Wilmot on October 31, Kerr humorously (intentionally or otherwise) noted that the fish were returned to Pat Hand, who sold them again despite the fact that "they were soft after two days being on exhibition and three days caught." Kerr bemoans the fact that no prize was awarded "For the simple reason! That no preparation was made before hand to do so!" Carrying on excessively, Kerr sulked, saying, "It is mighty hard, expensive and very discouraging to take a thing of this kind in hand, and then be sadly disappointed at the result. However! I shall try again! And Again! Until I carry my object triumphantly! No surrender—never!" I do not know what this says about Kerr. I mean, it

---
229   The Crystal Palace was opened on September 20, 1860, by Edward, the Prince of Wales, as an exhibition hall styled after London's Crystal Palace. Located on King St. W. at Locke St., it was demolished in 1891 and turned into Victoria Park. It is, at the time of writing, the subject of an archeological excavation

was a display of dead fish! What was he expecting?

In November 1875, Kerr was asked to obtain some speckled trout for Wilmot. He proceeded to catch thirteen and brought them back live to Hamilton, prior to shipping them to Newcastle. While waiting, he placed them in the pond at Court House Square in downtown Hamilton! This was neither the first nor the last time he resorted to this fish storage method. Imagine today if while sauntering beside the Gore Park Fountain you suddenly saw a school of live fish. I wonder what people would do? Run for their fishing rods?

By 1877 the first major crack appeared in the relationship between Kerr and Wilmot. Kerr had numerous fish guardians working for him in the fall to protect the salmon streams during spawning season, and he expected a lot of them. Wilmot had been put in charge of determining what the fish guardians were entitled to be paid, and based on Liberal frugality, he wanted to pay them less than half what Kerr had paid. Kerr wrote to the minister, saying, "I have no remark to make on Mr. S. Wilmot's low estimate of good and honest men's services for protecting a stream deserving protection... I shall make nocturnal visits myself for the protection of the creeks."

By 1878 a fish-breeding establishment was in operation at Sandwich[230] on the Detroit River under the auspices of Wilmot's protege, James Nevin. Nevin came to Hamilton in March and deposited sixteen cans containing two million whitefish fry into Burlington Bay. Kerr met him later in Toronto where he had brought 500,000 fry and "tenderly and carefully placed and committed them to their New Home in Lake Ontario." Kerr exclaimed, "I am delighted at the prospect of receiving these millions of Emigrants from the Detroit River." Kerr wanted "4 million for Niagara" and gave specific details as to how they could be brought by rail and deposited within one day.

As a postscript to this, Kerr reported that in September 1878 a young law student "deliberately drowned himself in the waters of B. Bay" and that they had used dynamite to recover the body. "The next day the

---

230 Sandwich is now part of Windsor. Named after the English town of Sandwich, in Kent, it was the western terminus of the GWR and thus well known to Kerr.

body was found floating with marks of the explosive dynamite found thereon." Trying to be somewhat delicate in the matter, Kerr noted that dead fish were recovered and that a "large quantity of fry, believed to be a portion of the young Sandwich whitefish deposited in the Bay by Mr. Nevin" were killed. Kerr wanted to "frown down a practice, if persisted in that will always be and prove so destructive to fishes." So, no more dynamiting for the dead of Burlington Bay!

In May 1878 Kerr once again broached the topic of creating a fish-breeding establishment on the Niagara River. He had a piece of the ordnance lands[231] in mind and wanted to have a personal discussion with Whitcher, the Commissioner of Fisheries, in Ottawa. As the impoverished Liberals were still in power, he wrote, "I hope to be able to do this without asking any outlay or expense from the fisheries department." The personal consultation would not happen until after the Grits were kicked out in September.

When visiting Niagara in March 1879 to catch some American poachers, Kerr took the opportunity to "inspect the springs at Fort George and the Ferry Barrack for a fish breeding establishment." He returned in July with a civil engineer to have a look around and to survey a piece of land in Niagara for the facility.[232] In September he met MP J. B. Plumb to line up some political support. He gave Plumb "the plans and description of about three and one half acres of Old Fort George, which he applied for as a fish hatchery."[233]

....

231   Ordnance lands consisted of property throughout the country that were reserved for military purposes. Sometimes they were leased out to private individuals.

232   It was to have been on Block "A" near the corner of Collingwood and Rykert streets in Niagara-on-the-Lake. It was 4 chains 90 links long (323.4 feet) by 3 chains wide (198 feet) and took in "the flats and the spring and the old Red Barrack," which today is known as Navy Hall, a National Historic site where Lord Simcoe and his wife had unhappily resided in 1790.

233   Josiah Burr Plumb (Mar. 25, 1815–Mar. 12, 1888) was born in the US, and he immigrated to Canada in 1865. He became a Conservative politician and was elected MP for Niagara. As a bachelor in Ottawa, he belonged to a drinking circle known as the "Jim Jam Club." After losing the election he was appointed to the Senate in 1885 and became Speaker, where he remained until his sudden death, just before Kerr, in 1888.

Annoyed that Wilmot's son, Charlie, had interfered with a licensed fisherman at Whitby, Kerr wrote to Whitcher: "Just tell young Wilmot to mind his own business, and you pay no attention whatever to what he says." Young Wilmot soon played a major role in the souring of the relationship between Wilmot Sr. and Kerr.

In May 1879, Kerr met Wilmot Sr. at Union Station, and they proceeded to Lambton on the Humber River to deposit "a large quantity of salmon fry in excellent condition." Kerr observed only a few large salmon in the river and had some doubt about the efficacy of the fish-breeding program, but he kept it to himself.

The fall exhibition in Ottawa took place on September 24. Wilmot had asked Kerr to secure some fish for him to have stuffed and exhibited. Kerr duly attended to the task and shipped the fish to Newcastle. Kerr noted, "After I returned home this evening, I found that I had travelled 38 miles [by horse and buggy] in procuring and expressing those fish for you and Mr. Whitcher, but I never care for that, where my friends are concerned."

At the last minute, Whitcher ordered Kerr to secure some live bass and bring them to Ottawa. Despite his doubts that it was possible to get live fish to Ottawa, Kerr began preparations. Getting a barrel in Niagara, he brought it by train to Hamilton and then headed out onto the bay with his own net to fish. On September 22, he was back on the bay fishing before hopping the train to Ottawa. There he took a carriage to the show grounds. He left Hamilton at 8:00 a.m. and got to the capital the next day at 7:30 a.m. He spent the next two days at the show and then at 10:30 at night caught the train back to Toronto. Did he go straight home for some well-deserved R & R? Nope. He headed to Toronto Island to do his duty. He was sixty-seven years old at the time.

In 1879 there was an abundance of whitefish in Lake Ontario, and Kerr felt, probably wrongly, that it was due to fish breeding and restocking. Proving that he was still on generally good terms with Wilmot, he wrote to the minister, saying, "The breeding of whitefish in the Newcastle fish breeding establishment, got up by Mr. Whitcher and placed under the vigilant superintendence of Mr. Sam Wilmot, has now become a great and magnificent success."

In his quest for a Niagara breeding establishment, in 1880 Kerr sought to buy a house in Niagara near the old ferry on which to erect a small hatchery. The owner, Mr. Andrew Heron of Isabella Street in Toronto, had not yet named his price, so Kerr promised to visit him. It turned out Heron did not own the 1.5 acres but had a long lease from the ordnance lands administrator, the Ministry of Militia and Defence, so Kerr applied for consent to assign the lease to him.

By May, Kerr had taken possession of the house and noted he had some trees pruned and fences repaired. He was also on the assessment roll, so he could now vote (legally?) in Niagara, as well as in Barton Township.

In October 1880, Kerr met with Wilmot in Toronto and introduced him to his son, Charles John Kerr. He tried to get Wilmot to hire him: "Saw Sam Wilmot, spoke for one of my boys." This resulted in a curious incident involving Wilmot's hatchery at Sandwich, run by James Nevin. Wilmot had agreed to the then twenty-six-year-old C. J. Kerr being apprenticed to Nevin "to learn your art and science of fish breeding" The younger Kerr took the train to Sandwich on November 6 and returned unexpectedly four days later, having borrowed five dollars from Nevin to get home.

Kerr later wrote to Nevin to apologize for his son's short stay, cryptically noting, "We can't help these things." What went wrong? Well, C. J. got married in May 1881, so I think he must have missed his girlfriend and my future great-grandmother, Helen Alicia Bensley.

That same month Kerr was again in Niagara, noting, "Paid Johnston Clench $10 on account of his good will for lot beside ferry lot, to pay him $40 more in January next." It is not clear if he was buying or leasing the property, but it was undoubtedly part of his doomed hatchery plan. Later that month he had his property surveyed and bought 350 pounds of barbed wire to fence it in, which he did in November with the assistance of C. J. Kerr.[234]

Late in the fall, the Department received a letter from John Davidson

....

234   C. J. Kerr was my great-grandfather. Had he gotten the job and moved away, I might not exist!

and George Sleeman, of Guelph, wanting permission to stock Puslinch Lake, near what used to be Hespeler, and Kerr was asked to investigate. Puslinch Lake feeds into the Speed River, which drains into the Grand River, thus breeding fish would populate a large river system. Kerr was amazed at the crystal-clear, spring-fed, 400-acre lake and highly recommended the petition and the two petitioners. Over the next few years, largely because of the Department's inactivity, it proved to be an underwhelming experiment.[235]

By the end of February 1881, Kerr still had not heard from the Department regarding Puslinch Lake, so he wrote a reminder to the minister. Still not having heard anything by March, Kerr enlisted Hamilton MP Kilvert to apply to the minister for 20,000 salmon and whitefish fry for Puslinch and asked Sleeman and Davidson for a $20 licence fee, thinking that if he set the plan in motion, the Department would have to consent. Kerr also noted in his letter to Kilvert that Davidson and his father "are good Conservatives, and the father is well and favourably known to Sir John for many years." (Did he mean Sleeman of Sleeman Brewery fame?) Sending the twenty dollars to Ottawa, Whitcher finally granted the application in April.

Kerr promised to get salmon and trout fry to Puslinch by May but was unable to deliver because Wilmot ran short. Sleeman and Davidson complained to the minister, and Kerr had to visit them personally to apologize and to promise he would deliver the following year. Before he saw them, he wrote to the minister, saying, "I feel regret, and sadly disappointed and humiliated about this, because when salmon fry were placed in Burlington Bay, I was then told by young Mr. Charles Wilmot, and the newspapers promulgated the same, that fry were also to be placed in Puslinch Lake."

....

235   John Sleeman (Aug. 1, 1841–Dec. 16, 1926) was the first and four-time mayor of Guelph. Sleeman was the son of John Sleeman, the founder of what became Sleeman Brewery. A famous supporter of baseball, he is in the Canadian Baseball Hall of Fame. Davidson was a retired colonel and insurance agent. Sleeman virtually controlled Puslinch Lake, owning the Lake Hotel and the small steamer, *City of Guelph,* that plied the waters. He would profit from increased fishing, so maybe his motives were not as pure as Kerr would have hoped.

Visiting Guelph to express his regret to Sleeman and Davidson about Wilmot's "oversight," Kerr recorded that "they are now perfectly satisfied." Kerr advocated that they should be given some authority over the lake, reporting that "they were subjected to much indignity and insult by the people" upon learning that no fry were to be planted and that "they nobly stood their ground under some abuse." Personal honour and integrity were very important in the nineteenth century.

Kerr heard that Wilmot had been superannuated, which meant he was granted a pension, and Kerr wanted one too. Noting that he was one of the oldest outside officers (and senior to Wilmot), he felt entitled to it, writing to Whitcher, "And although, always in good health, and able to do my duty, still, should an accident befall me where I became disabled, incapacitated and unable to work, after long services rendered, I feel now I ought and should have something solid to fall back on." It didn't happen. Instead, he worked himself to death.

In August, Kerr wrote to Whitcher to describe the Niagara property and to request that Wilmot or Nevin come to visit. Noting that he had expended $206 on acquiring and fencing the property, he reversed his previous position and wanted money from the Department. He claimed that "no member of my family will be connected with it. Mr. Wilmot can send one of his own people to attend to the fish, the house and grounds alone shall be mine." No wonder it never got approved if he couldn't keep his story straight about wanting or not wanting government money!

By the end of November, Kerr began to formulate in detail his plan for the fish hatchery, including what is now known as Navy Hall in Niagara, a former army barracks that Kerr had bought or possibly leased. Navy Hall still exists and is used as a rental hall for weddings and such, but it is no longer in its original location. Kerr gave its dimensions as twenty-four by one hundred feet. When I went to see the building, which is now south of the dock lands, I took a tape measure, and my wife and I determined that it is approximately these dimensions. He was going to use the building for his fish hatchery, to be run by one of his sons, Edward or Charles. The other son was going to seine fish adjacent to the railway lands by the lake. Kerr applied for a licence, but it doesn't appear that he got it. Another contradiction of his previous proposal.

In December, Kerr applied to the minister for permission to build his hatchery. He described the building and the adjoining lands: "I may as well candidly tell you, I wish to breed fish, on my own hook, on the best improved plans, for the benefit and the instruction of the public at large." Noting that he had the support of local MP, J. B. Plumb, he said, "any old cast off things from the Government fish breeding establishments will be thankfully received, and highly appreciated by me."

Hearing (falsely) that Whitcher was going to be superannuated (fired?) Kerr submitted his Christmas wish list on December 20, 1881. His first wish was to be reappointed overseer at Long Point. The second was that Puslinch Lake be set apart for Sleeman and Davidson, so they would control fishing. Third was his application for the fish hatchery, and the last was for his son to get a seine fishing ground at Niagara. Whitcher wasn't superannuated, but he also wasn't playing Santa. Never missing an opportunity to kiss ass, Kerr concluded, "I shall miss you very much if you leave the fishing department and I wish you every happiness the world can confer on you, Mrs. Whitcher and family."

In furtherance of his plan, Kerr spent December 23 and 24 at Nevin's fish hatchery in Sandwich to conduct a "close examination." On December 25, Kerr wrote a long letter to Whitcher describing what he regarded as almost a religious experience: "Although not in a church, here I observed some of the wonderful works of God, being carried out by the help, aid or direction of man, the agency of steam pumps and water, how sublime, indeed, to contemplate upon." Kerr noted 25 million whitefish eggs and recommended that the hatchery be more than doubled to hatch out 70 million.

Having heard nothing from the Department, as usual, Kerr wrote to Plumb asking him to shake up Whitcher. With his usual flattery, Kerr noted that, like Plumb, he was a staunch Conservative and that he had read Plumb's speeches in Parliament as reported in the newspapers and that they "are highly spoken of by every thorough Conservative with whom I have conversed. May a cabinet appointment be soon your reward." In March, Kerr met with Plumb and J. B. Geale, the ordnance lands officer, regarding getting a twenty-one-year lease for the ruins of

Fort George as part of his plan. It all came to nothing in the end.

In 1881 Wilmot advised Kerr that he had a large lot of salmon fry to deposit in Burlington Bay. Kerr wrote him back to advise that they would be devoured by the pike and bass, suggesting instead they be placed on the reefs of Lake Ontario. Contrary to all reason, Wilmot's son showed up with 20,000 salmon fry to deposit in the bay, and Kerr was forced to assist him! Another brick in the wall being built between Wilmot and Kerr.

In August, Kerr saw Plumb about the hatchery and requested he write to Whitcher again; however, this time he "wanted money to rig up a hatchery." I have no idea how he thought the Department would pay for something that they had not agreed to when he had previously offered to pay himself! When the Department advised they had no funds to assist him, Kerr wrote a saccharine letter to Wilmot requesting a $500 grant, noting, "for 15 years I have been advocating the erection of a small hatchery in my division, but to no effect."

Having met with no success, Kerr wrote a rather nauseating or sarcastic letter to Whitcher in March 1882: "I am so much in your debt for all your kindnesses that I must never forget you for the remainder of my days." Thinking words were not enough, Kerr also sent Mr. and Mrs. Whitcher a keg of "native wine" and a bunch of whitefish: "It will be from myself and no C.O.D." Finally getting to the point about the fish hatchery, he inquired if it was true that Whitcher believed the recommendation must come from Wilmot. In other words, whose bread should he butter?

In April 1882, Kerr assisted in the transporting and placement of 1.5 million whitefish fry in the Niagara River with James Nevins. He excitedly gave full details of how he met the train in Hamilton and continued on to the suspension bridge at Niagara Falls, where they would transfer the fry onto the train to Niagara-on-the-Lake and then with the assistance of friendly fishermen have them placed in the river. He noted, "I invited Judge Sinclair [of Hamilton], into the express car, to see the fry, he expressed his astonishment, as did Mr. D. B. Chisholm (remember this cad) and other gentlemen who saw them done the same." Then he requested but didn't get another 1.5 million fry for Port Dover.

He was successful in getting fry from Whitcher for Lakes Meadad and Puslinch and was told by Wilmot's son that fry could be obtained for Port Dover if Wilmot Sr. "gives the word." Kerr wrote to him, but Wilmot apparently did not give the word, which embarrassed Kerr, who had made promises to the Port Dover fishermen. If there was one thing Kerr hated, it was his integrity or his honesty being questioned.

Knowing that it never hurt to butter up the boss, Kerr promptly sent Whitcher and Bauset a turkey and Whitcher a keg of wine. The whitefish, which Kerr strangely described as "beautiful and handsome when I was placing them in the basket," also kept flowing to Ottawa!

In April, Kerr purchased or leased another piece of property in Niagara and sent Thomas Elliott a cheque for twenty dollars, asking him to give it to Robert Best along with a note for the remaining thirty dollars. There was a tenant, Mr. Purcell, "a pensioner from the Royal Canadian Rifles in Toronto, who will stay on for the time being, paying the property taxes and $12 a year rent." Still lacking permission from the Department, Kerr doubled down, to his future regret, and proceeded with his plan.

The *International Fisheries Exhibition,* under the patronage of Queen Victoria and the presidency of the Duke of Wales, was scheduled to take place at London in 1883. A scientific, cultural, and animal exhibition, it was held in South Kensington between May 12 and October 31 and was the largest special event in the world, attracting 2.6 million visitors. It featured exhibits from thirty-one countries and colonies, and it housed the largest aquariums in the world, holding 65,000 gallons of fresh and salt water. The Duke of Wales, Albert Edward (Bertie), became King Edward VII when Queen Victoria died in 1901.

Samuel Wilmot was the head of Canada's delegation, and his exhibit on fish breeding turned out to be the highlight of the event, even more so than the colony of live Canadian beavers that were also on display! Participants were invited to submit treatises for publication about pisciculture, which contributed to fish propagation efforts all over the world. Wilmot wanted a large exhibit of Canadian fish species and enlisted Kerr's assistance to obtain samples from fishermen and fish dealers. Kerr enthusiastically responded, vowing, "I shall do everything within my power in upholding the Honour of my Country."

Kerr and Wilmot met in Hamilton to put their heads together on how best to obtain the fish, cure them, and have them sent to England. Kerr thought he could rally the fishermen and fish dealers to help and obtain the best samples for exhibit to be shipped refrigerated. "Pack the fish fresh in ice, they will reach England same as fresh beef, all OK." Kerr sent notices to all his favourite fishermen to let them in on the plan, including his offer to pay them for the fish. Unfortunately, Kerr did not obtain a specific promise to be repaid by Wilmot.

Minister McLelan issued a proclamation on October 12 advising of the upcoming exhibition, and Kerr had sent it to all his favourites, including Cantwell, Elliot, Joseph Masters, and Richard and Robert Allan, all of Niagara. That same day, Wilmot met Kerr in Hamilton, and they proceeded to Port Dover to rouse the local fishermen. Kerr was also busy lining up a taxidermist for Wilmot and getting a miniature model pound net to go to London. There was also to be an essay contest with a one-hundred pound sterling prize, and Kerr asked the minister to be allowed to participate on the topic of "Relations of the State with Fishermen & Fisheries." It doesn't appear he ever got permission, but it would have been interesting to read what he had to say. Likely no government official had more interactions with inland fishermen than Kerr.

By 1882 it was becoming apparent that salmon breeding was not proving successful, and few, if any, salmon were spawning in the traditional salmon streams. Whitcher began to doubt the efficacy of the program and wrote about it publicly, which might have cost him his job. Kerr was ordered to discharge most of his Lake Ontario fishery guardians, which he did under protest and to great personal regret. Kerr also seemed to doubt Wilmot's commitment, noting how busy he was in getting fish for the 1883 London Fishing Exhibition and the fact that he had named a species of salmon "Wilmoti." The chasm was opening.

Despite these issues, Kerr continued to obtain items for Wilmot to take to London. On March 9, he wrote to wish him "a safe voyage and a happy, pleasant and triumphant return home again." Seeming to imply that he had been to England, Kerr also wrote, "You will be delighted to see England our Great and Glorious Motherland!" Was Kerr ever in England? I have no idea other than to probably get on the boat at Liverpool for the transatlantic crossing.

In 1883 Kerr wrote to newly appointed Senator Plumb and MP Rykert about the fishing hatchery, again seeking to obtain their assistance to persuade the Department to give him the green light. Kerr now wanted a twenty-one-year lease on all of the Fort George property, which was largely in ruins, as part of his plan together with his other two lots in Niagara that totaled three and a half acres. He promised his political support and noted how pleased the public would be with a fish hatchery. He also advised that he had been promised this and a $500 grant for start-up costs. In addition, he wanted a raise to $800 a year, noting his eighteen years of service, and he wanted a superannuation like Wilmot was going to get (a pension). Then he buttered Whitcher up with a keg of wine.

As his next foray to start up his fish hatchery, Kerr attempted to get the Niagara Town Council to sign a petition seeking the creation and funding of the Navy Hall-Fort George facility. Drafting the petition himself, Kerr enlisted Jim Cantwell in this mad scheme to get them all to sign, noting that he and Cantwell had voted for the councillors. As Wilmot was still away in London, he could not be of any help, not that he ever had been!

Things really started to get ugly in November 1883 when Kerr learned that Wilmot's son, Charles, had been involved in catching and selling salmon and whitefish during closed season at Meaford on Georgian Bay. Catching these fish during closed season was supposed to be allowed if Wilmot was extracting spawn or ova for the Newcastle Hatchery. Kerr heard that no spawn were harvested but that the fish had been sold for pure profit. Kerr had reliable sources at Georgian Bay, but this was still hearsay evidence, and he had to bide his time.

Wilmot heard of Kerr's criticisms and wrote an impertinent letter to the minister accusing Kerr of not knowing the facts and relying on the evidence "of jealous inside fishermen who have always been anxious to injure Meaford people and rob them of the privilege that has been granted to them." Those were fighting words for Kerr, who insisted that Wilmot "withdraw his language and apologize for using unfounded assertions" in his "intemperate, libelous, imprudent and uncalled for language." Kerr noted his view that the Georgian Bay fishermen "are all respectable, hard-working and well conducted men who stand up for their rights."

Kerr meticulously assembled the evidence he required to prove his point about twenty-eight-year-old Charlie Wilmot and F. O. Miller of Owen Sound turning a blind eye to the contraventions of closed season. How typical it seems even today that the only way to defend the indefensible is to attack the whistleblower and witnesses. *La meme choses...*

By the end 1883, Wilmot had returned to Canada to bask in the glory he had received in London for the exhibition. He did not pay Kerr or any of the other fishermen who contributed, and he did not share credit with anyone else for his triumph. As a result, combined with the culmination of the earlier disappointments, Kerr's relationship with Wilmot soured completely, never to be restored. In April 1884, on hearing that Wilmot might secure the position of commissioner of fishing, Kerr's response was "God Forbid." He stated his feelings in a letter to Bauset, who Kerr supported as the next commissioner, Whitcher having been "superannuated."

Wilmot had sent Kerr some of his pamphlets...

> *... with his compliments! If he is not ashamed of himself he ought to be! He made some bad speeches in England! After dinner speeches they are called there. Well it really is refreshing that I, poor ignorant mortal! Know a thing or two! It would have been more creditable for Samuel Wilmot, and for Canada, had he kept his tongue in his cheek about Mr. Whitcher and personal spleen! In England, allusions of that sort no one cares for! And amongst fishery officers in Canada... we are our own judges. Old friends, old acquaintances I shall never forget. Too much self in that animal for me."*

Ouch!

In May 1884 Kerr got a telegraph from newly "retired" Whitcher, and he wrote back, spewing more vitriol at Wilmot: "Fish breeding must change hands or it must be abandoned altogether!! Vengeance is mine, I will repay with the Lord[236] Sam Wilmot for his ingratitude to you! Who raised him up from poverty to applause will be henceforth held in contempt!!... He has completely forgotten himself, and more than that! Has forgotten every man who supplied him with specimens for the Exhibition!"

Despite the lack of any official success in setting up his fish hatchery, from time to time Kerr had work done in furtherance thereof. For example, he had his ferry lot fenced in, and he planted some fruit trees. In 1884 a curious incident occurred in which Alexander Keith (not the brewer) "willfully and maliciously" caused mischief to his property by cutting down a large number of Kerr's cherry and plum trees for no apparent reason. Kerr planned to have him charged before friendly JP William Kerby in St. Catharines. Ultimately, Keith and the widow Purcell were evicted for eight months of rent arrears, and their goods and chattels were "distrained against" (seized).

In a July letter to Bauset, Kerr roiled on.

> *I have never had a single word or letter from the Mr. Wilmot since he returned home from the Exhibition (he made of himself in London, England!) I now send you my claim for $30, it ought to be for $60–I suppose he had forgotten it. Everyone who supplied him with specimens are dissatisfied! For since his return home, he has never taken any notice whatever of them, not even so much as to send them the English version of himself. I wish for the fun of the thing, he would object to me being paid! And then you would see how I would batter him down! Even poor Thomas Elliott, of the Town of Niagara, fisherman, and out of his mind and imbecile for the past two years, supplied him with specimens of fish to the extent of $10.*

Returning to the topic in September, Kerr was thrilled to hear that Wilmot did not get the baronet appointment he had sought: "He did not get the baronetcy. Wonderful!!! I don't suppose he will attempt to get up specimens of fish for the Exhibition 1886. A few words from me

....

236 Deuteronomy 32:25

would kill him off it he attempts it."

In December 1884 Kerr sent a package of whitefish to S. P. Bauset from Killarney, and he couldn't resist taking a poke at Wilmot. He noted that the provider was the same man who sent fish to Wilmot, "for which, it is said **Gold Medals** were awarded at the great fishing exhibition 1883 at London, England… I hear no more of Exhibition Wilmot… I hope the minister will, through the recommendation of the Deputy Minister, promote me this year!! And then I hope I shall live to help you get up the Greatest Fish Show 1886, when the Department, Ottawa, shall receive all the honours! No scallywag for me!"

In an April 1885 memo to Bauset, Kerr recounted Wilmot's total failure regarding salmon and bemoaned his own fate: "I only wish I had the privilege of breeding fish at Niagara! Then I would leave a name and fame behind me!" In May, Kerr again wrote to Senator Plumb to renew his request for a promotion, which he thought was promised but delayed because of "Grit intolerance, and the trouble in the North West [Riel]… If you can obtain for me Old Fort George, at a small annual rent, I will fence it in and give the Government 4 votes from it [Kerr and his 3 surviving sons]. Now is a good time to repeat your application for the hatchery at Niagara. The dam across the creek at Newcastle Hatchery was carried away last winter and in consequence the fish eggs had to be moved to other Hatcheries."

Kerr heard that the Department was considering opening a hatchery in Owen Sound, and he was upset because Wilmot was involved and because he seemed to have again been forgotten about. Ever the optimist, Kerr said he was terminating his tenant at the old ferry lot because he planned to open his hatchery the following year. What upset Kerr was the devious nature by which Wilmot sought to obtain fish ova on Georgian Bay during closed season, which Kerr thought was just a ruse for illegal fishing. He wrote to Bauset, saying, "Until the Wilmot's are disposed of! No closed season will be ever kept in Georgian Bay. It was a cunning trick of theirs." Kerr reflects: "Since Wilmot named the salmon of Lake Ontario *salmon wilmotti* they have all nearly disappeared, and misfortune or bad luck seems to frown on them."

In December, Bauset sent Kerr a copy of a letter in which Wilmot apparently bragged about his exploits. Kerr caustically wrote back: "Wilmot has done well so far by stealing from the brains of his superiors. Just say nothing! But wait for his bombastic annual report and then we will see to whom he gives credit, you alone, for procuring this vast abundance of trout eggs! All himself. Sam Wilmot's assurance! To use an old Irish phrase, He has the assurance of the Devil."

In 1886 Wilmot sauntered into Kerr's territory and made a report alleging that Kerr had deceived the Ministry. Needless to say, Kerr was livid and wrote numerous negative comments about Wilmot, whom he referred to disparagingly as "the expert."

> *His disappointment was so great in not getting a baronetcy that his flimsy mind, talkative to a terrible extent at all times, was so overcome by the position he assumed at the Great Fish Expedition, that his intellect, if he ever had one before, was shattered! Or in plain language, he got so exalted that he was like the devil on two sticks, his time was altogether taken up now in pimping*[237] *after other men's affairs, who are his superiors . . . Sam Wilmot has got to be too big for his breeches.*

Apparently, Wilmot had other enemies such as J. S. Allen of Port Dover, and Kerr reported a March 1886 conversation with him: "Allen supplied Sam Wilmot with caviar and isinglass[238] for the exhibition in London. When Allen asked for his pay for it, Wilmot told him he never showed them! Allen told me the Wilmot's are damned queer people! Charley stops in a hotel in Newcastle, where he boards, while Sam and one of his daughters lives in the homestead and Mrs. Wilmot lives in Oshawa." I guess this was damned strange at the time! It is hard to imagine harsher language being used in the superficially polite nineteenth century. Unfortunately, we do not know whether Wilmot replied in kind.

In 1886 Kerr seemed to abandon any hope of establishing a fish hatchery in Niagara. He had experienced tenant problems for some time, and there appears to have been some vandalism, possibly related to him

---

237 "Pimping" in this context means pandering or procuring illicitly.
238 Isinglass is a translucent gelatin made from the air bladders of fish. Yummy!

helping the family of mentally afflicted Thomas Elliott. He wrote to Jane Elliott asking her to arrange for his handyman to tear down the tenant's house and board up the ferry house and the old barracks: "It is a rascally piece of business to see the property destroyed and handsome shade trees cut down! And this is the very thing that has happened since Mr. Elliott took ill! No wonder he expressed himself!!! 'It's now you will miss me.'" Kerr and Elliott's mutual enemies were the Boltons and Big Jim Cantwell.

Having visited Ottawa in March 1887 and being promised a promotion to inspector of fishing, Kerr revived his plan for a hatchery in Niagara. Writing to Bauset, Kerr opined,

> *I believe that Niagara is the best place for to have the Newcastle hatchery removed to. Meaford train station is at least one mile from the Lake or to any place the hatchery might be put. At Collingwood, it is or would be similarly situated! Whilst at Niagara it could be placed and located close to the railway station. And along with being useful in Niagara and made more productive in fish breeding, it will become a most attractive place, which would be a benefit to the people at large of Old Niagara. I have a building there you can have and Niagara River never goes dry, with no dam to be carried away. My son would take charge of the place and assist me.*

It was not happening.

In October 1887, Kerr was gobsmacked when he received a report from Samuel Wilmot regarding the fishway constructed in the Saugeen River at Southampton, which Kerr had inspected in the summer and reported on glowingly. Wilmot had found the fishway ineffective, which outraged Kerr, and he was determined to fight back. He wrote to Bauset: "I will never submit to a Star Chamber report against me by Sam Wilmot."

Kerr had superintended the fishway construction and noted that as far as he was concerned, Wilmot had not measured the fishway and that it should not be "condemned on guess work." Next, he wanted to know who Wilmot had spoken to, suspecting political motivation from hostile Liberals. Then things got personal and ugly as Kerr called Wilmot "the enemy" and ranted about him cheating the fishermen who got him fish for the exhibition.

> He is a regular fraud... Samuel Wilmot need not think, when he makes a lying report against me about the fishway, that I will allow myself to be trampled into the dirt by him. Where are the fish, the millions in his reports, he hatched out and planted, not so often in our lakes and public waters, as in private mud holes. I don't suppose Sam can find a **Wilmoti** any more in Lake Ontario!... Just let Sam Wilmot keep away from me! He and his son at the present day receive a good deal of public money for breeding fish and stocking our lakes with fish, which is a failure. Let Sam Wilmot look at home, read his fulsome reports, and compare what he has promised year after year, with what the present fish state of affairs are so far as his darling, humbug boy are concerned! Sam Wilmot would be better paid off [meaning retired], than be kept on to lie.

Calming down, a few days later Kerr wrote again, this time setting out in detail how and why the fishway was constructed and assembling a number of testimonials to its success. However, he could not resist taking another whack at Wilmot.

> I am informed that Mr. Samuel Wilmot expressed himself very freely on viewing the fishway and enquired who was the 'blessed Jackass' that built it. It was not exactly blessed but built much stronger. I have superintended the building of many fishways in my life, and although I lay no claim to the title of 'Professor,' I believe I know as much about fishways as some people do about fish culture and the propagation of **Salmon Wilmoti**.

Kerr got himself lathered up in a subsequent letter to Bauset: "Charles! Bring up the Theodolite!!! **Wales and I**, I am getting my lesson off by heart, such a d----d idiot." A theodolite is a surveying tool, so I am not sure what Kerr was referencing here, but he was clearly mocking Wilmot and his son. As for "Wales and I," I can only think that

Kerr was alluding to the king and his oldest son, the Prince of Wales, and Wilmot's royal pretensions.

Kerr was admonished by the deputy minister for his insulting language toward Wilmot, but Kerr was unrepentant. He wrote to Bauset: "Don't you think the Deputy ought first to call on the mighty big man, Sam, to withdraw his insulting language and unbecoming expression. A man who like Sam Wilmot, that boasts so much about his company keeping with Royalty when in England. Sam Wilmot must keep a civil tongue, as far as I am concerned, the fish breeding over which he presides is a failure, which nobody can deny!" This somewhat amusing exchange of insults between seventy-five-year-old Kerr and sixty-five-year-old Wilmot seems uncharacteristically juvenile for Kerr at least. I can't speak for Wilmot, who remained the superintendent of fish hatcheries until 1895. Kerr was correct, however, that Wilmot's salmon-breeding operation was a complete failure.

Deputy Minister Tilton asked Kerr to amend his letters, and Kerr reluctantly did so, but he couldn't help himself in taking another kick at the cat: "I consider there was no harm in letting **you** know what a precious humbug the fellow is, and in what light he, and his fish breeding experiments are held by an intelligent public in this part of the country. I am an older fishery officer than he! Major John Tilton... I have always tried to serve the Department honestly, faithfully and to the best of my intelligence which I apprehend is more than he could say." Na na na na! Enough already!

Apparently not. Kerr continued to smoulder about Wilmot and the deputy minister's rebuke: "It is unfair for the Deputy to place me at the mercy of such a reckless vagabond as Sam! Whose testimony could not be credited unless corroborated by reliable information from respectable persons. I am no tool in the Deputy's hands."

There was no reconciliation between Kerr and Wilmot, once good friends but now bitter enemies. Kerr's temper was on full display and is one of the blemishes on his personality. Perhaps this had something to do with his much promised but never delivered promotion or the Department's failure to allow Kerr to compete with Wilmot in fish breeding. Kerr, as we know, died in 1888, while Wilmot lived on, apparently successfully, until 1899.

334   Caught!

Fish hatchery at Sandwich (now Windsor), Ontario.

SALMON FRY.—On Tuesday Mr. John W. Kerr, Fishery Inspector at this port, received a telegram from Mr. Samuel Wilmot, Superintendent of all the Government fish breeding establishments in the Dominion, asking him to meet his agent at Toronto. Mr. Kerr did so, meeting Mr. Niven, of the Sandwich breeding grounds, but now stationed at Newcastle distributing salmon fry. These two gentlemen proceeded to the Humber, and near Howland's mills deposited 10,000 salmon fry, 5,000 of which were hatched from eggs brought all the way from British Columbia. The selection of Mr. Kerr to assist in this work is a tribute paid to his intelligence and experience.

Newspaper clipping found in Kerr diary. Salmon fry in the Humber River. ROM

Samuel Wilmot. Newcastle Historical Society

Wilmot's fish hatchery at Newcastle.

Navy Hall, Niagara on the Lake. Photo by Joel Kerr, 2019

Chapter 20

Ancient Order of Freemasons

The Masons are the oldest and largest worldwide fraternity dedicated to the brotherhood of man under the fatherhood of a Supreme Being. Originating in the UK in the early eighteenth century, they began to form lodges in Canada in the late eighteenth century. Many lodges in Canada formed under the authority of the Grand Lodge of Ireland.

It is not known whether Kerr was a member in Ireland or in London, Ontario, where he first resided. It is known that he was a founding member of St. John's Lodge #231 in Hamilton. With Masonry defined by a commitment to brotherhood and self-improvement, it seems to have been important to Kerr, and he certainly strived to live up to its standards.

Masons have certain methods of identification. For example, most of us have heard of the "secret handshake." If you Google it, you'll learn there actually were a number of handshakes in Masonic life dependent upon one's status as an apprentice or a master. In fact, one website shows various versions of the "secret handshake," which is quite detailed and somewhat convoluted.

Having met thousands of men in his long and active life, Kerr seemed to know who the Masons were. In writing to them, he would generally address his letters "Dear Brother" and end his letters "Yours fraternally." He would also sometimes draw a rudimentary compass and inset square, the universal Masonic symbol.

The Grand Lodge of Hamilton has existed since 1855 and still meets in a stone building on King Street West. If you pay them twenty-five dollars, they will send you what information they have about deceased members. So, I sent in my cheque, and a few weeks later I got an email response from Barb in the Grand Lodge Office. Kerr's mother lodge was Barton #6, and he belonged to two other lodges at various times for unknown reasons. It was noted that he attained the rank of Past Master, which I think means that at one time he must have been Grand Master of his lodge.

Not being particularly satisfied that my twenty-five dollars had been well spent, I decided to do some research of my own. The Hamilton Public Library has its catalogue online, so I found out that in their special collections they have a book entitled *The History of Free Masonry in Canada* by J. Ross Robertson. I handed the friendly lass in the Local History and Archives section the catalogue number, and a few minutes later she set on my desk two massive volumes, each containing over a thousand pages.

These well-thumbed and decaying tomes contain information on seemingly every lodge in Canada dating back to the 1700s. After looking through a large index, I eventually came across a section relating to St. John's Lodge #231 of Hamilton. In reading, I learned that the first meeting of St. John's Lodge was held on December 27, 1852, at Germania Hall on the northeast corner of John and Main Streets, Hamilton, and Kerr was in attendance. After an hour-long meeting, proceedings were adjourned to the City Hotel, where dinner was consumed and an "enjoyable evening" took place together with members of the "Strict Observance Lodge," whose Worshipful Master was Sir Allan MacNab. (I don't know what they were strictly observing or why other lodges weren't strict observers!)

At a March 1853 meeting, the lodge determined to acquire some Masonic regalia, and Kerr agreed to donate a Bible. Where he got this Bible is unclear, but I don't think he gave away his only Bible because much later in life he said that if he couldn't sleep, he read the Bible. Other donated items included a compass and ceremonial aprons. If you Google "Masonry," you can see pictures of members wearing these aprons, which are still in use today.

In 1854 Kerr was elected Worshipful Master. Some other employees of the GWR were also initiated, including company secretary W. C. Stevens and C. J. Brydges, who was the managing director and Kerr's boss. As noted in a previous chapter, he ultimately fired Kerr and about forty others as a result of a dispute in 1858. Possibly this explains why Kerr ultimately joined another lodge!

The Robertson history describes an amusing incident that took place in 1855. At the February meeting, a candidate for initiation was proposed and approved by the vetting committee. However, one member disapproved and indicated he would "blackball" the candidate, D. Murray.[239] When asked his reason, the objector indicated that Murray had misrepresented himself as a carpenter when he was really a "tucker" or a sort of male seamstress. An "animated discussion" took place, but Kerr seemed to have calmed the waters, and in the end he "shook hands" with the objector and "made ample apologies for the unpleasant as well as the warm expressions given to their feelings in the heat of discussion." You have to love understated Victorian language!

Apparently, this "discussion" was the subject of some conversation with uninitiated persons (a no-no), and after a committee was struck to investigate, it was determined that this warranted the "condemnation of every right-thinking Brother." Upon expressing appropriate "contrition," the guilty party was forgiven. This reminiscent of some humourous dispute among Fred Flintstone's Waterbuffalo brethren!

Masons typically celebrated the two St. John's Days, which were in June and December. The June date, June 24, was the day after Kerr's birthday. According to John J. Delaney's "Dictionary of Saints" Doubleday, 1980, there are 69 St. Johns. The one celebrated June 24th is John the Baptiste, who is reported to have baptised Christ as the Messiah. Other lesser known St. Johns include John the Dwarf, John the Good, John the Silent and John the Sinner. In 1855, because a member was away in England, it was determined to delay the event until July when the lodge members held "an excursion on the steamer *Arabian*."

....

239 The word "blackball" derives from a secret ballot where members would vote a white ball in acceptance and a black ball in denial.

No mention is made of where they steamed to, but probably a good time was had by all.

On December 12, 1879, Kerr wrote a peculiar letter to Mr. J. A. Malcolm, the secretary of St. John's Lodge: "Being the Oldest and a charter Member and Past Master of St. John's, please inform me why it is my name is omitted from The List of Most Worshipful Brethren eligible for the office of Worshipful Master. Yours fraternally, John W. Kerr P.M."

Knowing nothing about Masons, I Googled "Worshipful Master" and learned that this is the top dog in a lodge, and they can hold the office for one or two years. Masons ascend through various stations to reach the position, and when they relinquish it, they become Past Masters. The usual order of ascension is Tyler (guard) Steward, Deacon, Secretary, Treasurer, Junior Warden, Senior Warden, and Worshipful Master. Each position has its own "jewel" or emblem and specific duties. Some positions are not common to all lodges, such as a Marshal and Almoner.

What is unclear to me is why Kerr would be applying for Worshipful Master when he was a Past Master. Maybe one can hold the position more than once, and because Kerr was a bit of a megalomaniac, that would not surprise me. It is also unclear why he was left off the list. Was it an innocent omission or was he being blackballed?

In July 1884, Kerr attended the Grand Lodge meeting in Toronto. I think this was an annual meeting held at various locations in which all the Ontario lodges were invited to send delegates. Also in attendance were members of other North American Lodges and possibly from the Old Country. Each district rep gave a state-of-the-lodge address, and provincial or national issues were usually addressed.

Kerr's biography in the *Dictionary of Hamilton Biography Vol. II* notes he was buried with full Masonic rites, as was his son, George. Again, if you Google this you can see some videos of these rites, which are quite interesting in their symbolism. In a cryptic letter sent to Bauset in January 1875, Kerr said he attended a funeral but gave no details other than to note "It was only the second time in all my life I have attended a Masonic Funeral." That seems odd because by then he had been a mason for at least twenty-three years.

On September 21, 1885, Kerr wrote a letter to William Gibson of Beamville, sending him a "likeness" of his son, George, who had died on March 28, 1883. Gibson was born the same year as George (1849), and perhaps they knew each other. Kerr addressed the letter to "My Friend and Right Worshipful Brother," so obviously they were both Masons, as was George. Gibson was apparently the nephew of Kerr's good friend, Bob Gibson, and he was a successful businessman and politician. He was Liberal MP for Lincoln from 1891–1900 and was appointed as a senator in 1902. As a businessman he was a railway contractor and owned a quarry in Beamsville, together with being the president of the Bank of Hamilton. He was also the Grand Master of the Grand Lodge of Masons, so he was a pretty important guy. I wonder if Kerr knew he was a Liberal. Of course he would have known. In the nineteenth century, everybody knew everyone else's political persuasion.

One Masonic friend of Kerr's was J. W. Ranney of Ridgeway. A fisherman who was persistently late in paying his fees and frequently made false promises to Kerr for years, Ranney made a request to Kerr in 1887, to which Kerr replied,

> *It is forbidden by the Ancient landmarks of Freemasonry to do what you require of me. A Mason in the first place is bound to obey the laws of His Country! In the second place, I may candidly tell you, that I shall never mix up Freemasonry in my business as a Fishery Overseer. To do so would leave me at the mercy of the most unscrupulous people on the face of this earth. In all my travels as a man and a Mason of nearly 40 years, I have never met two dozen good Masons in all that time. I always try and take the advice of a good friend given me 49 years ago [1838] thus: "Place no confidence in man, for if you do, he will deceive you... and whenever I gave way to you and others, you have invariably always deceived me."*

This was a surprising comment from Kerr, who otherwise always seemed positive about his Masonic brothers. This rather negative view of humankind generally also seems uncharacteristic of Kerr's usually positive views on things in general. He may have just been trying to stir up his serial defaulter, J. W. Ranney. However, he mentioned this anecdote in several letters to others as well.

On an unrelated note, my maternal grandfather was a Mason, and my grandmother belonged to the Order of the Eastern Star, a companion order to the male-only Masons. At my mother's funeral in 1997, two elderly members of the Order showed up at the funeral home with a cheesy artificial floral wreath that they asked to place near the casket. At the end of the service, they politely asked if they could remove it and take it with them! I gather they needed it for the next funeral.

I have known a few Masons during my years as a lawyer, and I can honestly say that they were some of the kindest, most respectful people I have known. Not unlike J. W. Kerr.

CHAPTER 21

Kerr and Barton Township

In 1869, Barton Township consisted of all of Hamilton Mountain as far as Ancaster Township and most of what is now the lower city from east of Wentworth Street to the commencement of Saltfleet Township at Parkdale Avenue. On the south it was divided from Glanford Township by what is now Rymal Road. It gradually shrank out of existence by the 1950s as it was amalgamated with the city of Hamilton.

Barton Township Council was led by a reeve, and he and a number of councilmen met periodically to deal with local business. Kerr was a councilman at various times, but in September 1869 he was an auditor of the township. He and another auditor were tasked with conducting an investigation into the accounts of the former township treasurer, John Gage.[240]

John Gage was a member of the large and influential Gage family, and his son R. R. Gage,[241] was a lawyer who sat on council and who was evidently defending his father in regard to what were in effect allegations of misappropriation and corruption.

At the council meeting of September 27, 1869, held at the Mountain View Hotel, Kerr submitted the report that was the subject of an article in the *Hamilton Spectator* on September 28, 1969, which is attached,

....

240   John Gage (1819–1900)
241   Robert Russell Gage (1840–1918) was the son of John R. R. Gage. He sold part of his farm property to the City of Hamilton, and that property became Gage Park.

although a little hard to read.

The report found that John Gage of Bartonville[242] was indebted to the township in the astronomical amount of $904.78 in addition to the $954.97 he had already provided to his successor. Clearly written by Kerr, the report noted, "We have the honor to report that we have given Mr. John Gage ample time and opportunity to vindicate himself."

The *Spectator* reported, "A former treasurer had been ousted to make room for Mr. Gage, for the purpose of manipulation, and hence the unsatisfactory state of affairs. Rumbling rumours were deep and loud that a pair of cheats had been playing their little game. Now however, a family row had taken place and when rogues fall out, honest men get their dues." The family row was between Councillor Waddell and John Gage, who were related by marriage.

The meeting devolved into recriminations, threats, and actual violence between the newly elected reeve, Mr. R. R. Waddell,[243] and Joseph Rymal,[244] also a prominent citizen who commented on the "rotten state of affairs that had existed in the Township for some years past." The *Spectator* notes, "A most ludicrous scene took place to the admiration of all present and in which the Reeve got the worst... Robert R. Gage then entered the room and Waddell told him he was the greatest rascal he had ever met whereupon a general situation [brawl] ensued in which sticks were flourished [walking canes] and blows were struck before calm was restored." Who says municipal politics is boring? All of these men are memorialized in the venerable *Dictionary of Hamilton Biography*.

....

242 Bartonville below Hamilton Mountain was the commercial and business hub of Barton Township.

243 Robert R. Waddell was a politician and sometimes Kerr's lawyer. A Conservative like Kerr, he lost the 1882 federal election to Liberal Lewis Springer by forty-eight votes.

244 Joseph Rymal (Nov. 17, 1821–Dec. 15, 1900) was a farmer and a Liberal politician. He was MP for South Wentworth from 1867–1882. To his opponents he was an "Incorrigible wag," and to his friends he was "honest Joe." To friends he was also a "gentleman of large girth and genial countenance. To his enemies he was "lacking in education, polish and good manners." Kerr often quoted his exhortation, "Let him Rip," meaning let him go at it when he threatened to do something.

Kerr had apparently hired a man named John James Mason to assist him with the investigation. He rendered an account for forty dollars, which the council refused to pay. Kerr wrote to Mason suggesting he contact the provincial secretary to force the council to pay: "I am sure it will be paid, as the council cannot throw it aside."[245] It is not known whether John Gage ever repaid the large sum of misappropriated money. Matters like this seemed to have usually been settled privately, and no one probably even thought of calling the police because it was a "civil matter." In fact, I do not know if there were police in Barton Township.

In August 1870, Kerr applied to federal Minister of Agriculture Christopher Dunkin[246] to be appointed commissioner of census for the County of Wentworth. Kerr noted that he was an enumerator in the 1861 census for the Township of Barton. It is not known if he got the position, but it seems unlikely because there is no further mention of the 1871 census. The fact that he applied shows either how much he needed the money or how bored he was with farming his one hundred acres. Writing to his new boss, Minister Peter Mitchell, Kerr stated that the appointment "would in no way interfere with my present duties."

Kerr was involved with the establishment of schools in Barton Township before he got his appointment as fisheries overseer. In a later 1872 letter to Jacob Burkholder, Kerr noted that the school trustees leased the school, Barton School Section #3, from Burkholder Church and that part of the agreement was that the trustees would "keep the church in good repair." He warned them that they were not doing so, at least not to his satisfaction. Kerr's interest in schools may have been a result of the fact that he wanted his nine kids to have some education. None apparently had any higher education and they were a pretty undistinguished lot. However, some of his grandkids had illustrious careers, both good and bad.

....

245 The provincial secretary was then a senior cabinet position, roughly equal to deputy premier.
246 Christopher Dunkin (Sept. 25, 1812–June 6, 1881) was a lawyer and politician. Dunkin was the federal Minister of Agriculture from 1867–1871. The census was held every ten years and was then conducted by the Agriculture Ministry. The 1871 census was published in 1873. Curiously, Dunkin was an elected member of both the federal and Quebec governments at the same time!

For whatever reason, Kerr attached to his 1872 diary a newspaper account of a Barton Township meeting from February 1875. It seemed pretty routine, although Kerr did propose a motion to strip the Carbon Oil Company of its tax-free status. Kerr had tried to prosecute the company for polluting Burlington Bay but did not succeed. There are many ways to skin a cat and if he couldn't convict them, he could at least make them pay property taxes! It is also of note that the township made grants to poor people and then named them in the paper! I wonder why Patrick Langdon, "a poor man," only got $2 while everybody else got at least $4.

On October 27, 1874, Kerr, on behalf of the Barton council, attended the Saltfleet council meeting in regard to the bridge at Albion Mills. The mill was built around 1800, and the bridge crossed above Albion Falls, just as it does today. The center of a thriving commercial community, the bridge almost straddled the line between Barton and Saltfleet and was probably a shared responsibility to maintain. Noting that no other Barton councillors attended, Kerr was probably there due to the proximity of his farm, which was just a few miles from the falls and the decaying road.

In 1880 there is a cryptic entry in Kerr's diary: "Paid Harry Bryant $6.75 on account of Statute Labour." Not having heard of this I Googled it and found reference to the *Statute Labour Act*, which required every landowner to work for free for five days a year on roads and bridges. Failure to comply meant six days in jail, but landowners could pay someone else to do the work. Labour was worth about one dollar per day, so Harry did pretty well for himself! By the way, this Act is still in force in Ontario! You can Google it, and you will see that it is detailed, if archaic law.

On August 27, 1881, Kerr wrote a petition to the reeve of Barton Township, Thomas Lawry, regarding the "Mountain Drain." Any Hamilton Mountain resident over the age of about seventy will remember the Mountain Drain, which was built from near the edge of the escarpment at what is now Upper James to Buttermilk Falls, near Albion Falls. Apparently, the runoff from the mountain would frequently inundate the lower city, and an agreement was reached between the City and Barton Township to build and maintain this meandering ditch.

The petition notes, "And whereas the Mayor and the Corporation of the City of Hamilton have utterly failed to carry out on their part the agreement entered into. Your Petitioners pray for the Reeve and Council's immediate action in the premises; And your petitioners as in duty bound will ever pray." Unfortunately the signing page is not attached, so I can't say who the petitioners were, except of course, for Kerr, across whose property the ditch ran for a short distance.

On July 6, 1882, Kerr authored a petition to the mayor of Hamilton, Charles Magill,[247] and the Hamilton aldermen on behalf of the farmers, owners, and occupants of farms in concessions 2, 3, 4, 5, and 6 in Barton Township regarding the drain. It had been a particularly wet and cool spring and there was flood water on these farmers' fields. The drain had been only partially completed, and these men wanted it fully completed and that they be paid the same compensation as had been paid to farmers where it was completed. Kerr wrote,

> *Respectfully Sheweth: That they permitted your predecessors in office to enter upon their farms, on certain conditions, (never fulfilled) to make, build and construct a drain; so as to protect certain properties situated in the City limits of Hamilton. That by diverting the water from flowing down the Mountain, at the head of James Street, the property of Edward Martin Esquire, Barrister,[248] and several citizens have been saved and protected from damage and injury.*
>
> *That the said drain; "The Mountain Drain" has been well built, and constructed, as far as completed, and a stone dam, laid in mortar placed at its head on the Hamilton and Port Dover Road, near the Mountain View Hotel so as to stop all the water from descending into James Street, and the City of Hamilton; and thus force the water and all surplus water to run and flow east, through*

---

247 Charles Magill (Mar. 1, 1816–Dec. 1, 1898) Born in Ireland, Magill was a three-time mayor of Hamilton, a Mason, and a lieutenant colonel in the militia. His former house is now the ritzy Hamilton Club. Kerr knew him well. My grandmother was Georgina Magill, a relative.

248 Edward Martin was regarded as one of Hamilton's finest lawyers. He was a founder of the long-lasting law firm Martin and Martin.

and over and across our farms and properties which are situated east of the Hamilton and Port Dover Stone Road. That this drain has been made and finished all over and through farm lots Nos. 14, 13, 12, 11, 10, 9 & 8 in the fourth concession of Barton, and all the claims made on your corporation by the owners of these farm lots, to the extent of several hundred dollars, have been paid and satisfied by your predecessors to the satisfaction of all persons concerned. That then all further work ended on Lot number 8 in the 4th Concession.

That in consequence of the balance of work on this drain being left undone and not completed through, over and across Lots Nos. 7, 6, 5, & 4 in the 4th Concession and lots 3 & 2 in the 5th Concession; and lots 3 & 2 in the 6th Concession of Barton, as agreed upon with the Township Council of Barton; and with some of your petitioners, by your predecessors. Your petitioners crops! Wheat, potatoes, corn and barley have been injured and destroyed and become a total loss, by extra water from the finished portion of the drain coming down with a rush and flooding over the fields and crops of your petitioners. The unfinished portion of the drain in its present state is not sufficiently made for to carry off the extra water, and hence it floods all over the farms and lands of your petitioners. That your petitioners pray and desire that this repeated yearly damage, loss and injury be stopped immediately by the prompt completion of the unfinished balance of the Mountain Drain, down to the Hamilton and North Western Railway culvert, and settlement made at once as was agreed upon by Mr. Charles Foster and other aldermen, when prices for compensation were fixed and agreed to by some of your petitioners. And your petitioners want only British fair play! Just such, when agreed by and before your petitioners was afterward meted out, by the late Mayor and Board of Aldermen, to Mr. Joseph Jardine, Mr. James Jolley[249] *and*

---

249   James Jolley (1813–Nov. 28, 1892) was a Hamilton saddle merchant. He funded construction of the Jolley Cut toll road from his Hamilton Mountain home to the lower city.

Mr. Adam Inch,[250] *and immediately paid as settled upon before your petitioners; Your petitioners pray that no distinction be made in their case, but that all be treated alike! That your petitioners be, and receive at your hands, their fair and just due, the same as you have already conferred on Messrs. Joseph Jardine, James Jolley, Adam Inch, Mrs. Green, John Martin, Benjamin Hughson and James G. Unwin, through whose properties the drain was made and finished, and who were paid by the late Mayor and Aldermen for the privilege of permitting the drain being made through their respective properties.*

And your petitioners as in duty bound will pray.

Barton, 6th July 1882

Samuel Rendall	*Samuel D. Rendall*
John W. Kerr	*Daniel Flock*
Thomas Jaggard	*Lawrence Kennedy*
John A. Davis	*Robert Lowden*
Elijah S. Davis	*W. H. G. Secord*
Joseph Shutler	*Amos Burkholder*
George Bowman	*E. P. Barnes*
Wm. P. Bruce James Watt	*Robert Watt*

This is long-winded and perhaps the worst example of Kerr's writing. Its legalistic tone was probably familiar to the contracts Kerr would have seen when working for the GWR. It is not known if compensation was ever paid, but it took a few more letters by Kerr to get the ditch completed.

On July 2, 1883, Kerr was obligated to write again to the mayor of Hamilton to complain that the Mountain Drain committee had still not finished its work, with the result that water was pooling on his property and the property of his neighbour, Samuel Rendall, due to spring

....

250 Adam Inch (1857–1933) bought a one-hundred-acre farm on Hamilton Mountain in 1875 when he was allegedly seventeen. His family later donated what is now known as Inch Park, where I swam and played hockey as a kid.

flooding. Estimating his loss at $1,200, Kerr railed that it wasn't just some act of providence but was brought about by a breach of contract and gross negligence by the committee, and Kerr was not going to wait any longer before taking action.

By November 21, Kerr had largely achieved his objective because the City had been spurred into action by threats of a lawsuit: "I will thank you very kindly to continue the work of cleaning out the Mountain Drain through my farm and through Mr. Samuel Rendall's farm. This fall our crops were very much injured by last spring's freshet, If you continue your good work you will have done me and my neighbour a very great kindness indeed beside carrying out our arrangement with your solicitor to Alderman McLagan, chairman of the services and Mountain Drain, City of Hamilton." The Mountain Ditch was not filled in until the 1950s when housing development took off on Hamilton Mountain.

As should be evident by now, Kerr took a great interest in pollution coming from Hamilton's burgeoning industry but usually from the perspective of fish welfare. In October 1884, Kerr examined the state of Hamilton's sewers and noted they were "a standing disgrace to the Board of Health, of the City of Hamilton, and although the mayor and aldermen of Hamilton have been petitioned by fourteen medical practitioners, and by others! All residing in the City and the locality! Still nothing has been done to abate such a dangerous and filthy nuisance."

The petition, which Kerr likely wrote, indicated "There have been several cases of malarial fever, typhoid fever and ague![251] And no wonder!! When we are compelled to have 2/3 of the City sewage placed right in our midst, which is contrary to by law. The residents of this part of the City feel alarmed, especially on account of the great amount of sickness that has prevailed during this part of the summer."

The problem was that the city's ashes were being dumped in Land's Inlet at the bottom of Wellington St., creating a dam that did not allow the broken Depew St. sewer to reach the water, and the sewage was pooling on the surrounding land. Therefore, the lye resulting from the ashes was killing the fish, and the ponded sewer water combined with

....

251   Ague was a fever marked by alternating sweating and chills.

the "fish stench and nuisance, was causing disease." Even almost 150 years ago, municipal council was not paying adequate attention to sewer water!

On October 14, Kerr found Peter Connors, a carter [driver] for the Board of Health dumping ashes in Land's Inlet and had him summonsed up before Police Magistrate Cahill for contravening the *Fisheries Act*. The case was adjourned to allow the aldermen, the Board of Health, and reporters from the two local papers to report, which they did and Connors was acquitted for unstated reasons. The Rules of Evidence may not have yet been fully developed! Reporters are generally not witnesses!

Kerr was admonished by the deputy minister for having gotten involved in this sewer matter, which was properly the matter for the Board of Health, but Kerr stood his ground and claimed, disingenuously, that his case had nothing to do with the sewer but only with the ashes being dumped into Burlington Bay. Thumbing his nose at the minister, Kerr snorted, "I done my duty. I am satisfied. Outside of the fisheries, the Board of Health may act as they please."[252]

In March 1884 Kerr wrote a letter of reference for Mrs. Wheeler, who ran a hotel on Burlington Heights, to Mr. J. W Murton, chairman of commissioners at Hamilton, excerpted below.

> *I would like very much, if you can possibly do it, that you will be pleased to grant Mrs. Wheeler a [tavern] licence for this year, 1884. When out on Burlington Bay and the Dundas Marsh, in my official capacity I have often been glad to stop into her Hotel on the Heights– get something to eat, warmed up at a good fire, and off to away again with renewed vigour. She has always been very attentive to me whenever on such occasions I visit her place, and appears well adopted for Hotel Keeping. On the whole, the public speak well and favourable of her. I would like very much to see her obtain a licence.*
>
> *PS This is the first favour I have asked you for in your official capacity.*
>
> *John W. Kerr.*

....

252 Using the word "done" rather than "have done" was the only common grammatical error Kerr generally made.

Favouritism seemed to be the order of the day back then. To some extent it still is today but maybe not so much in government. It seems peculiar that Kerr would have to ask a favour to get Mrs. Wheeler a license when there were so many unlicensed taverns such as on the Beach strip.

During Kerr's life the province leased the Burlington Beach strip to the City of Hamilton, and it rapidly developed into a vacation getaway and a place for summer day trips. Kerr had to occasionally remind builders and developers that the water was licensed for seine fishing on the lake side and that a sixty-six-foot fishery reserve existed on both sides. In 1885 the City expanded their water intake capacity by building a crib farther out in the lake from which to run a line to the filtering basin. Kerr wrote to City Engineer William Haskins on June 30 to remind him of this and to suggest that the line be located on the division line between seine licences so as to disturb the fishing as little as possible.

Kerr's home was almost directly above the city reservoir, which was built halfway up the escarpment to store water pumped from Burlington Beach. Through the "instrumentality of a cat," it had been discovered that there were fish in the reservoir, and Kerr was curious as to how they got there. On August 9, Kerr wrote to the deputy minister to provide an explanation:

> Sir:
>
> With reference to my report to you of the 7th instant, I beg to state further for your information that the reservoir from which the City of Hamilton is supplied with water situated within 400 yards of my residence in the Township of Barton is pretty well stocked with these inferior shad [small fish]! Besides numerous other fish.
>
> I may here report for your information that the filtering basin situated on Burlington Beach and the reservoir are fully 4 miles apart.
>
> The filtering basin is about 800 or 1000 yards long, wide and deep and made by excavation! Several feet below the surface level of the waters of Lake Ontario. It is from the lake the water filters in through the beach and embankment of sand and gravel to

this basin and from which it is pumped both by night and by day through a large pipe up into the reservoir from which, as well as from the Pumping House near the beach, the water is distributed all over the City of Hamilton. There is no connection at present between Lake Ontario and this filtering basin!

However, I may here report that a few years ago, before the present filtering basin was enlarged and the water got very low in the basin and lake, a large wooden pipe was put in connecting the waters of Lake Ontario with the filtering basin so as to keep up the supply of water for pumping.

It must be through this large wooden pipe that the shad got into the filtering basin and were pumped from there in the water into the reservoir. The suction from the lake to the basin through this pipe when the sluice was raised was quite forceable.

Mr. William Calder, the caretaker and superintendent of the reservoir and grounds told me that he first discovered the shad in the reservoir through the instrumentality of a cat.

Mr. Calder has informed me some of the shad are 8 inches long and several of them have died in the water of the reservoir during this current year and were found by him floating there.

Respectfully submitted, John W. Kerr, Fisheries Overseer.

Now just hold on here! Dead fish in the city water reservoir? I don't think the citizens of Hamilton would be too happy to hear about that. Second, this does not seem to be even remotely possible that live fish could be pumped four miles to the reservoir, even if there were fish in the filtering basin. Kerr didn't seem to contemplate the possibility that a few live fish were thrown in the reservoir by mischievous boys. Maybe that is why reservoirs are now covered!

As a final task in 1885, Kerr was asked to comment on a proposal by Thomas Jackson, a surveyor and civil engineer, who proposed to drain Dundas Marsh and convert it into farmland because it was "a sheet of stagnant water considered to be a source of great evil during the hot months of the year." Kerr gave a thorough history and summary of the Desjardins Canal and how it would be impossible to drain the marsh. I sent a copy of the long letter to the curator of the Dundas Museum but received no response. If anyone wants to read the whole thing, it is in vol. 13 on p. 1,093. Thanks for crickets, museum guy or girl!

In May 1886 the bridge over the Mountain Drain (now at Buttermilk Falls) had collapsed, and the Township had to repair it. Kerr wrote to lawyer R. R. Waddell, who was the lawyer for the Road Company.

> *I understand it is your intention . . . to put in large pipes on the Concession Road and under your stone road. The consequence has been, and will be, if pipes are put in there and continued there! My fields and crops are sure to be flooded over, injured, damaged and destroyed; which they have been recently by a water rush. A culvert large enough to carry off the large volume of water that accumulates there after a freshet, swelled by such great rains as we have had recently is more preferable. I hope I am not intruding in calling your attention to these matters.*

When Kerr built his house in 1855, Concession Street went no farther than his place or perhaps that of his neighbour, Samuel Rendall. However, by 1886 it appeared that Barton Township wanted to extend it to run along the Mountain Brow, presumably as far as Albion Falls. There was a road allowance there and in December Kerr wrote to Robert D. Bensley[253], the township clerk, to get a copy of the by-law. This presumably would have been of some benefit to Kerr, so I assume he was in favour of it. Today Mountain Brow Blvd. provides a scenic view of the Red Hill Creek valley. Its modest 1950s home are gradually being replaced by monster homes.

As a ratepayer, Kerr seems to have taken a continuing interest in Barton schools, and he wrote a letter complaining about the 1885 annual meeting. Addressed to School Inspector J. H. Smith, I've included this amusing letter in its entirety:

---

253 "Robert D. Bensley (1839–1892) was the father of Helen Allena Bensley, who married my great-grandfather in 1885. My middle name is Bensley!"

Dear Sir:

I am requested to tell you that a Public Notice for to hold the annual school meeting for the election of a trustee and for other business on Wednesday the 30th of December last in the school house in S.S. #3 on the Mountain, Township of Barton. It was duly posted up in 3 conspicuous places within said Section.

When the rate payors arrived there, at the appointed time, it was found arrangements had been made for to carry things with a high hand and contrary to law.

A person named Wilson Crockett, imported from the City of Hamilton, a pliant tool, placed as Chairman, in the exuberance of his position, called our respected rate payor, Samuel Rendall, <u>a liar</u>! Crockett, it is said, paid no school tax for the year 1885. Unbecoming language for such a meeting was freely used and might have led to a breach of the Peace being committed, but for the forbearance of the rate payors of the School Section, opposed to such improper and illegal proceedings, withdrawing from the meeting.

Chris Solversburg was re-elected trustee in a rapid hurry - declared to be so elected by Crockett before the legal time to announce the same had arrived! Witnesses are prepared, I understand to prove all this.

It is reported after the meeting closed, Solversburg adjourned to the City of Hamilton, imbibed freely of the ardent [alcohol] and was driven to his house in an unconscious state of intoxication.

I may tell you in years past I succeeded in having this S.S. #3 set apart and layed off and I disapprove of such improper conduct being carried on.

Messrs. David Flock, Samuel Rendall and others who are large rate payors like me within the section, claim British fair play and I in their behalf and my own ask you to enquire into this matter.

On your answering this letter, I will furnish to you the names of

> the rate payors present as witnesses willing to assist you. For my part, I was 145 miles away from the School Section, when what I am instructed to tell you all happened! Hoping you will make the enquiry and stop such smart practice in future, I am Sir, Your Obedient Servant, John W. Kerr.

Who says school board meetings are boring?

The last bit of Barton business Kerr was to conduct was the annual meeting of S. S. #3, which was held in the schoolhouse on Mohawk Road on December 28, 1887. Kerr was elected chairman of the meeting, and his son, Fred, also attended as a member. Not surprisingly, Kerr kept the minutes, although Robert Nichols was elected secretary! It appears to have been routine business that year. No shenanigans! Kerr would be dead less than five months later, and he was probably grooming his son, who did not yet have children, to take over his role in school affairs.

These Barton and Hamilton vignettes are only known because they are randomly included in Kerr's fishery diaries. If he had kept a general diary, who knows how much more we might have learned!

Mountain ditch at Upper Gage Avenue. From "Mountain Memories."

ANOTHER ATTEMPT TO LEVY TRIBUTE.

Alderman Waddell and Mr. Carpent[er] [h]aving failed in securing all the avenues [to] [t]he city, and thereby levying tribute on a[ll] [w]ho enter or depart, have got up anoth[er] [s]cheme to effect the same end. Under th[e] [p]eculiar Act which enables them to assum[e] [an]d make toll leviable, without the consen[t] [of] the rate-payers or travellers, they hav[e] [n]otified the Council of the township of Barto[n] [th]at they are about to take possession of [a pi]ece of road leading into the city by th[e] [w]ay of the Albion Mills, and running alon[g the] brow of the mountain. Mr. Kerr, th[e] [Fis]hery Inspector, is the ostensible operato[r in] this little game. But the Council of Bar[to]n, are, I am informed, aroused. And th[e] [ob]ject of all these speculators to levy tribut[e] [wil]l certainly be defeated by a meet[ing] of the Council called together by the [Ree]ve, Mr. Loury.

Newspaper clipping found in Kerr diary. Mountain toll roads were very unpopular. ROM

Barton Township Council.

BARTON, Feb. 22, 1875.

The Council met pursuant to adjournment; the Reeve in the chair; all the members present.

Moved by J. W. KERR, seconded by J. E. LOTTRIDGE, That whereas By-law No. 57, exempting from municipal taxation the Carbon Oil Company's manufacturing establishment, which is situated on a part of lot No. 10, in the second concession of the township of Barton, during the years (A. D.) 1870, 1871, 1872, 1873, and 1874, be it resolved, That that the term of years for which By-law No. 57 was passed having expired on the 31st day of December, 1874, the Assessor be instructed to assess the said property for the current year, and that this Council be ordered to write him accordingly.—Carried.

Moved by J. W. KERR, seconded by THOMAS MACKLEM, That By-law No. — be now introduced for fixing the salaries of township officials by this Council for this current year. —Carried.

Moved by J. W. KERR, seconded by J. E. LOTTRIDGE, That the By-law fixing the salaries of Township officers, be now read a second and third time; the blank to be filled up in the By-law, it be passed, signed and sealed.—Carried.

Moved by WILLIAM HILL, seconded by J. E. LOTTRIDGE, That By-law No. 103, for opening the original road allowance between Lots 10 and 11, in the 8th Con. Barton, be now read a first time.—Carried.

Moved by J. E. LOTTRIDGE, seconded by THOMAS MACKLEM, That the By-law 103, to [...]

[...] MACKLEM, That the Reeve do issue his order on the Treasurer for the undermentioned sums:

Mrs. Tosh, a poor widow	$5 00
Thomas Unwin, a poor man	5 00
Mrs. Jane Williams, a poor woman	5 00
John Meeks, a poor man	5 00
Patrick Langdon, a poor man	2 00
William Nelson, a poor, sick man—wood	4 00
R. D. Bensley, for provisions, funeral expenses to Geo. Hunt and family	13 25
Samuel Glazzard, repairing culvert	8 00
The Times Office, for printing Minutes for 1874	30 00
Messrs. Hart & Rawlinson, do do	1 37
Widow Duggan, a poor woman	4 00
Alfred Perkins, a poor man	5 00
Jacob Heff, removing fence	3 00
Mrs. Broadwater, a load of wood	4 00

—Carried.

Moved by J. W. KERR, seconded by THOS. MACKLEM, That the agreement entered into at the time of the formation of Union School, Section No. 5, by Deputy-Reeve, R. D. Bensley, 'o Barton, and Alonzo Egleston, Reeve of Ancaster, be carried out by this Council, and that Col. Aikman be instructed to do so.—Carried.

Moved by J. E. LOTTRIDGE, seconded by WILLIAM HILL, That this Council do now adjourn to meet at John Kerr's Hotel, on the 29th of March next, at 10 o'clock a. m.—Carried.

On motion, the Council adjourned until Monday, 22nd day of March next, then to meet at John Carr's Hotel, at 10 o'clock a.m.

THOMAS LAWRY, Reeve.
J. H. BURKHOLDER, Township Clerk.

Newspaper clipping found in Kerr diary, from Hamilton Spectator. Account of Barton Township Meeting Feb. 22 1875. ROM

Chapter 22

Alcohol!

Kerr was opposed to excessive alcohol consumption and frequently noted illicit taverns, particularly on Burlington Beach. Taverns were everywhere, which seems to indicate that alcohol was cheap and readily available. He occasionally noted men with alcohol problems and usually admonished them to sober up. An early example is from June 1868 when the government received yet another complaint about Kerr's activities. Regarding the complainant, Kerr responded, "I wished to see him reform and be what he ought to be **(a sober industrious man)** but my exertions on his behalf were of no avail. "Drink has been the bane and cause of this man's misfortunes—**nothing else!**"

In April 1869 Kerr noted the connection between alcohol consumption and domestic violence. In regard to Burlington Beach fisherman William Podkins, who was two years in arrears on licence fees, Kerr said, "He drinks the money. I met him upon the beach. He was drunk and told me he would fish where he had a mind to in defiance of the government and me. Tis true that he has a poor blind wife for he knocked that last good eye out of her head with a blow from a block of wood he threw at her some years ago in one of his drunken tantrums." In May Kerr revoked his licence, but he got it back by sobering up.

It was not just the working class who had problems with alcohol. In June 1869, Kerr was in court with his nemesis lawyer, Charles A. Sadlier. Kerr reported, "The conduct of the attorney was most unbecoming, unprofessional and drunken... C.A. Sadlier, well corned, appeared for the defendants."

One of Kerr's good friends on Toronto Island was fisherman David Ward. However, in August 1870, Kerr had to warn Ward about his drinking. Writing to another friend, Patrick Gray, Kerr stated, "unless David Ward gives up drinking and drunkenness altogether you will please tell Billy Ward [his son] I shall not give him a licence next year."

Another drunken fisherman was fellow Irishman Patrick Hand of Winona. In an October 1871 letter to him, Kerr noted he was two years in rent arrears: "My Dear Paddy—The rent must be paid; you must become sober and attentive to your fishing, or you must stop fishing altogether." Returning to the topic in 1881, Kerr wrote again to Hand threatening to cancel his licence for various infractions: "You had better turn your hand to something else, besides fishing for a living."

Later, Kerr observed that Hand had "turned back to drinking, and drunk repeatedly, again! And again!! You and another man are the only men who sell fish, and get drunk, **so look out.** I only have to write the word to Ottawa and that is the end of you." They continued to have a curiously ambivalent relationship, alternating between affinity and admonition.

In August 1872, Kerr remarked about Burlington Beach fisherman James Waddell "who has been drunk and drinking for the last three weeks." In 1882 Kerr made reference to Harry Whitehead, a bookkeeper in Port Dover, who "destroyed himself, he was a very fine fellow, but sad to tell you, he took lately to hard fits of drinking, as I have heard."

For the longest time, I thought Kerr was a teetotaler, so to my surprise I learned in 1879 that he took brandy as a medication! On getting ill while on a trip to Ridgeway he reported he was "obliged to drink Brandy to cure my bowel complaint."

Kerr began to send casks of "native wine" to his superiors in Ottawa, namely, Whitcher and Bauset, usually for free and shipped by train. George Barnes had opened Barnes Winery in St. Catharines in 1873, and perhaps that was the source of Kerr's acquisitions. In a chatty 1882 letter to Bauset, he described the wine.

> About the wine, it is called "dry." Temperance people say, and they quote from Scripture: "look not in the wine when it is red!!"[254]

....

254 Proverbs 23:31

> Timothy wrote "we should take a little wine for our stomachs sake!"[255] The Angel, I think it was, in speaking of St. John the Baptist, said he should never drink wine nor strong drink! And the Holy Ghost should be with him. Ah, but give a good horn of that wine made by Our Lord and Saviour himself, from the water at the marriage in Cana in Galilee—so much said about all good wine.[256]

Kerr seemed to be grappling with the inconsistent biblical positions regarding alcohol consumption. Later Kerr commented on the winery.

> *There is still about 50,000 gallons of various kinds of wine, where I got that I sent you. Except to go in there occasionally and drink a couple of glasses of it. I hardly ever touch it. It is all kept in large hogsheads[257] until drafted off in to kegs to be sent away. It will keep better in the keg: but then I sent it to you for to drink! Or as the Old Song says "Jolly mortals fill your glasses, noble deeds are done by wine!"[258] For my own part I believe this Native Wine is a good thing! Hence why I sent it. However, last year when I was sick, the doctor ordered me to drink but Brandy and I did, and aided by powerful medicine it cured me!!*

By 1883 Whitcher had been superannuated, which may have meant retired or fired. He wrote to Kerr in 1884 to advise that his wife was ill. Kerr wrote back: "I sent you a 5-gallon keg of that nice wine for my sincere friend, Mrs. Whitcher. For a sick person it cannot be surpassed—so at least Doctors say!" Sending a keg to Bauset, he noted, "Doctors say it is better than medicine." I don't know what kind of doctors Kerr was listening to!

In a playful letter written in October 1884 to a friendly Killarney fisherman, Kerr asked,

---

255   1 Timothy 5:23
256   Cana was where Jesus turned the water into wine when it became evident the wine at a wedding was going to run out. It is considered his first public miracle.
257   A hogshead is a large wooden cask, typically holding sixty-three US gallons.
258   A song based on the 1785 Robbie Burns poem "The Jolly Beggar."

> *Will I send you a keg of wine in case you don't feel well during next winter? Just let me know what Mrs. Cameron has to say on the subject! Don't fail!!! I don't recollect if I wrote you that on my way home from Killarney on May 31st I took <u>bowel complaint</u> and it was a full month before I got rid of it! I suffered a good deal! Some people said change of water but my own candid opinion it was <u>Egans Beer</u>! It could not be your oysters! For like the Priest and tea leaves–I only drank the broth!!*[259]

In 1886 Kerr again sent Cameron a five-gallon keg of native wine, saying, "during the cold winter, shut in from the outside world, when you occasional partake of a little of the wine, for your stomach's **sake,** you will I am sure think of me."

Bauset had trouble sleeping, so Kerr advised him to drink some bottles of Guinness XXX Porter to help. He acknowledged he had once resorted to this cure by drinking six bottles. His advice was to drink a single bottle at dinner because Guinness had a "drowsy" quality about it.

When Whitcher was near the end of his life in 1888, Kerr sent him a five-gallon keg of wine to help him recover, but it was too late. Whitcher wrote back to thank Kerr but noted he was too ill to drink. He died just a few days later at a relatively early age. I think Whitcher liked his drink. Remember, he once spent five weeks shooting ducks at Long Point, which was a notoriously boozy group of rich guys.

So, to summarize Kerr's position, drinking alcohol to excess to get drunk is bad; drinking alcohol in moderation for medicinal purposes is good! I can agree with most of that!

....

259   I couldn't find a reference to Egan's beer, the priest, or the tea leaves.

— An Irishman, having signed the pledge, was charged soon afterwards with having drank. "'Twas me absentmindedness," said Pat, " an' a habit I have of talkin' wid meself. I sed to meself, sez I, 'Pat, coom in an' have a dhrink.' 'No, zer,' sez I, 'I've sworn of.' 'Thin I'll dhrink alone,' sez I to meself. 'An' I'll wait for yez outside,' sez I. An' whin meself cum out, faith, an' he was dhrunk."

Newspaper clipping found in Kerr diary. This joke must have amused Kerr. ROM

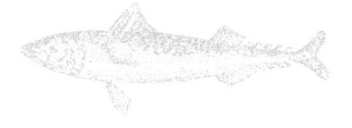

CHAPTER 23

The Strange Saga of Simcoe Kerr

William Johnson Simcoe Kerr (1840–1875) was the grandson of Joseph Brant (1743–1807) and the son of William Johnson Kerr (1787–1845) who had married Brant's daughter, Elizabeth. Upon his father's death, Simcoe Kerr, who was then an infant, became heir to the Brant estate by native tradition.

Joseph Brant (who led an incredibly colourful life) wanted to settle down in the late 1790s and proposed to buy about 3,500 acres at the northeast edge of Burlington Bay from the Mississauga Natives. Governor John Graves Simcoe would not allow a purchase transaction between Natives, so he bought the property and gave it to Brant who built a large house there, in which he died in 1807.

The Brant estate had been largely sold off by the 1860s, but Simcoe Kerr retained about seventy acres, which included a swampy area known as Brant's Pond (later Kerr Pond). Simcoe Kerr was in the militia and was a lawyer who also served as reeve of Nelson Township, now part of the city of Burlington.

The problem began on April 29, 1870, when Kerr seized the illegal net of serial offender, Benjamin Joyce, near Brant's Pond. A scuffle ensued, and Kerr noted "threats bad, oaths worse." Kerr had Joyce summonsed, and in court a few days later, Joyce had his lawyer, Simcoe Kerr, with him. For whatever reason, J. W. Kerr had the impression "that Simcoe Kerr has encouraged this man Joyce to violate the Fisheries Act."

Kerr then received two letters from Simcoe Kerr (the two men were not related) in which Simcoe alleged that Kerr seized the nets on Brant's Pond (variously referred to as Kerr's Pond) which he claimed as private property. Kerr responded, "this is the first time Simcoe Kerr has claimed this pond which is no pond at all but an arm of the Bay that runs in towards Wellington Square[260] to a point, with Burlington Beach on one side and the Brant farm on the other."

Kerr elaborated: "Simcoe Kerr has not only claimed this pond or water of the Bay as his private property but it is said that he claims all of B. Bay and part of Lake Ontario, adjacent thereto, as an Indian Reserve. He causes a good deal of annoyance by encouraging this man Joyce to violate the Fisheries Act." Kerr believed that Joyce, whose licence had been cancelled, "at the instance of Simcoe Kerr, fished all through closed season and caught bass." This was a challenge to the Department's authority that Kerr could not tolerate.

On May 9, Simcoe Kerr had J.W. Kerr summonsed to appear before JP John Wesley Hopkins for theft of Joyce's net. On May 10, Joyce, in a court in Hamilton, was convicted and fined by Police Magistrate Cahill. Kerr wrote to the minister: "I am compelled to say to you that in consequence of the stubborn and self-willed determination of this man to fish and trade in fish in defiance of the law and my authority, I had no other alternative left me but to stop his career by the severe measures I have reported to you." Joyce indicated his intention to appeal.

On May 11, Kerr appeared in court in Halton before Hopkins, and his lawyer advised Hopkins that it was Kerr's duty to be on Burlington Bay seizing nets. Kerr snorted, "The Magistrate, however, contented himself by saying I had no right, nor authority to go on the Bay at all." All the relevant sections of the *Fisheries Act* "had no influence over him—He would try the Governor General if arraigned before him." Needless to say, Kerr was convicted and fined sixteen dollars plus costs (or twenty days in jail!)

On May 14, Kerr seized another of Joyce's nets under a warrant from James Cahill, and Joyce was taken into police custody by Kerr with the assistance of two Hamilton police constables. Suddenly, a Port Nelson

....

260 Wellington Square was then the name of what would become the city of Burlington.

(Burlington) police constable and Ben Joyce showed up before JP Cahill with a warrant signed by JP Hugh Cotter of Halton authorizing the search and seizure of the net from the Hamilton police! The request for this warrant was signed by Simcoe Kerr. The police station and the constables' homes were duly searched before the net was located at a local livery stable. Enlisting the willing help of Dan McGwynne (remember him?), the nets were taken back to Halton.

Kerr wrote, "The whole proceedings... are so strange and obstructive to me in the discharge of my duties... Something must be done to stop Mr. Hopkins in his wild, mad career." Then Kerr appealed his conviction. Writing to Minister Mitchell, he said, "I hope Mr. W. J. Whitcher, or some competent person, will be at once appointed to enquire into the strange proceedings of all the persons named to you in my letter, so that justice may be done." In furtherance of this, Kerr paid for a copy of the evidence that Hopkins had received in court to pass on to his boss as proof of this miscarriage of justice.

Commenting on Joyce's appeal, Kerr pleaded,

> *Some more reliable remedy must be found to put a final stop to contraventions of the Fisheries Act... It is of no earthly use in going into the Court of Quarter Sessions before Judge A. Logie unless the Attorney General or Eminent Counsel is sent there by the government to prosecute, and if the convictions are quashed, to move the cases to the Court of Queen's Bench*[261]—*Such has always been my sad experience of Judge A. Logie and his court."*

Kerr went to war against JP Hopkins, sending the evidence and witness statements to the Department and to John Hillyard Cameron, MP for Peel and associate of Sir John A. MacDonald:[262] "I hope and entreat of the Department to teach Mr. Hopkins as new lesson–He is the only magistrate in all my district 'until recently' [Hugh Cotter?]

....

261   The Court of Queen's Bench was then the Supreme Court of Ontario.
262   John Hillyard Cameron (Apr. 14, 1817–Nov. 14, 1876) was an Irish Protestant Conservative politician (just like Kerr!). He was the MP for Peel from 1867–1872. His career was impeded because he was Grand Master of the Orange Lodge.

who treats me in such a manner as to try and debar me, by this fine, from doing my duty." If the conviction stood, Kerr would have likely lost his job, so the stakes were high.

Circumventing the Court of Quarter Sessions, Kerr's lawyer, "a clever and competent man," brought an appeal to the Court of Queen's Bench for *certiorari*, a legal procedure to literally "make more certain"[263] by quashing an unlawful ruling. Returning again to the topic of Hopkins, Kerr railed, "I hope something will be immediately done… to put a final stop to the very great annoyance I am continually made the subject of by Mr. J. W. Hopkins."

On June 4, Kerr seized Joyce's nets for a third time for fishing without a licence and had him summonsed. Appearing in court as counsel for Joyce, Simcoe Kerr requested an adjournment "to produce some old documents to prove that he is the lawful owner of Kerr pond." Kerr noted that it was the same net previously seized by him: "I have the net and ropes now in my possession, in my own house, and I am determined to hold them until confiscated."

Regarding Joyce, Kerr opined that

> *Mr. W. J. S. Kerr has been making a tool of this man so as to establish his legal claim to that portion of B. Bay known as Kerr's Pond… He has advised Ben Joyce to the unlawful course he has been pursuing–and because I will not permit it, I am put down as having some selfish ends to accomplish… I have had to bear a good many insults in connection with Mr. W. J. S. Kerr and Ben Joyce in this matter. And it is not the first time I have had to stand fire. I will endeavour to meet any and all that may be hurled at me in a becoming manner and with good grace.*

Soon there would be more to come.

Kerr then proposed that the Ministry pass a regulation outlawing

---

263 A writ of certiorari still exists today under a different name, but is a rare legal proceeding. It is a prerogative or special writ, like habeas corpus, to immediately quash a decision made without jurisdiction. It literally means "to make certain."

private fishing ponds. They didn't, but they did later propose that Kerr Pond be "set aside" for fish propagation. Kerr was pleased and suggested that the entire Bay and Dundas Marsh be set aside as well, contrary to his previous position in 1869.

Appearing at Quarter Session on June 15, the Joyce convictions were all quashed. Kerr moaned,

> *The case was not submitted to a jury at all. Judge Logie refused to hear my evidence altho' I was the person who found the fish in Mr. Joyce's possession, because I was interested as complainant to half the fine... In order to maintain me in my position it has now become necessary to make regulations... to counteract Judge Logie's view of the law in such cases. I don't want ½ the fines–strike ½ the fines to the prosecutor out of the Fisheries Act... Although the cases were ably pleaded by Mr. O'Reilly for the Department, I never felt smaller in my life and evidently I had not a foot to stand upon, so to use a common phrase.*

Not prepared to lie down and admit defeat, on June 20, Kerr obtained and sent to the Department "an abstract from the original patent from the Crown made to Captain Joseph Brant, from Peter Russell, President of Upper Canada and dated the 14th of February, 1798." Kerr noted that the original 3,450 acres had been reduced to "about 70 acres held by Mr. W. J. S. Kerr, all the rest of the immense property has passed out of the family. Never to return." Kerr wanted to know what the Ministry thought about the claim.

On August 3, 1870, Kerr was invited to Ottawa where he met Minister Peter Mitchell, for the first and possibly only time. Kerr reported, "He was very glad to see me. Stated so. He introduced me to his daughter. He appears to be a fine man. Talked about Simcoe Kerr's claim to the Bay fishery near Wellington Square."

After a lull in the festivities, things heated up in October. Kerr and his sometime assistant, Fred Corey, were on Lake Ontario, north of the Burlington Bay Shipping Canal, hunting for nets belonging to Ben Joyce and his family. Joyce's fishing licence had been canceled in 1868 and given to Dan McGwynne, who had apparently reformed his evil ways. The seized nets were transported to Kerr's home, and then Joyce and Simcoe Kerr got to work getting warrants issued to search Kerr's house for illegally seized nets. The warrants were signed, naturally, by JPs Hopkins and Hugh Cotter.

Before those warrants were executed, Simcoe Kerr, Joyce, and others descended upon McGwynne and seized his nets. Kerr reported,

> ... at 10:00 p.m. Simcoe Kerr came along with 5 other men. S. Kerr was armed at the time with a revolver... and ordered his men to seize and take up 400 yards of net. This the men in the boat did immediately while the men on the shore made McGwynne a prisoner... Simcoe Kerr asked McGwynne for his licence and why he did not lease from him instead of from the Department through me, who he stigmatized in unmeasured terms and language. I cannot account for Mr. S. Kerr's conduct except that, as McGwynne says, he was drunk at the time.

Laying the blame at the feet of Simcoe, Kerr wrote to Whitcher.

> I attribute the proceedings of Mr. Kerr, who styles himself the Chief Magistrate of Nelson, he being the Reeve, to the manner in which Hugh Cotter, J. Wesley Hopkins, J. P., and Judge Alexander Logie have from time to time acted with this man, Ben Joyce, and others, to suppress and force down the Fisheries Act... Ben Joyce and his sons openly say they will fish and shoot the first man who takes up their nets again. And that Mr. W. J.S. Kerr bid them do so and he will bear them harmless. Shoot or shoot not, I shall endeavour to do my duty feeling as I do hope that my conduct will be borne out by you and the Department.

Joyce then boldly appeared before JP Hopkins to act on the warrant to search Kerr's house. As recorded by Kerr,

> I heard they were coming in at my gate and I went out to meet them, when they explained to me the object of their mission. On going out of the house I ordered the doors to be shut and locked. I

informed them that I seized the nets by the power invested in me under the fishery law and my appointment, that I did not steal them, that I had them in my possession and would not give them up until the proper time arrived. I had the nets in my house at the time but the constables did not break open the doors, had they done so, I should have resisted them.

Kerr then wrote to the minister seeking permission to "employ half a dozen policemen to establish Mr. Dan McGwynne in his fishery and protect him there for a few nights in case I find it necessary to do so." It apparently wasn't necessary because the next act in the melodrama was for Joyce to get another warrant to search Kerr's home: "On this day three constables again made their appearance at my house with Ben Joyce and his son, with a search warrant to take the nets stolen from the property of W. J. Simcoe Kerr in Lake Ontario. Fortune again favoured me, they were observed coming, the doors were shut against them— they tried to obtain admittance, failed in the attempt and then went away. The warrant is signed by Hugh Cotter and J. Wesley Hopkins."

Hoping that the Department would "take measures to stop these magistrates from annoying me and my family," Kerr vowed, "I don't want to take the law in my own hands. If I would I should stop it very quickly." As a former chief constable in the Irish Constabulary, Kerr was not a man to be fooled around with. He and his family were armed, and he knew how to shoot!

Then Kerr arranged to have the confiscated nets taken from his house to the railway station "and conveyed them away to a place of safe keeping and beyond the reach of two magistrates who do not yet know the difference between a seizure of nets legally made by me, and the same nets sworn to be feloniously stolen by Ben Joyce. It always seems to be correct that Messrs. Cotter and Hopkins encourage the crime of perjury in these cases."[264] [265]

---

264 Besides being a justice of the peace, Hugh Cotter was also the postmaster and a produce and lumber merchant. Everybody in the nineteenth century had multiple jobs!

265 John Wesley Hopkins was born on Dec. 14, 1825, and died in 1871, to Kerr's relief.

By late October 1870, Simcoe Kerr seemed to want to make peace. Running into Kerr in downtown Hamilton, Kerr said, "Mr. W. J. Simcoe Kerr hailed me on James Street and wished me to come down to Ottawa this week with him to have a final settlement made about his fishing property on B. Beach." Kerr was having none of it: "I replied I had no business to Ottawa and was not aware that he had a fishery in the public waters there on the Beach." To the minister, Kerr advised, "Mr. Simcoe Kerr will endeavour to get you to acknowledge his having some title to the premises where he has none whatever." The war raged on.

Obtaining a copy of the information sworn before Hopkins that resulted in the warrants to search Kerr's house, he railed to the minister.

> Mr. Hopkins knows very well that when I seize nets for contraventions of the Fisheries Act, I don't steal them, I act openly. The course Mr. Hopkins pursues toward me is vexatious, obstructive and malicious. It's done to perplex, annoy and retard a final and fixed establishment of our Fisheries Act. But for Mr. Hopkins uncalled for interference on behalf of a few lawless fishermen, urged on and countenanced by him to break the law... these illegal acts would have terminated long ago... I hope to be equal for every emergency which may turn up. Threats to shoot and drown are publicly talked of by Ben Joyce and his 3 sons if I attempt to seize any more nets belonging to him or them... we shall see!!"

In his annual report for 1870, Kerr expresses appreciation for the minister having instructed County Attorney Sam Freeman to inquire into the conduct of Hopkins and Cotter. On March 13, 1871 Kerr crowed that his conviction, on appeal to the Court of Queen's Bench, "was quashed absolute. So much for the local Magistrate's stretch of power in a wrong direction."

You would think this would be the final act in this almost humorous grudge match, but no. On May 23, 1871, "the Deputy Sheriff of the County of Wentworth accompanied by Benjamin Joyce came to my house and place of residence, which they entered and searched for nets seized and confiscated in 1870. It appears in this latter instance the seizure was made under the authority of a Writ of Replevin.[266] As a matter of course, nothing was found, I having the things removed to a place of safekeeping some months ago."

Amusingly, Kerr recorded that Joyce himself was of so little value that he "had to get 2 solvent persons to give security for $700 to bear the Sheriff harmless, for his illegal proceedings against me." This means Joyce had no money and no assets. I wonder who those two solvent persons were. Perhaps Simcoe Kerr and one of the justices of the peace. I'm betting that Kerr was not home at the time of the search, or their might have been fireworks.

In July 1871, Kerr reported a curious reversal in his relationship with J. P. Hopkins. Finding two men illegally fishing at Burlington Beach, Kerr got into a scuffle and noted,

> *These men obstructed me in the discharge of my duty, assaulted me and refused to open a box in which they had the fish locked up. I was obliged to leave the scene of occurrence and obtain the personal aid of John Wesley Hopkins, J. P. I succeeded in finding the fish they had caught with the assistance referred to ... Squire Hopkins gave me his valuable aid and assistance–he got out of bed and came with me to the scene of occurrence and remained by me until I found the concealed fish. I may add that both men were drunk at the time, just sufficient to put them in fighting order.*

Hopkins died before the end of the year of unknown cause, perhaps somewhat redeemed in Kerr's eyes.

As a last hurrah, Joyce sued Kerr in the Court of Common Pleas in October 1871. Kerr predicted "I shall badly beat Benjamin Joyce in this suit."[267] The case was scheduled to be tried in November, but it was not reached, meaning it would be adjourned to the next sitting. Kerr suggested that the minister authorize him to return the nets to Joyce: "By

....

266   A *writ of replevin* is a legal proceeding to summarily secure the return of personal property wrongfully seized.

267   The Court of Common Pleas was established in Ontario (Canada West) in 1849 to assume part of the caseload of the Court of Queen's Bench.

doing this you will stop all further annoyance to me, and I presume, put a final end to the law suit."

Kerr observed, "I have been subjected to gross insult and annoyance since May 1870. I have been charged with stealing those things by a partisan, ignorant local magistrate who issues search warrants to ransack my house and premises. That Magistrate, John Wesley Hopkins, is **now dead and gone.** I can therefore afford to lay the matter before you in a Christian and becoming spirit." Another good, sensible compromise by our boy.

Summarizing the matter in February 1872, Kerr wrote,

> *Mr. Benjamin Joyce has seen his folly out, his false friend Simcoe, he says, has deserted him. Poor Hopkins is dead. The Honour of the Department has been upheld by me, subject, however, to gross insults and great annoyance of both myself and family. I have the consolation of knowing that I have done my duty and did not yield an inch, I hope, at least, my conduct has merited the approbation of the minister and the Department. Benjamin Joyce and his sons have applied for their licence for year 1872.*

Kerr attached to his diaries an article about "Toadies," possibly in reference to Mr. Joyce, but other toadies were about, as we have seen at Toronto and Niagara.

In May 1873, Simcoe Kerr wrote to the minister offering to lease Brant's Pond to the Department to permit them to create a fish nursery. Kerr was asked to respond, and he wrote back to the minister to remind him that the pond was set aside for fish propagation by a proclamation on August 23, 1870, and to remind him as to why. Kerr huffed again that Simcoe Kerr didn't own the pond and that it is not even surrounded by his lands. Kerr concluded, "For many reasons which have come to my knowledge, I cannot recommend Brant's pond for the purposes referred to by Mr. W. J. Simcoe Kerr beyond what the proclamation already gives the Department, control over the waters of the same."

Simcoe Kerr wrote back to allege that the Department (i.e., J. W. Kerr} was incapable of protecting the pond from fishing which really set Kerr off on a tear: "I look upon this language of Simcoe Kerr as futile, trifling and worthless, emanating as it does from an unreliable source... Why! This is all bosh!—to my certain knowledge, not one single fisherman has ever gone there and only once have I found a small piece of net set therein, a farmer's net."

Kerr noted the "strenuous exertions" Simcoe Kerr had used to induce people to fish on the pond but that...

> ... not even Benjamin Joyce, nor his boys, could be induced to fish there upon his invitation... Mr. S. Kerr, to use a common phrase, is now on his last legs and his letter is merely an attempt to raise the wind, to get a money consideration from the Department, if he found you or I silly or simple to help him with his nefarious purposes. In his Indian cunning he even offered myself a consideration [bribe] if I would assist him by a report favourable to this attempt of his at blackmailing. But then Mr. S. Kerr is not accountable for any bad or good thing he does, as I may candidly tell you, he is hardly ever sober. He has squandered away all his property, he will shortly have nothing left... where he resides is mortgaged for double its value.

Ouch!

Simcoe Kerr was dead by 1875. To quote the *Grateful Dead*, "What a long strange trip it's been!"

CHAPTER 24

A Melancholy Accident on Burlington Bay

Kerr was an astute observer of wrongdoing and injustice. On this subject, on July 2, 1870, he wrote to the minister the following letter, which I have reproduced in full:

> Sir:
>
> I beg most respectfully to draw your attention to a most melancholy accident that happened on Burlington Bay whereby three children, daughters of Thomas Swinyard, late Manager of the G.W. Railway at Hamilton, were drowned by the capsizing of the pleasure boat, Empress, on Monday evening last between the hours of 8 and 9 o'clock p.m.
>
> It appears that this melancholy accident happened in consequence of the unstable state of the vessel capsizing by a sudden squall, in consequence of being rendered dangerous by oversparring and overcanvasing.[268]
>
> I heard it was only the fourth time the Empress was sailed in the Bay; on two other occasions of these before this she capsized. As a person expressed to me "you might as well place three yards of canvas on a cockleshell."

---

268 Meaning too many masts and sails.

My object in writing you in this matter, foreign to the fisheries branch of the Department, is that I believe a competent person should be appointed from the Marine Department to examine the pleasure yacht Empress. She is not a safe, seagoing vessel.

Such men as Mr. H.L. Bastien, who owns the Empress, and every other person situated as he is keeping for hire and renting out boats for a consideration, should be by law to have and keep only safe and proper boats, well-formed and well maintained.

This boat in her present state is very unsafe. John Roche who steered this boat on the late sad occasion, is reputed as ignorant of the first principles of a sailor. He is fond of liquor and it is reported he was drunk on that late sad occasion.

Mr. Thomas Swinyard had his 6 children out with him, Mr. Fred Ritchie, the Post Master, was there besides John Roche, who steered the boat and three innocent little girls to a watery grave. When the accident happened all were precipitated into the water, the boat turned completely upside down on four of the children. A boy dived from under the boat and was saved, but sad to relate, the three girls were drowned.

Mr. Swinyard, Mr. Ritchie and the two other children in Mr. Swinyard's arms, besides Roche, were thrown clear of the boat when she went over. They were saved by the lucky proximity of a small yawl they had attached to the stern of the sailing yacht, and the speedy succor of a man who put out in a boat to their rescue from Brown's wharf situated ¾ of a mile from where the sad accident happened in the Bay.

Six persons in all were saved, while three as already shewn, were drowned. This man deserves the Humane Society medal, which I recommend to your notice.[269]

Two of the bodies were found, they were grappled by hook

---

269 The Humane Society bronze medal was introduced in 1837 and was awarded for bravery in saving lives.

and line.

In a conversation I had with the Mayor, George Morrison, he says he has no jurisdiction over the waters whatever but thought that perhaps you as Minister of Marine had. If so, I have taken the liberty to write you for a remedy.

John W. Kerr

This incident demonstrates the fragility of life in the 1800s and how unregulated things were at that time, leading to terrible results. It is not known whether the rescuer was awarded the medal, but it is highly unlikely that an investigator was appointed because "accidents" happened all the time. Human life was cheap. Only when civil litigation lawyers began to achieve some success in the courts and awards were granted for negligent conduct did safety standards begin to appear, both in law and in practice. Now we see civil litigators as greedy ambulance chasers (and some are), but many are responsible, sensitive, and sensible lawyers. If you suffer an injury as a result of someone else's negligence or malfeasance, hire a lawyer carefully, not just from TV ads. If you have a trusted lawyer, ask what he or she thinks. In Hamilton we all know one another or have ways of finding out. You can check out lawyers online, but in my experience, most reviews are by disgruntled former clients with an axe to grind. Remember, no lawyer wins all cases, and many losses are not the lawyer's fault! Oh, and a final word of advice: hire a local lawyer and one who will help settle the case rather than fan the flames of litigation to the benefit of no one but the lawyers. Sorry about this rant!

A Melancholy Accident on Burlington Bay 377

Bastien boat houses, Burlington Bay. Hamilton Public Library.

Postscript

Following his father's death in 1888, thirty-five-year-old Frederick Kerr stepped into his father's shoes and took over the position of fisheries overseer. He was invited to visit Ottawa in May to discuss matters, but he was generally treated shabbily by the Department. His appointment wasn't confirmed until nearly a year after his father died, and he was not paid for many months, typical of the disorganized nature of the federal government.

His district was substantially reduced, and by February 1889 he was perplexed at the strange way the Department was treating him, not knowing where he was at or even if he was going to be kept on. On being formally appointed, he wrote to Deputy Minister John Tilton to thank him but groused about his salary: "Although I admit that the salary is comparatively small, still I am not complaining as to that." He also noted some special duty and requested "a little extra remuneration."

In June 1889 he wrote to a friend: "I am very glad to hear that you were appointed collector of customs. It is a great deal better than Fishery Overseer in my opinion. No trouble on your mind or abuse as it is in the fishing business." That month Fred achieved his crowning glory when he rented a boat at Port Colborne and seized 1,000 yards of American nets set in Point Abino Bay on Lake Erie, something his father often dreamed of but never accomplished. For this he was "highly commended" (but not paid any extra).

Travelling to Ottawa for a second time in December 1889, he met the minister, who promised to increase his salary "without any hesitation." After he requested an increase to $500 from the $250 he was being paid, the Ministry granted him an extra $50. Some things never change as far as unfulfilled promises are concerned. In applying for more money, Fred noted that he had helped his father for over fifteen years and that he had "acquired the experience which my father's extensive and general knowledge of the fisheries enabled him to teach me." Fred also noted that he was an up-and-coming young man who had been voted deputy reeve of Barton.

Like his father, Frederick recognized the overfishing, especially in Lake Erie, where he recommended the gradual reduction in the number of pound nets. He also continued his father's tradition by sending Bauset the occasional keg of "Haskin's Best Native Wine, the sample that I hope to have at my wedding when I become eligible for marriage." He got married in 1892 and had two daughters.

Frederick also inherited a bit of his father's feisty defensiveness. When he was attacked in a letter by Fisheries Overseer Sharp, a man J. W. Kerr had little, if any, respect for, Fred fired back, noting that he had started work at age thirteen and had had little time for "bumming." Of Sharp he noted, "He used to wear a white choker like an 'old deacon' and carried a black bottle in his coat pocket, especially when the Scott Act was in force and it was hard to get a drink."

Like his father, Fred had an affinity for the common man. In 1891 the Department cancelled spearfishing on Burlington Bay, but Fred worked to get it restored by writing a long letter to Bauset. He noted that most of the spearfishermen were bricklayers, masons, and farmers who had no work in the winter and caught fish to put bread on the table and that if not fishing they would otherwise just lounge around taverns. The order was rescinded. J. W. Kerr had made the same argument years before, without success.

A good Conservative like his father, Fred worked to re-elect MacDonald in 1891, but Sir John A. died soon after the election, on June 6, 1891. Fred dealt with the same squabbles amongst many of the same fishermen, and he continued to attend to the interest of Mrs. Elliott and her family. Echoing his father, he wrote on April 27, 1891, "She is a very poor, hardworking, industrious woman with a large family to provide for, burdened with an insane husband who has been a raving maniac for the last 10 years." I can find no record in Fred's diaries of the Boltons or Cantwell because Niagara was not part of his reduced district.

Fred seems to have been fairly efficient in enforcing the law, and like his father he kept a lot of newspaper clippings of his exploits. He also seemed to stay on the farm and was responsible for operating it with his five spinster sisters and his elderly mother, who died in 1907. Fred also visited the mills in his district and tried to keep the sawdust and mill debris out of the streams and rivers. He noted many mills closing due to a lack of available timber, as his father had predicted.

Fred's diaries are also available online, though I admit I have not read them all. That may be a project for somebody else. There is a curious gap in that the diaries from 1892–1895 are missing. They also end in February 1898 when Fred may have handed the job off to my great-grandfather, Charles John Kerr, whose diaries, if they ever existed, have not been preserved. Fred died in 1902, and his younger brother, Charles, died in 1942 at age eighty-seven.

Barton Township was fully absorbed into the City of Hamilton by the 1950s. The GWR became part of the Grand Trunk Railway and then the Canadian National Railway. They still have a large staging area at Stuart and Bay Streets, but most of the buildings, including the offices and the roundhouse, are long gone. My father, Frederick Bensley Kerr, had the railway in his blood but opted instead to be a tool and die maker at Westinghouse, a job he hated. When I was about seven or eight years old, he used to take me to the Bay Street Bridge over the lines of tracks and sadly point out the steam locomotives being cut up for scrap.

Although I do not know many of J. W. Kerr's heirs, it seems that some of the children and grandchildren of his third son, Charles John Kerr, became notable, some for better and one for worse. George Robert Vandeleur Kerr was treasurer and vice president of Westinghouse Canada before he died of a stroke in 1937 at age fifty-five. Several of his sons became famous medical doctors and reside in British Columbia. Robert "Kerr" Morrow was a grandson of C. J. Kerr, and before his death in 2018 he became the longest-serving mayor of Hamilton (1982–2000).

Then there was John Bensley Kerr, my partial namesake. Born into this family of solid upper-middle-class workers, the grandson of J. W.

Kerr did not want to wait or work for status but instead opted for a life of crime as "Canada's Most Daring Rumrunner," so named by author C.W. Hunt in his book *Whiskey and Ice*, Dundurn, 1995. Falling in with Rocco Perri, Hamilton's most notorious gangster, Kerr and others took enormous chances to run boatloads of Canadian hooch into the United States during prohibition for big payoffs. Of course, Canadian distillers and brewers were complicit in this scam, and everyone knew they were as dirty as the boat boys.

John Bensley Kerr's luck held for almost ten years but ran out in the winter of 1929 when he died on Lake Ontario, either accidentally in a boat accident or intentionally by murder. When his body was found in the ice a few weeks later, it was impossible to determine the cause of death. He had earned enough money to support his wife and daughter for over forty years.

Conclusion

So, what can I say about the long life of John William Kerr that could be considered objective and neutral, even though I am neither of those things? First, the things I regret, such as the fact that I know so little about his early life or his thirteen years in the Irish Constabulary. Although not an important historical figure, he was such a good and interesting writer that I wish he had kept more diaries. There were other exploits in the RIC that he refers to but doesn't describe. I still do not know the true circumstance of him and a second wife fleeing Ireland.

Second is the fact that we only have his words, for the most part, because none of the letters he received from the Ministry or from anyone else have been preserved. All we have are occasional quotes by Kerr from those letters. It is maddening that these were not retained, and it is often like fighting with one arm tied behind one's back trying to determine what the Ministry expected of him.

The index on the website says there are two boxes at the ROM, so I thought I may have to go to hated Toronto to see what they contained. Instead I contacted the ROM, and they had a look for me, but I was advised that they only hold the hundreds if not thousands of receipts that Kerr obsessively retained. I didn't contact the National Archives (though maybe I should have) to see if they have any of Kerr's stuff. I just assumed the papers of an insignificant federal employee would not have been of any interest and, therefore, not retained.

Overall, Kerr's impact was probably insignificant. He may have temporarily slowed down the decline of the lower lakes' fisheries, but decline they did, to the point of virtual oblivion, at least from a commercial perspective. In regard to pollution, he may have had some impact because some of the most egregious aspects of fouling this planet are now, for the most part, a thing of the past, at least in most of the developed world.

I think his legacy is more of a personal nature. He was a supremely decent man in a species of often indecent beings with a probably limited future on this planet. I've often wondered what contemporaries thought of him, and I think they would generally have a grudging respect for his integrity, hard work and his kindness to others. For me, it was a privilege to read his words, and I'd like to think I am a better person for having done so. So, to J. W. Kerr, it's "Hip, hip, hurray! No surrender, never!"

Hamilton, Ontario, January 2021

Kerr's gravestone, with wrong date of birth. Hamilton Cemetery. Photo by Steve Burditt, 2020

384   Caught!

Kerr house, with author by the door. Photo by Kristen Kerr, 2020.

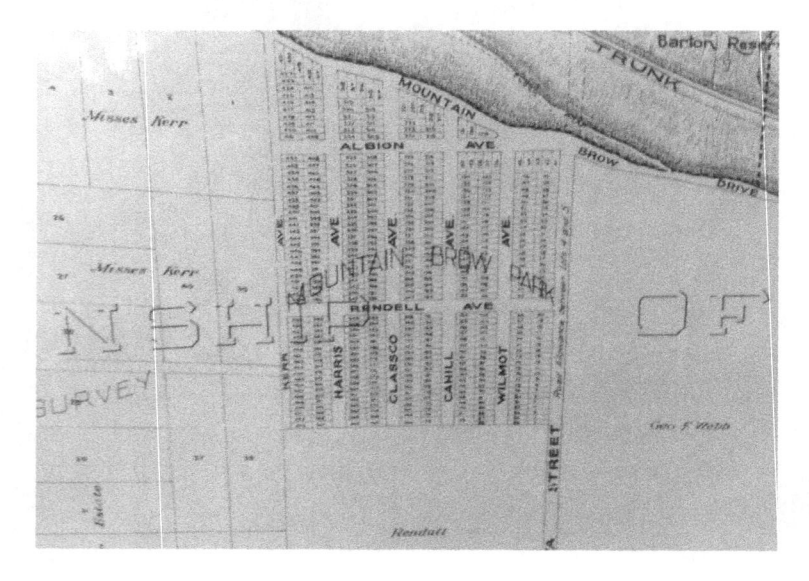

Proposed subdivision of part of Kerr farm, 1922. Hamilton Public Library.

How I Wrote This GD Book

I grew up on a small part of my great-great-grandfather's farm on Upper Gage Avenue. After my great-grandfather died in 1942, the remnants of the Kerr farm were divided amongst family members, and my grandfather got a parcel on which he built his house at 401 Upper Gage, and my father later built our house at 431 Upper Gage. A few other family members were on the property that I never knew, but most of the farm was sold to land developers. John William Kerr's house at 988 Concession Street was sold out of the family, but I always knew it was the original family home, and I had some idea that he was "a somebody" a long time ago.

Somehow, I knew that Kerr's diaries had been put on microfilm and that my dad's cousin, Eleanor (Kerr) Morrow, had paid for a copy to be provided to the Hamilton Public Library. But as I said in the introduction, reading long documents on a microfilm reader is torture. So, when I learned the diaries were online, I determined to read them, all 9,472 handwritten pages! (Many with two letters per page.)

As I read on my computer or notebook, I would summarize what I thought was of interest on pads of foolscap. That took a hell of a long time! After about seven pads, I was done, and I even carried on a ways with the diaries of Kerr's son, Frederick, who took over upon his death in 1888.

Then I thought about the topics I would cover because I did not want to just write a chronological summary of his career as fisheries overseer. I began to learn about his earlier career in the Royal Irish Constabulary and as chief engineer for the engineering department of the GWR as he would tantalizingly disclose from time to time in his letters or diaries. I colour-coded my notes based on topics so as not to miss too much of anything when I started typing.

Other than newspaper articles and some marginal collateral material about Barton Township or the Masonic brotherhood, there was no information except as Kerr chose to reveal it and hardly any responses to the thousands of letters he wrote, for they were not preserved. So, the picture I have painted of Kerr is largely his own, and we know how dangerous that can be. I have tried to be objective, but I have to admit that I am an unabashed fan, with reservations. When I finished his life story in the letter books, I felt sad, but I began to write seriously then, knowing as much about him as I ever would. As I wrote, I read the diaries again to make sure I had the quotes right and that I understood the bigger picture because some events continued over months or years.

My research was not as extensive as I would have liked. I re-read some Canadian history and read about the GWR and commercial fishing and the Long Point Company. Most of my footnotes are from articles that I found on the Internet about the places he visited or the people he knew. I visited some of his hangouts and took some pictures of some things that still remain.

This big, garbled book is the result and it is not intended as an academic work. I was merely trying to tell the story of what I think was a remarkable life, not important historically or politically but maybe important in a human context. To sum it up, my impression is that J. W. Kerr was a very decent man, perhaps typical of his age, who always tried to do his best, to do his duty for his government, his adopted and much-loved country, and most importantly, for his fellow man, even to the very end. And so mote it be!

Fishing spear from the Hamilton Museum of Steam & Technology NHS artifact collection. Spear originally was from John P. Smith & Co. in Dundas. Photo courtesy of the Hamilton Civic Museums collection.

Acknowledgments

This book would not have been possible with the aid and assistance of a number of persons and institutions. First and foremost, my wife Deb, who not only encouraged me in the endeavour but who was also virtually ignored during the long hours spent reading Kerr's diaries and writing his story. I would read and write at almost any hour of the night or day but often spent five or six hours straight at my computer without moving. When she would come upstairs to go to bed she would invariably ask, "How's it going?" to which I would invariably and dismissively snort "Fine." I apologize for my rudeness and thank you for not being more intrusive.

I owe a debt to my late Great-Aunt, Eleanor Morrow, who, as I understand it, paid to have a copy of the microfiche from the Royal Ontario Museum sent to the Hamilton Public Library containing the diaries. Were they not here in Hamilton I would likely never have learned of them many years ago and set my mind towards reading them.

The Local History and Archives department of the Hamilton Public Library is a fantastic resource and the staff are very helpful. Virtually all of my collateral research was done there and it is a great room in which to think and reflect.

My good friends, Ted Arnold and Sue Andrews are to be thanked for their assistance. Ted is my sometime travelling companion who doesn't mind a jaunt around assisting me with research. Sue is my Ancestry guru who provided me with Kerr's family tree, which allowed me to hopefully keep things straight about the family.

My daughters, Kristen and Jasmine Kerr, were invaluable for their computer skills in navigating the arcane world of modern publishing and just generally to assist with my virtually non-existent computer skills. Kristen's husband, Steve Burditt, is also to be thanked for improving some of the photo images that I had taken on my out-of-date cell phone.

Thank you also to Alan and Laurie Huurman, the current owners of the Kerr home, for allowing my daughter and myself to tour their magnificently restored residence and take some pictures. While thoroughly modernizing the home they have maintained many of its original features including pine floors and 12" baseboards!

Thanks to Terry Boulton (a relative of the notorious Bolton Brothers) and the Niagara on the Lake Historical Society and Museum for assistance with the Niagara aspects of the narrative and for their keen interest in Niagara History.

Finally, thank you to all the staff at Friesen Press for their professional work in putting this book together and correcting a litany of my mistakes.

Joel B. Kerr
November 1, 2020

Index

Acton, Ont., 260
Albion Falls Mills, 346, 354
Ascension, Church of, 50, 148
Atkinson, Isaac, 249

Backhouse, John A., 102, 119, 146
Bailey, Dr. T. Melville, 7
Baldry, Joan, 49, 50, 53, 62, 63, 66, 78, 87, 93, 112
Ballinahown, Westmeath, 15
Barnes Winery, 359
Barton Township, 4, 343
Bastien, H. L. (Boathouse), 58, 100, 375
Bates, John, 43, 46, 47, 78, 85
Bauset, Simon Peter, 54, 103, 119, 152, 157, 172, 187, 199, 201, 209, 220, 230, 231, 237, 242, 272, 327
Beardmore Tannery, 259
Bensley, Robert D., 354
Big Creek, 90, 246, 262
Bingham, Charles L., 119, 141, 145, 146, 148, 174, 241

Birley, Norris F., 94, 99
Black, Joe, 115, 128 138
Blaine, James, 78, 85, 110
Blake, Domenic "Edward", 202, 209
Bolton, Charles, 196
Bolton, John "Jack", 120, 128, 129, 145, 149, 152, 168, 171, 172, 173, 175, 181, 192, 194, 196, 203, 212, 219, 221, 223, 228, 231, 241, 331
Bowers, Owen, 146, 173, 174, 175, 279
Brampton, Ont., 133
Brant, Joseph, 363
Bright House Hotel, 113
Brydges, Charles John, 3, 25, 26, 27, 293-298, 339
Buchanan, Isaac, 24, 26, 139, 292, 294
Buffalo, N.Y., 21, 121, 132, 151, 263, 309
Bull, Harcourt Burland, 28, 40, 81
Burkholder, Jacob, 345

Cahill, James, 42, 43, 45, 56, 58, 64, 78, 85, 87, 90, 108, 177, 178, 216, 245, 249, 351, 364
Campbell, William, 178, 184, 208, 214, 217
Cantwell, "Big Jim", 9, 49, 63, 67, 120, 128, 129, 145, 147, 152, 153, 156, 169, 171, 172, 176, 181, 193, 200, 203, 204, 210, 279, 331
Carbon Oil Company, 99, 245, 346
Carbery, Bishop James, 9
Cardwell, Ont., 217
Carling, John, 22, 238
Carpenter, F. M., 114, 230, 231
Cashmere, Ont., 233, 277
Charleton, Benjamin, 89, 99
Chisholm, Daniel Black, 73, 95, 99, 178, 188, 323
Clark, John T., 26, 293
Cleveland, Grover, 285
Collingwood, Ont., 105
Coote's Paradise, 108
Corey, Frederick, 44, 64, 84, 95, 139, 367
Cowan, William, 247
Credit River, 88, 247, 255
Crerar, John, 216, 267
Crockett, Wilson, 355
Crooks, Adam, 149, 153, 231
Crystal Palace, 300, 315

Daly, Kearan, 16
Davidson, John, 319
Delhi, Ont., 262
Derror, David, 86, 140, 142
Desjardins Canal, 48, 81, 296, 354
Dickens, Charles, 307
Dictionary of Hamilton Biography, 7
Dobbie, Thomas, 207, 243
Don River, 254
Dublin, Ireland, 8, 9, 12
Duffin's Creek, 52
Dundurn Castle, 24
Durham, Earl of, 22
Durnan, George, 235
Dynamite, 108, 318
Dynes, John, 58-59, 62, 64, 77, 81, 82, 85, 219
Dynes Tavern, 139

Egan, Dan, 33, 35
Egar, Benjamin, 113
Elliott, Thomas and Jane, 9, 49, 60, 120, 128, 143, 145, 147, 150, 168, 174, 175, 176, 181, 194, 196, 200, 219, 221, 222, 328, 331, 379
Emery, William Y., 207, 219, 241, 283, 285, 288
Ennis, Sir John, 17
Enniskillen, County Fermanagh, 11
Erie Canal, 21, 308

Index   391

Fenian Raids, 172
Ferguson, Dr. Charles F., 215, 229, 263
Fermanagh County, Ireland, 7
Flock Road, 41
Fort George, 12, 14, 317, 323, 328, 329
Foster, Sir George Eulas, 75-76, 212, 230
Foulds, Ben, 51, 63
Fraser House Hotel, 284

Gabriel, Joseph, 140, 142, 171
Gage, Andrew, 144, 216, 288
Gage, John, 343
Gage, Robert Russell, 343
Gage, William J., 79, 82, 84, 140, 248
Galt, Ont., 59, 61, 78, 85, 88, 247, 312
Gates, Joe, 90
Georgian Bay, 104, 111, 120, 180, 236
Gibbons, James, 15
Gibbs, Thomas N., 128
Gibson, William, 341
Gifford, Benjamin Meade, 173
Gilbert, Richard, 107, 184, 186
Gillespie, George H., 269
Glassco, Capt., 30
Goderich, Ont., 189, 239
Gooderham's Distillery, 183, 255
Gordon, Thomas, 232

Grand Bend, Ont., 240
Grand River, 55, 59, 67
Grand River Navigation Company, 61, 67
Gray, Patrick, 50, 51, 56, 65, 101, 135, 138, 145, 185
Griffith, Henry, 102, 119
Guelph, Ont., 85
Gunsell, John, 155, 183, 185, 203, 233, 238

Hamilton Cotton Works, 257
Hamilton Institute for the Insane, 194, 221
Hamilton & North Western Railway, 105, 113, 219
Hamilton Street Railway, 3
Hand, Patrick, 177, 359
Hanlan, Edward "Ned", 50, 135, 138, 185, 235
Hanlan, John, 51, 52, 57-58, 65
Harold, Rev. P. J., 204
Harris, Chester, 177
Harris, Edward, 271, 274
Harris, Robert William, 292
Harvey, Sir John, 12, 215
Helmer, William, 99, 103, 146, 147, 155
Hopkins, John Wesley, 44, 45, 46, 51, 54, 58, 62, 364–371
Hull, Wellington, 255, 259
Hutchinson House, 10, 22, 199, 201
Hutchinson, Jimmy, 205, 222, 282

Huurman, Alan & Leslie, 289

Inch, Adam, 349
International Fisheries
  Exhibition (1883), 324
Irish Potato Famine, 10
Irving, Emilius, 64

Jackson, Frank, 144
James, Rev. Solomon, 187, 304
Jolley, James, 348
Joyce, Ben, 58, 363

Kearney, Joseph, 16
Kerr, Archibald, 266
Kerr, Charles John, 2, 7, 86, 255, 276, 318, 380
Kerr, Clara Augusta, 287
Kerr, Edward Thomas "Ned", 103, 215, 239, 276, 286
Kerr, Emily Jane, 278
Kerr, Frederick, 7, 84, 144, 243, 263, 276, 309, 378–380
Kerr, George, 55, 84, 176, 277, 278, 280
Kerr, Gordon, 289
Kerr, John "Uncle", 10, 21, 207
Kerr, John Bensley, 380
Kerr, Louisa, 278
Kerr, Mary Eliza (Winslow), 11
Kerr, Dr. Robert Bews, 7
Kerr, W. "Simcoe", 66, 305, 363

Kerr, Thomas Cockburn, 266
Killarney, Ont., 179, 185, 236
Kilvert, Francis Edwin, 198, 208, 213, 228, 230, 320

Lang, William "Billy", 136, 155
Lawe, Henry, 118, 156
Lawry, Charles, 251
Lawry, Thomas, 346
Lazier, Stephen Franklin, 249
Leamington, Ont., 92, 210
Leary, William, 271
Leckie, John, 239
Logie, Judge, 51, 59, 367, 368
London, Ont., 22, 23, 233
Long Point, Lake Erie, 47
Long Point Company, 62, 266–275
Lord's Day Act, 50, 81
Lottridge, George, 64
Lottridge, Thomas, 140
Lutz, Morris, JP, 110

MacIntosh, Dr., 250
Mackenzie, John I., 167, 246, 250, 266
MacNab, Sir Allan N., 24, 25, 28, 30, 267, 292, 294, 338
Magill, Charles, 347
Marsh, Alfred, 167
Marsh, Leonard, 65, 80
Martin, Edward, 347
Martin, Richard, 83

Masonic Order, 213, 337–342
Mason, John James, 345
Mason, William, 251
Masters, Joseph, 168, 192, 205, 282
McBride, Alexander, 199, 201, 209
McCrea, W. Allan, 156, 170, 210
McCullough, A.B., 36–38
McGillivray, Duncan, 43
McGregor, Sir Duncan, 15
McGywnne, Dan, 58, 87, 108, 365, 368
McKinnon, Alexander, 240, 242
McLelan, Archibald Woodbury, 74, 197, 212, 325
McNair, Samuel, 110, 178, 216
McMaster, D., 191, 238
McMichael, John, 208
McQuaig, John, 28, 30
Medcalf, Francis Henry, 101
Middlesex Militia, 13
Miller, George, 105, 221
Miller, James, 106, 117, 327
Mitchell, Peter, 4, 71-73, 365, 367
Morrow, Eleanor (Kerr), 2, 385, 387
Morrow, Robert, 2, 380
Mowat, Oliver, 184
Mountain Drain/Ditch, 346
Mountain View Hotel, 343, 347

Muir, James, 189, 191, 196, 198
Mullingar, County Westmeath, 2, 7, 8, 13, 15
Mulvany, William Thomas, 11, 283

Nath, "Dutch Pete", 106, 118, 129
Navy Hall, NOTL, 14, 317, 321
Nelson, Viscount Horatio, 5
Niagara Historical Society, 168
Niagara River, 48, 121, 263
Noble, Charles & James, 133, 180, 186, 236
Norfolk County, 85, 99, 141
North West Rebellion, 197, 201, 262

Ocean House Hotel, 99, 112
O'Reilly, Judge, 64

Paisley, Ont., 191, 253
Parson Brothers, 248, 251
Patton, James, 111, 119, 180, 182, 201
Pelee Island Lake Erie, 210
Penrose, Gen'l William Henry, 183
Phoenix Park, Dublin, 20
Plumb, Josiah Burr, 17, 150, 153, 154, 158, 194, 205, 215, 243, 317, 322, 326

Podkins, William, 358
Point Abino, Lake Erie, 121, 126, 379
Pope, James Colledge, 74–75, 126
Port Burwell, 207
Port Colborne, 39, 61, 121
Port Dalhousie, 106, 118
Port Dover, 32, 55, 61, 90, 195, 324
Port Maitland, 55, 85
Port Rowan, 90
Port Stanley, 10, 20, 21, 90, 284, 286
Progreston (Carlisle) Ont., 178, 208, 287
Proud, Andrew, 285
Puslinch Lake, 320

Queen's Royal Hotel (NOTL), 129

Ranney, John W., 126, 183, 186, 341
Redhead, John, 219
Rendall, Samuel, 349, 354, 355
Ribbonmen, 16, 47
Robertson, Thomas, 184
Robinson, John Beverley, 57–58, 61, 112
Rondeau Bay, Lake Erie, 92
Roscommon, County, Ireland, 16

Royal Irish Constabulary, 2, 10, 15, 18
Ryerson, Dr. Egerton, 268
Rykert, John Charles, 158, 194, 205, 215, 229
Rymal, Joseph, 344

Sadlier, Charles, 43, 50, 59, 66, 85, 87, 108, 179, 250, 358
Sarnia, Ont., 199, 238, 243
Sauble River, 195
Saugeen River, 191, 235, 253
Scott Act, 262
Seagram's Distillery, 258
Shaftsbury Hall, Toronto, 167
Shannon River, Ireland, 10, 15, 47
Sharp, David, 174, 194, 195, 239, 379
Shawanaga, Ont., 187, 304
Sherman House Hotel, Fort Erie, 234
Sherman's Inlet, Hamilton Harbour, 248, 254
Silver Star Oil Company, 254
Sleeman, John George, 320
Smith, Sir Albert James, 73-74, 98, 101, 120
Smythe, William Barlow, 14
Snook, William, 146, 155
Solversburg, Chris, 355
Standard Insurance Company, 278
St. John's Day, 339

St. John's Lodge, 231, 338
St. Catharine's Game Club, 93, 106
Stipe, Simon P., 139, 140
Stoney Creek, Battle of, 12
Stuart, Dr. James W., 144, 146, 149
Sturgeon, 151
Swinyard, Thomas, 374

Thames River, 77-78, 88, 103, 233, 274
Thompson, George, 95
Thompson, William A., 60
Tilton, Major John, 189, 200, 210, 217, 221, 230, 323, 378
Tisdale, Colonel David, 229, 266, 273
Tiverton, Ont., 240
Toronto, Ont., 48, 49

Van Wagner, Peter, 45, 49, 103
Vincent, General John, 12

Waddell, Robert R., 46, 154, 169, 344, 354
Wadsworth, Chester, 142, 171
Wadsworth, John, 86, 142
Wallace, William, 158, 167
Ward, David, 50, 65, 136, 151, 359
Ward, William, 112, 116, 185, 235
Wardell Family, 194, 211

Watt, Robert, 130
Welland Canal, 35, 44, 86, 121, 293
Wentworth Fish & Game Protection Association, 135, 176, 178, 184, 185, 208, 217
Whitcher, William Frederick (W.F.), 17, 37, 42, 48, 53, 55, 56, 65, 80 83, 98, 103, 115, 120, 148, 170, 200, 241, 243, 268, 318, 360
White, Thomas, 243
Wilcox, James, 115
Wilkinson, J. S., 212-213
Williams, James Miller, 99, 245, 250, 253
Williams, John, 110
Wilson, Capt. Joseph, 186, 189
Wilson, Dr., 200
Wilmot, Samuel, 13, 37, 81, 213, 214, 235, 238, 242, 311
Windsor (Sandwich) Ont., 24, 92, 316
Winona, Ont., 44
Winslow, Alicia, 11
Winslow, Mary Eliza, 8, 10, 20
Woodruff, Sheriff Samuel, 273
Woolard, W.B., 239
Wooten, Edward, 156, 171

Zimmerman, Samuel, 27, 293, 308

CPSIA information can be obtained
at www.ICGtesting.com
Printed in the USA
BVHW030535240321
603292BV00006B/12

9 781525 585036